Building on the Past

OTHER TITLES FROM E & FN SPON

European Directory of Property Developers, Investors and Financiers 1993
2nd edition
Building Economics Bureau

The Idea of Building
S. Groák

Investment Appraisal and Financial Decisions
4th edition
S. Lumby

Land for Industrial Development
D. Adams, L. Russell and C. Taylor-Russell

Marketing the City
The role of flagship developments in urban regeneration
H. Smyth

Microcomputers in Property
A surveyor's guide to Lotus 1-2-3 and dBase IV
T.J. Dixon, O. Bevan and S. Hargitay

The Multilingual Dictionary of Real Estate
L. van Breughel, R.H. Williams and B. Wood

National Taxation for Property Management and Valuation
A. MacLeary

Property Investment Decisions
S. Hargitay and M. Yu

Property Development
3rd edition
D. Cadman and L. Austin-Crowe
Edited by R. Topping and M. Avis

Property Investment and the Capital Markets
G.P. Brown

Project Management Demystified
Today's tools and techniques
G. Reiss

Property Valuation
The five methods
D. Scarrett

Rebuilding the City
Property-led urban regeneration
Edited by P. Healey, D. Usher, S. Davoudi, S. Tarsanoglu and M. O'Toole

Risk, Uncertainty and Decision-making in Property Development
P.J. Byrne and D. Cadman

Spon's Budget Estimating Handbook
B.S. Spain

Transport, the Environment and Sustainable Development
D. Banister and K. Button

UK Directory of Property Developers, Investors and Financiers 1993
7th edition
Building Economics Bureau

Urban Regeneration
Property investment and development
J. Berry, W. Deddis and W. McGreal

For more information and other titles please contact: The Promotion Department, E & FN Spon,
2–6 Boundary Row, London SE1 8HN, Telephone 0171–865 0066

Building on the Past

A guide to the archaeology and
development process

Greg McGill

The College of Estate Management
Reading, UK

E & FN SPON
An Imprint of Chapman & Hall

London · Glasgow · Weinheim · New York · Tokyo · Melbourne · Madras

Published by E & FN Spon, an imprint of Chapman & Hall, 2–6 Boundary Row, London SE1 8HN, UK

Chapman & Hall, 2–6 Boundary Row, London SE1 8HN, UK

Blackie Academic & Professional, Wester Cleddens Road, Bishopbriggs, Glasgow G64 2NZ, UK

Chapman & Hall GmbH, Pappelallee 3, 69469 Weinheim, Germany

Chapman & Hall USA, One Penn Plaza, 41st Floor, New York NY 10119, USA

Chapman & Hall Japan, ITP-Japan, Kyowa Building, 3F, 2-2-1 Hirakawacho, Chiyoda-ku, Tokyo 102, Japan

Chapman & Hall Australia, Thomas Nelson Australia, 102 Dodds Street, South Melbourne, Victoria 3205, Australia

Chapman & Hall India, R. Seshadri, 32 Second Main Road, CIT East, Madras 600 035, India

First edition 1995

© 1995 Greg McGill

Typeset in 10/12 pt Times by Cambrian Typesetters, Frimley, Surrey

Printed in Great Britain at the University Press, Cambridge

ISBN 0 419 17690 X

A catalogue record for this book is available from the British Library

Library of Congress Catalog Card Number: 94–79769

∞ Printed on permanent acid-free text paper, manufactured in accordance with ANSI/NISO Z39.48-1992 and ANSI/NISO Z39.48-1984 (Permanence of Paper).

Contents

ENGLISH HERITAGE

From the Chairman

We greatly value our archaeological heritage for the link it provides to our history, not only through individual monuments and buildings but also because of the way past occupation has influenced the modern countryside and townscape through field patterns, street plans, major monuments such as cathedrals and collections of buildings. We recognize the importance of these various aspects under both general planning legislation and specific measures such as the scheduling of ancient monuments, the listing of historic buildings and the designation of conservation areas.

Until November 1990, scheduling was the one statutory mechanism which guaranteed that the case for the preservation of archaeological remains was fully considered – a tool available only to the Secretary of State. In 1990 the Secretary of State published PPG-16 on *Archaeology and Planning* which gives advice to developers, planning authorities, archaeologists and other interested parties on archaeology in the development process. The PPG confirmed the materiality of archaeology in the planning system but also placed it firmly on the centre stage of the development process.

As the statutory advisers to Government on archaeological matters, English Heritage also provides advice to planning authorities and developers. We view our role as reconciling the legitimate tensions which can occur between the need for economic development on the one hand and the preservation of our archaeological heritage on the other.

This book will assist in the process of increased understanding of each other's problems and as such I commend it to a wide audience and wish it every success.

JOCELYN STEVENS CVO
Chairman of English Heritage

Acknowledgements

I have received help and advice from many individuals and organizations and I am grateful to them all. More especially I would like to thank David Chapman, John Dillon, Tim Dixon, Peter Fasham, Richard Hall, June Hargreaves, Katie Jones, Andrew Lawson, John Oxley, Robert Pilcher, Bill Trench, Karl Wiggins and the College of Estate Management. I would also like to reserve a special thank you to Alison Andrews and to my wife Sheila, without whom this book would not have been possible.

List of acronyms

AAI	Area of Archaeological Importance
AC	Law Reports, Appeal Cases, House of Lords
ACA	Association of Consulting Architects
ACAO	Association of County Archaeological Officers
BEC	Building Employers' Confederation
BLR	Building Law Reports
BPF	British Property Federation
BRE	Building Research Establishment
CAO	County Archaeological Officer
CASEC	Committee of Associations of Specialist Engineering Contractors
CBA	Council for British Archaeology
CBI	Confederation of British Industry
CD	Contractor's Design
CIOB	Chartered Institute of Building
DA	Development Area
DCF	Discounted Cash Flow
DLG	Derelict Land Grant
DNH	Department of National Heritage
DoE	Department of the Environment
DoT	Department of Transport
DTI	Department of Trade and Industry
EA	Environmental Assessment
EAGGF	European Agricultural Guidance Fund
EC	European Community
EGCS	Estates Gazette Case Summaries
ERDF	European Regional Development Fund
ERM	Exchange Rate Mechanism
ESA	Environmentally Sensitive Area
ESF	European Social Fund
EU	European Union
EZ	Enterprise Zone
FASS	Federation of Associations of Specialists and Subcontractors
FF	Fixed Fee (Form of Prime Cost Contract)
GC	Government Contracts
GDO	General Development Order

GIS	Geographical Information Systems
GLC	Greater London Council
IA	Intermediate Area
ICE	Institution of Civil Engineers
IDO	Interim Development Order
IFA	Institute of Field Archaeologists
IFC	Intermediate Form of Building Contract
JCT	Joint Contracts Tribunal
LBC	London Borough Council
LIBOR	London Interbank Offered Rate
LPA	Local Planning Authority
MAFF	Ministry of Agriculture, Fisheries and Food
MAP	Management of Archaeological Projects
MC	Management Contract
MW	Minor Works
NPPG	National Planning Policy Guideline
NRA	National Rivers Authority
PAN	Planning Advice Note
PPG	Planning Policy Guidance
RCAHMS	Royal Commission on the Ancient and Historical Monuments of Scotland
RCAHMW	Royal Commission on Ancient and Historical Monuments in Wales
RCHME	Royal Commission on the Historical Monuments of England
RIBA	Royal Institute of British Architects
RICS	Royal Institution of Chartered Surveyors
RTPI	Royal Town Planning Institute
SCAUM	Standing Conference of Archaeological Unit Managers
SDD	Scottish Development Department
SMR	Sites and Monuments Record
SOEnD	Scottish Office Environment Department
SPZ	Simplified Planning Zone
SSSI	Site of Special Scientific Interest
UCO	Use Classes Order
UDP	Unitary Development Plan
USM	Unlisted Securities Market
VAT	Value Added Tax
YAA	York Archaeological Assessment
WO	Welsh Office

List of figures

List of tables

Introduction

It has been said that more of our heritage has been destroyed in the past 30 years by new development than was previously known to exist. Whether or not this is true there can be little doubt that the destruction that occurred during this period encouraged the conservation movement. Concerned initially with protecting historic buildings it has spread to all aspects of our environment including archaeology. We can confidently say that the desire for the protection of our heritage is now deep-rooted in society.

At the same time there has rarely been a time like the present when new development has been so necessary. Many buildings in our towns and cities, constructed in the late nineteenth and early twentieth centuries are now coming to the end of their useful lives, with many in need of repair or renewal. There is also an urgent need to replace disused industrial and other buildings and to revitalize many inner-city areas and ageing infrastructures.

Against this background it is perhaps not surprising that a conflict of interest should develop between those who wish to protect the archaeological resource and those who wish to develop land. On the one hand there will be those who genuinely believe that protecting what is there should take priority over change and new development. They argue, sometimes to the extreme, that development projects should be prevented if destruction of archaeological remains is the likely outcome. Conversely, there are those who see progress in development as paramount. They see archaeological investigation as abstract and unnecessary, arguing that little additional information can be obtained from out of the ground. In between are the many who wish to see buildings, roads and other structures provided where they are needed, as efficiently and as effectively as possible, whilst taking into account the need to protect the environment.

These different viewpoints clearly reflect different attitudes to the environment shaped, no doubt, by a variety of interests. Economic, social, moral, cultural, educational and other factors will all have had a part to play with variations in attitude occurring according to personal background, different perceptions, local circumstances and the passage of time. They show that development and archaeology cannot and should not be seen in isolation from each other and other matters.

Significantly, and this is the key, they suggest that attitudes to archaeology and development can change. If opinions can alter through time then it is possible for us to become more aware of the role of the archaeologist and the importance of archaeology in the same way that we can become more aware of the need for development and the concerns of the developer. Of course, we cannot predict all of the issues nor assess all of the implications and we cannot say for certain how one set of actions by a developer will affect archaeology or *vice versa*. Every site will have its own problems requiring its own solutions. But what we can do is seek to improve the situation. If we accept that new development is necessary, and I think we should, we need to look at how archaeological considerations can be satisfactorily accommodated in the development process.

This is the underlying theme of this book. The aim is to try and reduce the uncertainty and misunderstanding that can exist between archaeologists, developers and those who have to advise or control development. Directed at increasing the knowledge of each group of the roles and concerns of the other parties, my hope is that it will increase understanding and provoke thought for the mutual benefit of the archaeological and development processes.

In pursuit of this aim the book is divided into three Parts. The first looks at archaeological considerations: the intention is to direct the developer's attention to archaeological investigation. Chapter 1 gives an outline of archaeological thinking, paying particular attention to the build-up of knowledge and how it has changed over the years according to circumstances. Essentially it draws attention to the need for early evaluation which Chapter 2 looks at in more detail. Types of site, how they are formed and how to evaluate what lies beneath the ground without actually excavating sites form the main areas of study. Chapter 3 moves on to examine excavation at those sites where this is deemed necessary. Drawing attention to the need for pre- and post-excavation work it seeks to identify the many problems that can arise. Finally, in Part One, Chapter 4 looks at archaeological contracts with the aim of bringing to the notice of developers the codes of practice and the contractual matters that may need to be taken into account when seeking professional archaeological advice.

Part Two looks at public controls. Chapter 5 sets out the roles of central government and the local planning authority before moving on to outline the relevant Acts of Parliament. Here we find that the ancient monuments legislation and the planning Acts are the most important, with the subsequent Chapters in this part of the book dealing almost exclusively with them. Public policy is very much the key, which is what Chapter 6 looks at. This is followed in Chapters 7 to 10 by a study of how monuments are protected and how planning applications, where necessary, are determined. Within this Part I have also thought it necessary to look at the ways in which environmental assessment might be used and how planning gain operates. These are matters that are increasing in importance and accordingly are looked at respectively in Chapters 9 and 10.

In Part Three the line of enquiry is very different. Whilst accepting that public controls are necessary, it is what actually gets built on the ground that is important. Here I am very much aware of the need to set archaeology and planning in a wider context, and especially within the context of the development process. Other matters can be equally, if not more, important to the developer and present the construction and property industries with all sorts of problems. They are matters which archaeologists, planners and decision-makers ought to be aware of.

With this in mind Chapter 11 provides an overview of the development process and the inevitable booms and busts of the development cycle. This sets the scene for what follows, where Chapter 12 looks at some of the problems and pitfalls of project management. Chapter 13 looks at possible design solutions for protecting as much as possible of the archaeological resource.

Construction contracts follow in Chapter 14, where the aim is to draw attention to the main concerns of the developer, the types of contracts that are available and how archaeological matters may be addressed in the clauses. Finally, in Chapters 15 and 16, we look at financial considerations: first, factors influencing costs and second, sources of development finance. This provides the background for an appraisal where examples are used to give an indication of the possible financial effects of archaeology on development.

Archaeological Considerations

PART **1**

The development of archaeological thinking | 1

1.1 THE MEANING OF ARCHAEOLOGY

Archaeology means, quite simply, the study of human material remains. More commonly it is thought of as the study of buried remains, standing ruins and other surviving objects of past human activity although the Oxford English Dictionary defines archaeology slightly differently. It states that it involves the systematic description or study of antiquities where the aim is to find out more about different periods of the past.

Some might argue that archaeology is a branch of history but whereas the historian will seek to obtain a picture of all manner of historical events including natural occurrences, a large part of the archaeologist's activity concentrates on humans' past activities and their impact on the landscape. Other life forms are also important, particularly in the prehistoric period, but the archaeologist is primarily interested in the past achievements of humans and how societies and communities evolved over the years. The main aim is to obtain and interpret information with timing, techniques and location forming key elements in this quest for knowledge.

1.2 THE QUEST FOR KNOWLEDGE

The quest for knowledge of archaeology, as we know it today, ostensibly started some 200 years ago. Before then the Bible formed the main source of information about past societies and seventeenth century theologians had calculated the creation of the Earth at 4004 BC. At the beginning of the nineteenth century people were either unable or unwilling to believe the greater antiquity of the human race. To go back before 'the present world' of the Bible was unheard of. It was considered unchristian and undermined the Christian faith, a powerful and compelling influence. It challenged established thinking and needed people of great courage to come forward. Not surprisingly, archaeological study was almost non-existent and grew very gradually.

In effect, it started with the collection of objects such as coins, works of art, pieces of pottery, sculptures and other curios which were being discovered. Many were collected out of curiosity, but as more and more were accumulated people started to ask questions about where they came from, how they were made, what age they represented and so on. Collection was no longer enough.

In this search for knowledge the Industrial Revolution was of fundamental importance. Quarrying for building materials, the building of the canals and later the construction of the railways all resulted in the removal of large volumes of earth. Cuttings exposed all sorts of buried objects lying either just beneath the surface or at various depths in the ground. It also became apparent that deposits of sand, gravel, clay and limestone were the result of the ordinary deposition of sediments. This was not generally realized until the 1830s, when Charles Lyell (1797–1875) published *The Principles of Geology*. He showed, for the first time, that geological evidence appeared in sequence in a simple undisturbed series of layers. It is said that Charles Darwin (1809–1882) was influenced by Lyell's studies of geology and that they may have formed the catalyst which led to Darwin's general theory of evolution. In any event they posed new questions about the chronology of human societies and how cultures developed. They showed that the history of the Earth was much longer than had previously been realized.

Ironically it was the canal and railway building and other developments which helped to advance archaeological thinking. If development had not taken place the opportunities for archaeological investigation would not have been so great and one conclusion must be that, whilst development can destroy evidence and can be a nuisance, in the advancement of archaeological knowledge it is a necessary nuisance.

As personal wealth increased in the nineteenth century, in part from the growth of industry and commerce, so exploration and excavation were able to expand. Archaeology began to take on a more scientific role with people such as Pitt-Rivers, Evans and Petrie providing new information. They showed that with a methodical approach to excavation and detailed recording, new levels of accuracy and discipline could be obtained. Pitt-Rivers (1827–1900), for example, accurately recorded every specimen and artefact collected, making detailed drawings and descriptions of all excavations. Evans (1851–1941) similarly paid attention to detail, attaching great importance to all finds no matter how trivial. Equally, they recognized the importance of the publication of that detail.

Another key figure was Petrie (1853–1942). As an archaeological surveyor who made the first accurate survey of the pyramids, he developed a system of sequence dating. In his book *Methods and Aims of Archaeology* he set out four principles for archaeological investigation which are just as relevant today:

1. that care must be taken of the monuments being excavated;
2. that special attention must be paid to the collection and description of everything that is found;
3. that detailed and accurate surveys should be undertaken together with careful planning;
4. that all information should be published as quickly as possible.

Of course, not all the early approaches were so scientific. Schliemann (1822–1890), for instance, was more interested in pursuing a particular objective. Fascinated by the stories of ancient Greece and particularly those of Homer's Troy, he set out to find the truth about Troy. He sought to distinguish myth from reality and, in the process, destroyed much of the evidence without making a methodical record. However, despite the different approaches, these examples show a science emerging to confront traditional beliefs. In their different ways they demonstrate an objective approach to archaeology, tending towards a detailed description of data. Making use of scientific methods, they argued that the facts spoke for themselves.

These methods also proved to be successful in the development of techniques. As excavation proceeded and further discoveries were made and published, important breakthroughs in the ability to date the past, the development of aerial photography and other techniques of investigation were made. However, they revealed a reliance of factual information which some would argue put too great an emphasis on the detailed description of data. In fact, it was becoming apparent that the steady collection of data, in itself, did not appear to be leading to major advances in knowledge. The argument was growing that the pursuit of knowledge could not progress simply as a result of collecting more and more data, but that the development of theory and ideas was equally, if not more, important.

Alongside these developments in archaeology, considerable environmental change was taking place. Social, economic, political and physical factors were all having an impact on where we lived, worked and played. This was especially so after the Second Word War when many war-damaged buildings and sites needed to be redeveloped and new buildings constructed. It was also a time when nationwide land use controls were introduced. The Town and Country Planning Act 1947 required, for the first time, that planning permission be obtained for new development, but an important feature of that Act, which is sometimes overlooked, is that it introduced a system of compensation and betterment. This had the effect of dampening the supply of new buildings although demand continued to grow; the gap between supply and demand grew wider. This continued until the 1950s when the restrictions on supply were lifted. The betterment levy was abolished thereby opening the floodgates for development. Local authorities and developers alike became actively involved in promoting and implementing development projects. A lot of land was cleared for development and many sites earmarked for **comprehensive redevelopment**, a term used to describe large scale demolition and, in many cases, high-rise development. New construction techniques encouraged this and tall buildings became commonplace in many towns and cities, frequently requiring deep foundations.

One site that was cleared for redevelopment in 1954 is where the Temple of Mithras was discovered. Located at Cannon Street in the City of London, it generated considerable public interest, so much so that time was set aside for excavation and public viewing of the uncovered Roman remains. Inevitably there was a delay to the redevelopment of the site but, contrary to popular belief, this only lasted three weeks and related solely to a small part of the site. Some in the development industry, however, saw this as a disaster, which is not altogether surprising considering the uniqueness of the situation. Discovery and delay on anything like this scale had not happened before although they were certain to happen again.

Elsewhere other activities were gaining momentum. Significant among these was a new type of archaeological research project at Winchester. Under the leadership of Martin Biddle, excavations were carried out at a number of sites within the city to establish its historical geography. Detailed investigations were made with great precision and discipline covering a range of historic periods from the Iron Age through to the Roman, Anglo-Saxon and Medieval periods. They provided archaeologists with many new insights and greatly advanced the cause of urban archaeology.

As archaeologists were becoming more aware of what was happening, much of the urban fabric was already in the process of being destroyed. The removal of restrictions in the 1950s together with a booming economy resulted in many buildings being demolished to be replaced by new high-rise buildings, new highways, new underpasses and other structures. In many towns and cities little regard was paid to their historic character and much that was important historically was destroyed or left to deteriorate. The situation regarding archaeological remains was even worse.

The reaction to this destruction encouraged the conservation movement. It led to increasing calls to protect the environment which were directed initially at saving historic buildings and areas, although gradually extended to archaeological sites. The delay was probably due to the fact that most archaeological remains were hidden underground, in contrast to buildings which, by their very presence, constantly remind us of our heritage. To some extent it will have been a matter of 'out of sight, out of mind'. Certainly this will partly explain why so many archaeological sites were destroyed in the boom period of the 1950s and 1960s. However, by working in an urban environment many in the archaeological world were beginning to realize how much modern developments could damage or destroy archaeological remains and how important some of these sites were.

This destruction helps to explain why many locally based archaeological units came into being in the 1970s. Established primarily to publicize the destruction and to record as much as possible of what remained before it was destroyed, they also sought to rescue the archaeological resource. They were the originators of rescue archaeology.

1.3 RESCUE ARCHAEOLOGY

As the Winchester project was reaching fulfilment, so sites in other towns were beginning to be investigated. By 1970 the total in England had reached 23 and archaeologists were formulating ideas about how to investigate urban sites. New ideas about archaeology were being published in archaeological journals with the effect that minds began to concentrate on how to develop strategies and methods of investigation. As Carver (1987) later reported, three ideas dominated the strategy of the 1970s: 'think big', 'think history' and 'think rescue'.

In many ways these three ideas sum up what rescue archaeology was all about. Many archaeologists were beginning to conclude that the purpose of archaeology in towns was to provide knowledge of their history and that by examining archaeological remains a story of the growth and development of towns could be obtained. In other words, to use Carver's phrase, there was a need to think history.

However, if the history of a town or city was to be established it also became necessary to think big. Within an urban area each site that was and still is investigated can only provide a small part of its history. If archaeologists want to find out more about a town it is necessary to investigate as many sites as possible. In a sense each site is a piece in the urban historical jigsaw where the picture is only revealed when accumulated information is put together.

The problem with history, however, is that it contains many pictures. For every period of history there are different stories to tell, which means that more than one picture is needed if the history of a town is to be ascertained. To get the full story it becomes necessary to extract a whole series of pictures for the different historical periods. It means that just as each site should not be seen in isolation from its surroundings so each period of history should not be isolated from other periods.

In terms of **rescue** this was and is not an easy thing to do. It means that a strategy has to be devised for each historic area. Decisions have to be made about which periods to investigate, where to dig, what to look out for and how to retrive and assemble information. Initially this proved difficult. From 1969 onwards, excavations commenced at sites in many towns and cities such as Chelmsford, Exeter, Nottingham, Southampton, Poole, Gloucester and parts of London. Operating independently of each other, units sought to retrieve as much archaeological information as possible before it was destroyed although they were frequently hampered by lack of money, trained staff and limited resources. Often a practical and pragmatic approach was required such as was beginning to take place in cities like York and London. The York Archaeological Trust, for example, put great emphasis on excavating those sites and strata that were about to be destroyed by new development. At the Museum of London an attempt was made to devise a strategy for excavators to work from.

Of course, these and other units were not without their problems. Pressures to develop land meant that difficult decisions had to be made. Archaeologists in London and York, as in other towns and cities, were often restricted in where they could excavate. They were dependent on the developer, the vagaries of the market in providing sites for excavation and the attitude of the local planning authority. In the 1970s it was difficult to get access to sites and conditional planning consents requiring excavation were rare or non-existent. Few developers could afford the delay and many local planning authorities did not recognize archaeology as a material planning consideration in the determination of planning applications. Meanwhile, urban renewal programmes, redevelopment and new building continued apace.

During the 1970s and 1980s circumstances changed. Many newly qualified archaeologists were appearing on the scene and keen to investigate new sites. By 1981 as many as 124 towns had been or were in the process of being investigated (Carver, 1987) with the growth of interest matched by a growth in excavation. This in turn was matched by a growth of information although this was not always clear at the time. Much was not published and there was a need to analyse existing information. Some archaeologists were also convinced that to excavate as much as possible was not the answer. They counselled change, arguing that there should be a change of emphasis away from simply collecting everything to collecting what was needed and to make it publicly available in the context of an overall strategy. Not all of the changes, however, were to serve the cause or the advancement of archaeological investigation: not initially, at least.

1.4 STRATEGIES IN THE 1980s

The thrust for these changes began in 1979: first by the Labour government's introduction of the Ancient Monuments and Archaeological Areas Act 1979; second, by the new Conservative government's approach after it won the general election later that year.

The calls for greater protection of archaeological sites had eventually worked through the governmental system, although when it came the changes were viewed in different ways. Whilst some considered the Ancient Monuments and Archaeological Areas Act 1979 to be a significant step towards protecting archaeological remains others thought its measures were insufficient to make any real impact.

Principally, the 1979 Act consolidated earlier legislation relating to ancient monuments. Important among the changes to monument protection were the redirection of funding powers towards specified projects and the need to obtain the consent of the Secretary of State for any proposed works to scheduled monuments. Previously owners had only to give three months notice of their intentions to carry out such works.

A new initiative was the extension of protective measures to certain areas known to be archaeologically important. Defined as Areas of Archaeological Importance, the Secretary of State became empowered to designate these areas where this was thought appropriate. Areas in ten historic cities were put forward although only five were chosen for designation, namely Canterbury, Chester, Exeter, Hereford and York. Within these areas time and access (but no money) became mandatory for rescue archaeology.

Immediately after the introduction of this Act the Conservative government came to power. Under the leadership of Mrs Thatcher a whole new policy approach to government was introduced. Politics decreed a lessening of public controls over enterprise and the use and development of land. The market place was to be given a greater say in when, where and how land should be developed.

One impact of these changes was to produce the recession of the early 1980s, leading to a gradual decline of traditional industries with the consequent run-down of large urban and inner-city areas. The relaxation of controls was, of necessity, targeted at these areas, although it was limited. Aimed principally at enterprise zones and urban development areas – which were restricted in number and area – it meant that many other areas received little benefit. The result was that archaeologists had difficulty funding projects and developers were often unable to provide financial support for archaeological investigation. This was not surprising since the main aim was one of supporting the rebuilding of urban areas. Urban regeneration took priority over preservation.

The mid-1980s saw the partial reorganization of local government and further relaxations of control. The GLC and metropolitan counties were abolished, simplified planning zones were introduced, and changes of use from all sorts of industrial buildings to offices were automatically granted planning permission in a new Use Classes Order. When the boom came in the late 1980s the combined effect of these changes resulted in widespread development. Sites in many towns and cities, including historic cities, witnessed a plethora of new buildings.

The problem was not so much that new buildings were being erected. In many cases it was their sheer size and number and the fact that foundations needed to be sufficient to carry the increased loads that were the problem. Deeper foundations, with the occasional underground car park, meant that many archaeological remains were destroyed. In a sense it was similar to the industrial revolution of the nineteenth century and the development of the 1950s and 1960s. The main difference was that the impact on archaeology was recognized which led to increased calls for protection of the archaeological resource.

1.5 A NEW STRATEGY FOR ARCHAEOLOGY

The publication in November 1990 of *Planning Policy Guidance Note 16* (PPG 16) provided a great boost for archaeologists. By formally recognizing archaeology as a material planning consideration in the formulation and implementation of planning policy, it has given the archaeological profession a greater say in the development process and a new strength of purpose. It has meant that archaeological considerations cannot be ignored when development is proposed, although this recognition has not been without its problems.

On the positive side, the PPG has introduced greater clarity of purpose and enabled archaeological thinking to influence and be influenced by the planning process. A logical consequence to investigation is the reduction in need for excavation. By a process of elimination, based on the principle that preservation *in situ* is preferred to recording what is there, the comprehensive excavation of sites now only proceeds as a last resort when deemed necessary.

The problems stem from this greater involvement and relate to expectations and attitude. Differences of opinion as to how archaeological considerations should be taken into account when development proposals affect archaeology can now be detected. There is a feeling among some archaeologists that insufficient attention is given to archaeology when planning applications are determined. They see a number of authorities acting virtually indifferently to archaeology, taking little or no account of archaeological considerations. They complain that insufficient attention is paid to archaeology in comparison to other planning matters. Other archaeologists see things differently. From their experience they find planners responding positively to archaeological interests, although they acknowledge that this response does differ from authority to authority.

In talks with planners and developers the views expressed are often quite different. All see archaeology as one of the considerations to be taken into account in the determination of development proposals although many see other considerations as being more important. Frequently social and other environmental factors carry more weight, the argument being that archaeology has not been ignored but has been given due consideration.

Differences of opinion such as these are not surprising. Different specializations, interests, training and educational programmes generate different expectations with greater importance being given to particular interests. Archaeologists will almost inevitably attach greater weight to archaeological matters in the development process in the same way that planners will put more weight on regulating development in what may be termed the public interest. Developers, intent on making a living by providing buildings and other structures for present day society, will similarly take a different view.

What is more clear is that archaeology and development can no longer be separated. Just as development, as stated earlier, is seen as a recognized nuisance in the advance of archaeological knowledge, so too can archaeology be seen as a recognized nuisance in the development process. The key, however, is to recognize that this nuisance has its limits. Preservation *in situ* is the preferred option, indicating that attention should focus on how to preserve archaeological sites when this is deemed necessary, and on ways of ensuring that destruction, without recording what is there, is kept to a minimum.

REFERENCES

Carver, M. (1987) *Underneath English Towns: Interpreting Urban Archaeology*, Batsford, London.

DoE (1990) *Planning Policy Guidance Note 16: Archaeology and Planning*, HMSO, London.

FURTHER READING

Barker, P. (1982) *Techniques of Archaeological Excavation*, Batsford, London.

Daniel, G.E. (1975) *A Hundred and Fifty Years of Archaeology*, Duckworth, London.

Greene, K. (1990) *Archaeology: An Introduction*, Batsford, London.

Hodder, I. (1992) *Theory and Practice in Archaeology*, Routledge, London.

Jones, G.D.B. (1984) *Past Imperfect: The Story of Rescue Archaeology*, Heinemann, London.

Lowenthal, D. and Binney, M. (eds) (1981) *Our Past Before Us: Why Do We Save It?* Temple Smith, London.

Rahtz, P.A. (ed.) (1974) *Rescue Archaeology*, Penguin, Harmondsworth, London.

Archaeological investigation | 2

There are many types of archaeological remains of every period. Upstanding remains are the most obvious but many others such as ancient settlements are to be found all over the countryside and underneath our towns and cities. Sites also vary enormously in their state of preservation and can range from well preserved wetland sites to others which are virtually unrecognizable because of the erosion that has occurred. They cannot all be investigated in the same way and different approaches must be adopted in the way sites are discovered or how further information about them may be obtained.

Each of these aspects of investigation is comprehensive, which is why, in this Chapter, the aim is to look at the principles involved in site investigation. The idea is to look first at how sites may be formed in order to give developers and others an insight into where they might be found and how deep finds might be. This is followed by an appraisal of the types of the many sites that may be encountered: records show that there are over 700 000 known archaeological sites in Britain. Large parts of Scotland and Wales, however, have never been surveyed, suggesting there could be more.

Against this background of how sites are formed and what they might consist of, the next stage is to see how they might be found. Several methods of investigation are available ranging from the very simple to the very complex. They include the use of instruments designed to detect what lies beneath the ground without actually disturbing it, although it must be remembered that these cannot provide a complete picture. All information obtained in this way must be treated with caution as archaeological artefacts can be missed and readings misinterpreted. Finally, as part of the investigation there is a need to look at the costs involved and the main factors influencing those costs. The problems associated with excavation are looked at in the next Chapter.

2.1 HOW ARCHAEOLOGICAL SITES ARE FORMED

Why an understanding is important

If we are to find out how archaeology may affect development projects it is important to understand how archaeological sites develop. The more we know about them the better it will help us to tackle the problems that might arise. It should make it easier to understand the evidence that is recovered and lead to a greater awareness of the relative importance of a site. An understanding can also be used to help in deciding how best to proceed and where to make further investigations or where to excavate. This can benefit the advance of research and could be less disruptive of the development process.

The formation of archaeological sites

Essentially archaeological sites are formed in one of two ways. Either remains are deliberately buried or they are buried by accident. Sometimes both occur at the same time and certainly both are helped by nature.

Of the remains that are deliberately buried, by far the most common are interred human remains. Burial mounds, funerary chambers and graveyards regularly occur throughout the land but all kinds of objects ranging from a single pot to a wealth of precious possessions can be buried with or alongside human corpses. In addition, many other remains can be buried deliberately during the life of a community. Rubbish tips and refuse pits are good examples which can reveal a wealth of information.

As far as accidental burials are concerned it is amazing how many occur. Even buildings constructed of stone can disappear from the surface, for once they cease to be occupied disrepair and decay begin: as timbers rot, so doors, windows and eventually the roof will collapse; fallen woodwork will decay more quickly; soil will be blown in and plants take root; vegetation will produce a rich bed for more plants which, together with frost action and the freezing of trapped water, dislodge masonry and stones; walls will start to crumble and so begins an almost endless cycle of natural decay.

In many cases this process of natural decay is assisted by human interference. Ruins of buildings, for example, provide a ready source of stone for further building work without having to search or quarry for it. It is easily accessible which means that the amount of stone can be reduced rapidly thereby accelerating the rate of decay.

Once under the ground decay continues at a greater or lesser extent depending on several factors. These include the acidity and permeability of the soil, the extent to which the ground is waterlogged and, of course, the nature and substance of the discarded objects. Organic matter will decay more quickly than inorganic material so that an object such as a timber post will eventually end up as a dark stain in the earth; iron will rust and cause staining; precious metals will survive more easily. Pottery and stone are the best survivors.

As a rule, the greater the acidity of the soil the quicker the decay. By contrast, the more airtight the conditions the greater the degree of preservation. Thus in wet sites where anaerobic, that is, airtight conditions exist, timber, leather, textiles and plant matter can all be preserved although, when such material is exposed to the air, decay can set in very quickly.

The process of levelling is another factor which has contributed to the formation of archaeological remains. When new buildings were contemplated, not only was masonry taken from sites but many were levelled to provide a platform for new buildings. This could have involved a levelling-up or a levelling-down of the land depending on the topography of the area. Undulations in the ground or valley sites and the proximity to a river may have resulted in the filling in of land to avoid flooding. Sometimes restrictions on the removal of debris will have resulted in a gradual rise in ground level. Chester is a good example where this has occurred, although the process will vary from town to town and within different parts of the same town.

The age of a town and its importance during different periods of history will also affect the depth of deposits. For example, at Aylesbury, where Medieval deposits exist, strata can be found at depths of 1–1.5 m (3–5 feet) whereas in Droitwich, which has Roman origins, remains can be as deep as 5 m (16 feet) below ground (Carver, 1987). Thus, the formation of archaeological sites will depend very much on the length of time remains have been left untouched, soil conditions, the underlying natural topography and the length and period of occupation.

2.2 TYPES OF ARCHAEOLOGICAL REMAINS

Prior knowledge of the type of archaeology to expect at a development site will be of considerable benefit in assessing its importance. It can help archaeologists and developers to assess what it will mean in terms of time, money, effort and the use of other resources.

Sometimes the nature and importance of an archaeological site will be instantly recognizable, but more often it will not. Clues, however, will be present. The location and character of an area can provide useful information. They can tell us why a site was established and perhaps why it continued or failed to continue to flourish. For instance, it may have been located for defensive reasons (a prominent elevated site), as a focal point for communications (at a river crossing), as a site for agricultural production, or because of its proximity to timber or minerals. By studying the character and nature of the surrounding area it should be possible to get an idea of why a site was established. English Heritage have recognized the importance of this by identifying eleven main types of area or topographical zones where different types of archaeological sites might occur (English Heritage, 1987):

1. **Wetland and waterlogged areas**
   Sites in these areas were often used as hunting grounds and sources for food and raw materials. They are where wood, leather, rope, spears, spades and many other finds have been found, which, when studied and properly analysed, have helped to build up a picture of the climate, vegetation and wildlife encountered by earlier generations. The fact that they are waterlogged has meant that material in them has usually been well preserved although when exposed to the air they tend to decay quickly. From an archaeological point of view they should be kept wet or covered with vegetation to prevent drying and erosion by the wind.

   Important wetland areas include the Somerset Levels, the Fens of East

Anglia, the Humber Basin, other low-lying areas and many mires and bogs in northern Britain. Much in the north has not been surveyed.

2. The coastal zone

For thousands of years the coastal zone was the point of entry and exit for Britain. It formed a line of defence and was also a major communication link and a source of raw material. Accordingly, evidence of a wide range of past human activity can be found in this: castles and fortifications for defence; lighthouses and harbours for transportation and trade; and salt-pans and fish traps as reminders of exploitation for food.

The coastal zone is an area which has not received a lot of attention in the past but coastal and other erosion and a growing awareness of the potential of this area, particularly for leisure and recreation purposes, indicate that it is likely to be an area of increasing importance in the future. English Heritage are currently showing an interest in the zone.

3. The offshore zone

This is another area of increasing interest. Apart from many historic wrecks, the topography of the inshore sea bed may contain a variety of information that is well preserved. Estuaries and other intertidal areas such as the Solent are places where evidence of earlier occupation may be found. Headlands and other dangers to navigation may also prove fertile ground for archaeological investigation, with other territorial waters (within the 12 nautical mile limit) tending to be less significant.

4. Rivers and lakes

Rivers and lakeland sites have always provided food and raw materials. As a means of and as barriers to movement and communication they have also formed a focus for human settlement providing a wealth of archaeological information. Types of remains associated with riverside occupation include bridgeheads, centres for fishing, the locations of markets and associated activity and habitation.

Riverside sites are also prone to deposition of mud and silt, especially after times of flood. Layers of alluvium can build up and hide earlier remains with the result that archaeological remains may be well preserved. Care should therefore be exercised when rivers are dredged or river banks cut back, excavated or improved.

5. Old pastures

In prehistoric and Medieval times land in England was commonly used for grazing purposes; less so in Scotland and Wales. Beneath it many forms of archaeological sites can be found because of the nature of this use of land where the shallow root systems of grass and turf have helped to preserve them. Some of the best ancient field systems are to be found in these areas together with deserted villages, means of enclosure, boundary dykes, old tracks, Roman camps and castles. Many of these sites remain in reasonable condition because the land is still used for grazing purposes.

6. Ploughed landscapes

More land is used for farming than for any other use and it is not therefore surprising that ploughed landscapes should contain a wealth of archaeological sites. These can range from earliest prehistoric farmland enclosures to buildings of the Middle Ages. Roman occupation was also common in these areas and many villas and temples were built within them and may still be found. Larger settlements have also been unearthed and deserted towns and cities can lie beneath the soil. Some of these sites stand out as islands within a sea of cultivated land, but the majority are hidden from view. Occasionally, ploughing may bring remains to the surface or even destroy them. Some sites may be revealed by crop marks, which are referred to later.

Many rural areas are now well documented although there may still be gaps in the archaeological record. Wessex and East Midlands are two areas that have been extensively investigated. Elsewhere the record is not so thorough, indicating that we can, in the short-term, expect to see regional and chronological imbalances, at least until the Monuments Protection Programme is completed (Chapter 6). Landscapes that have only recently been ploughed are likely to contain better preserved sites and may therefore be a focus for attention.

7. Woodland

In earlier times, woodland covered much of the country. Timber was a widely used resource and created much employment. It was a ready supply of fuel which led to the introduction of early industrial processes such as charcoal burning, pottery making, woodworking and basketry. Iron-smelting and quarrying activities were often located in or near woodlands.

Woodland sites and particularly ancient woods are likely to contain a wealth of archaeological sites. These can include hill-forts, camps, boundary earthworks and hunting lodges. Roads and settlements were also built to service the above crafts and industries.

8. Lowland heaths

The lowland heaths in evidence today were largely created by over-exploitation of the soil. This was begun in prehistoric times by early farmers, primarily in southern England. Settlements and burial mounds show that occupation was widespread during the period 2000–1000 BC.

Later prehistoric times saw the establishment of enclosures, hill-forts and small industrial sites in what were discovered to be mineral-rich areas. Potteries, brickyards, peat-drying and even mining and quarrying activities have all been found to exist in these areas. Timber may have been one of the resources over-exploited in these areas.

9. Upland areas

Whilst many upland areas today appear desolate and inhospitable this has not always been the case. When the climate was warmer than it is today many upland areas were relatively densely populated areas, particularly in the south-west of England such as on Dartmoor. A variety of activities took place in these areas and, because stone was the main building material, much of the evidence from these periods is still visible. Barrows, enclosures, stone circles, cairns, hill-forts, settlements, field systems, mines and other remains have all been found.

Surveys carried out in the north of England have shown that new earthworks may be discovered in areas threatened by forestry, reservoir construction and other large-scale developments. The same could equally be true in Scotland where many prehistoric sites are known to exist.

10. Industrial landscapes

Bearing in mind that the industrial revolution began in Britain it is not surprising that there should be widespread interest in industrial heritage. Today, however, the interest goes beyond the industrial revolution and three types of industrial landscapes are regarded as being particularly important.

The first concerns the metal-extraction industries. Britain was renowned for lead mining in the Roman period and the concern today appears to centre on advancing our knowledge of the scale, character and duration of such early and subsequent metal-extraction industries.

The second area of interest is water power. Whilst the canals of the eighteenth and nineteenth centuries today generate much interest from the development industry as a focus for urban renewal it is the use of water as an early power source that is regarded as archaeologically important. Water-mills of all types and descriptions, the different ways in which they were used, and how water was managed through ducts, channels and even lifted are subjects for investigation.

Thirdly, there is an interest in the manufacturing processes used during the industrial revolution. The ways in which energy was generated and how machines were used for one or more purposes are increasingly seen as important in our post-industrial society. Many people now desire to find out how things were done and how one innovation led to another. Today, interest is growing in the agriculture, charcoal, chemical and extractive industries, engineering and manufacturing processes, the transport and distribution industries and water, sewerage and other services.

11. Townscapes and urban areas

Many modern towns and cities are the product of centuries of occupation. Most came into existence in the ninth and tenth centuries, initially as centres of defence and later developing into market towns. Market charters or borough status began to appear in the late twelfth and early thirteenth centuries which encouraged settlements to grow and expand. Distinctive street patterns emerged and when a new building was required it was usually constructed on the site of an earlier building, making use of its foundations for support. Much of the archaeology was, and still is, close to the surface.

There is now a realization that all historic towns, whatever their size, can provide a wealth of knowledge about the past. Indeed, historic townscapes are now one of the most important areas for archaeological investigation although there are limits to what can be achieved. The random and haphazard manner in which sites are brought forward for development make it unrealistic to expect that many sites can be examined. The opportunities to investigate are limited suggesting that an overall strategy be put in place, relating not just to the town or city but to wider geographical areas.

2.3 HOW SITES ARE DISCOVERED

Myth has it that archaeologists have a hunch about where to dig and are rewarded with fantastic discoveries. In practice the situation is very different. Basically, archaeological sites are discovered either by accident or by design. They can be discovered by anyone (they often are) and it does not have to be an archaeologist who finds them.

Many sites are already known. They stand out above the ground and are visible for all to see, like Stonehenge, or they are hidden but their presence is nevertheless evident because of the lie of the land. We may sense that something is there but we are not quite sure what it contains because the site has not been excavated. Many sites fall into this category.

A large proportion of newly discovered sites are found by systematic fieldwalking. Others are found by accident depending largely on how the land is used and whether it is being altered in some way. In open countryside discovery can be from ploughing, quarrying, dredging, construction works or by erosion. Many Roman villas have been found after ploughing. Quarrying and dredging operations have been important in revealing prehistoric finds such as fossils, and new motorways and trunk roads have sometimes been notorious in unearthing important finds.

In other areas site evaluations will generally indicate what to expect although accidental discovery can still occur. As bulldozers begin to clear and prepare a site for development, unexpected finds can sometimes be revealed. For example, at Alington Avenue, Dorchester, initial investigations from a magnetometer survey and trial trenching carried out in 1985 suggested little in the way of significant finds (Figure 2.1). It was only when development was about to commence that substantial remains, including many human burials, were discovered. Further investigation revealed a far more complex site, as can be seen from Figure 2.2, where over 50 human corpses were discovered. Discoveries such as this will, today, be rare because of the ways in which site evaluation is undertaken. Nevertheless, unexpected finds can still occur indicating the need for caution and early research.

Desk-top studies

A desk-top study will initially involve the archaeologist in an examination of many documents and records including old library and archive material, maps, ground and aerial photographs, manuscripts and, for coastal and

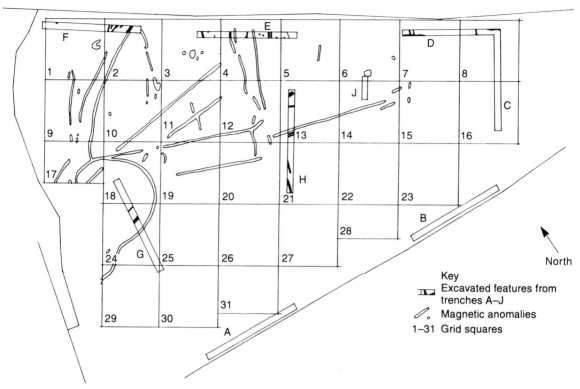

Figure 2.1 Alington Avenue, Dorchester: results of trial trenching and magnetometer survey. (Source: Wessex Archaeology.)

inshore areas, old charts. These will frequently help to identify the location of burial grounds, forts, hamlets, parishes, field boundaries, long-established lanes, footpaths and other signs of past human activity. Early editions of maps may indicate the position of former buildings at a site and original field names may provide clues about earlier occupation. Some names may suggest earlier discoveries of building debris (e.g. Chapel Field, Tile Field) or activity (e.g. Kiln Field). Old charts may similarly indicate the position of wrecks or former watercourses where early occupation or activity occurred. Aerial photographs can also be useful in this respect, as shown in Figure 2.3. An interesting feature about this photograph is that the modern farms are not just located alongside the modern fenland road but are adjacent to the former watercourse which can be identified.

Many archaeological sites have been excavated over the years with varying degrees of success and with varying amounts of information recorded. This, however, is to be expected. Apart from the obvious fact that different sites contain different amounts of detail it is also likely that thoroughness of investigation will not always have been the same. GIS, however, may change all this. The York Archaeological Assessment (YAA), for instance, can rapidly produce data combining archaeological information with other criteria such as topography and cityscape (Miller, 1994).

One aspect of record keeping that could be very useful is borehole logs

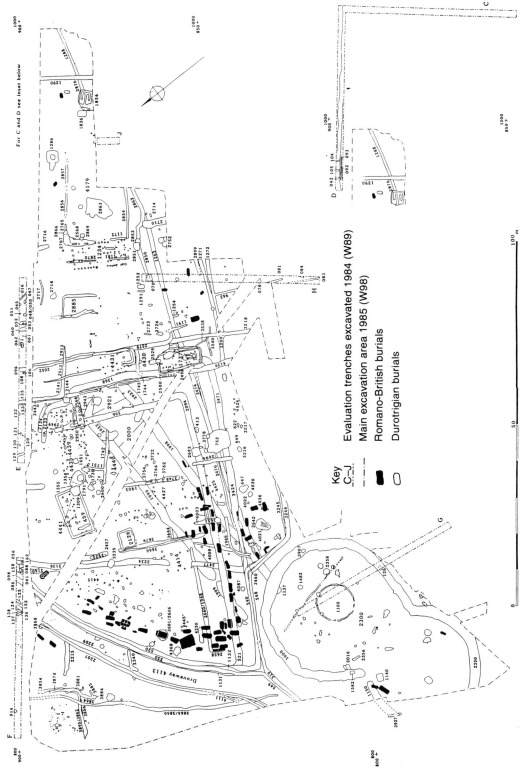

Figure 2.2 The Dorchester site after excavation. (Source: Wessex Archaeology.)

Key

C–J   Evaluation trenches excavated 1984 (W89)

     Main excavation area 1985 (W98)

     Romano-British burials

     Durotrigian burials

For C and D see inset below

Figure 2.3 Soil marks at Littleport, Cambridgeshire: an example of soil marks where the lighter toned silt of the former Little Ouse river which dried up in the seventeenth century is clearly visible. Note the siting of the modern farms within the broad banks of accumulated silt. (Reproduced with permission from Cambridge University Collection of Air Photographs: copyright reserved.)

supplied by developers or, in some cases, landowners. Such information could provide evidence of occupation, or lack of it, thereby saving time and money. The desk-top study should, of course, identify statutory protection and local policy issues, most notably local planning policy, and should be undertaken at the earliest opportunity. It is far preferable to do this at the assessment of feasibility stage rather than at the expensive detailed planning stage.

The Sites and Monuments Record (SMR)

The SMR is a comprehensive local authority record of known archaeological sites in Britain. It is compiled largely by archaeologists employed in local government working in conjunction with the government's national heritage departments and agencies (English Heritage, Historic Scotland and Welsh

Historic Monuments (Cadw)), and it forms the basic source of information about all known archaeological sites and spot-finds in the area of each local authority. In England the records are usually kept by the county council although in London and the metropolitan areas the situation is different. In London the SMR is maintained and administered by English Heritage and in the other metropolitan areas the SMRs are jointly maintained by the metropolitan boroughs. In Scotland the records are kept by most of the regional councils and elsewhere by Historic Scotland. In Wales four archaeological trusts (covering the whole country) are responsible for collecting this information: these are Clwyd-Powys Archaeological Trust, the Gwynedd Archaeological Trust Ltd, the Dyfed Archaeological Trust Ltd and the Glamorgan-Gwent Archaeological Trust Ltd.

The SMRs generally identify and include whatever information becomes available and are constantly updated as a result of casual finds, excavations, aerial photography and other survey work. They form an invaluable service to developers, landowners and consultants who wish to find out more about sites, what they contain or what may be expected.

SMRs normally contain five main components:

1. Ordnance Survey base maps on which are plotted archaeological sites and finds;
2. other maps and drawings at various scales detailing specific information about individual sites;
3. a database (often computerized) which summarizes what is known about given sites and where additional information may be found;
4. photographs including aerial photographs, photographs of survey work or photographs used to monitor site excavations and conditions;
5. drawings and other graphic material.

One of the aims of SMRs is to distil what is known about the archaeological potential of any given site and to direct enquirers to other sources of information. In this respect the computerized database – Figure 2.4 provides an example – is often produced and given to enquirers.

Fieldwalking

Fieldwalking is the word used to describe the systematic collection of artefacts from the surface of the land and frequently cultivated fields. If and when discoveries are made, or where some parts of a field or area appear more promising or more accessible than others, a system of recording is used to enable others to locate the position of finds at a later date. Recording what is found is also important because it can be used to establish the density of those finds and suggest areas for further investigation or where to undertake a sampling strategy. It would also be useful to record the position of any buildings and give an indication of the levels involved. Time of year and recent ploughing will indicate the circumstances in which finds were discovered.

The method of recording would normally be based on a grid system set out either in line with the orientation of the field to be surveyed (as in Figure 2.5)

Berkshire SMR Number: 02539 . 02 . 500

Photographic records :   Bibliographic records :   Archive records :

| Site name: COLEY PARK FARM, READING. | Parish(s): READING; | ; | Nat grid ref: C 470660 171990 | Site/find: S | Area status: | Legal status: |

Periods: SAXON   Period Qualifier: ?   No. items: 1   Type: STRUCTURE: COMPONENT: Planform :

Class: Material: Colour: Decoration on type:

Description: UNDERLYING RIVER SILTS IS A RICH ORGANIC LAYER, POSSIBLY REPRESENTING AN EARLY CHANNEL WITH MAN MADE BANK. THIS LAYER CONTAINED A STAKE AND SOME MID SAXON POTTERY.

Boundary/Line :1.   2.   grid coordinates 3.   4.   Dimensions:units: Type & size: 1.   2.   3.   Area :   Weight: Altitude: from 40 to   (M)   Aspect: Slope :   Alignment:

Formcodes and date: EXCAVATED SITE 0/1985   Condition codes and date: UNKNOWN 0/1985 TWA   Excavator and date: 0/1985   Landuse and date: Water code: RIVER distance : 1 units : M   Further action?

Drift geology: ALLUVIUM   Base geology :   Soiltype : ALLUVIAL GLEY SOILS   Landclass: Compiled by: DCH 28/09/87   Checked by : / /   Amended by: / /   / /

Berkshire SMR Number: 03942 . 02 . 000

Photographic records :   Bibliographic records : Y   Archive records :

| Site name: LECKHAMPSTEAD | Parish(s): LECKHAMPSTEAD; | ; | Nat grid ref: C 443900 176000 | Site/find: S | Area status: | Legal status: |

Periods: 11TH CENT   Period Qualifier: A   No. items: Type: SETTLEMENT: Planform :

Class: Material: Colour: Decoration on type:

Description: 'LECANESTEDE' RECORDED IN DOMESDAY. LATER VARIANTS OF THE NAME INCLUDE 'LECHHAMESTEDA' (1167), 'LEKHAMSTEDA' (1176), AND 'LECKHAMPSTED' (1316). THE NAME DERIVES FROM THE SAXON 'LEAC', MEANING LEEK OR GARLIC. ALL INFO FROM GELLING. THE GIVEN NGR IS FOR THE PRESENT VILLAGE, BUT SEE SMR 3942.01 & 2665.

Boundary/Line :1.   2.   grid coordinates 3.   4.   Dimensions:units: Type & size: 1.   2.   3.   Area :   Weight: Altitude: from to   (M)   Aspect: Slope :   Alignment:

Formcodes and date: DOCUMENTARY SOURCE 0/1086   Condition codes and date: Excavator and date: Landuse and date: Water code: distance : units :   Further action?

Drift geology: CLAY WITH FLINTS   Base geology :   Soiltype : PALEO-ARGILLIC BROWN EARTHS   Landclass: Compiled by: PF 29/05/90   Checked by : / /   Amended by: / /   / /

Figure 2.4 Extracts from the Berkshire SMR. (Reproduced from records of Berkshire County Archaeologist.)

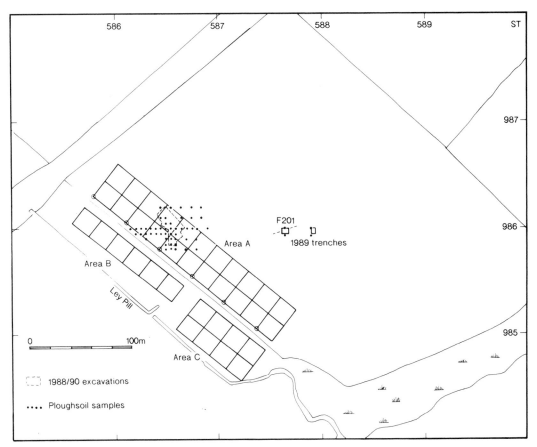

Figure 2.5 Location of geophysical survey and plough soil samples at Woolaston, Gloucestershire. (Reproduced from M.G. Fulford and J.R.L. Allen, Iron-making at the Chesters Villa, Woolaston, Gloucestershire: Survey and excavation 1987–1991, *Britannia XXIII*, 1992.)

or on a north/south and east/west axis based on the national grid. The advantage of the former is that it can be easier to establish in the field; however, the latter method enables different sites to be related to each other more easily.

Aerial photography

It is remarkable how much can be discovered about a site from the air. Patterns which are not recognizable from the ground and landscape details which are too small to be shown on maps can all be revealed. Indeed the examination and interpretation of aerial photographs is one of the main techniques in use today to locate and understand archaeological sites in the countryside. It can supplement ground observations and allow rapid recording of vast areas of the countryside, although much will depend on how the land is used and the procedures that are adopted. A few comments are in order.

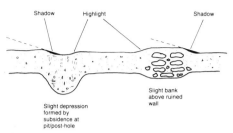

Figure 2.6 Shadow site.

How land is used

The way in which the countryside is used will influence what is revealed by aerial photography and how it should be interpreted. There are three conditions which apply, namely:

1. where ancient earthworks remain intact (a **shadow site**);
2. where the land is cultivated but not growing a crop (a **soil mark site**);
3. where crop growing occurs (a **crop mark site**).

Shadow sites

Where there are ancient earthworks, aerial views can amplify ground surveys and reveal details of slight features and indentations that are hard to discern from the ground. Shadow photography, as the name implies, identifies features because shadows are cast over the ground where there are mounds or depressions. In addition, taken from afar, as it were, aerial photographs can give an overall picture of a site showing how different features relate to each other and to the surrounding landscape. The shape and form of historic or prehistoric settlements may be outlined, as shown in Figure 2.6, to the extent that judgements can be made about the location of buildings, defences and other features. It is a method that is useful for the study of hill-forts and, more importantly, for the study of low banks, ditches and walls remaining from abandoned settlements and field systems.

Soil mark sites

Disturbance of the ground usually affects the colour of the surface soil. When earth is ploughed, the soil which is turned up will be a different colour to that which has not been touched. Similarly, the deeper the ploughing the greater the chance that the ploughed soil will be another colour. Sometimes these differences in colour can reveal past disturbances of the ground. Where human occupation has occurred, soil from old earthworks, ditches, burnt fragments and other remnants may be brought to the surface by ploughing as shown in Figure 2.7.

In addition it is also possible, by studying soil mark sites, to detect changes in the landscape. In the Fenlands, for instance, marks in the soil have revealed the position of former creeks and rivers traceable by the meandering lines of silt. Figure 2.3, referred to earlier, illustrates a good example of this.

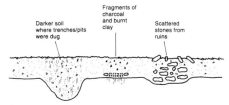

Figure 2.7 Soil mark site.

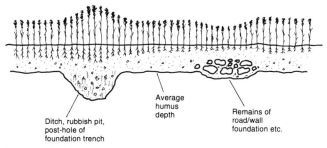

Figure 2.8 Crop mark site.

The archaeologist can learn a lot from these discolourations but it is often only possible to detect them from the air. When on the ground it can be very difficult to discern any changes and particularly any pattern to the changes.

Crop mark sites

Crop marks are the patterns that can be observed from growing crops. They result from soil disturbed by earlier human settlement which has affected the content of the soil in some way thereby affecting plant growth. A former ditch or pit, for example, is likely to have a greater depth of topsoil than the surrounding area and to retain more water and plant nutrients, thereby encouraging plant growth. Conversely, earlier settlement consisting of stone foundations, cobbled yards or old roadways is likely to restrict crop growth. It will be visible as areas of less luxurious or even stunted plant growth as illustrated in Figures 2.8, 2.9 and 2.10.

Crop marks can develop at almost any time but will generally be most noticeable in early summer, when differences in the rate of growth will be most pronounced. The degree of drought will also be important. Depending on the stage of the growth cycle, the extent of drought will greatly increase the colour variation as plants with a better supply of water will tend to grow more quickly and ripen at different times.

Aerial photography can reveal these differences, although care needs to be taken in interpreting what is there because other factors can also influence what appears on a photograph. Geological patterns, land drains, agricultural practices, pipelines and even previous fairground activity can all produce unusual crop or soil marks similar to those produced by archaeological remains.

Figure 2.9 Romano-British agriculture revealed at Sutton St Edmund, Lincolnshire. (Reproduced with permission from Cambridge University Collection of Air Photographs: copyright reserved.)

Procedural matters

It is worth noting that timing and the angle at which photographs are taken will be important. Time of day and of year can produce different results in the same way that oblique photographs will produce different information from vertical photography. Degree and angle of sunlight, weather, the seasons and the extent of plant growth will all have an influence. Changes in ground level and the angle of photographs can also cause distortion, indicating that care must be taken in the use and interpretation of aerial photographs.

Remote sensing

Remote sensing operates on the principle that anomalies in the normal or expected physical or chemical make-up of the soil can be detected. Brought about by past human activity and occupation, instruments or tests can be used with varying degrees of success to measure the extent of that activity. Essentially there are five ways in which this might be done. They are:

Figure 2.10 Crop marks at Brampton, Huntingdon: note the rings in the field to the left of the main road and where one has been cut through by the estate road. (Reproduced with permission from Cambridge University Collection of Air Photographs: copyright reserved.)

1. to measure the resistance of the subsoil to the passage of an electric current (known as **resistivity surveying**);
2. to measure variations in the magnetism of the ground (**magnetic scanning**);
3. to measure the physical properties of the topsoil (by **magnetic susceptibility**);
4. to interpret reflected radio signals (generally referred to as **ground-penetrating radar**);
5. to assess the chemical composition of the soil (referred to as **chemical analysis**).

An important feature of these techniques is that they can provide quick results although prior thought will be needed in order to decide which method to use. Information from the desk-top study, local geology, ground cover, the nature of the proposed development and planning time-scales will all have to be taken into account where large development sites such as a housing scheme or mineral extraction will require different strategies and targets to that required for linear sites such as pipelines or road proposals.

Resistivity surveying

Resistivity surveying measures the resistance of the ground to an electric current. The process works on the principle that some features will interrupt the flow of current thereby increasing the resistivity of the ground whilst other features will reduce the resistance. The method involves the insertion of an electrical current into the ground with the reply measured to reveal anomalies. Walls and dry conditions will normally result in higher resistance responses with wet conditions producing a low resistance.

A problem with this method is that many factors can influence the passage of the current, making it difficult to identify what has caused the anomaly. Stony soils or soil containing boulder clay, for example, can give erratic results which can be difficult to interpret. Sandy soils can also produce a high resistance to the current and recent rainfall can make interpretation difficult.

Experience suggests that resistivity surveying is most useful where linear features such as a road or walls are expected. By taking measurements in a straight line or a series of straight lines across a known or suspected feature a reasonably accurate picture can emerge. Each line would appear as peaks and troughs on a graph indicating the change of level of resistance to the current. Interpretative skills will be important.

Magnetic scanning

Magnetic surveying is similar to resistivity in that it too measures variations in the soil. The difference is that it measures changes in the magnetism of the ground by looking at the effect deposited materials can have on the Earth's magnetic field, which runs in a known direction and can be calculated at any given place or time. If artefacts and features from past human activity lie buried in the ground they can alter the magnetic field depending on the strength of magnetism emanating from the deposited material. It can be either positive or negative and increase or decrease the strength of the Earth's magnetic field.

If the aim is merely to locate a known feature then this method can be very useful. If, on the other hand, an interpretation of what lies beneath the ground is required, then the process becomes more difficult. Factors such as depth and area of disturbed land, the size of any feature, the nature of the past human activity and the content, looseness and water content of the soil and its surroundings become important. They can require different types of magnetometer to be used although the fluxgate gradiometer appears to be the most popular. A pottery kiln, for example, will produce a strong magnetic anomaly because of the fired clay and brick structure.

Magnetic susceptibility

Rather than measure changes in the Earth's magnetic field associated with buried features, magnetic susceptibility is concerned with measuring the effects of human activity in the soil. Forming a prospecting technique in its own right, the aim is to measure changes in the physical properties of the soil and its susceptibility to past occupation. Three intensities or sampling intervals can be used, referred to as coarse, medium and fine. In the coarse method the interval of measurement will be between 10 and 50 m depending on the size of the project. It will provide background information and help show where more detailed investigation should be undertaken. The medium density will be carried out at a ground interval of 10 m or less in order to define areas of activity, whilst the fine sampling interval would be undertaken at approximately every metre, in order to produce specific information about a small site. This last approach, however, will not always be appropriate, especially where ploughing has redistributed the soil. An example based on magnetic susceptibility is shown in Figures 2.11 and 2.12. Based at the same site as shown in Figure 2.5 the results of the survey for Areas A, B and C in the earlier drawing are shown in Figure 2.11, with their interpretation shown in Figure 2.12.

Ground-penetrating radar

Just as radar relies on sending out short radio waves or pulses which are reflected back from objects, so ground-penetrating radar transmits and receives radio waves at regular intervals. The time it takes for the reflected radio wave to bounce back depends on how deep the object is, although readings can be difficult to interpret, particularly if buried remains are deep or lie beneath other objects or if they are not solid. As Gaffney and Gater (1993) recognize, some claims for the success of this technique have been overstated. Difficulties in interpretation and exact depth resolution do not always make this a cost effective technique.

Chemical analysis

Chemical methods of detection are another means of trying to find out what lies beneath the ground although they tend to be most useful in connection with human or animal activity. When human and animal matter decays, phosphates are deposited in the soil which can then be collected and analysed for its phosphate content. The more phosphate that is discovered the greater will have been the activity.

If small samples of soil are collected and tested, either on site or in the laboratory, and a careful record made of the position and depth of each sample, then it is possible to get an idea of the level of past occupation. The main difficulty, however, is that it is not possible to distinguish between human or animal remains without further evidence. If a large amount of phosphate is discovered there is no way of telling if it was caused by human activity or if the area was used, say, for keeping livestock. However, if careful records are made of other finds or if the method is used in conjunction with one or more of the other techniques, it may be possible to obtain a better appreciation of the activity that occurred at the site. In general it is a quick, cheap and useful way of identifying where activity occurred.

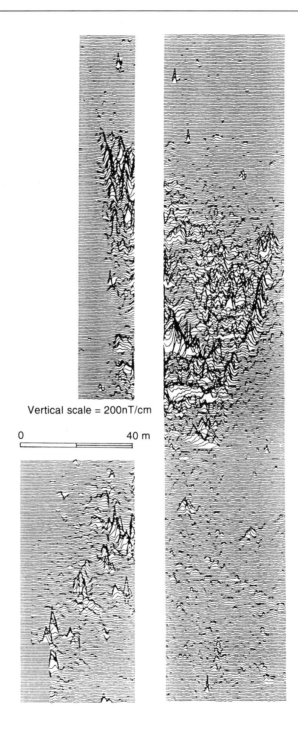

Vertical scale = 200nT/cm

0   40 m

Figure 2.11 Results of the magnetometer survey at Woolaston, Gloucestershire. (Reproduced from M.G. Fulford and J.R.L. Allen, Iron-making at the Chesters Villa, Woolaston, Gloucestershire: Survey and excavation 1987–1991, *Britannia XXIII*, 1992.)

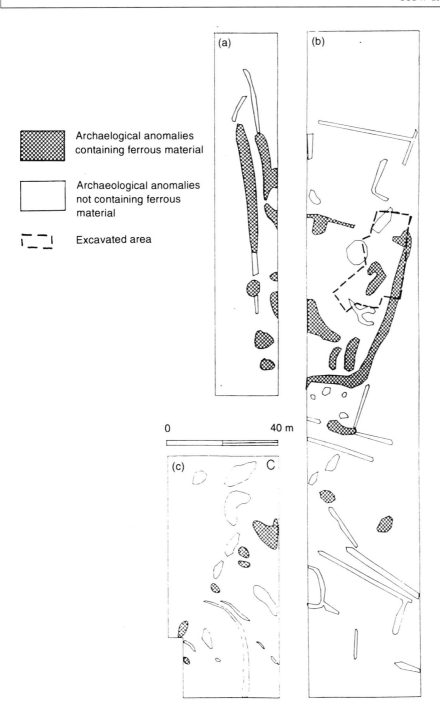

Archaelogical anomalies
containing ferrous material

Archaeological anomalies
not containing ferrous
material

Excavated area

0   40 m

Figure 2.12 Interpretation of the magnetometer survey at Woolaston. (Reproduced from M.G. Fulford and J.R.L. Allen, Iron-making at the Chesters Villa, Woolaston, Gloucestershire: Survey and excavation 1987–1991, *Britannia XXIII*, 1992.)

Trial trenching

Anomalies in the ground obtained from remote sensing together with information from the desk-top study can be tested by trial trenching. Based on a careful analysis of the above and in respect of where development is proposed, it should be possible to devise a sampling strategy whereby trenches normally one metre wide are dug. These would be where archaeologists judge that past activity was most intense and where the best results are expected. Care, however, must be taken because information can be misleading, as was shown earlier in Figure 2.1 and 2.2.

2.4 CHOOSING AN APPROACH

The aim of investigation will be to extract as much information about a site as possible within the time and resources available. The investigation will be influenced by what is proposed at a site and how extensive development might be.

Ideally, background research will have incorporated a desk-top study where the SMR, aerial photographs and other sources would have been examined to help decide how to proceed. Type of soil, the possibility of obstructions, the relevant periods of history likely to be found at a site and the possible depth of finds might be revealed by this study and suggest a course of action. They may give an indication of the archaeological importance of a site although remote sensing and trial trenching would have a greater impact. Each of the techniques has its advantages and disadvantages but the most striking thing about them is the extent to which they complement each other. There is little overlap, which highlights the need for early research in order to choose the most appropriate course of action. It also suggests that the most complete picture would be to make use of all of these techniques although time and money will frequently prevent this: skill and knowledge in these matters will be crucial if the best results are to be achieved.

2.5 THE COSTS OF INVESTIGATION

Many factors contribute to the costs of archaeological investigation. No two sites are the same and local circumstances will always differ. The information that is required, the ease with which it can be obtained, the archaeological content, site factors and how the investigation is conducted will all vary from site to site. They indicate that it is not possible to predict what the cost of investigating or excavating a site will be. On the other hand, it is possible to identify the main cost elements and the factors which influence them.

The cost elements

The costs of archaeological investigation can be broken down into cost elements, the number of which will depend on the significance of the archaeological evidence. The more important a site the greater the number of elements that will apply. Eleven significant cost elements can be identified:

1. **Examination of the archive**

   The compilation of information about a site takes time. Commonly referred to as a desk-top study it will require an examination of all available records of a site, such as the SMR, estate records, archive material, tithe maps, planning policy, the planning register and so on. Available from county, regional (Scotland) and district records, local libraries and other sources, not all of it will necessarily be published nor readily available. It forms the starting point of enquiries and should always apply.

2. **Purchase of information**

   Some of the most useful information may need to be bought. Aerial photographs, reports of earlier excavations, drawings and other records, whether in private or public ownership, may occasionally have to be purchased before it can be used. Even an SMR search can cost money as some authorities now charge for this service. Where purchase is necessary it may be possible to reach agreements on the exchange of information, although it is as well to check wherever possible on its content beforehand. The information may not be suitable or appropriate to the occasion.

3. **Preparation of preliminary findings**

   As part of the initial evaluation process it is advisable to proceed step by step where the findings from the archive and other initial information can be carefully studied. If a logical sequence of events is pursued it can show how far the investigation needs to go and where it becomes unnecessary to continue. A preliminary report can help in this respect. It can highlight the possible or probable importance of a site and point to the direction for further investigation.

4. **Non-intrusive site investigation**

   Site investigation is a key component of archaeological evaluation. Costs, however, can vary enormously where different techniques, as we have seen, can produce different results. Ideally several methods should be used, including fieldwalking, soil sampling and geophysical techniques. Much will depend on the nature and content of the soil, subsoil and the types of finds and artefacts lying within it. Waterlogged ground will affect resistivity whilst wetland sites will present difficulties of access and recording. They are sites where geophysical prospecting will present problems and where trenching would probably produce better results provided the water can be kept at bay.

5. **Compilation of evaluation report**

   At many development sites an evaluation report is now a necessary prerequisite to the submission of a planning application. By bringing archive information and site investigation together it should reveal the expected archaeological importance of a site and indicate whether and in what circumstances excavation would be appropriate. In short, it is the report to indicate whether further work is necessary and the options available to the developer. At 1990 prices, Ove Arup (1991) reported the

Table 2.1 An example of evaluation costs in connection with a proposal to construct a 1.5 km long by-pass (submitted for competitive tender)

Desk study	£600	6.2%
Preliminary field visit	£150	1.5%
Trial trenching	£5900	60.8%
Report preparation	£2800	28.9%
Archive deposition	£250	2.6%
Total	£9700	100%

cost of an evaluation report to be in the range of £10 000–50 000 although some archaeologists would consider this estimate rather high. One recent example (shown in Table 2.1) produced an estimate of £9700 although confidentiality restricts identity. It does, however, give an indication of what to expect, bearing in mind the comments made earlier about variations in cost.

6. Examination of the specification

Some authorities prepare archaeological briefs and specifications aimed at spelling out their requirements for site investigation and possibly excavation. Designed to produce from the evaluation the necessary data to enable informed decisions to be made on any development, there will be times when a developer will want a second opinion from an archaeological consultant concerning the content and requirements of a specification. Concerns about value for money, the time-scales involved and the possible impact of archaeology on site development will be key factors where a second opinion could be of particular benefit to the developer.

7. Site excavation

If remains are to be destroyed and cannot be preserved *in situ* and an evaluation supported by planning requirements indicates that excavation is necessary, then careful planning will be essential if unnecessary costs are to be avoided. Generally, excavation is the most expensive part of any archaeological investigation, frequently running into six figures (sometimes seven). It is where factors such as the area(s) to be excavated, the resources required, funding, the location of facilities and the possibility of adverse weather will need to be taken into account if costs are to be kept to a minimum. They are matters which are looked at in more detail in Chapter 3.

8. Collection and storage of information

It follows that artefacts and other finds discovered at a site need to be collected, conserved, stored and analysed. Less obvious perhaps to the developer is the fact that some finds need to be protected from the air as quickly as possible and that convenient facilities for washing, packing and storing will need to be provided. Existing buildings on a site can be invaluable in this respect although rural and submerged sites present more of a problem. The provision of site huts and/or distance to the laboratory may have to be costed.

9. **Conservation and analysis of information**

The preservation and analysis of finds is often a time-consuming process involving detailed specialist knowledge and equipment. It is where adequate facilities need to be available but where they cannot always readily be provided. The analysis of excavation results, however, is of great importance. In the same way that a developer would expect borehole samples to be examined and reported upon, so a proper assessment of excavation results should be conducted so that discoveries crucial to the understanding of a site can be selected for analysis.

Normally the larger archaeological units will have their own in-house facilities where conservation and analysis is an on-going activity. For smaller units this facility may have to be contracted out and financial contributions may need to be sought towards the cost of analysis and testing of finds. Either way it can be an important cost element especially if information is to be published. Reference to English Heritage's *Management of Archaeological Projects* (1991) would help.

10. **Publication and publicity**

Publication is seen by many as the important end-result of the investigative process although it is where costs can, again, vary enormously. Apart from obvious variations due to the nature and extent of excavation and the information retrieved from a site, there are less obvious problems associated with where and what to publish and the timing and costs of publication. For professional bodies this should not be a problem but for those archaeological units run by small groups of dedicated amateurs differences of opinion can occur over what and where to publish. Should a national archaeological journal be approached or should the information be published in a local newsletter or publication that is produced on an *ad hoc* basis? Small points, perhaps, but they indicate that publication can be far from straightforward.

11. **The archaeological unit**

The type of archaeological unit and the way it is organized can have a bearing on cost. Administrative and other costs will be the same as in many businesses and consultancies and will be absorbed into the overall income and expenditure of the unit. Efficiency and effectiveness of operation will be key factors but so too will the size of the unit. Some organizations because of their size will have very few overheads and be able to provide a cheaper service. Size, however, might mean that they are good at providing some services but less good at providing others. A small unit, for instance, might be very good at initial site evaluation and the examination of reports in a consultancy capacity. A larger unit would probably be better at managing an excavation and providing a comprehensive service. Consideration, therefore, should be given to the nature of the advice that is sought and the type of unit to provide it.

Factors influencing the cost of investigation

Each of the cost elements identified above can be subject to a number of influences. No matter that the element can differ because of what is required, several external factors can also affect the costs of investigation. Significantly, they can apply individually or in combination thereby increasing the scope for archaeological costs to vary. The main factors are as follows:

1. **Location**

    The location of a site can clearly affect the costs of investigation. Isolated and remote sites will inevitably involve more travelling time, sometimes across difficult terrain, and lead to additional transport costs, the transportation of equipment and finds over greater distances, additional accommodation requirements and other overheads. The ability and motivation to undertake work in out-of-the-way places, notwithstanding weather conditions, will differ from organization to organization, amateur and professional. When it comes to tendering, well-organized local units will often be at an advantage.

2. **The type of advice sought**

    The advice sought by developers can range from a simple critique of an archaeological specification to a full-blown, large-scale, time-consuming site excavation. In between there will be a number of alternatives, but as the extent and importance of the archaeological resource will not generally be known in advance, initial ideas about the extent of advice sought can easily be superseded. What might originally have been thought of as a straightforward evaluation could evolve into a more complex search for information and require a change of plan. Variations could occur because of the perceived importance of a site and, significantly, the statutory requirements that might be imposed through planning or other controls.

    Related to the type of advice that might be sought is where the requests come from. Here one of the larger archaeological units revealed that for the 1992–93 period some 40% of the threats to archaeology came from development projects, 15% from roads and 6% from golf courses (Table 2.2). Admittedly this is not a complete picture and will contain geographical bias, but it is an example of where concerns came from in 1992. It would also be interesting to see how these figures differ between the regions and how they may vary over time.

3. **The availability of information**

    Current information about a site will depend on the extent of past investigation and what the records show. Whether public or private they may be limited in scope, such as the casual discovery of coins from

Table 2.2 Sample of development threats to archaeology in 1992–93

Development	50	40%
Roads	19	15%
Services	20	16%
Golf courses	7	6%
Mineral extraction	8	6%
Other	21	17%
Total	125	100%

Source: Wessex Archaeology

fieldwalking, or they may contain a detailed account of earlier excavations. A site could have been extensively excavated many years ago and provide a mine of information waiting to be tapped – the excavation of the Roman fort at Malton, North Yorkshire in the 1920s is one example. Today, at first glance, it virtually gives the impression of a site suitable for development. Past information indicates otherwise.

4. The nature and type of site

We know that historic remains can come in all shapes and sizes. They also vary enormously in importance and the information they contain. Furthermore, many modern boundaries do not respect historic boundaries, with the effect that neighbouring development sites can produce vastly different amounts of archaeological information. Extent and type of occupation, depth of discovery, historic periods, the extent of previous destruction, the size and location of the site being considered for development are factors which can all have an impact on the information retrieved.

Another factor which can be even more important is ground conditions. Waterlogged sites and those with a high water table where anaerobic conditions exist will inevitably contain more preserved and worthwhile information. They are sites where archaeologists are likely to want to spend as much time as possible extracting as much information as possible. Archaeological investigation at such sites will frequently be longer and cost more money, although the site evaluation, if it has been done properly, should have revealed these differences.

5. Resources available to the investigation

Time, money, people and equipment are the main resources, all of which can vary according to location, size of investigation, likely or known importance of a site, time of year, information available, type of site, the organization of the archaeological unit and the need to subcontract specialist services. The combined effect of these factors can dramatically affect the costs of investigation, indicating that money spent on early evaluations is usually money well spent.

6. Accessibility

If a site abuts the public highway and the developer has complete control of access and is willing to allow an archaeological investigation to proceed, then access should not present a problem. Apart from possible technical difficulties caused by underground or overhead services, security, rights of way and related matters, it should be possible to freely enter and leave a site for the purposes of archaeological investigation.

Difficulties, however, can arise where the developer does not own the land or all of it up to the public highway or where he does not yet own all of the land. One of the points about archaeological investigation is that it ought to start at the earliest opportunity, which could be while the developer is still negotiating the purchase of a site. One or more third parties could be involved and be unwilling to allow access. In some cases the people involved might even be unwilling to accept cash payment.

Conclusions on costs

The factors contributing to the cost of an archaeological investigation are many and varied. Different circumstances will apply to each site and there can be no hard and fast rules as to what the costs will be. The only thing that is certain is that the costs will always vary, although if the above factors are born in mind we should at least be able to appreciate why they vary. Finally, as a last resort, there is also the possibility of a second opinion, albeit at a price.

REFERENCES

Carver, M. (1987) *Underneath English Towns: Interpreting Urban Archaeology*, Batsford, London.

English Heritage (1987) *Ancient Monuments in the Countryside*, English Heritage, London.

English Heritage (1991) *The Management of Archaeological Projects*, English Heritage, London.

Fulford, M.G. and Allen, J.R.L. (1992) Iron-making at the Chesters Villa, Woolaston, Gloucestershire: Survey and Excavation 1987–1991. *Britannia* XXIII, pp. 159–215.

Gaffney, C.G. and Gater, J.G. (1993) Practice and method in the application of geophysical techniques in archaeology, in *Archaeological Resource Management in the UK: An Introduction* (eds J. Hunter and I. Ralston), Alan Sutton, Stroud.

Miller, P. (1994) Dig or pile? *Planning Week*, Vol. 2, No. 43, 27 October 1994, RTPI, London.

Ove Arup & Partners *et al.* (1991) *York development and archaeology study*, Ove Arup, Manchester.

FURTHER READING

Aston, M. and Rowley, T. (1974) *Landscape Archaeology*, David & Charles, Newton Abbot.

Barker, P. (1977) *Techniques of Archaeological Excavation*, Batsford, London.

Barker, P. (1986) *Understanding Archaeological Excavation*, Batsford, London.

Haskell, A. (ed.) (1993) *Caring for the Built Heritage: Conservation in Practice*, E. & F.N. Spon, London.

Hunter, J. and Ralston, I. (eds) (1993) *Archaeological Resource Management in the UK: An Introduction*, Alan Sutton, Stroud.

Miles, D. (1978) *An Introduction to Archaeology*, Ward Lock, London.

Muir, R. (1983) *History from the Air*, Michael Joseph, London.

Rahtz, P. (1985) *Invitation to Archaeology*, Blackwell, Oxford.

Riley, D.N. (1982) *Aerial Archaeology in Britain*, Shire Publications, Aylesbury.

Webster, G. (1974) *Practical Archaeology*, Adam and Charles Black, London.

Archaeological excavation | 3

As far as excavation is concerned the ideal situation from an archaeological point of view would be to extract and record as much historical information as possible from a site. In practice, this is rarely achieved. The natural effects of erosion and chemical action can destroy a lot of information, but human actions both past and present have been equally if not more damaging. The Victorian period is often thought of as being particularly destructive of archaeology but many recent buildings have been just as bad. Those constructed during and since the 1960s with basements and pile foundations will undoubtedly have destroyed much of what lay beneath the ground.

Today the situation is somewhat different. Planning policy, which is discussed in Chapter 6, now seeks to preserve archaeological remains *in situ* with excavation and recording principally taking place where development causes unavoidable destruction. Yet, at sites where archaeology is known to exist, some destruction will be unavoidable. The building of foundations, infrastructure projects and mineral extraction will inevitably damage part of the resource. Depending on the type and location of development this could be extensive or small scale.

At the intitial appraisal stage of development there will, on occasion, be a need to plan for excavation. For many developers it will need to be undertaken as quickly as possible although excavations which are hurried or incomplete can destroy vital clues. Careful recording will reduce this but is it necessary to extract every pebble and every grain of pollen from a site? Many would argue that it is not. Apart from grounds of cost it is sometimes argued that it is simply not essential to the furtherance of knowledge.

The availability of resources can also be a concern and we can, in effect, deduce that a rushed minimalist approach to excavation prior to loss by development and a full and thorough excavation of a site, by themselves, are not the answer. One is restricted too much by time, the other by a lack of resources. They indicate a need to optimize the collection of information.

3.1 STRATEGY FOR ARCHAEOLOGICAL EXCAVATION

The theory of optimization means that there ought to be a plan of action for archaeological excavation. Rather than dig wherever and whenever the opportunity arises, for whatever period, one argument is that there should be an overall strategy which identifies those sites worthy of excavation and those that are not. Of course, this is not simple, indeed some would argue that it is not possible. However, it does pose a number of questions about excavation. Apart from asking whether it would be better not to excavate at all and preserve remains *in situ*, other questions about where to locate development, the likely archaeological importance of a site and what information is required or sought become important. They indicate that there is a need to work out carefully where and what to dig.

A carefully devised strategy has advantages for the archaeologist and the developer. By identifying sites or areas for excavation it can help to concentrate minds on what to dig and how to go about it. It can also help to reduce uncertainty for the developer although this cannot always be the case, especially now that archaeology is recognized as a material consideration in the planning process. But by concentrating minds it should make potential difficulties and problems easier to identify and understand.

Such a strategy must form part of the ideal. In reality we need to look at the current issues involved in excavating sites and what to do with the information that is received. In this Chapter, therefore, we start by focusing on where and what to dig. This is followed by a look at some of the main things that need to be thought of in advance, such as the setting of objectives, how an excavation may be managed, the carrying out of background research and how a dig might be funded. This then provides a background for looking at how to go about the dig itself and how to collect and record information. Post-excavation work involving the bringing together of information also forms a key part of the process.

Where to dig

In one sense, where to dig can be considered irrelevant because rescue excavation will be dependent on where development is proposed. On the other hand, knowing where to dig can be important for two reasons. First, developers will want to know which sites are important for archaeological investigation and second, they will generally want to know which parts of a site require excavation.

Such questions must rely initially upon investigations and evaluations referred to in Chapter 2. The desk-top study would have identified important locations, and the remote sensing techniques those parts of a site most likely to produce results. But developers may still ask questions about whether every site that becomes available ought to be excavated or whether fewer sites should be excavated in greater detail.

There are arguments both ways. By looking at all of a town, its assets and character can be appreciated, whereas if part of a town is studied in greater detail a better understanding may be obtained of how that area evolved. Other arguments can also be present but to pursue either approach successfully and economically it would be advisable, indeed necessary, to find out as much as possible about an area in advance.

Fortunately, we know how deposits build up and how to interpret them.

We know that they do not build up in a regular and constant fashion and that archaeological remains are unevenly distributed both in quality and quantity. Some sites will hold little information, others will contain a lot, whilst information recovered at others will indicate how worthwhile excavations in an area may be.

This range of possibilities means that it is necessary to think ahead about what may lie beneath the ground and what the archaeologists want to extract from it. There will be a need to study past urban characteristics to see what attributes a town contains. Historically it could relate to a single period or, more commonly, to several historic periods over a time span from, say, the Romans up to the present day. Settlements of later periods will be superimposed on top of earlier settlements and it could be a question of which period or periods to investigate.

In this respect much will depend on a variety of factors. The type of settlement, the amount of evidence already obtained about different historic periods from other sites in the locality, ground conditions and their likely consequential effect on the survival of evidence, together with personal preferences and motives of the archaeologist, will all have a part to play in the choice of location. All of these and more can affect where to dig and whilst much information will be available thorough the SMR and other sources it is as well for the developer to be aware of these influences.

What to dig

In many ways the conditions applicable to site selection apply to what to dig within a site. Often particularly in an urban context it will relate to a multi-period settlement where a choice may have to be made over which period or periods of history to investigate. Generally, excavation would extend down to the level of destruction by development although this may not always be possible. Sites with a long historical background can present archaeologists with a number of options. They may be able to investigate ancient Briton, Roman, Anglo-Saxon, Viking, Medieval or later periods but not have time to thoroughly investigate all of them. Sites with a shorter historic background should present less of a problem although this need not be the case.

Size of site can also be important. Many archaeologists, but not all, believe that the larger the continuous area of excavation the more complete and less distorted the records will be. Experience shows that where there is a vertical edge or baulk there is some loss of evidence because:

- erosion will occur at the edges of the vertical face;
- the area behind the baulk has not been excavated;
- there can be difficulties in matching two separated areas of excavation;
- few archaeological sites will match modern site boundaries.

Where excavation is divided into trenches or trial pits considerable information can be missed. Smaller areas will almost always give partial and possibly misleading information, as we have seen in Figures 2.1 and 2.2. Another difficulty associated with excavating a site relates to the build-up of evidence. More recent deposits tend to be on top and excavators have to dig backwards

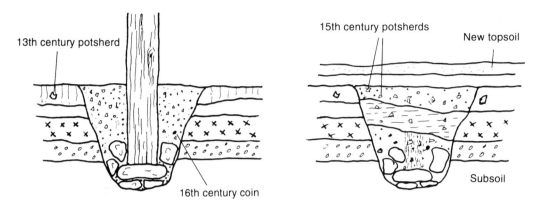

13th century potsherd

15th century potsherds

New topsoil

16th century coin

Subsoil

Figure 3.1 The effects of back-filling on strata.

in time. The historical development of a site is usually revealed in reverse order and yet this is not always the case. The common sense notion is that in a series of layers, the ones at the bottom will be earlier than the ones on top. However, archaeologists know that this is often not true. Older material can quite easily be found at a higher level and rather than refer to 'layers' or 'strata' archaeologists use the word **stratification** to convey the importance of interfaces between layers. Figure 3.1 indicates what this means. It shows a post-hole where surrounding earth has been back-filled with the result that objects from relatively recent periods can be discovered at a lower depth than artefacts from earlier periods.

This point has important implications for excavation. First, it means that excavators need to be aware of the fact that more modern finds can be found deeper in the ground. Second, it shows that excavation must be undertaken carefully, slowly and painstakingly if it is to be successful. Third, that the horizontal record of a site should be given more importance than the vertical, and finally, that a great deal of forethought must be given to where to dig on a site.

3.2 PLANNING AN EXCAVATION

The most important message to be received from considering where and what to dig is that pre-excavation planning is necessary. Irrespective of whether an excavation requires no more than a few volunteers at a site or a director managing a major project with full-time paid assistants, a plan of action will be required. Someone will be needed to take responsibility for the project to ensure that the necessary research is carried out, that the excavation is properly set up and run and that the results are fully written up and published. To ensure that an excavation runs smoothly, attention needs to be paid to the setting of objectives, the appointment of a team, background research, funding, organization of the dig itself and the site archive. They are sometimes collectively referred to as the project design or research design.

The setting of objectives

Archaeologists have found from experience that what needs to be done at an excavation and then sticking to it can be difficult. Problems arise or circumstances change, dictating a different course of action which deflects from their original ideas and produces different results. From experience they have found it necessary to set objectives for an excavation as a whole: about what to look out for, what to do when other factors intervene and so one. There is a need to define objectives against which the excavation, as it proceeds, can be judged.

These objectives will be influenced by several factors. Practicalities, academic interest, personal motives and the resources available to the excavating organization will all be relevant. So too will the nature of the site. As excavation proceeds unexpected finds or difficult site conditions may require the objectives to be reviewed or redefined. Soil conditions may slow down the rate of excavation. There may be a need to put more emphasis on a different period of history or it may be advisable to excavate a different part of a site. Alternatively, some finds may be more intact or appear more fashionable than others or it may suit the archaeologists to pursue a different line of enquiry. If objectives are made clear at the outset these would help guide subsequent changes of direction.

Appointing the team

In order to achieve the set objectives it is necessary to select the right team. A site director, with appropriate knowledge and experience and who can communicate with others, will take overall responsibility for the management and running of an excavation. The quality of the excavators and other supervisors will also be important but not to the same extent. The ability to detect that something is important will be an asset, but it will be for the site director to lead on this and give directions.

The success of an excavation will also depend to a large extent on how effectively the team work together and communicate with each other. The ability to get on may be cited as important but far more significant will be the flow of information through regular meetings. These should concentrate on:

- maintaining a constant critical view of the project and how the objectives are being met;
- monitoring progress and expenditure of the excavation and how they accord with the forecast;
- keeping members of the team informed of progress by others involved in the site;
- ensuring that appropriate professional standards are being met;
- informing and involving team members in any adjustments to priorities, timetabling, methods of investigation or the availability of resources.

Background research

The more information that can be obtained about a site the better will be its excavation. Preliminary investigations will be essential, requiring an analysis of all available records and a site investigation. Old maps and drawings, museum archives, aerial photographs, geological conditions and soil characteristics should be investigated for an indication of what might be revealed and to help provide an insight into the depth of what may lie beneath the ground. An examination of the SMR, site evaluation and newly emerging GIS methods such as the York YAA will constitute important aspects of this work. It may also be necessary to check town and country planning requirements.

A physical inspection of the site should be made. Where trial trenching and boreholes are undertaken as part of the excavation their location and setting should be examined as part of the site investigation. The immediate surroundings and neighbouring sites should also be checked so that ideas can be formulated about safe depths for excavation near buildings, whether shoring or underpinning is needed and the means of access.

Quite often it will not be possible to excavate all of a site. The existence of buildings, the unwillingness of a site owner or the lack of resources can all restrict where excavation takes place. If this is the case, more attention should be paid to background research and evaluation. It can help identify those parts of a site likely to produce the best results or suggest an order of preference for excavation if the best parts of a site are not available.

Funding an excavation

In the present economic climate where public funds are severely restricted and where developers are often expected to pay for archaeological investigation from anticipated (not actual) profits, consideration of how an excavation is to be funded is vital. Without sufficient funds it will not be possible to mount an excavation at the desired level and, indeed, in some instances, it may be more appropriate not to mount an excavation at all. If only limited work can be done on site this could be counter-productive to the pursuit of knowledge. It could conceivably destroy more than it finds, suggesting that preservation *in situ* should be pursued. Policy objectives, therefore, must take funding into account, where two considerations will be paramount – where the money is to come from and how it is to be spent.

Sources of finance

Over the years the balance of funding for archaeological investigation has undergone substantial change. Up to and including the 1980s, the bulk came from central government but more recently the onus has been transferred to the developer and other sources. The main sources can be identified as:

- **The developer**
  On the basis that development projects frequently destroy archaeological evidence many see the developer as a necessary and desirable contributor

to the funding of archaeological investigation. On the 'polluter-pays' principle the argument is that he or she should pay rather than the money come from public taxation. Ove Arup (1991), however, found that developers felt they should not pay the full cost of preserving the archaeological heritage. Whilst there was a willingness by many developers to accept the costs of evaluation, Ove Arup found that there was a reaction against bearing the full cost of archaeological excavation.

- **Central government**
  Funding decisions are now based on strict criteria relating in part to the importance, condition, rarity value, vulnerability and potential of an archaeological site, but more specifically to threatened sites. Value for money, careful targeting and a lack of an alternative sponsor mean that only the most worthy causes will receive money from the government. In line with PPG 16 and continuing pressure on overall resources, the emphasis is shifting away from more traditional recipients of government grants towards bodies and organizations concerned with securing the protection of important sites and the retrieval of valuable information. The aim is not simply to direct grant aid where it is desirable but where it is essential and where there is no alternative.

- **Local authorities**
  Whilst money can, in theory, be made available for archaeological investigation, local authorities are themselves in a difficult position when trying to target limited resources. Bearing in mind their many other responsibilities, some authorities might take the view that the expenditure of considerable sums of money on archaeological excavation where development is proposed should not be forced on the local community. Yet, no authorities are likely to consider the matter lightly. Views have been expressed about the possibility of extracting a levy on all development (Ove Arup, 1991), a matter not without its problems, as we shall see in Chapter 6.

- **Other sources**
  These can include civic and amenity organizations, academic institutions, individuals, charities and business interests. Money may be raised through public subscription, donation, appeal, sponsorship, the sale of merchandise and publications or the charging of entrance fees. Frequently, however, it will be made available for research purposes, particularly if an investigation is being undertaken at a site of high national importance rather than for rescue operations where development is proposed.

The costs of excavation

In the assessment of cost it is not just staff, equipment, accommodation and administrative costs that have to be considered. Factors such as time of year, location and the type of site must also be taken into account. These can have quite an impact on the number of hours required for excavation. Some tools and equipment needed for an excavation may have to be hired whilst others

Table 3.1 Example of archaeological excavation costs at a proposed quarry site

Fieldwork			
Staff	£14 000	47%	
Support	£ 7 000	23%	(accommodation, vehicles, etc.)
Specialists	£ 600	2%	(including monitoring by LPA)
Site costs	£ 1 400	5%	(including site huts, toilets, tools, etc.)
Plant hire	£ 7 000	23%	
	£30 000	100%	
Overall costs			
Fieldwork	£30 000	60%	
Assessment	£ 7 000	14%	
Analysis	£13 000	26%	
	£50 000	100%	

(Source: Wessex Archaeology.)

may be provided by a developer. Safety considerations, insurance, shoring, site accommodation, electricity and other overheads all indicate that careful assessments will have to be made if realistic estimates are to be obtained. Table 3.1 shows an example of excavation costs in connection with a proposal to develop a 100 hectare site for quarrying purposes. It must be emphasized, however, that no generalizations should be read into these figures as a neighbouring proposal could have totally different requirements. No two sites are the same.

At waterlogged sites costs increase. Apart from the additional cost of pumping out water there will most probably be further expense due to the fact that finds will be better preserved. Almost inevitably more time will be required to excavate such a site thereby adding to labour costs and hire charges. Furthermore, post-excavation costs are also likely to be more expensive. Greater care in preservation will be needed and if unique well-preserved environmentally sensitive evidence is to be protected there could be an ongoing cost in perpetuity.

These additional costs suggest that excavation be kept to a minimum, possibly by preservation *in situ*. However, if potential sponsors are to be approached a realistic assessment will have to be presented for sufficient money to be received. Assessments which are over-optimistic could be counter-productive and be of little benefit in the long run.

Organizing the dig

Once information about where and how to excavate a site has been worked out, together with an estimate of the costs involved and the time available for excavation, the planning of the dig can start. Decisions will have to be made about exactly where to dig and at what depth to commence serious exploration. It may be necessary or desirable to remove soil to a predetermined level below ground or to phase the excavation.

Consideration will also have to be given to where to store unwanted soil and where and when shoring will be required. Ground water could present a problem and require pumping arrangements. This could become a contributing factor influencing the manner in which a site might be excavated. So too could adverse soil conditions. Although minor points, they do show how attention to detail is important.

As excavation proceeds so recording of information and the removal and conservation of finds will take place. Techniques of conservation will be important, as will storage and retrieval systems. In addition, consideration must be given to time and cost constraints, requiring a level of monitoring appropriate to the size of the dig. Regular meetings and the dissemination of information both up and down the chain of command will be needed to ensure a satisfactory outcome. Some form of chart or similar graphic presentation would be advisable, especially if the following are important and need to be indicated:

- the range of tasks required for the excavation;
- the sequencing and relationships between these tasks;
- the amount of time allocated to each task;
- the personnel allocated to the different tasks;
- the critical path indicating where the least amount of float is available between tasks;
- detailed cost projections indicating where and when cash payments and receipts will be required.

The site archive

All the data gathered from an excavation needs to be quantified, indexed and preserved. This will constitute the field record of the excavation and must be available for subsequent research and interpretation. Consideration, there-fore, should be given as to how this is best achieved, for it is vital that it is maintained in optimum condition and not altered or tampered with in any way. If material is to be removed or even discarded from the archive this must be recorded.

The archive should be compiled by those most closely involved in the excavation as soon as possible after it is completed. An account should be prepared summarizing the site, the excavation, what was expected and what was found. It should include a record of the range, quality, condition and any

Table 3.2 Contents of an archive

- a copy of correspondence relating to the investigation
- a summary of the site objectives
- survey reports (geophysical, boreholes, etc.)
- site notebooks
- original photographs of the excavation
- drawings of the site
- artefacts and ecofacts from the site
- original finds records
- conservation records including X-rays
- records of skeletons
- computer discs
- other information retrieved from the site
- a detailed summary and index of the above

other relevant detail of the artefacts and material collected as indicated in MAP 2, prepared by English Heritage (1991). In addition there should be a recognition that this initial interpretation may change as and when analysis and assessment of the site are undertaken (Table 3.2).

3.3 TECHNIQUES OF EXCAVATION

Understanding sites

Visitors to archaeological sites often ask if anything interesting has been found by which they usually mean skeletons, coins or upstanding remains. They tend to think in terms of immediate appeal or intrinsic value. In response, excavators list the 'vital statistics' of a site: one skeleton, two brooches, four coins or whatever. Some, on the other hand, may give a detailed account of the importance of a site or talk at length about a particular item found on it. They will be revealing their own interests in contrast to those of the visitor or developer who may regard the amount of time an archaeologist spends at a site as unnecessary. This will be especially so if the amount of information is negligible. The visitor or developer may also conclude that if more time was spent actually digging a site less time would be wasted.

Yet it is the details – animal bones, charcoal, nails, pieces of pottery, soil samples and others – that will reveal so much about a site. The sight of an archaeologist carefully collecting samples of soils may appear unimportant but each sample will consist of more than just earth. It may contain tiny fragments of many types of material such as fibres, decayed mortar or pollen grains, which together can provide remarkable evidence. Pollen grains alone, when analysed, can reveal a great deal about climate and ancient vegetation and help to build up a framework for the past environment of a site.

The ability to ascertain a chronological framework is one of the major roles of archaeology. In any study of the past, time is an essential dimension where the sequencing of events is all important. When archaeologists excavate a site they do not have historical events to work to but must find some other means of constructing an historical framework. The only material in sufficient quantities lies in the ground.

Pottery is usually regarded as the most useful material. The reason for this is relatively straightforward. From different levels on a site pottery of different kinds can be compared with that found at other sites in the area. Changes in design and decoration can then be used to produce a sequence which can be used for subsequent finds in the area. Figure 3.2 shows how a chronology can be build from incomplete information from each site.

This example illustrates the importance of recovering information as well as objects. If finds are recorded and later compared with information received from other sites or, indeed, the same site at different times, the sum of information may be greater than the parts. By recording and analysing what might appear to be of little interest to, say, a developer, the archaeologist could contribute substantially to the advancement of knowledge.

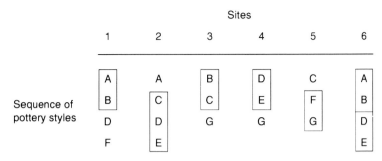

Figure 3.2 The sequencing of information: the letters A to G represent seven different styles of pottery and the numbers 1 to 6 represent six sites where excavation has taken place. The stratification of pottery is indicated by the vertical columns of letters with overlapping sequences ringed. (Redrawn from K. Branigan, *Archaeology Explained*, published by Duckworth, 1988.)

Stratification

Evidence from a site is not straightforward. It may appear to come in layers but this is rarely the case, as shown in Figure 3.3. Layers of history merge into one another or even become inverted with earlier historical evidence discovered above more recent material. Often features do not interrelate making it very difficult to interpret what has been found, raising questions about the date of finds and the periods or duration of occupation. Large sites can be particularly difficult to interpret and lead to speculation about what has been discovered.

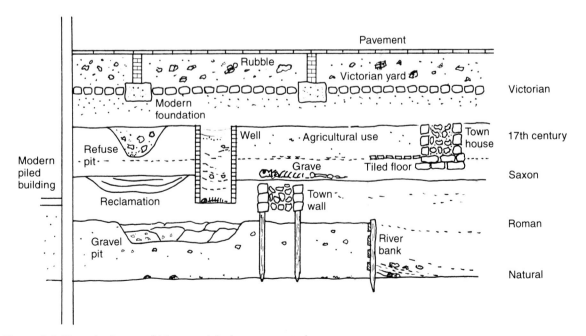

Figure 3.3 How the layers of history might be represented.

One technique aimed at reducing this speculation (and finding out more about a site) is stratification, referred to earlier, briefly. Defined as the successive layers of the Earth's surface, either artificial or natural, revealed by excavation, it is used to elucidate and interpret relationships between artefacts. Successive finds will not necessarily lie on top of each other but will relate in different directions according to the activities and actions that took place at the site. The back-fill for a post-hole, as we have seen from Figure 3.1, or a silted-up ditch can result in later deposits becoming buried more deeply than earlier ones. Thus the archaeologist, apart from taking care over the nature, colour and texture of the soil, will also be thinking about the possible sequence of past events and how finds might relate to each other. This, of course, takes time.

The other point about stratigraphy is that it is the horizontal record that is important. Vertical wall faces or the sides of a trench may be very interesting but more substantial information will be unearthed only through methodical and careful horizontal scraping away of the soil, making use of adapted skills, local knowledge and experience and recording as much as possible.

Recording

Excavation by its very nature is destructive. Once a site has been excavated it is gone for good and cannot be retrieved. For this reason full recording of what is discovered is vital. The search for information is concentrated on what remains of human activity and recording as much as possible in the time available. But the excavator will also be looking at what is not there. Negative evidence can present itself in different ways and can be just as important. It can be used to illustrate how a site developed or to show where gaps occur in the evidence. The archaeologist may have expected to see the remains of a wall but excavation may reveal none. If nothing else, the recording of this fact will enable the archaeologist to be more objective and thorough in the recording of a site and, when coupled with other available information, be of benefit to those who analyse the information after the site has been destroyed.

The elements to preservation by record are fourfold, consisting of the written, drawn and photographic record and the collection of finds and other archaeological evidence.

The written record

The written record contains all the immediate descriptions of a site and will be found on standard record-sheets, less formalized notes, day-books and other written material made up by anyone working on a site. It should include an account of progress together with a record of the thoughts of the site director and others involved in decision-making. Increasingly, it may also include tape recordings used alongside notebooks, to be transcribed at a later date. These may be used to capture immediate thoughts which might otherwise be forgotten.

One advantage of using standard forms is that it makes it easier to compare information from different sites. It can also act as an *aide memoire* for the person filling it in. By drawing attention not just to the matters that need recording but to those that might have been overlooked or expected but not discovered, it can provide both positive and negative evidence. Linked to a computer it can be particularly useful in the analysis of information.

The drawn record

This consists primarily of plans of all or parts of a site and of one or more features in it, showing them in the context of their surroundings or individually in as much detail as possible. Features may include walling, pits, post-holes, burials or specific items found on site and drawn separately from their context. Plans are normally drawn at a scale of 1:20 with smaller features where more detail is required at a scale of 1:10. It is important that drawings of different parts of a site are to the same scale and cross-referenced to the written record and any photographs that are taken. In this way they will go a long way to preserving by record what is destroyed.

The photographic record

Photographs relating to the written research and drawings can delineate features and different aspects of a site precisely. They have the specific advantages of speed, lighting, colour and angle. They can emphasize shape and surface texture and can be taken at an angle, vertically or stereoscopically to highlight or reveal different aspects of a site. Oblique photographs can show what a site looks like and the relationships between features both on and off the dig. Vertical photographs, in contrast, will be closely related to plans and drawings and can be used to supplement them. If they are used jointly, or stereoscopically, as in a grid of overlapping photographs, they can be useful in the recording of surfaces and features and act as a check on the accuracy of the drawn record. Finally, they can be of value when information is published. Whether in books, museum displays, the SMR or to supplement talks and lectures, the photographic record will undoubtedly be an invaluable aid to the archaeologist.

3.4 THE ARCHAEOLOGICAL EVIDENCE

Much speculation can develop over what is found at archaeological sites and can lead to problems for the developer. It can cause delay to development projects and, in extreme cases, lead to abandonment. It indicates that the interpretation of archaeological evidence must be undertaken with great care and is an important task which archaeologists must face. It would benefit developers to have a sound understanding of what is revealed and its likely importance.

The archaeological evidence obtained from sites can be said to fall into four broad types, namely deposits and structures, finds, human remains and environmental evidence. How they are interpreted will depend on the nature and location of the material, its relationship to other evidence and its degree of preservation. Some evidence, such as the physical remains of buildings, will be relatively easy to interpret, others such as discoloured earth, less so.

Deposits and structures

Early structures were built of stone, timber or other material such as clay, mud and reeds. Of these, stone structures are the easiest to recognize and excavate. Unearthing them can be visually impressive and, therefore, tempting to undertake. This temptation, however, can lead to poor results. In the past, one common technique was to dig a trench until a buried wall was struck and then to follow the wall, digging along each side until other walls were revealed. This process continued until as much of the walls as possible was uncovered and a plan of the building emerged. The effect, however, was that vital information between walls and relating to occupation was removed, making it almost impossible to ascertain what happened at a site and difficult to reappraise at a later date. It produced quicker results with the emphasis very much on quantity rather than quality.

Stone can be used in a variety of ways for construction purposes, ranging from dry stone walling, which relies on gravity and friction for its stability, to fine cut stonework using a bonding agent for added strength. Technique of construction might suggest that it symbolizes wealth and lead some to think that it conveys status although this will often be far from true. If stone was convenient it was used. Instead of constructing buildings in stone, it was quite feasible for foundations only to be used in this material. Timber tended to be more common but if a site was uneven stones could have been used to level it for a timber-framed construction.

Timber, in contrast to stone, is preserved only in exceptional circumstances. If it has not been kept in very wet or very dry condition it decays and perishes, especially in a temperate climate such as that of Britain. Foundations of different shapes and sizes will have been necessary depending on local circumstances. Individual post-holes are the most common but larger buildings or defences will have required trenches and additional support. The size, depth and frequency of post-holes can give some indication of what may have been constructed although, again, great care needs to be taken in the interpretation. Differently sized timbers decay at different rates; replacement post-holes may have been needed for a variety of reasons thereby increasing the number to more than was necessary. Similarly, rigidly jointed non-loadbearing timber-frames will have relied more on their joinery for support than earthbound upright posts.

Other materials such as sun-baked clay, mud and reeds all have limited lives and do not survive well. Thus, as far as structures are concerned, stone is the most impressive evidence of earlier occupation. Its scope for information, however, tends to be limited.

Finds

The term **finds** is generally used to mean all portable objects which are found in an excavation. It includes all sorts of fragments which can be classified in two main ways – either by the material from which they are made or by function. In the case of the former, they can be bone (combs, pins); bronze (brooches, buckles, pins); iron (nails, spearheads); flint (knives) and so on. In respect of function they may be classed as weapons, coins, ornaments, tools, pottery, etc.

Finds can tell us about activities that took place at sites and the nature of a culture. They can help tell us how advanced a community was in technical innovation, fashion, wealth creation, trading and more. The emphasis, however, is on help. Finds in themselves cannot be conclusive and assumptions will have to be made. The context of the surroundings in which they are found therefore becomes important, together with accurate recording.

Another feature of finds is that once unearthed they can deteriorate rapidly. Iron and bronze objects, in particular, will need on-site treatment. Others will merely need cleaning: this can be wet or dry depending on the material and its condition. Many will be fragile and need extreme care in their handling, transportation, storage and conservation.

Human and animal remains

The sight of a human skeleton always arouses interest, particularly among visitors to an excavation. Apart from the age and sex of an individual, the cause of death is a major point of enquiry. The possibility of foul play is often raised but this curiosity is probably linked more to human interest and how people survived than to morbid curiosity.

When examining a human skeleton, the first thing a pathologist will do is establish its sex. Male and female characteristics are easily distinguishable in several parts of the body, most notably the pelvis and skull, from which a reliable indication of sex can be made. Age is more difficult. Estimates have to be made based largely on the wear and tear of teeth and the degeneration of bones in the body. An examination of the build-up of tooth enamel and the density of blood-carrying channels in bones are two ways of estimating the age at death, although the results will only be approximate.

Information about the cause of death and the society in which the individual lived will be fragmented. Generally it will not be possible to establish the cause of death although sometimes skeletal remains will provide an answer. Gashes in a skull and the broken remains of a spearhead stuck in a bone are signs of sudden death. More frequently it may be possible to gain knowledge about attitudes to death and customs of a society. The mode of burial, the elaborateness of a tomb, the presence (or absence) of grave goods and the depth and size of a burial chamber can all provide clues, but when only one or a few skeletal remains are examined there can be little overall information of the society in which the individual lived.

What this tells us again is that careful recording is vital. Observation concerning the lie of the bones, the depth of burial and any unusual elements are all crucial to a better understanding of what may have happened (Figure 3.4). If all of these and other factors are recorded, then, as and when further burials are discovered over time, so an overall picture will gradually emerge from which more reliable assumptions can be made.

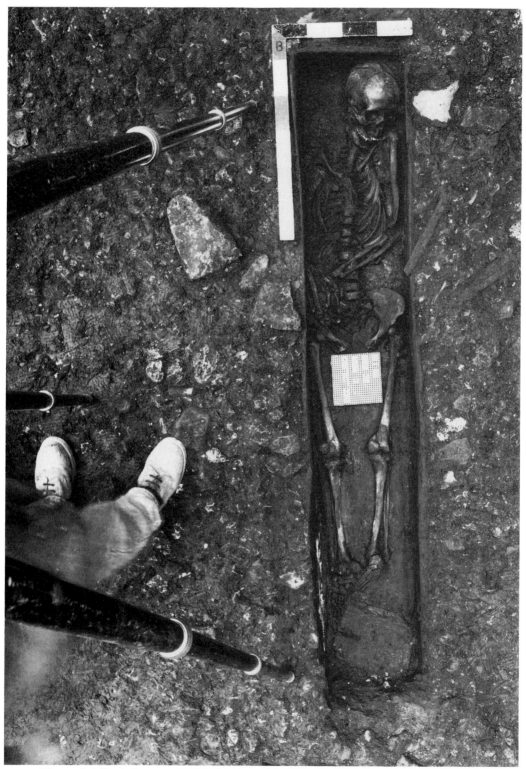

Figure 3.4 Buried corpse at York: note the size of coffin, lie of the bones and surroundings.

Environmental evidence

So far we have concentrated on human artefacts and remains. Human activity, however, does not operate in a vacuum. The environment in which we live plays an important part in how we survive and occupy our time. Thus the livestock we keep, the food we grow, the amount and type of grassland or woodland that is used, the animals that are hunted or fished and patterns of trading in commodities all become important. By examining all available evidence from fish bones to salt it is possible to build up a picture of the natural environment and the ways in which it was used to support human habitation.

3.5 POST-EXCAVATION WORK

Although the period of excavation may seem long to the developer it amounts to only a small fraction of the time an archaeologist will spend investigating a site. We have already seen that a considerable amount of preparatory work needs to be done before excavation can commence, but a great deal more time needs to be spent once the excavation is over. Depending on the size and importance of a site and what is retrieved from it, a number of post-excavation activities will have to be undertaken. These will include the washing, sorting and cataloguing of finds, the drawing of many items, the examination of soil and other samples, the preservation of finds in the laboratory and the careful marshalling of evidence for publication and research purposes.

Interpreting the evidence

Archaeologists have said repeatedly that an excavation is only as good as its recording system. If the position, extent and characteristics of all finds, materials and other matter and the context in which they are found are not meticulously recorded by all means available, the ability to interpret the evidence afterwards will be greatly diminished.

Whilst this is undoubtedly true there are two other factors which must not be overlooked. Underlying all practical and theoretical discussions about an excavation is the fact that when buried deposits are revealed, subjective perceptions will be difficult to avoid. Artefacts cannot always be immediately identified and although training in stratigraphy will provide many answers there can be no substitute for experience. To see how buildings decay, how layers of occupation accumulate, how depressions of all kinds silt up and how other processes help to form an archaeological site are important in understanding what is there.

The second factor is observation. Linked very much to recording and experience is the ability to observe the slightest change in the ground. The history of archaeology shows all too clearly how much information can be lost at an excavation simply because of a lack of observation and judgement. Excavators and their supervisors not only need experience but observation as well. Coupled with an understanding of how archaeological sites are formed and how buildings used to be constructed, informed experience will be used to recognize what is happening at a site.

Experience and observation underlie the importance of good recording. Linked with a record of initial thoughts, detailed field drawings and photographs and the archaeological evidence, they should help dispel doubts about how a site was made up. With time for analysis and the application of common sense, with perhaps some lateral thinking, a reasonable interpretation of what has been found should emerge.

Dating the past

The ability to date archaeological evidence is a major factor in the organization of archaeological evidence. By knowing how old a series of artefacts are, we are helped to understand the way in which a civilization progressed and the speed of development.

Basically there are two ways in which finds can be dated. One involves a careful study of an accumulation of deposits and the relationships between them; the other adopts a more absolute method using scientific techniques and analysis. On a single site, the study of the relationship between deposits will reveal which are the earliest and those that are later in origin. A sequence of deposition can be identified but if this is done for a number of sites, as discussed earlier and shown in Figure 3.3, further comparisons can be made. By constantly handling and studying various materials archaeologists will get to know the forms, decoration and other features of many artefacts and develop an understanding of items from different periods.

This approach may seem vague and unscientific but it is not and good results can be obtained. It certainly works well in situations where a lot of evidence has already been obtained and where the time and distance between the culture being dated and our own is not great. In Roman Britain, for example, where much evidence already exists, it forms the backbone for the historical dating of Romano-British deposits. Where the culture under examination is prehistoric and the links are more tenuous, it becomes more difficult to date finds using this technique. A more scientific approach becomes necessary, as indeed it must, even for Roman and more recent times, if an absolute chronology is to be established.

One of the important things about scientific methods of dating is that they do not have to rely on established links or the sequence of events. Instead of giving relative dates they concentrate on absolute dates, although, having said that, relative dating is still important, especially if used in conjunction with scientific methods. When the two methods are combined a better picture of events can be built up and possibly convey the tempo of life. In the development of civilization it becomes important to know if a technological change took 50 or 200 years to achieve.

Several scientific dating techniques are now available (Figure 3.5) and the situation is still changing. Their most spectacular successes have been in dating prehistoric cultures although it should not be forgotten that almost all of these techniques were first validated by using previously known samples.

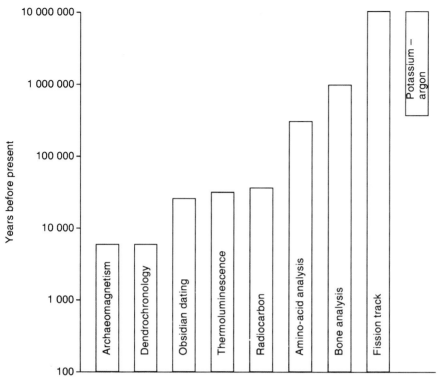

Figure 3.5 Ranges of application of scientific dating techniques. (Adapted from K. Green, *Archaeology: An Introduction*, published by Batsford, 1990.)

Another important point is that different techniques can only examine certain types of material. Dendrochronology, for instance, must make use of timber while archaeomagnetic dating is particularly useful for dating pottery and kilns where magnetic traces are to be found.

Publication

The publication of archaeological information is crucial for the advancement of knowledge, where two main strands can be identified. One is academically based where specialized knowledge or discussion is provided. This may deal with specific aspects of archaeology such as expanding the knowledge of a particular historic period or area or as a discourse on method – scientific dating or techniques of excavation are two examples – where the aim is to improve the retrieval of information for the benefit of others. The archaeological archive and the SMR would form key elements of the knowledge base although publication in newsletters and professional journals will be just as important.

The other strand to the advancement of knowledge is more general. Instead of dealing with certain aspects of archaeology in great detail (although this should not be ruled out), it seeks to inform the public about archaeology. Books, leaflets, photographs and films are examples where information in a highly readable or picturesque way is presented to inform and entertain the public. It may be presented in publications or be displayed at sites or in museums or it could be put on film.

Separate from these issues is the question of presentation. Obviously funds and costs will be important but lively and imaginative presentations do help to promote archaeology. It is not easy to picture buildings from holes in the ground yet with careful and imaginative expertise much can be achieved. Books, articles in magazines, leaflets and architectural drawings reconstructing the past are all common examples while the use of scale models, full-sized replicas and television programmes further illustrate the role and importance of archaeology in our society. They can have a tremendous impact.

There is also the realization that archaeological remains can all too easily be lost without record being made. Significantly, public concern over the loss of archaeological remains has grown over recent years and has voiced the need for constant record keeping. Coupled with advancements in the pursuit and gathering of information together with improved techniques of presentation, the publication of information, in whatever form, of threatened and saved sites seems set to continue.

REFERENCES

Branigan, K. (1988) *Archaeology Explained*, Duckworth, London.
English Heritage (1991) *Management of Archaeological Projects*, English Heritage, London.
Greene, K. (1990) *Archaeology: An Introduction*, Batsford, London.
Ove Arup & Partners *et al*. (1991) *York Development and Archaeology Study*, Ove Arup, Manchester.

FURTHER READING

Barker, P. (1977) *Techniques of Archaeological Excavation*, Batsford, London.
Barker, P. (1986) *Understanding Archaeological Excavation*, Batsford, London.
Carver, M. (1987) *Underneath English Towns: Interpreting Urban Archaeology*, Batsford, London.
Clark, A.J. (1990) *Seeing Beneath the Soil*, Batsford, London.
Harris, E.C. (1979) *Principles of Archaeological Stratigraphy*, Academic Press, London.
Rahtz, P. (1985) *Invitation to Archaeology*, Blackwell, Oxford.
Webster, G. (1974) *Practical Archaeology*, Adam and Charles Black, London.

Archaeological contracts 4

Whenever development is likely to disturb or remove known or presumed archaeological remains it is important that arrangements are in place to deal with any problems that may arise. These can occur for a variety of reasons depending on and including what is discovered, the siting and importance of any remains, publicity, the need to investigate further and the effects of the weather on excavation. We cannot fully anticipate every eventuality but a mechanism needs to be found which is capable of tackling problems expeditiously, in a socially acceptable manner and with the minimum of disruption to development. This is where contracts become desirable although the matter is far from simple.

Before any archaeological contract is entered into between a developer and an archaeologist there are a number of matters that need to be considered. First and foremost is what sort of advice is required and by whom? Is an archaeological consultant required to give advice at the pre-planning application stage or does it relate to an excavation that cannot be ignored? Secondly, who should be approached for advice and what standards can be expected?

In an attempt to answer questions like these, three broad subject areas need study. The first hinges on the need for advice. If a contract is to be entered into between a developer and an archaeologist, thought needs to be given to the type of organization that requires the advice, what their requirements are and what they may expect.

The second issue is the advice that may be received and the rules or codes governing that advice. Much has been said in recent years about competitive tendering and the problems this can pose for the archaeologist. Conflict of interest has been mentioned but whilst some of this concern may be unwarranted it is nevertheless something which ought to be looked at.

Finally there is the contract itself. Since people are fallible and because extraneous factors can have an adverse effect on what happens, a mechanism by which archaeological investigation and excavation can proceed at a site must be carefully thought out so that potential problems can be contained. These are the matters which we shall look at in this Chapter.

4.1 THE NEED FOR ARCHAEOLOGICAL ADVICE

Many people want to know more about archaeological sites for a variety of reasons. Some will be committed to finding out as much as possible about a site whilst others will have only a passing interest. This could be in respect of archaeology itself or what a site can tell us. Different groups will have different interests.

Alongside these interest groups will be those who want to know more about the archaeology of a site, not so much for archaeological reasons, but in the way that it might affect other ideas about land. A prudent developer, for instance, will want to know as much as possible about the archaeological content of a site in order to help assess its development potential. Other interests can also be present where, broadly speaking, four main groups with interest in the land can be identified:

1. Landowners

Landowners will want to know what lies beneath their land primarily so that they can decide what to do with it. Some may contemplate development either for their own use and enjoyment or they may wish to sell it. Others may wish to improve the drainage of the land or plough it for agriculture. Occasionally a landowner may wish to investigate the archaeological resource and get a research organization to do this or may simply just want to know how significant a site is archaeologically. Generally speaking the owner will want to ascertain the relative or likely importance of a site either for philanthropic reasons or to extract some form of gain from it.

2. The developer

There are many different types of developer, ranging from a householder who wants to build an extension to a government department wishing to undertake a major infrastructure project. All will have their reasons for wanting to develop a site and archaeology is unlikely to be one of them. Occasionally there may be a desire to incorporate archaeological remains into a scheme but as a rule archaeology will be seen as a constraint on development. The need will be in trying to find out how much of a constraint there is, what effect it will have on their proposals and what needs to be done about it.

3. National and local government

Governmental organizations, in addition to taking on the role of developer, will more frequently act as regulators in the public interest. The concern will be to ensure that what is proposed at a site is appropriate, taking environmental and other considerations, including archaeology, into account. There will be a need to know how important or significant a site may be in archaeological terms so that correct measures can be taken to control development.

At the national level, archaeologists are employed to assess the quality and quantity of the archaeological resource and to advise officials, politicians and other decision-makers on policy matters and how to proceed. At the local level, planning authorities and other regulatory organizations will want to know how important different sites are and how best to control development, with archaeology as one of the factors to take into account. Some, most notably county councils, will employ archaeological staff.

4. Other professionals

Practising lawyers, surveyors, architects, planners and other professionals will occasionally need archaeological advice for their clients. The advice sought will vary according to their clients' interest and could include all of the above groups. In addition they may be engaged to advise third parties such as objectors to a development proposal or institutions who may be concerned about archaeological implications in the management of property portfolios.

4.2 THE NATURE AND TYPE OF ADVICE

When development is proposed and archaeology is a consideration the advice sought about archaeological matters is likely to focus on one or more of the following matters:

1. the historical importance of a site, the historic periods present or most likely to be found, together with an indication of the prevalence, frequency and significance of each historic period;
2. the likely importance of a site for the advancement of archaeological knowledge;
3. whether the archaeology at a site is of national, regional or local importance;
4. the likely archaeological importance or otherwise of different parts of a site where development is proposed;
5. if some parts of a site are likely to produce more or less worthwhile information about the archaeological resource;
6. an indication of where development will cause least harm to archaeological remains;
7. where excavation could or should take place;
8. the geographical extent of excavation necessary to achieve identified archaeological objectives;
9. the time required to carry out an excavation;
10. the likely cost of an excavation;
11. possible alternative costs for more or less thorough excavation(s) of a site;
12. the extent and nature of public controls that may be used at a particular site in order to achieve archaeological objectives;
13. the possible cost implications to the developer of an archaeological investigation at a site where development is proposed.

Two main motives will influence the interest groups seeking this information. One will be an interest in archaeology for its own sake – either for investigative reasons or in terms of how to protect it – and the other will relate, usually, to an ulterior motive. The interest will not be so much a concern about archaeology – although this may be present – but in how it may affect what can be done with land. Can a site be developed and if so in what way? What constraints will archaeology inflict upon any development or other proposals?

From these motives we can see that the archaeologist will be required to advise in one of two capacities. Either it will be in what may be described as a curatorial role or it will be on a contractual basis.

The archaeologist as curator will be responsible for the protection, conservation and management of the archaeological resource. Often in an official or statutory capacity, he or she will be employed to set briefs and specifications for archaeological work to be carried out by others acting as contractors and to monitor and archive that work. Alternatively the advice will be directed at decision-makers who determine development proposals. As protectors of the archaeological resource they will advise on statutory public requirements and duties and on the archaeological significance of a site with a view to protecting remains either *in situ* or by record.

In contrast, the archaeologist as contractor will be employed to advise a client, usually a developer, on what should or should not be done at a site where archaeological remains exist or are expected to exist and where development is proposed. Acting as a consultant, he or she may be approached directly by a developer to investigate a site or may have tendered for such work in competition with other archaeologists. Rather than approach just one firm a developer may approach several in order to introduce a competitive edge and possibly save money.

4.3 COMPETITIVE TENDERING

This is a subject which has caused much concern to many archaeologists, some welcoming the opportunity to compete for business, others alarmed at the possible implications for archaeology. Viewpoints have differed substantially, leading to arguments about the meaning of competitive tendering and what should be done about it. Yet whilst ideas can differ, competitive tendering will usually involve one of two things: either the preparation of a detailed specification against which competing archaeologists bid to do work or organizations are asked to indicate the work they propose to undertake and to price it in competition with other firms.

For some this is seen as a problem. As an inevitable consequence of developer funding brought about, in part, by PPG 16 (see Chapter 6), they view competition as the cause of a decline in standards, price wars and the erosion of the public interest. They see competition not so much as where two or more organizations compete anonymously in sealed bids against a highly detailed brief, but rather as a less formal process (Buteux, 1991). They are concerned that the client – as paymaster – is able to exercise choice in the same way that he or she might choose an architect. Is this a bad thing?

From the developer's point of view, if competent and accurate advice is obtained in a professional manner, competitive tendering must surely be a good thing. On the other hand the cheapest may not always be the best. On the basis of 'you get what you pay for' – although this is not always the case – the developer should look very carefully at what is involved. The content of a bid, past experience of the archaeologist and recommendations should all be checked. From the archaeological point of view, competitive tendering will be more important in relation to the scope for research, where it should take place, how it is to be funded, and whether there may be specific adverse effects.

The scope for research

One of the concerns about competitive tendering is its effect on research. The promotion of good research is a primary objective of many archaeologists, particularly the Council for British Archaeology (CBA), where the interest is in archaeology as a subject rather than the people or organizations who practise it. Whilst developer-funding creates scope for competitive tendering, it can result in a minimalist approach to research and exacerbate the existing situation.

Financial contributions by developers will almost always be related to rescue archaeology but this will be on a site-by-site basis as and when development proposals in archaeologically sensitive areas come forward. It is not related to any overall strategy for research and will not take into account any disparities between regions, urban and rural areas of types of site. Thus, with developer-funding becoming more widespread (Lambrick, 1991) money for archaeological investigation is likely to become more dependent on the general prosperity of the economy and the profitability of development. Furthermore, as developer-funding extends to public bodies, the scope for archaeological research may become more piecemeal. On the other hand, some archaeologists also recognize that without developer-funding the situation concerning archaeological research could be even worse.

Territoriality

One of the criticisms of competitive tendering has been that it can lead to the appointment of archaeological organizations who are cheaper to employ but who lack local knowledge and experience, working outside their territory. The argument has been that outside organizations may fail to consider the importance of a site in areas with which they are unfamiliar and yet many archaeological units and university departments have been working away from home for many years without such criticism. A lot of good archaeological research has been undertaken by units in this way and the criticism now seems less valid. It would seem that it stems primarily from developers and others who are not so much concerned about territoriality but value for money. Working away from home might engender higher costs although much depends on the nature of the advice that is sought: for site evaluation there may be little difference whereas excavation costs will usually be greater where a non-local unit has been appointed.

The effects of competitive tendering

An assumption by those fearing competition is that decisions will be made on the basis of cost and that whilst this will not be a concern to some developers there will be others who will seek to minimize or get rid of the archaeological constraint in the cheapest way possible.

Competition clearly has its advantages and disadvantages. Whilst it can help to reduce costs there is a concern that this could lower standards. The argument is that not all units will necessarily have the same technical knowledge, period specialization, experience and equipment to undertake the various types of surveys and analyses that are necessary, with the result that capabilities and results will differ. This is at a time when increasing complexity and variety of investigations requires increasing specialization although expertise can be subcontracted.

The scope for improvement

There is no reason why standards of archaeological work should not be maintained or even improved with competitive tendering. The key to improvement, however, will rest on the application of the following four regulatory requirements:

1. **The establishment of an independent regulatory framework**
   When curatorial advice is needed, the ideal situation would be for it to be independent of any archaeological contracting role where financial or other interests will be present. If it is not and the same investigating unit takes on both roles – as with the Welsh archaeological units – it is possible for a conflict of interest to arise. Fortunately, procedural arrangements are now in place to help overcome this although there will still be a need for personal professional integrity. A more satisfactory approach would be for the curatorial role to be separate and independent of the contractual role, as now applies in most areas.

2. **The maintenance of performance standards**
   At a time when quality assurance is important, and where disparities exist in technical and academic standards (Lambrick, 1991), it is imperative that performance standards regarding investigation are established. Applicable to specifications, evaluation, excavation and publication, the maintenance of minimum standards will be needed to overcome differences in specification, report-writing, interpretation and analysis. Without it, some form of licensing of contracting archaeologists may be necessary.

3. **The publication and examination of work**
   An important factor in the maintenance of performance standards will be the prompt publication of works. Needed for examination by peer groups and others, delay will make it more difficult to judge the quality of the work that is produced. This could apply to archaeologists engaged in curatorial or contracting work where the need for early assessment could be more important and occasionally critical.

4. **The consistency of standards**
   In addition to the maintenance of standards is the need for consistency. Differences of approach can occur between one geographical area and another where different curatorial standards may be adopted by local

authorities. If regulatory measures are to be introduced – and this would appear desirable – then there ought to be a system for ensuring that standards are consistently maintained.

4.4 CODES OF PRACTICE

Because archaeological remains are an irreplaceable, finite resource and because they form part of our common heritage, archaeologists and developers, collectively and individually, can both be said to have a responsibility to protect, investigate, or allow to be investigated, the archaeological resource for the benefit of society. In addition to what might be required by legislation both have a duty to ensure that information is retrieved or protected. The obligations imposed on them, however, are not always the same and there will, no doubt, be differences of opinion as to what they should be. Nevertheless, it is worth looking briefly at these obligations.

The archaeologist's codes

Essentially the archaeologist is faced with two codes, one of professionalism in the course of work – **the code of conduct** – and one concerning the method of investigating a site – **the code of practice**. The duties and responsibilities they impose overlap but both have their differences and implications, which the developer should be aware of.

The code of conduct

The archaeologist's code of conduct laid down in *Bye-Laws of the Institute of Field Archaeologists: Code of Conduct* in 1988, rests on four principles relating to behaviour, the archaeological resource, professionalism and the dissemination of information:

1. **Behaviour**

   The IFA principle on behaviour states:

   > The archaeologist shall adhere to the highest standards of ethical and responsible behaviour in the conduct of archaeological affairs.

   There are various aspects to this principle including acting responsibly, a duty of care and compliance with the law. Of particular importance to development and developers is the need to be adequately qualified and the requirement of confidentiality of information.

   It is the responsibility of the archaeologist to inform current or prospective clients or employers of any inadequacies in his or her qualifications to do a job and where additional professional advice, if any, should be sought. This latter approach is more likely to happen, but if this is not possible an alternative might be to arrange to modify the work or to subcontract part of it.

   As far as confidentiality is concerned, the archaeologist should seek to ensure that employees, colleagues, associates or others involved in a site investigation do not reveal confidential information gained from a project.

2. The archaeological resource

The second IFA principle states:

> The archaeologist has a responsibility for the conservation of the archaeological heritage.

Advances in the study and practice of archaeology are the *raison d'être* for archaeologists. In striving to conserve archaeological sites and material for study or enjoyment the professional aim will be to protect what is there. This will be for both now and for the future, from which it can be argued that preservation *in situ* rather than preservation by record should be pursued, unless destruction is unavoidable. It suggests that reasons other than archaeology can and will be present when decisions concerning development proposals are made.

3. Professionalism

The third duty on the archaeologist is that he or she:

> shall conduct his/her work in such a way that reliable information about the past may be acquired, and shall ensure that the results are properly recorded.

This, perhaps, is the most straightforward of the code's principles, although it requires that records, including artefacts and results from the laboratory, be maintained in good condition. Curatorial care and storage conditions will be important and all information should be readily available for study and examination. Developers should be aware of these needs.

4. Dissemination of information

The publication of archaeological information and records may not, at first glance, appear to some to be as important as the other three principles. The IFA, however, gives it equal status when its fourth principle states:

> The archaeologist has responsibility for making available the results of archaeological work with reasonable dispatch.

The availability of information will be of great importance to historians, other archaeologists and developers. If requests for information are honoured, not only can this be invaluable but it should significantly help improve standards of investigation. It could also strengthen the case for competitive tendering.

One problem that can arise relates to timing. Difficulties over publication can crop up for a number of reasons, as recognized by the IFA when it states, in its code of conduct, that failure to publish the results of data derived from an investigation more than 10 years after completion shall be construed as a waiver of the archaeologist's responsibilities. It goes on to state that in the event of failure the archaeologist responsible should, if requested, hand over the information for another archaeologist to analyse and publish. This is tantamount to a recognition that delays, even as long as this, can happen.

One problem that may arise and be associated with delay is the nature of the contractual obligation imposed on an archaeologist. A client seeking archaeological information about a site may wish to keep it private and confidential. It may not suit his or her interests as a landowner or prospective developer. If the landowner thinks it might reduce the value or if a developer thinks it might significantly increase the costs, they may seek to impose conditions in the contract aimed at restricting or preventing publication.

In this situation the code states that an archaeologist should not accept conditions which require the permanent suppression of archaeological discoveries or interpretation. This suggests that temporary suppression may be acceptable but how temporary is temporary and how might this be interpreted by different parties? One answer will no doubt be to suppress it until the completion of development but perhaps the decision should rest on the importance and rarity of the information.

Codes of practice

Just as the archaeologist has a code of conduct to adhere to, there is a code or rather codes of practice which should be followed. Essentially there are three: the first is again produced by the IFA (1990), the second by the British Archaeologists and Developers Liaison Group (1991), a permanent body initiated jointly by the British Property Federation and the Standing Conference of Archaeological Unit Managers (SCAUM) and the third by the Welsh archaeological trusts. All three apply where an archaeological investigation is proposed at a site where development or redevelopment is to take place. They do not affect statutory requirements as may be found in the Ancient Monuments and Archaeological Areas Act 1979, or the planning Acts, but are intended as measures of good practice. In the words of the Group the main objective is 'to ensure long-term understanding, goodwill and co-operation between archaeologists and those involved with development'.

The main factors in these codes can be grouped into those that need to be taken into account prior to excavation on site, those during a dig and those after it has been completed. Some aspects will be ongoing. They are as follows:

1. Prior to excavation

The main considerations, prior to excavation, relate to the gathering and dissemination of information and agreeing on what should be done. If the archaeologist is to give advice about a site, sufficient information must be obtained so that objectives can be defined. These need to be discussed at an early date so that the archaeologist can advise on the steps that will be necessary. Both parties will need to establish what is involved including the costs of investigation, funding and possible tax benefits from voluntary contributions. The duty on the archaeologist will be to see that the above are adequate. A brief should be prepared with the archaeologist advising on the steps necessary to acquire information, the adequacy of the brief, the ownership of finds, access to the site and advance warning of entry on to a site. Written agreement on the above will be essential.

2. Duties during excavation

During excavation the archaeologist has a duty to inform the developer/ client as soon as possible of any discoveries. At the same time he or she should not get involved in any publicity or campaigns aimed at preserving remains *in situ*, and should avoid any criticism in public. Whilst under contract, co-operation with the developer in accordance with the agreed programme is vital, as is the need to co-operate with other interested parties such as English Heritage, Historic Scotland or Cadw and the local planning authority. Where a need for preservation is identified the archaeologist should take into account the effects on the developer and in particular the cost implications. Early assessment and decision-making in consultation with the developer is essential. The archaeologist should also respect the need for confidentiality.

As excavation proceeds a comprehensive and fully integrated archive record must be made. The archaeologist should also monitor progress to ensure that the work conforms with the brief and specification. If work needs to be altered or conflicts with the agreed programme the archaeologist must bring this to the attention of the parties involved.

On occasion there may be a need or a desire on the part of the archaeologist or developer to exhibit, promote or display archaeological work. This could be during or after excavation but co-operation between the parties is necessary and the archaeologist, if promoting the idea, should ensure that any contractor's programme is not adversely affected.

3. Duties after the completion of excavations

Apart from the possibility of exhibitions and displays already mentioned, the main concerns will be to ensure that information is analysed promptly with full acknowledgement given to the developer in all relevant publications. Archive arrangements and ownership of finds will have been agreed already but the duty on the archaeologist will be to see that arrangements are properly carried out within a reasonable time period.

The Welsh code of practice

In Wales, the four Welsh archaeological trusts (listed on p. 21) are in the interesting position of taking on both the curatorial and contractual role. By providing advice and guidance to planning authorities, landowners, statutory bodies and developers in the handling of archaeological matters, they may get involved in archaeological assessment, evaluation and investigation. As such they have to take care to ensure the two roles are kept separate, a point recognized in the Curators' Code of Practice which seeks to complement the other codes mentioned in this Chapter. The main points in the Welsh code are shown in Table 4.1.

Table 4.1 The Welsh code of practice

1. The curatorial staff of each Trust will provide impartial and independent advice on the archaeological implications of proposed developments.
2. The curatorial staff of each Trust will normally provide a brief for archaeological assessments, field evaluations and investigations, as appropriate.
3. The curatorial staff of each Trust will be responsible for approving the detailed specifications designed to satisfy an archaeological brief.
4. The curatorial staff of each Trust will advise those wishing to commission particular pieces of archaeological work of their freedom of choice in the selection of a contractor. (Names of individuals and organisations working in this field may be obtained from the Institute of Field Archaeologists.)
5. Where a Trust is contracting to undertake a particular piece of work, it recognises that those intending to commission such work may wish to engage an independent archaeological consultant to assess a specification of works intended to satisfy an archaeological brief, to monitor the progress of the work, or to advise on the recommendations for any further action.
6. The curatorial staff of each Trust have full authority to ensure that an archaeological brief is adequately fulfilled at all stages, irrespective of the contractual arrangements.
7. The curatorial staff will seek amendments to, or if necessary reject, any contracted piece of work which they consider does not fulfil the archaeological brief.
8. The curatorial staff will be solely responsible for determining any recommendations for further action arising from an assessment or field evaluation report prepared by an archaeological contractor.

Source: The Welsh Archaeological Trusts

Duties of the developer

There are three main codes for the developer, one relating to all work involving archaeology, one relating solely to mineral operators and the third to water operators.

The developer's general code of practice

This is to be found in the document produced by the British Archaeologists and Developers Liaison Group (1991), where the following practical measures are recommended for developers:

1. **Seek early professional advice**

   Many developers now seek advice about archaeology although not all do so at the earliest opportunity. Adequate time is not always allowed with the result that difficulties and delays sometimes arise. Developers are strongly advised in the code to seek professional advice from organizations such as English Heritage and others as appropriate concerning the extent and importance of the archaeological resource and what needs to be done about it.

2. **The advantages of negotiation**

   There is no obligation on developers to discuss the history and archaeology of a site with approved archaeologists although the advantages of early negotiation are fairly obvious. Open discussion into the likely archaeological importance of a site can lead to time and cost savings. Buildings and foundations can be sited and designed to minimize impact and consideration can be given to any planning restrictions and conditions that may apply.

3. Community benefits of co-operation

The code points out that there can be political and community benefits to the developer and archaeologist if they co-operate with the planners and local councillors. Both may be more receptive to developers' requirements if archaeological considerations are researched and remains are protected or allowed to be recorded for the benefit of society. Early agreement can smooth the passage for subsequent approval, and there could be other spin-offs from co-operation.

4. Statutory requirements

Archaeological sites can be affected by various statutory requirements and the developer will need to ensure that these are complied with. These can arise under the Ancient Monuments and Archaeological Areas Act 1979 relating to scheduled monuments and designated areas of archaeological importance; the planning Acts, where conditions and other obligations can be attached to permissions to develop land, and other lesser known statutory provisions which are referred to in Part Two.

5. Preservation and presentation

Partly as a means of overcoming archaeological objections, one option developers are advised to consider in the code is the incorporation or display of important remains in their projects. The preservation of significant surviving structures *in situ*, if sympathetically done, could make a project more attractive both visually and financially.

6. Communications

Where excavation is to take place the code stresses the importance of drawing up good lines of communication between all staff working on site, senior management and the principal archaeologist so that any problems that may arise can be dealt with expeditiously and not hold up development.

7. Recording arrangements

Where the developer is funding an archaeological investigation copyright of all reports and archive material will remain with him. The code, however, suggests that arrangements be made for copies of all original material to be deposited at an approved museum, the local SMR and the appropriate national commission: the Royal Commission on the Historical Monuments of England, the Royal Commission on Ancient and Historical Monuments in Wales or the Royal Commission on the Ancient and Historical Monuments of Scotland. In Scotland it will also be necessary to nofity the procurator fiscal about certain finds.

8. Importance of care

Articles found at a site which are not treasure trove nor, in Scotland, *Bona Vacantia*, will be the property of the site owner, who will be entitled to do what he or she wants with them. The site owner is, however, encouraged in the code to donate as many as possible to the approved museum which holds the excavation records and to make available the remainder – as a gift or loan – to an approved museum for research and study purposes.

9. Publicity and publication
It will often be in the developer's interest to give support and to pay special attention to publicity and the publication of archive material. Press releases issued jointly with the archaeologists working at a site and agreed statements concerning any discoveries will generally be good for public relations. The publication of material should also be supported and the code points out that this should be considered as an essential part of the costs of investigation.

The code of practice for mineral operators

This code, published by the Confederation of British Industry (CBI) in April 1991, overlaps in many ways with the one above although there are significant additional points. Directed primarily at mineral operators these are:

1. to check the SMR before undertaking mineral exploration in order to establish whether the work would affect a site of archaeological interest, as defined in the Town and Country Planning General Development Order 1988;
2. to consult with the planning authority to see if proposals for mineral development will affect any known or likely site of archaeological interest;
3. to allow the archaeologist access to the proposed site;
4. to supply additional information, when requested, to the local planning authority. They may require an evaluation to be made incorporating remote sensing, trial trenching or other appropriate techniques;
5. to consider the need for environmental assessment;
6. to show, in accordance with any environmental assessment or evaluation, how archaeological interests are to be accommodated in the proposal;
7. to consider offering financial or practical assistance to any archaeological investigation although the code adds that 'the decision to make such contributions is a matter for the operator in each case';
8. to use their best endeavours to restrict access to any archaeological investigation at a site to personnel approved by the archaeological contractor or body and to discourage access by other groups or individuals;
9. to accept that archaeologists can have legitimate interests in wishing to examine sites which have already been approved for mineral workings and that access should be allowed when consistent with safety and operational requirements.

In addition to the above the CBI has also produced a checklist of matters for agreement. Aimed at helping operators to prepare agreements for archaeological investigation, the matters listed in the code are shown in Table 4.2.

The water operators' code

The Water Act 1989 imposes a number of general duties on the National Rivers Authority (NRA), water and sewerage undertakers and internal drainage boards in respect of conservation, public access and recreation. In connection with these duties the government produced in 1989 a Code of

Table 4.2 Checklist of matters for agreement prior to investigation

- the archaeological project design which should provide for recording, analysis and interpretation of the results of the investigation
- the timetable for the project which should cover each phase of the investigation
- the methods to be used for such operations as soil stripping, excavation and reinstatement by the archaeological contractor
- definition of safe areas and access routes for the archaeological contractor and any related visitors
- compliance by the archaeological contractor and any related visitors with the operator's requirements
- procedures for deciding the ownership and conservation arrangements for artifacts recovered during the investigation
- rights of publication and rights to the results of the investigation
- the archaeological contractor's insurance cover, particularly against third party claims
- clear arrangements for funding where necessary, including specific definition of sphere of financial responsibility where funding is to be shared between several parties

Source: CBI (1991)

Practice for the authority and undertakers with separate advice on conservation guidelines produced for the drainage boards.

Within the Code of Practice, five areas of concern are identified, all of which can have implications for archaeology. They relate to:

1. **Operating within a planning and management framework**

   Here the relevant bodies in the discharge of their environmental duties are required to develop a framework for policy making, procedures and management. As part of this they must:

   - establish channels for consultation and liaison with all relevant organizations, groups and individuals;
   - integrate land use and management plans for sites where archaeology is a significant factor;
   - set up training and research programmes for staff;
   - devise ways of disseminating information about their plans.

   The code recognizes that conflicts of operational, environmental and recreational considerations can rarely be reconciled without due planning, consultation, training and publicity.

2. **Conservation and enhancement of the environment**

   Many operations and activities of the relevant bodies can affect archaeological sites and other sensitive areas. As such, certain general and specific requirements are set out in the code relating to new schemes and works. The general ones require careful consideration to be given to:

   - the design of works and use of land which could adversely affect the character of ancient monuments;
   - works aimed at lowering water levels which could cause drying out and decay of archaeological remains;
   - ways and means of protecting monuments and other archaeological sites;

- the recording of sites of archaeological significance in consultation with specialist bodies such as the CBA;
- the establishment, where necessary, of heritage reserves for ensuring the protection, management and public interpretation of archaeological sites and features;
- how future routine maintenance works will be carried out whilst ensuring that conservation duties are not overlooked.

More specifically the code requires, for the management of water resources, water supply schemes, sewerage and sewage disposal schemes, pipe-laying and bankside activities, that:

- proper and adequate consultation takes place in advance;
- archaeological considerations are taken into account;
- environmental assessment is undertaken where schemes will have a significant effect on the environment;
- existing archaeological features are retained wherever possible;
- the impact of a project which could affect archaeology indirectly (e.g. the hydrological regime where water abstraction is proposed) is fully considered;
- that the routes for new trunk mains and sewers and other construction programmes are checked and every effort made to by-pass or minimize damage to the archaeological resource;
- the incidence of bank erosion through the harmful effects of boat traffic and any implications for archaeology are fully taken into account.

3. Preservation of public access

As part of their public access duty relevant bodies should adopt, wherever reasonably practicable, a number of duties in respect of archaeological sites including:

- appropriate management and signposting;
- the creation of heritage trails;
- the creation of formal displays;
- the provision of facilities for the study of the archaeological resource.

When operations require public access to be terminated or modified consultation with the appropriate body is recommended.

4. The use of water and associated land for recreational purposes

In pursuit of recreational objectives the relevant bodies are asked to provide recreational facilities in the best possible manner taking archaeology, social importance, recreational needs and other factors into account. Thus, care should be taken in respect of the siting of car parks, toilets, picnic sites and so on and their possible effect on archaeology.

5. Duties in special areas

In the vicinity of ancient monuments owned by a relevant body or others, the code states that the appropriate national agency (English Heritage, Historic Scotland or Welsh Historic Monuments (Cadw)), should be consulted if there is any doubt about the importance of a particular site and the effect of works on it. Where works directly affect a site the code reminds operators and the NRA that any work which has the effect of demolishing, damaging, removing, repairing, altering, adding to, flooding or covering it will require scheduled monument consent. The code also draws attention to planning requirements, which are matters looked at in Part Two.

4.6 CONTRACTS

The nature of a contract

One of the problems associated with development and archaeology is uncertainty. A requirement to excavate a site where development is proposed can present a number of problems for both the developer and the archaeologist. Not all of the answers will be known in advance and frequently there will be no way of telling what they could be. Both will want to protect their interests as much as possible.

The commonest way to do this is for the parties to enter into a contract to secure whatever is required in a manner that is acceptable to both. The contract will be a legally binding document bestowing benefits and limitations on them although, for it to be legally enforceable, three things have to be shown to exist. There has to be:

1. an unconditional offer from one party to do something;
2. an unconditional acceptance of that offer by the other party;
3. a valuable consideration must be passed or be promised to be passed between the two parties.

To satisfy these requirements a contract can be oral or written. Both are equally binding in law although with oral contracts there is the obvious problem in proving what was said. The matters may appear to be uncomplicated, particularly with small contracts, but this can be far from the case. A written contract is more precise and easier to interpret.

An offer by one party must spell out what is required. It must define what needs to be done and make it clear to both parties what is required of them, and when they must do it. Inevitably prior to its conclusion there should be discussion and negotiation about the terms of an offer. It makes sense to agree as much as possible beforehand although there will still need to be clauses covering such matters as time periods for compliance, means of acceptance and default.

Matters to be included in a contract

The following provides an outline of the main components of a contract for archaeological services.

The parties involved

The agreement must spell out the names and addresses of the parties to the contract. Normally this will be the archaeological organization and the developer although there may be a need to include the landowner, tenant or agent (architect, surveyor) acting for the developer. If agricultural land is to be excavated it is essential that any tenant of the land is made aware of what is proposed although the tenant need not necessarily be a party to the agreement.

Preamble

The preamble should indicate what is proposed. This would include the developer's proposals or works at the site and the nature of the archaeological investigation: this would be in respect of on-and-off-site surveys, excavations and report publication, as appropriate. Reference should also be made to any statutory requirements pertaining to the site such as a conditional planning consent and definitions and terms used in the contract. By defining and interpreting key terms this will help to avoid any subsequent confusion over responsibilities and duties. It is likely that a schedule would be attached to the contract defining some of these matters in more detail.

The site to be investigated

The site and extent of the archaeological investigation must be clearly defined. In some city centre or urban sites this may be easy to identify but normally a plan or an Ordnance Survey map to an appropriate scale would be needed. This would be especially important at open land or greenfield sites. In addition the plan ought to show existing buildings, the area(s) to be excavated (or surveyed), the boundaries of the site, where live services are located, where sewers may be found, where topsoil is to be deposited and where there are changes in land ownership. If site huts are necessary the area of land where they are to be located should be identified, as should the means of access into the site.

In some instances it will be useful to specify the minimum or maximum depths for excavation, the former so that mechanical diggers can be used, the latter because of existing structures or known maximum depth of occupation.

Period of investigation

The date for starting the investigation must be stated, either as a fixed date or a date determined by the completion of some other activity at the site. The duration of the investigation should also be spelled out with a completion date or maximum period of occupation after entry specified. An allowance for an extension of time to the licence period should also be considered, as should the possibility of premature termination, delay or postponement. As with construction contracts, which are looked at in Chapter 14, arrangements should be made to cover default procedures, the giving of notice and claims for default.

Consents and access

The archaeologist must be allowed access to as much of the site as is necessary to carry out the investigation. This should include getting to a dig across private land, not all of which may be in the same ownership. Identifying land for the deposit of soil, site infrastructure works, administrative and on-site conservation accommodation should also be considered as more than one owner may be involved.

Where licences or consents are required the developer would normally be responsible for obtaining them and for associated costs. There may also be a need to ensure that access can be obtained after the expiry of an investigation period so that continued observation can be undertaken – this could be needed to satisfy a condition of planning consent. The proviso would be that it should not interfere with the development programme.

In consideration of access it may be necessary to specify entry points into a site, where and when vehicles may be used and if visitors and the general public are to be allowed. The latter might be favoured by the archaeologists at some sites – possibly for publicity or financial reasons – but it is a matter that must be weighed up carefully. Matters of insurance and where and when such access is possible would have to be taken into account and allowed for, as necessary, in the contract.

Rights and duties of the archaeological contractor

It goes without saying that the archaeologist should exercise all reasonable skill, care and diligence in the performance of the work. The contract, however, whilst stating this, may impose limitations on the activities of the archaeologist. It might, for instance, stipulate reasonable requests of the developer or impose limits on the depth of investigation. Normally these would not have any implications but there may be times when a conflict of interest arises. In such cases the archaeologist's code of conduct and the joint code of practice should apply.

The archaeologist's rights of access should not be interfered with during the access period although this would apply only to persons duly authorized onto the site. Safeguards against unauthorized access will have to be maintained and the archaeologist may have to consider safety and security matters and identify where agreement is necessary.

Other matters which the archaeologist may need to remember are any conditions pertaining to scheduled monument consent, licences under the disused burial grounds legislation, planning permission and any other consent. These might require agreement on site with officers of the relevant regulating body present at any meeting. There could also be concern about the removal of finds or other operations affecting a site. If pipes, cables, drains, sewers or other apparatus are damaged, the archaeologist would be expected to ensure that the relevant statutory body or undertaker is notified immediately.

Obligations of the developer

In addition to ensuring rights of access for the archaeologist during the excavation period, and such later period as may be required by statute, the developer should also make provision for access before excavation commences

Table 4.3 Facilities that may be provided by the developer

Soil stripping machinery (e.g. JCB)	Water pumps
Spoil removal	Storage pallets
Lighting	Wheelbarrows
Hoardings	Electricity supply
Fencing	Water
Sheet piling	Hose pipes
Shoring	Dumper truck
The provision of shelters	Planks
Roofing	Temporary trench protection
Offices	Security (gate, availability of keys etc.)
Toilet(s)	

so that the archaeologist can examine the site. The depth of existing foundations, the existence of cellars, the routes of pipes, cables and other services and where demolition is proposed should all be checked. Apart from anything else this could save time later and be of financial benefit to both the developer and the archaeologist. The developer may also need to make certain equipment available to the archaeologist. Normally specified in a schedule to the contract, the matters that might be included are shown in Table 4.3.

Inspection and monitoring of the site

The developer and/or the agent must have the right to inspect the archaeological activities taking place at the site. Monitoring in accordance with the requirements of any planning permission or scheduled monument consent may also be necessary and in some cases the developer may wish to engage an independent archaeological consultant to monitor events. The contract should make provision for access to the site to allow this to take place.

Financial arrangements

Who pays for what, when and how, together with the sums involved, are important considerations that must be addressed in the contract. The following factors may have to be taken into account:

1. **Price**
   Normal practice is for the contract to state the sum to be paid by the developer to the investigating organisation. Generally a fixed price would be adopted where the archaeologists agree to undertake the investigation for a specified sum. This would include pre- and post-excavation work.

2. **Payments**
   The payment of this sum may be all at once or in stages. If the investigation is large or important it could involve extensive conservation work and analysis of the finds with publication some time later. In such cases it would be appropriate, certainly from the developer's point of view,

to pay in stages with part at the beginning of investigation and further specified sums paid on specified dates. Agreement would be needed on frequency, due dates, the basis for making a claim and whether the payments are to be made in accordance with a programme or costs incurred. The date for final account should also be stated.

3. Retention monies

It would normally be advisable for certain monies to be retained until reports are completed. Without a clause of this nature the incentive to complete could be reduced and delay in publication could occur.

4. Interest payments

In the event of contractual payments not being made by the due date it would be expedient to allow for interest to be paid on any overdue amounts.

5. Penalties

Archaeological investigation can delay a development programme. This is explicit and accepted in the contract. Less certain are other delays caused a) to the development process by an extension of the archaeological programme or b) to the archaeological programme itself by actions, or lack of action, associated with the development project. In both cases it may be necessary to make provisions for penalties in the archaeological contract with appropriate limitations for unforeseen and unreasonable events.

6. Extras

Some archaeological investigations may result in a need for special conservation work, additional storage costs, the display of finds or other presentation and publicity. From an archaeological point of view there may be a case for seeking additional payments to cover all or some of these matters although care should be taken in planning such extras. The developer could reasonably argue that additional income, such as the sale of publicity material should be split or, as a minimum, cover the extra costs involved. A more appropriate course of action would probably be to make allowances for any extras in the original sum. This could be on a percentage basis or as a fixed sum.

7. Compensation

It is possible for crops, land drains, fences, underground services, paths and other features both on- and off-site to be damaged by archaeological activities. Tenants' rights could also be interfered with, as might happen if a private right of way was accidentally blocked or a gate left open. Claims for compensation could arise and there may be a need to make financial provision for this in the contract.

Work practices

Good work practices will normally be implied in archaeological contracts but sometimes special consideration may need to be given to certain activities or actions, for example:

- keeping paths and access ways clean and clear of obstructions;
- installing special shoring for earthworks, site huts and paths;
- removing ground water above a certain level;
- preventing silt and sludge from entering drains or pumps;
- ensuring that the site is safe and secure.

These are some of the matters that may need to be made explicit. In addition, reference may need to be made to the reinstatement of land and/or buildings. Normally the archaeologist would be responsible for the back-filling of excavation works although this could be done by the developer as an additional facility. Again, it would make sense for the contract to indicate who is to be responsible for this work in clear and unambiguous terms.

Assignment

As with development projects there will be occasions when certain aspects of archaeological work may need to be subcontracted: the moving of earth, dewatering, fencing or an academic input are examples. Normally applicable to larger projects, although one or more of these could be equally applicable to smaller ones, there will be a need to ensure that such matters are included in the contract. The normal form would be to receive the written approval of the developer who should not withhold it unreasonably. The contract should also specify that the archaeological contractor be responsible for the acts, defaults or negligence of any subcontractors.

Liabilities and insurance

The archaeological contractor will normally have to indemnify the developer against any expense, liability, loss, claim or proceedings arising in respect of personal injury or death arising out of the archaeological investigation. The exception would be when any act of the developer or the developer's employees, through omission or neglect, causes injury or death. In such a situation the developer would be responsible. A similar approach would apply to property.

Archaeological discoveries

Any archaeological remains or archaeological discoveries except those declared by Coroner's Inquest to be treasure trove, and discovered in the course of investigations, are normally taken to be the property of the landowner. Upon discovery, whether by the contractor or developer, each party would normally be expected to notify the other. In some cases, such as with the discovery of Roman mosaics and other ancient remains, it would be reasonable to expect the archaeologist to examine and record such antiquities for up to 14 days or other reasonable period after discovery. Reasonable assistance should be afforded and allowed for in the contract.

It is often requested and indeed expected that ownership of all such discoveries would be transferred unconditionally to a local or named museum for public display and safekeeping. The contract could make reference to this.

Records and reports

The archaeological record of an investigation will be of various sorts including written notes, drawings, photographs, plans and, possibly, audio and video tapes. Samples of selected materials for display purposes and a variety of publications (books, leaflets, etc.) could also be included with back-up copies deposited with a suitable museum and the appropriate SMR. From these the contractor would be expected to produce for the developer a draft and then final report of the investigation. The contract would refer to the need for the distribution of copies and the publication of material to be agreed in writing. It might also specify dates or deadlines for submission and agreement. It would be appropriate for these matters to be addressed in the contract.

Settlement of disputes

In the event of any dispute arising out of a contract it would be normal for the matter to be resolved by arbitration. The arbitrators decision would be final and binding on the parties with any costs borne equally between them.

REFERENCES

The British Archaeologists and Developers Liaison Group (1991) *Code of Practice*, (3rd edn), BADLG, London.

Buteux, S. (1991) Competition in archaeology: a pragmatic approach, in *Competitive Tendering in Archaeology*, RESCUE and SCAUM, Hertford.

Confederation of British Industry (1991) *Archaeological Investigations: Code of Practice for Mineral Operators*, CBI, London.

Department of the Environment; Ministry of Agriculture, Fisheries and Food; Welsh Office (1989) *The Water Act 1989: Code of Practice on Conservation, Access and Recreation*, HMSO, London.

Institute of Field Archaeologists (1988) *By-Laws of the Institute of Field Archaeologists: Code of Conduct*, IFA, Birmingham.

Institute of Field Archaeologists (1990) *By-Laws of the Institute of Field Archaeologists: Code of Approved Practice for the Regulation of Contractual Arrangements in Field Archaeology*, IFA, Birmingham.

Lambrick, G. (1991) Competitive tendering and archaeological research: the development of a CBA view, in *Competitive Tendering in Archaeology*, RESCUE and SCAUM, Hertford.

Welsh Archaeological Trusts (1992) *Curators' Code of Practice*, Welsh Archaeological Trusts.

FURTHER READING

Chadwick, P. (1991) Competitive tendering in archaeology: the curator's role, in *Competitive Tendering in Archaeology*, RESCUE and SCAUM, Hertford.

Darvill, T. and Atkins, M. (1991) Regulating Archaeological Work by Contract. *Institute of Field Archaeologists Technical Paper Number 8*, IFA, Birmingham.

Swain, H. (ed.) (1991) *Competitive Tendering in Archaeology*, RESCUE and SCAUM, Hertford.

Public Controls

PART

2

The framework of control 5

The need to know more about the past, a dislike of unnecessary destruction and a general concern about protecting our heritage linked to tradition, continuity, attitude and other personal interests have to be considered alongside the demands for adequate housing, commerce, retailing, manufacturing, roads, infrastructure and other societal needs. Inevitably, as new buildings, roads and other infrastructure projects are required, conflicts of interest will arise between the needs for new development and the preservation of archaeological remains. It means that if archaeology is to be protected some form of public control needs to be applied to ensure that new buildings are built in the right place with a minimum adverse effect on the archaeological environment.

Legislation, of course, exists for this purpose but it is complex in two main respects. First, there are a number of Acts of Parliament relating to different aspects of development and it is not always clear when each or any one should apply. Second, within these areas of legislation, and most notably the planning Acts, the procedures are complicated and sometimes difficult to understand. There is a need for clarity on both counts.

In this Chapter the objective is to try and make sense of this complexity. Initially the aim is to look at the organization and role of central government, which is followed by that of the local planning authority. Being very much involved in regulating development and protecting the environment, the former can be identified as setting the policy and legislative framework for how land should be used, with the latter basically deciding how individual sites should or should not be developed. The authority must operate within the legislative framework set by government although there are a number of Acts which can affect archaeology, as outlined later in the Chapter. Subsequent Chapters look at detailed policy, the mechanisms of control, the need for consent and how development proposals are determined, taking archaeological considerations into account.

5.1 THE ORGANISATION AND ROLE OF CENTRAL GOVERNMENT

As there is no written constitution defining the powers of central and local government in Britain, power derives from the legislation that is enacted by parliament and through common law. The former sets the framework which decides how government is to be organized and function, the latter helps to guide decision-making by setting precedents. England, Scotland and Wales have their own legal and administrative arrangements which add to the confusion. Within England two government departments are responsible, in different ways, for archaeology, the main one being the Department for National Heritage (DNH) with the Department of the Environment (DoE) taking on a more indirect role. Other departments also get involved but to a lesser extent. In Scotland and Wales the Scottish Office Environment Department (SOEnD) and the Welsh Office (WO) respectively are the responsible departments.

Department of National Heritage

Previously part of the Department of the Environment, the DNH came into being on 3 July 1992 charged with overall responsibility for the arts, museums and galleries, heritage, the export licensing of works of art, antiques, sport, tourism, press freedom, film and broadcasting. Under the direction of the Secretary of State for National Heritage, the department aims to conserve, nurture, enhance and make the cultural heritage more widely accessible. In the words of the department's information sheet, it seeks to create conditions which:

- will preserve ancient sites, monuments and historic buildings and increase their accessibility for study and enjoyment both now and in the future;
- maintain, increase and make available the national collections of books, works of art, scientific objects and other records and artefacts of the past and of the present;
- encourage the living arts to flourish – including the performing arts; the visual and plastic arts; broadcasting; film; and literature;
- increase the opportunities for sport and recreation both for champions and for the general public;
- attract a wide range of people from this country and abroad to enjoy and enrich our national culture.

In the pursuit of these aims the department is organized into four groups as shown in Figure 5.1. It is also responsible for two executive agencies and 42 non-departmental public bodies and public corporations.

The group responsible for matters relating to archaeology is the Heritage and Tourism Group, where the Heritage Division is directly responsible for:

- government policy on the conservation of monuments;
- the scheduling of monuments and sites;
- sponsorship of English Heritage, the Royal Commission on Historical Monuments of England, the National Hertitage Memorial Fund, the Redundant Churches Fund and the Royal Fine Art Commission.

The Royal Estates Division is responsible for the protection and preservation of the Occupied Royal Palaces and certain historic buildings and statues.

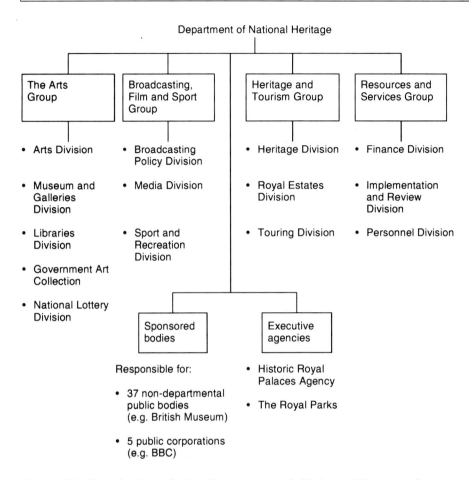

Figure 5.1 Organization of the Department of National Heritage. (Source: Department of National Heritage.)

The Department of the Environment

Under the direction of the Secretary of State for the Environment the central theme of the DoE, established in 1970, is to protect and improve the environment of England. Other objectives are also present where we find that the following areas of concern can have implications for archaeology.

Local government
Important aims of government are to oversee the structure and areas of local authorities, to prescribe their powers, to define their boundaries (this is currently under review) and to establish the financial basis within which they must operate. All of these can affect the role and ability of local authorities to deal with archaeological matters.

Planning
Government responsibilities relate to providing national and regional policy guidance issued primarily through circulars and Planning Policy

Guidance Notes (PPGs), the review of the planning system, the co-ordination of strategic planning (although local authorities approve plans) and the determination of 'called-in' applications and appeals. That can all have a major impact on archaeology as we shall see in subsequent Chapters.

Inner cities

Here the initiatives relate to policy for inner-city areas, the urban development corporations, the co-ordination of urban regeneration programmes and grants and the setting up of and policy for enterprise zones. Aimed at supporting and encouraging development, the weight given to archaeology may be less than in other areas.

Housing

A prime aim of government is to ensure that there is an adequate supply of land for housing. Located where they are most needed, new dwellings may be found within established built-up areas or at greenfield sites where archaeology can frequently be a material consideration.

Countryside

Committed to protecting the countryside, the department is responsible for policies, among others, aimed at safeguarding the best landscapes, ensuring good agricultural and forestry practice and for the funding and promotion of practical conservation work. Some of these actions can help or hinder the archaeological resource.

Pollution control

The need to protect people and the environment from the harmful effects of human activity is now recognized in government policy and legislation. Less clear is how the environmental element relates to the protection of archaeological remains from, say, chemical leacheate action.

Promotion of the construction industry

Recognized as an important part of the department's work, especially within the European context, the promotion will be in the context of and subject to normal environmental constraints operating on development. Sometimes of greater interest will be the large construction research programmes undertaken by the Building Research Establishment (BRE). By examining building materials, construction techniques and defects and their possible remedies, there may be scope for seeing how elements of this could be transferred to protecting the archaeological resource.

Policy guidance

Split into policy and procedural guidance, although it is not always easy to separate the two, we find that the most significant instruments of guidance as far as archaeology is concerned stem from:

● **Planning Policy Guidance Notes**
First introduced in 1988 these now form the main element of government policy over land use in England and Wales. The most

important one as far as archaeology is concerned is PPG 16, *Archaeology and Planning*, published in 1990, although others can have implications for archaeology.

- **Mineral Planning Guidance Notes**
  There are a number of guidance notes relating solely to mineral extraction because of the complexity of the subject. These spell out national policy in detail, setting out site requirements through to reinstatement when mineral extraction finishes.

- **White Papers**
  These are published from time to time to show what the government intends to do. They are principally statements of intent where the government publicly makes known its ideas for future policy and legislation. The best known and the one most relevant to archaeology is *This Common Inheritance: Britain's Environmental Strategy* (DoE, 1990).

- **National Planning Policy Guidelines**
  These apply solely to Scotland and are similar to the planning policy guidance notes issued in England and Wales. They relate to policy issues of particular relevance to Scotland such as those relating to oil-related development. A draft policy guideline relating to archaeology and planning was published in 1992.

- **Planning Advice Notes**
  Again these relate to Scotland but as the name implies, they are aimed at giving advice to planning authorities, developers, land-owners and professional advisers about various matters relating to the use and development of land in Scotland. A separate PAN on archaeology and planning was published in draft form in 1992.

Other departments

Other government departments can become involved in archaeology but only when activities for which they have responsibilities come into contact with archaeological sites and monuments. Departments that can be involved include:

- Ministry of Agriculture, Fisheries and Food (MAFF), in respect of environmentally sensitive areas and the way land may be farmed;
- Department of Transport (DoT), in so far as proposed trunk roads, motorways, ports and airports may affect archaeological sites;
- Department of Trade and Industry (DTI), in respect of the location of industry and incentives to develop land, and matters formerly the responsibility of the Department of Energy concerning the generation and supply of energy where they may intrude on ancient monuments and other archaeological sites.

The Scottish Office

The Secretary of State for Scotland presides over a multi-function Scottish Office which contains different departments. The department responsible for archaeological matters is the SOEnD which has wide-ranging powers relating to planning, land use, conservation and heritage. In effect it is similar to the combined responsibilities of the DoE, DNH and DoT in England. National planning guidelines and policy documents are produced by the department and a large proportion but not all the legislation concerning development and archaeology is separate from that in England and Wales. Historic Scotland acts as the executive agency under the wing of the SOEnD responsible for scheduling ancient monuments and for the management and protection of archaeological sites.

The Welsh Office

The office does not have such a long history as the Scottish Office and has fewer responsibilities. The Secretary of State for Wales is responsible for the Welsh Office, but all of the legislation concerning land use, planning and archaeology is the same as for England, where the relevant Acts apply to both countries. Guidance on the other hand is often separate and there is also a separate Land Authority for Wales which can and does acquire land for development purposes. Welsh Historic Monuments or Cadw is the executive agency which carried out the statutory responsibilities for the Secretary of State for Wales in respect of protecting, conserving and presenting ancient monuments and other historic sites in Wales.

5.2 THE ORGANIZATION AND ROLE OF LOCAL GOVERNMENT

How local government is organized

A key responsibility of the government is to determine the way in which local government operates. It defines the responsibilities and boundaries of local authorities which in turn decide the policies for areas of land and individual sites and how these policies should be implemented.

The authority most directly involved in archaeology is, of course, the local planning authority but there are different types with different responsibilities. We find that there are regional, islands, county, district, metropolitan district and London borough councils with planning functions together with urban development corporations, certain national parks authorities and the Broads authority in East Anglia. Parish, town and community councils do not have decision-making powers or responsibilities as far as planning is concerned although they often get involved and make their views known, via a consultation process.

In most areas there is, at present, a two-tier system of planning control. The upper tier looks at planning in a strategic context: it consists of the counties in England and Wales and the regions in Scotland. At the lower tier we find that, for most areas, it is the district councils which get involved in detailed local planning.

In the densely populated parts of England, generally referred to as the metropolitan areas, and in the sparsely populated parts of Scotland, a single-tier system is in operation. The London borough councils and the metropolitan district councils take on both a strategic and local role in the control of land use in their respective parts of England. In Scotland's remoter areas the regional councils take on all the planning functions and responsibilities.

Both tiers have their advantages and disadvantages. Under the two-tier system there is sometimes confusion about the responsibilities of the respective tiers, which is one reason why local government is now under review. With the single-tier system there is less confusion over responsibilities, but more concern about the way in which strategic planning is pursued. Not, perhaps, so important for archaeological considerations although strategies and consistency of approach to archaeological investigation can be important strategic issues. With the emphasis on detailed planning at the district or borough level, strategies for development and conservation can be more difficult to implement.

Finally, in respect of government reorganization, there is speculation and some concern about the eventual outcome. If the system is to become a single-tier system of unitary authorities, as is widely predicted and now being proposed in many areas, it will be a question of how archaeological considerations are to be treated. Will decisions be more parochial in character and less consistent between areas and locations? If they are, will this lead to a lack of consistency, greater uncertainty and perhaps less fairness for archaeologists and developers or will the government get more involved through its regional offices to provide strategic guidance? Only time will tell.

The role of the local planning authority

The main aim of planning is to regulate the use and development of land in the public interest. This is exercised through the local planning authority which decides, in accordance with the responsibilities set down by government, how land within its area ought to be used. In theory a system of statutory development plans is required, setting out the policies, priorities and objectives of the authority. Decisions are then made in accordance with those policies, priorities and objectives.

That is the theory. In practice the planning system is more complicated than this. Policy may be expressed in different plans or, alternatively, there may be supplementary guidance which an authority uses to assist in the determination of development proposals. Development control can be just as flexible.

The development plan

The development plan, which is the main vehicle for expressing planning policy, comes in different shapes and sizes and is rarely a single document. It also varies in different parts of Britain. In most parts of England, all of

Scotland and all of Wales it consists of two plans, namely the structure plan and the local plan. In the metropolitan parts of England it comprises just one document known as the unitary development plan or UDP. Figure 5.2 shows where these plans operate.

For their respective areas, development plans provide the main planning policy guidance on the location, amount, type and appearance of development. They specify where development should or should not go and indicate how certain matters are to be dealt with, such as the protection of buildings, landscapes or archaeological remains. At the strategic level, in structure plans and part 1 of the UDPs, they prescribe broad principles for decision-making: where development should be located and the broad types of constraints that should apply. At the local level, in local plans and part 2 of the UDP, more detailed consideration is given to planning issues and options. This is where sites and areas are identified for specified uses and where constraints on development such as those relating to archaeological investigation are indicated and explained.

Supplementary planning guidance

Irrespective of whether there is a development plan, a local planning authority may produce supplementary planning guidance. This will either spell out detailed policy guidance for a particular site, as in a development brief, or it will relate to a particular type of development as in a design or subject guide. Both types of guidance can be relevant to archaeology. A development brief will indicate the planning objectives and constraints applicable to a site and could make reference to archaeology. A subject guide might signify how archaeological evaluation is to be tackled in the development control process.

Planning policy, wherever it is found, should provide the framework for rational and consistent decision-making. But essentially it is a framework. Through a statutorily adopted and approved development plan it aims to provide all concerned – developers, archaeologists, residents, amenity societies, business interest and those responsible for providing roads and public buildings – with a measure of certainty about the development and use of land in the foreseeable future. However, such plans may not and often do not specify all the criteria for the control of development. They can give guidance but they cannot and do not specify precisely every aspect of control. They do not, for example, specify which building materials should be used at different sites or the conditions to be attached to every planning permission. They are more general than that, allowing each scheme to be determined on its particular merits.

Development control

Development control is that part of the planning process dealing with a) planning and other applications for development and b) enforcement of planning control, for example, where development has been undertaken without permission.

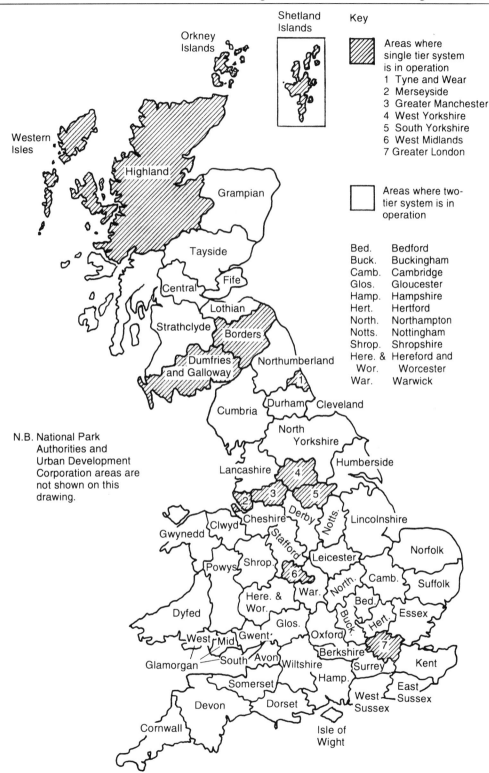

Figure 5.2 Location of the different planning systems in Britain.

Table 5.1 Decision-making powers of the different types of local planning authorities

	Type of authority	Decision-making powers
1.	County and regional councils (except the three Scottish rural regions of Borders, Dumfries and Galloway and the Highland region)	Applications relating to mineral extraction and waste disposal
2.	The remaining three Scottish regions (identified above) and the Islands authorities of Western Isles, Orkney and Shetland	The determination of planning applications and all other development control matters under the planning Acts
3.	District councils	The determination of all applications except those relating to mineral extraction and waste disposal
4.	Metropolitan district councils	The determination of all applications for planning permission and all other development control matters
5.	London borough councils	The same as the metropolitan districts
6.	Urban development corporations	The UDCs in England are responsible for all development control matters (in Cardiff it is the city (district) council which determines applications)
7.	Joint planning boards (Lake District and Peak District National Parks) and the Broads Authority	The determination of applications in consultation with the appropriate district authority (with some variations on procedures)

In 1992 over 500 000 planning applications were received by local planning authorities in England; nearly 40 000 and nearly 48 000 in Wales and Scotland respectively. About 150 or 0.03% were referred to the Secretaries of State, with planning authorities using their powers to determine the rest. Determined mostly by district councils – the relevant authorities for determining different applications are shown in Table 5.1 – some 80% were approved.

In exercising their powers to determine these applications, authorities generally consider each application on its merits, taking into account local planning policy contained in the development plan and any other relevant consideration. There is a presumption in favour of proposals which are in accordance with the development plan, and a presumption against those not in agreement with it. The planning Acts, however, state that material considerations may make it necessary to depart from these presumptions thereby allowing some leeway in decision-making. Thus there exists a degree of flexibility and uncertainty in the planning process. As we shall see later in Chapter 10 this has implications for both archaeologists and developers.

5.3 LEGISLATION AFFECTING ARCHAEOLOGY

There are, in essence, three ways in which land use legislation can be used to guide and control development whilst at the same time taking archaeological considerations into account. It can be:

• Mandatory, where policies relating to the use and development of land and the protection of the environment, including archaeology, must be prepared and implemented. Principally this will apply to planning controls where the planning Acts spell out that policy relating to the use and development of land must be formulated in local plans and used to guide and control development.

- Discretionary, indicating that there is no compulsion as to what must be done. Here we can think that whilst policies must be prepared by planning authorities there is discretion over the content of these policies. Broadly speaking, as long as they work within the guidelines set by government they are free to decide what to include in their development plans and other policy documents.
- Enabling, where planning authorities and other agencies can seek to encourage activities to control development (by agreement or otherwise) such as allowing archaeologists to enter sites for the purposes of investigation or excavation. How they seek to do this will depend very much on local circumstances which can vary enormously.

Parliament can and does issue a mass of legislation aimed at covering many aspects of everyday life. In connection with the use of land and matters relating to archaeology, four sets of legislation can be identified: the protection of ancient monuments; town and country planning powers; countryside legislation; and the operation of energy and utility companies.

The ancient monuments legislation

The principle aim of this legislation is to protect important archaeological sites from damage or destruction. The following Acts are the most relevant.

The Ancient Monuments and Archaeological Areas Act 1979

This is the main Act concerning known archaeological sites. Relating to all of Britain it consolidates earlier legislation dating back to the Ancient Monuments Act 1882, the first Act to be introduced and aimed at protecting ancient monuments.

The 1979 Act, in broad terms, seeks to do three things. First it is designed to protect archaeological sites by providing for the listing or scheduling of nationally important ones. Any work proposed to a site on the schedule must first receive **scheduled monument consent** from the appropriate Secretary of State. This may or may not be forthcoming depending on how the monument is affected.

Second, it makes provision for the funding of archaeological investigation by enabling the relevant agencies to undertake or assist in the cost of investigating any land thought to contain anything of archaeological interest. The agencies currently involved are English Heritage, Historic Scotland and Cadw.

Third, the Act also conveys certain rights to excavate and record in designated archaeological areas where remains can be expected but are not necessarily known in advance of excavation. Known as **Areas of Archaeological Importance** (AAIs), they are to be found in five cities only: Canterbury,

Chester, Exeter, Hereford and York. Within these areas designated by the government, developers have to accept that archaeological investigations can proceed whether they like it or not.

The National Heritage Act 1983

This Act made a number of minor amendments to the 1979 Act and established the independent Historic Buildings and Monuments Commission, otherwise known as English Heritage. This body is charged with a number of responsibilities including the following:

- to secure the preservation and enhancement of ancient monuments in England;
- to encourage the management of ancient monuments;
- to promote the public's enjoyment and to improve their knowledge of ancient monuments.

The Protection of Wrecks Act 1973

In a manner similar to the designation of archaoelogical areas under the 1979 Act, the Protection of Wrecks Act 1973 empowers the appropriate Secretary of State to designate an area of the sea around a wreck as a protected area. Within it, salvage and other operations are restricted unless a licence has been obtained to explore and investigate. The aim is to ensure that historic, archaeological and artistic objects or evidence are not unwittingly or unnecessarily damaged.

The burial grounds legislation

The protection given to burial grounds is slightly different to buried or submerged objects and other finds in that in addition to protecting buried remains from development the legislation also makes provision for the removal and reburial of human remains. Different Acts of Parliament apply in accordance with these two separate requirements. The Burial Act 1857 regulates the removal and reinterment of human remains by the use of a licensing system, whilst the Disused Burial Grounds Acts of 1884 and 1981 regulate what must be done when buildings are proposed at cemeteries and other burial grounds.

The planning legislation

Throughout Britain a number of Acts relating to planning are in operation but for the purposes of archaeology three are of particular relevance.

The Town and Country Planning Act 1990

This Act, which is the principal Act in England and Wales, sets out the requirements for the preparation of policies relating to the use and development of land. It states that policies should be prepared by local planning authorities and incorporated into development plans. It gives a broad indication of the matters to be included in these plans and specifies what local planning authorities can and must do in the control of development. It is where archaeology can be taken into account as a material consideration in the determination of development proposals. The Planning and Compensation Act 1991 made a number of amendments to this Act.

The Planning (Listing Buildings and Conservation Areas) Act 1990

This Act, which also relates to England and Wales, covers the special extra provisions relating to **listed buildings** and **conservation areas**. It does not directly take archaeological matters into account although it can have an indirect bearing. By imposing constraints relating to the character and appearance of development at historic buildings and in conservation areas, these additional controls can affect the ways in which archaeological investigation is pursued.

The Town and Country Planning (Scotland) Act 1972

In Scotland the bulk, but not all, of the legislation concerning the use and development of land is contained in separate Acts of Parliament. The Act of 1972 is the principal Act, although a number of amendments have been made to it, including those introduced by the Planning and Compensation Act 1991. The Scottish legislation is similar to that in England and Wales in that it adopts the same principles of both the English Acts above with just minor variations in detail.

Countryside legislation

This is aimed at both protecting resources and controlling development. It is mainly concerned with the natural beauty and amenity of the land but there are, nevertheless, aspects of it which relate to archaeological interests.

Coastal Protection Act 1949

This Act makes it unlawful to excavate or remove any material, other than minerals more than 50 feet below the surface either on, under or forming part of the seashore. The Minister (now Secretary of State) for Transport has certain rights to undertake operations but for others an order must be made specifying what development can proceed, with areas clearly defined at the seashore. Thus if archaeological remains are found at the seashore an element of protection could be given under the Act.

Forestry Act 1967

Aimed principally at afforestation, management and the protection of forests, the relationship to archaeology applies when land is to be acquired for forestry purposes. Compulsory purchase powers cannot be used where there is an ancient monument or other object of archaeological interest.

Countryside Act 1968

As part of the legislation relating to the enjoyment and protection of the countryside this Act enables planning authorities or others to provide study centres, tourist or other facilities in national parks. These facilities are to enable people to learn about the history, natural features, flora and fauna of the national park and objects of architectural, archaeological or historic interest to be found in them. Its role, therefore, in respect of archaeology is primarily related to education and learning.

Land Drainage Acts 1976 and 1991

Under the 1976 Act drainage boards and other drainage authorities are given extensive powers to clean, repair, maintain, deepen, widen, straighten or otherwise improve existing watercourses. Provision is also made for the construction of new works but none of this work can contravene the ancient monuments legislation. So that drainage authorities are aware of these requirements the government has produced guidelines (since 1982) which show how to meet these conservation duties by setting out best practice. In 1988 a revised document *Conservation Guidelines for Drainage Authorities* was published making it clear how these duties relating to archaeology should be exercised.

The 1991 Act extends the duties of internal drainage boards to the extent that they must consider the desirability of protecting and conserving buildings, sites and objects of archaeological interest. Public access for visiting or inspecting such sites must also be maintained and taken into account when development is proposed.

Wildlife and Countryside Act 1981

This Act seeks, among other things, to conserve or enhance the natural beauty and amenity of any land in the countryside by the use of **management agreements**. Made with any person having an interest in land, such agreements can impose restrictions on methods of land cultivation, agricultural land use and rights over land. Obligations to carry out operations or do other things appropriate to protecting historic components of the landscape can be imposed.

Agriculture Act 1986

This Act makes provision for the designation of **Environmentally Sensitive Areas** (ESAs) by the Minister for Agriculture, Fisheries and Food, where it is considered desirable to conserve, protect, enhance or restore imortant wildlife, historical or landscape features. These can include scheduled or unscheduled archaeological sites.

The method of protection is by agreement where a conservation plan is prepared as part of a management agreement aimed at adopting particular agricultural methods and at identifying features and sites suitable for protection where agricultural practices will be restricted.

Natural Heritage (Scotland) Act 1991

As part of its duties to protect the natural heritage of Scotland, this Act requires Scottish Natural Heritage to take account of the need to conserve sites and landscapes of archaeological interest. Thus to an extent it complements the Agriculture, Wildlife and Countryside Acts, but in a Scottish context.

Legislation relating to energy and public utilities

In the provision of public utilities, statutory undertakers have responsibilities concerning conservation. The most important are those relating to the coal industry and the electricity and water companies.

The coal industry Acts

Under the Coal Industry Nationalization Act 1946 a licence is needed before a number of mining and incidental operations can proceed. However, as a result of the Coal Industry Act 1990, any person who holds or applies for a licence must have regard to the desirability of protecting sites, buildings and objects of archaeological interest. Where relevant, proposals must include measures aimed at mitigating any adverse effects.

The Coal Mining Subsidence Act 1991 applies where scheduled monuments (and ancient monuments under the care of the Secretaries of State) are affected by subsidence damage. A duty is imposed where it is reasonably practical and in the public interest to restore any such monuments to their former condition before damage by subsidence occurred.

The Electricity Act 1989

Under this Act persons and companies licensed to generate or distribute electricity above stated limits (specified in section 38, Schedule 9 of the Act) must have regard to the desirability of preserving, among other things, geological or physiographical features of special interest and of protecting sites, buildings, structures and objects of historic or archaeological interest. In addition they are required to do what they reasonably can to mitigate any adverse effect on such sites, objects, etc. The Secretary of State for Trade and Industry (formerly the Secretary of State for Energy), when considering any application for a licence, must also have regard to the above.

As part of the licence application process, prospective licence holders must, after consultation with the relevant and respective national agencies (English Heritage etc.) prepare a statement setting out how they are to perform their duties concerning the above.

Water Act 1989

Under this Act the conservation duties imposed on the privatized water companies and the NRA are slightly different. There is still the duty to have regard to the desirability of protecting and conserving sites, buildings, structures and objects of historic and archaeological interest, but in addition to their setting and amenity value there is the added duty to consider access for the public to visit or inspect any such site, structure or object. If initial proposals have any effect on such freedom of access the implications of this must be considered.

Where land is to be disposed of in designated areas – national parks, areas of outstanding natural beauty and sites of special scientific interest – statutory procedures allow the above duties to be transferred to future owners by management agreements or through covenants governing public access, future land use and encouraging good conservation practice.

Separate from this is the requirement of statutory undertakers to take into account a code of practice prepared by the government in 1989. Similar to guidelines for drainage authorities, it provides comprehensive advice on all of the functions, operations and duties under the Act. Part of the code seeks greater integration of conservation issues into the planning and operation of these functions and duties. The aim is to encourage positive conservation as opposed to reacting against threats to development.

Water Resources Act 1991

This Act contains a similar requirement to the Water Act 1989 in that the same duty to protect and conserve buildings, structures, sites and objects of archaeological interest still applies. The difference is that any proposal relating to the functions of the authorities is now considered.

Two things are significant about the above legislation when development is proposed. First, some Acts will be more relevant than others, depending on the nature, type and location of the project. Second, archaeology is clearly becoming more important to developers, as witnessed by the increasing number of Acts in recent years, as shown in Table 5.2.

Secondary legislation

An important aspect of British legislation is the way government makes provision for orders, regulations and directions to be made. Generally they stem from Acts of Parliament such as the above, but sometimes they have to be made as a result of European Directives. Both make provision, or require the appropriate Secretary of State, to publish statutory instruments dealing with a particular matter in far greater detail than would be expected in any one Act of Parliament. Whereas the latter provides the basic legal framework, statutory instruments provide the detail for day to day decision-making and procedural matters. Prepared by government departments they are sometimes referred to as secondary legislation. Examples include the Use Classes Order and the General Development Order under the Town and

Table 5.2 The main Acts containing archaeological implications for development projects

Agriculture Act 1986
Ancient Monuments and Archaeological Areas Act 1979
Burial Act 1857
Coal Industry Nationalisation Act 1946
Coal Industry Act 1990
Coal Mining Subsidence Act 1991
Coastal Protection Act 1949
Countryside Act 1968
Disused Burial Grounds Act 1884
Disused Burial Grounds Act 1981
Electricity Act 1989
Forestry Act 1967
Land Drainage Act 1976
Land Drainage Act 1991
National Heritage Act 1983
Natural Heritage (Scotland) Act 1991
Opencast Coal Act 1958
Planning and Compensation Act 1991
Planning (Listed Buildings and Conservation Areas) Act 1990
Protection of Wrecks Act 1973
Town and Country Planning Act 1990
Town and Country Planning (Scotland) Act 1972
Water Act 1989
Water Resources Act 1991
Wildlife and Countryside Act 1981

Country Planning Acts and the Environment Assessment regulations emanating from the 1985 EC Directive on the environment. All three are referred to in later Chapters.

REFERENCES

Department of the Environment, MAFF, WO (1989) The Water Act 1989: *Code of Practice on Conservation, Access and Recreation*, HMSO, London.
Department of the Environment *et al.* (1990) *This Common Inheritance: Britain's Environmental Strategy*, HMSO, London.
Department of National Heritage (1992) *Information Sheet*, DNH, London.

FURTHER READING

Fairclough, G. (1990) Countryside legislation and statutory codes of practice. *Conservation Bulletin*, Issue 11, pp. 12–13, English Heritage, London.

6 Policies for archaeology and development

Controls over the use of land cannot operate in a vacuum. Whether they are private or public there has to be a policy framework within which decisions are made. This applies to archaeology just as much as it does to development although obviously the objectives will differ. For archaeology they will be geared to protecting remains and to increasing knowledge. For development the main aim will be to ensure that new buildings and infrastructure are provided where they are most needed.

In many ways these objectives conflict. New buildings, because of their size, complexity, the need for secure foundations or the locations that are chosen, will, on occasion, destroy archaeological remains. The aim of policy must be to minimize this destruction whilst allowing development to proceed.

The ways in which this conflict might be tackled is the theme of this Chapter. The intention is to consider policies for archaeology and development; to establish what they require and how they may be used in the development process for the preservation of remains as well as the provision of buildings and other works. Essentially, there are three levels at which public policy operates: namely, at the international, national and local government levels, deriving from European Union policy initiatives, British government policy and the policies of local planning authorities.

6.1 POLICY AT THE INTERNATIONAL LEVEL

In 1991, The European Convention on the Protection of the Archaeological Heritage adopted, with the approval of Ministers of the European Union and the UK government, a document aimed at protecting the archaeological heritage. The main points in the report, as highlighted by Wainwright (1992), can be summarized as:

1. the maintenance of an inventory of the archaeological heritage of each country;
2. the designation of protected monuments, sites and areas;
3. the mandatory reporting of chance archaeological discoveries;
4. the making available of new discoveries for examination;

5. the prior authorization of the use of metal detectors and other detection equipment;
6. an integrated approach to the conservation of archaeological sites;
7. the installation of a mechanism which allows the impact of development to be assessed;
8. the provision of public and private financing arrangements for archaeological research and conservation;
9. the prevention of illicit circulation of archaeological elements.

In pursuit of an integrated approach to protection each party to the agreement undertook to pursue the following:

1. to combine and reconcile archaeological and planning requirements by ensuring that archaeologists participate in the development of planning policies and strategies for the conservation, protection and enhancement of archaeological sites;
2. to ensure that archaeologists participate in development schemes where relevant;
3. to ensure that sufficient time and resources are made available for the study and publication of findings;
4. to ensure that full consideration is given to an assessment of the impact of development proposals on archaeological sites;
5. to assess the feasibility of conserving the archaeological heritage *in situ*.

With regard to the financing of archaeological investigation, research and conservation the agreement sets down the following guidelines:

- there should be public financial support for archaeological research from national, regional and local government;
- suitable measures should be adopted to ensure that the total costs of rescue archaeology arising from major public or private development schemes are covered by public or private sector resources as appropriate;
- provision be made in the budgeting of major schemes for preliminary archaeological investigation, a scientific record of what is found and for the full publication of findings.

From this statement of intent we can see that the European approach, which is now largely adopted in British government guidelines, sets out broad principles for protection with particular emphasis given to the involvement of archaeologists in the development and planning processes and to the financing of archaeological investigation. In respect of the latter it clearly puts the burden of funding archaeological activities squarely on to those responsible for major development projects. Included in this funding are the costs of assessment, the identification of data, the production of a research archive and the publication of a final report. It does, however, raise questions about what is meant by major development projects: how big is major? The agreement is not clear on this although it is an important point. Should public money be used for the research element and private funds for rescue or should the balance be split differently? Again, is it possible to separate these costs and if so, how and who decides?

There is also a question of where the money is to come from for schemes which are both research- and rescue-orientated. Whilst there will be those who will argue that the developer should contribute to all of the costs on the basis of the 'polluter-pays' principle, no doubt there will be others who will say that funding should be divided proportionately or equally between the public and private sectors. These are questions which cannot easily be resolved although they may sometimes produce answers related to the principle of inability to pay.

6.2 GOVERNMENT POLICY

Government policy concerning archaeology is to be found in a range of documents produced by different government departments and several quangos. The most significant document is *Planning Policy Guidance Note 16* (PPG 16), *Archaeology and Planning*, produced separately for England, Scotland and Wales. Each is worded slightly differently although the basic aims remain the same.

Alongside the PPG is the White Paper on the Environment *This Common Inheritance* (HMG, 1990), several Minerals Policy Guidance Notes, a Planning Advice Note on archaeology produced in Scotland and a number of other documents prepared primarily by English Heritage, Historic Scotland and Cadw. Between them they constitute a formidable stock of comment and advice relating to the preservation, protection, education and enjoyment of the archaeological resource. Within each of these areas are many matters where policy guidance is available or, in some cases, still needed.

With regard to preservation, the main concerns are with the designation and scheduling of sites for protection; programmes for the protection of monuments; assessments of the survival of existing monuments; and the management of the archaeological resource.

Protection, the second area of concern, permeates all of these but is primarily aimed at protecting archaeological sites from human activity and development proposals. It focuses on rescue archaeology and is where the planning system becomes important. Planning policy and how it is used to determine development proposals are key features but so too are the practical aspects of protection. Here any study cannot ignore how archaeological sites and their protection are to be funded.

As far as education and enjoyment are concerned, research and analysis are important together with the development of the archaeological archive. The collection and dissemination of information depend on government policy which ensues that academics, developers and others can examine and be aware of the archaeological resource. Enjoyment will be aimed principally at the general public.

Separate from these policy objectives, but equally important, is government policy concerning the use and development of land. Here a range of advice is provided by way of planning policy guidance notes, circulars and ministerial statements. Many relate to individual subjects such as housing, green belt, transport or retail development but more significantly there are guidance notes such as PPG 1 and PPG 12 which lay down general principles for development which are significant because the case for archaeology often has to be judged against them.

General statements of intent

The government's general proposals concerning heritage are outlined in the White Paper on the Environment which states, in respect of preserving and enhancing the best of our heritage, that the main aims are:

- to look after properties in government care;
- to promote the enjoyment and understanding of the heritage;
- to encourage private sector efforts and to make financial assistance available to help meet the extra costs of maintaining and restoring the heritage;
- to identify and record the best of the heritage;
- to ensure that it is properly protected and preserved by the legislative system.

Archaeological remains, because of their irreplaceability, form a crucial part of this heritage. As the only evidence of prehistoric periods, appropriate management to ensure their survival is seen as essential, as supported by the government when it states that they form part of our sense of national identity and are valuable both for their own sake and for their role in education, leisure and tourism. PPG 16 (Para. 6) adds that 'they can contain irreplaceable information' and that 'care must be taken to ensure that archaeological remains are not needlessly or thoughtlessly destroyed'.

At first glance we could be forgiven for thinking from this that all archaeological sites must be protected. The phrase 'not needlessly or thoughtlessly destroyed', on the other hand, suggests that once need and thought have been given to archaeological remains their removal or destruction might be possible depending on prevailing circumstances. It hints that where development is needed, policies should make adequate provision for it whilst at the same time taking into account the need to protect the environment. As stated by the Department of the Environment, public controls should:

> operate on the basis that applications for development should be allowed, having regard to the development plan and all materials considerations, unless the proposed development would cause demonstrable harm to interests of acknowledged importance. *PPG 1, Para. 5, 1992*

adding that the planning system:

> fails in its function whenever it prevents, inhibits or delays development which should reasonably have been permitted. *PPG 1, Para. 5, 1992*

Inevitably not all archaeological remains can be saved indicating that a balance needs to be struck between protecting archaeological remains and allowing development, a point clearly recognized by the government when it states:

> where nationally important archaeological remains, whether scheduled or
> not, and their settings are affected by proposed development there should
> be a presumption in favour of their physical preservation.
>
> *PPG 16, Para. 8, 1990*

From this we can conclude that the general presumption about protection is
starting to get clearer. The emphasis is on nationally important remains, the
implication being that the presumption in favour of protection need not
necessarily apply to remains that are not of national importance. A second
inference is that nationally important sites do not have to be on a register or
schedule of ancient monuments – these are looked at in some detail in the
next Chapter – but can be anywhere and as yet unknown or unrecognized,
although deemed to be of national importance once discovered. Thus the
identification or scheduling of nationally important sites has to form a key
element of government policy.

The scheduling of sites

The scheduling of archaeological sites involves a number of detailed
considerations about their rarity value, diversity, condition and vulnerability
as we shall see in Chapter 7. At a more general level, the key issue is one of
importance where sites of national, regional, or local significance can provoke
different responses from the government.

For sites of national importance there is a presumption in favour of their
physical preservation and a presumption against developments which would
have a significant impact on their integrity or setting. Such sites are put on a
schedule, although not all nationally important remains meriting preservation
are yet scheduled. Where such remains have been identified by the national
agency, English Heritage, Historic Scotland or Cadw, and the information
made available to the planning authority, the authority is required to operate
a similar presumption in favour of protection.

Where sites are of local importance only they will not merit scheduling
under the criteria for national importance. Here government guidance states
that there should be a presumption in favour of preservation (i.e. a
presumption against proposals which would involve significant alteration or
cause damage) through the medium of the development plan (SOEnD, 1992).
In cases involving archaeological remains of lesser importance the way to
proceed will not always be so clear and planning authorities will need to take
archaeological advice.

One point about the above needs mentioning. It relates to the fact that
some monuments, whilst perhaps of national importance, may not be
scheduled. For example, minerals can only be extracted where they are found
and some major projects (e.g. roads) will be restricted in where they can go:
there are occasions when monuments even of national importance should not
be protected under the scheduling procedures. Rather than protection *in situ*
they will be subject to investigation and recording as recognized by the
government when it states:

> The preservation *in situ* of important archaeological remains is always to
> be preferred where feasible, particularly in relation to nationally

important sites. Where this is not possible, an archaeological excavation incorporating the recording and analysis of remains and publication of the findings may be an acceptable alternative, although always less preferable from the archaeological viewpoint.   *SOEnD, Para. 17, 1992a*

Making use of local planning policy

The government places great emphasis on the planning process for protecting archaeological sites. The inclusion in the principal planning Acts, by the Planning and Compensation Act 1991, of the requirement that local plans must be produced and the increased weight given to the development plan when determining planning applications confirm this. They make it important, among other things, for plans to incorporate robust and relevant policies for the preservation of archaeological sites and monuments.

In particular the government states that structure plans should:

- take full account of the implications for scheduled archaeological remains and other nationally important remains, at present unscheduled, in considering possible locations for new development;
- contain general protection policies for both nationally important remains and their settings and also unscheduled sites of more local importance, and their settings;
- include general policies requiring the excavation and recording of such sites where the primary aim of preservation has not been possible. *SOEnD, 1992a*

and that local plans should:

- include policies for the protection, preservation and where appropriate, enhancement of all nationally important sites of archaeological interest and their settings;
- include policies for other unscheduled remains of more local importance, identified as particularly worthy of preservation;
- include policies requiring the excavation and recording of such sites where the primary aim of preservation has not been possible;
- define the areas and sites in the proposals map to which the policies apply making a distinction between sites of national importance and other sites.   *SOEnD, 1992a*

It is noteworthy that the Scottish guidance differs slightly from the English. Whilst the former states that policies should relate to both nationally and locally important sites in development plans, in England such a distinction is not made. Instead the DoE (1990), whilst acknowledging that nationally important scheduled remains should normally be earmarked in development plans for preservation, declares only that unscheduled remains of more local importance may, in appropriate circumstances, be identified in development plans as particularly worthy of preservation.

Thus, while local planning authorities in Scotland are advised by the government to identify all archaeological sites and areas, whether of national importance or otherwise, in their local plans, in England the decision is left to each authority to decide. They can choose to make the distinction if they so wish.

Planning applications

In addition to providing guidance on the content of development plans, government policy relating to the implementation of local planning policy is equally if not more important when it states:

> The desirability of preserving an ancient monument and its setting is a material consideration in determining planning applications whether the monument is scheduled or unscheduled *PPG 16, Para. 18, 1990*

Clearly there can be no doubt about the relevance of archaeology as a factor to be taken into account in the determination of development proposals. Less clear is the weight to be attached to this factor. For instance, the government states in PPG 16, Para. 27 that the case for preserving archaeological remains must be assessed on the individual merits of each case, taking into account the archaeological policies of the development plan together with all other relevant policies and material considerations. Included within these considerations is the intrinsic importance of the remains, weighed against the need for development.

This question of weighting is considered in more detail in Chapter 10. However, the following general rules appear to form a substantial part of government policy where planning authorities are advised to:

- seek early discussions with prospective developers;
- consult the local authority archaeological officer and, if appropriate, or where necessary, the relevant government agency;
- request the prospective developer to provide, where appropriate, an archaeological site evaluation;
- ensure that relevant information on the cultural heritage is taken into account in any environmental assessment that may be required (this is looked at in Chapter 9);
- where physical preservation is not feasible, ensure the developer make appropriate provision for the excavation and recording of the remains.

In contrast, one thing that authorities are requested not to do is include policies in their development plans requiring developers to finance archaeological works in return for planning permission (PPG 16, Para. 25). However, whilst specifically not making any reference to funding archaeological investigation the note subsequently implies that this may be acceptable in certain cases. By stating that a non-profit-making community body, a charitable trust, a housing association or an individual may experience difficulty in raising funds for an excavation and subsequent recording, the implication is that profit-making bodies should pay. Funding, therefore, appears to be based on the ability to pay or perceived ability to pay although the archaeological merits of a site will undoubtedly also be important.

Another conclusion to be drawn from this advice to planning authorities is that in certain circumstances it would be appropriate to refuse permission for development if it will destroy archaeological remains. It shows that there can be no absolute rule as to whether remains should be preserved intact or whether development should proceed in a prescribed way at a predetermined location. It emphasizes that presumptions only can be made and that early consultation and evaluation are prerequisites to success.

Rescue archaeology

Rescue archaeology forms an important part of government policy although less so that it once did. Despite the fact that excavation can itself destroy sensitive information, when a site is threatened by development the recording of what is there will nearly always be preferable to destruction without any record. When all attempts to protect what may be regarded as an important site, through scheduling or the planning process, fail, **preservation by record** is likely to be the preferred option. This is the post-PPG 16 approach.

Frequently preservation by record will be restricted to an examination of what is to be destroyed on only part of a site. Sometimes, however, a case may be made for undertaking a thorough and comprehensive excavation. The objectives of those involved together with professional and subjective judgements and motives will be important factors yet, whilst the government puts great store on these matters, planning authorities are allowed to put their own interpretation on how to pursue rescue archaeology. This can vary enormously.

Managing the resource

Many archaeological sites need care and management. In addition to scheduling, many sites of national, regional and local importance are recognized by the government as needing proper management for their future well-being. Government agencies play an important part in nationally important sites but other agencies and local authorities often need to be involved in managing these and other sites depending on the identification of priorities and the availability of resources.

An important aspect of management is assessing the significance of sites. As we have seen in Chapter 2 the SMR provides information on known archaeological sites from which it will be possible to get some idea of their relative importance. Alongside this is the government's **Monuments Protection Programme** and **Survival Assessment Programme**, aimed respectively at the scheduling of further archaeological sites and at studying what happens to monuments after they have been given statutory protection. The latter is particularly pertinent because, as stated in PPG 16, 'Monuments can be seriously damaged by neglect and need constant minor repair to prevent their deterioration'.

Grassed sites can be vulnerable to damage by neglect and owners, who are primarily responsible for upkeep, are advised to pay special attention to this. Government advice and financial assistance is available but only within tightly prescribed limits. Grants may be given for repair, recording or the consolidation of monuments and management agreements may be arranged by governmental sources to encourage beneficial management.

The Monuments Protection Programme

The protection of monuments forms a major part of management. An important aim of government is to retain a representative sample of sites for future generations, which means that sites must be kept under review by an appropriate mechanism. Principally this involves the scheduling of monuments but as only some 21 000 sites out of a possible 700 000 are scheduled, a case for more scheduling can easily be made.

This, in fact, is a major aspect of the Monuments Protection Programme. Currently under way it has been suggested that up to 50 000 sites in England alone may be protected under the scheduling procedures. Thus more widespread controls over sites and areas of land containing important archaeological remains are inevitable indicating that owners, whether public bodies or private individuals, will have to pay more attention to archaeology in the future.

The Survival Assessment Programme

One factor of concern to the government has been the speed with which monuments have been lost. In recent years many have been destroyed, which prompted the assessment programme. Starting from a pilot project in Wiltshire, the aim has been to quantify the archaeological record in terms of:

(a) the changing state of knowledge concerning the nature and scale of the archaeological resource;
(b) the rate of loss and damage to monuments and the causes for this;
(c) the condition and survival of the known existing resource;
(d) the level of success of measures designed to improve the management of archaeological sites   *English Heritage, 1991a*

The assessment programme, in addition to the above, is also aimed at giving pointers for the future allocation of resources – both staff and financial – to governmental, voluntary and private organizations and, ultimately, to report on the findings of the project.

Funding

There are two main aspects to government policy over funding. One is to give guidance to interested parties about where and when funds might be used for archaeological preservation and the other is to decide how much and in what circumstances public money should be spent by the government for investigation, research and protection.

Advice to others

A major objective of government policy is to secure the preservation of archaeological remains *in situ*. Where this is not possible the aim is to preserve by record the evidence of prehistory and history before a site is destroyed. The recording, however, is expensive, particularly in historic urban areas which are rich in deposits. It is also, by definition, destructive of the remains which it seeks to preserve, which means that money needs to be well spent.

In the early 1980s the bulk of funding came from central government although more recently the emphasis has shifted towards the developer. Based on the principle of the 'polluter-pays' and in part due to a lack of public money some planning authorities have sought to require funds from private developers for archaeological investigation including excavation and publication of results. This, however, is not without its problems as we shall see later in this Chapter.

Partly in response to these actions the government indicated in PPG 16 that planning authorities:

> Should not include policies in their development plans which would require developers to finance archaeological works in return for the grant of planning permission. *PPG 16, Para. 25, 1990*

Where it is decided that preservation *in situ* is not justified and that development which will result in the destruction of archaeological remains should proceed, the PPG adds that the authority would be justified in satisfying itself before granting permission that the developer has made appropriate and satisfactory provision for the excavation and recording of remains. Significantly the PPG adds (Para. 25) that where the developer is a non-profit-making organization, such as a housing association or charitable trust, which is unable to raise the necessary funds for excavation and subsequent recording, or an individual who similarly does not have the means to fund such work, an application may be made to English Heritage for financial assistance.

In other words the 'polluter-pays' principle is modified to the 'polluter who is able to pay' or more correctly to the 'polluter-who-is-thought-to-be-able pays'. On many occasions and particularly in times of recession it is by no means clear which developers would fall into this category. Nevertheless, the policy exists although as we shall see in later Chapters, the developer is faced with a number of risks and uncertainties when engaged in a development project making it difficult for him to forecast profits and viability accurately.

Government funding

Government policy regarding its own finances is to allocate funds for recording those sites which cannot be preserved, where destruction is taking place and where the agencies involved do not have sufficient resources to deal with the problem (English Heritage, 1991c). It is aimed at selected sites where all possibilities for saving a site have been exhausted.

The government also commissions projects which enable it and its agencies to carry out their statutory duties and to fund particular research problems. In addition, there may be cases where these agencies are prepared to offer financial assistance. These tend to fall into two main classes:

Table 6.1 Archaeological grants paid by English Heritage 1992–93

	Number		£
Recording	32		1 066 303
Assessment	23		751 100
Analytical	94		2 204 607
Evaluation	2		19 159
Survey	28		876 166
Local authority	21		197 636
Farm survey grants	11		57 968
Presentation grants	1		2 460
Miscellaneous	20		244 772
Establishment	1		85 000
			5 505 175
Trunk road schemes			
Recording	13	1 255 908	
Assessment	3	43 196	
Analytical	7	107 273	
		1 406 378	
			6 911 553

Source: English Heritage

- those where the archaeology demands an investigation clearly out of proportion to the proposed development;
- where unexpected and important evidence emerges following the grant of planning permission and where existing resources put aside for archaeological investigation are insufficient.

One type of development warranting and receiving considerable grant aid is trunk road projects. In 1990–91, for instance, the total grant for projects in advance of trunk road schemes in England was £726 702 distributed between 9 survey grants, 17 excavation grants and 12 post-excavation grants. At the same time English Heritage donated an additional £5 186 211 in rescue grants between a further 172 projects. By 1992–93 trunk road schemes supported by grant had been reduced to 23 but the total amount increased to £1 406 378. Similarly the total rescue grants in England also increased in 1992–93 with Table 6.1 showing the 1992–93 position.

The investigation of archaeological sites, whether by survey, excavation, analysis, recording and publication accounts for a large part of English Heritage's budget. The rescue grants programme dominates these activities but, as can be deduced from Table 6.2, several related activities cumulatively make up nearly 30% of the archaeological budget. Significant among these are the costs of maintaining and recording properties in public ownership, scientific analysis by the Ancient Monuments laboratory and the Monuments Protection Programme. The backlog report grants relate to unpublished projects undertaken between 1938 and 1973 although these have now been completed. The publication costs are aimed at defraying the costs of publishing reports on work previously funded by the government.

Table 6.2 The allocation of resources by English Heritage 1989–93

	1988/89 £'000	1989/90 £'000	1990/91 £'000	1991/92 £'000	1992/93 £'000
Rescue grants	5 478	6 058	5 550	6 881	6 912
Properties in care: archaeological recording	656	989	974	886	594
Ancient monuments laboratory contracts	625	745	678	773	928
Monuments protection programme	534	659	441	215	185
Consultants and fees	476	497	341	306	121
Greater London SMR	289	333	340	287	214
Publications	255	211	241	221	202
Ancient Monuments and Historic Building recording	256	260	165	301	229
Central Excavation Unit	134	140	132	116	118
Backlog report grants	174	195	100	72	40
Storage grants	68	28	52	133	72
Oxford training course	21	25	28	25	26
Totals	8 966	10 140	9 042	10 216	9 701

Source: English Heritage

6.3 POLICIES OF LOCAL PLANNING AUTHORITIES

The main impact of policy is at the local level where local planning authorities decide what will be allowed at different locations. They enable developers and archaeologists to identify with varying degrees of certainty the chances of their objectives being met. By indicating the main criteria against which development proposals will be judged they should enable applicants to form an opinion as to how their proposals will be determined.

Policies will, of course, vary from authority to authority, but those relating to archaeology are likely to be aimed at preserving remains irrespective of their national importance. The fact that many sites cannot reasonably be assessed will, for many authorities, be of little consequence. The aim will normally be to establish what can or should be done depending on local circumstances.

Another factor which underpins the importance of local policy is the requirement that it must be the first consideration of the planning authority whenever development proposals are to be determined. The Planning and Compensation Act 1991, by amending the principal Acts of 1972 (Scotland) and 1990 (England and Wales), makes this clear when it states that decisions on planning application must be made in accordance with local policy (in the development plan) unless material considerations indicate otherwise.

Basically there are two areas of concern that need to be addressed. The first relates to the types of policies that may be adopted by local authorities and the second to how they might be applied in selected areas. The matter of how policy may be challenged is a separate issue not covered in this book.

Types of policy

One of the aims of local planning policy is to protect both scheduled and unscheduled sites. However, because of statutory protection given to the former under the ancient monuments legislation, and the greater number of the latter, many authorities tend to stress and seek to protect the unscheduled and locally important majority of sites. Their importance, setting, educational and tourist value become significant factors where policies can range from broad principles of protection to site-specific requirements concerning matters such as archaeological evaluation, the degree of destruction that may be permissible, the excavation of sites, recording by record and the funding of archaeological investigation and research. Below, we look first at the general policies that may be found followed by those that are more site-specific.

Policies of a general nature

In an analysis of planning policies concerning archaeology, six main areas of general importance can be identified in structure, local and unitary plans.

1 The recording of archaeological sites

As a matter of strategic planning and as a precursor to more detailed policies which state what should be done when archaeological remains are encountered, planning authorities may require archaeological sites to be identified in local and unitary development plans. A policy such as the following can often be found:

> The local planning authorities will seek to identify, record and protect archaeological sites, monuments and historic landscapes.

Directed at district councils, we can see that this policy is aimed at all archaeological sites and not just scheduled monuments.

2 A presumption against development

One of the basic aims of planning is to protect the environment. This is recognized by the government in its planning legislation and by local planning authorities in their development plans. Relating to both the natural and built environments it is perhaps a foregone conclusion that policies such as the following, directed at archaeology, are to be found:

> Development proposals which could result in damage to, or the destruction of, sites of archaeological importance will normally be refused.

or

> The local planning authorities will seek to ensure that historical archaeological sites, features and areas deemed to be of national or county importance are protected from development.

In the two examples, taken respectively from the structure plans for North Yorkshire and Somerset, the authorities are seeking to set the scene and do not qualify the archaeological sites in any way. Yet if the policies are applied literally it would appear that planning permission ought to be refused if damage is likely. PPG 16, on the other hand, states that the case for preservation must be considered against all other relevant planning considerations. This indicates that policies worded in this way and concerned with archaeology should not be strictly interpreted – the word 'normally' provides the clue – but judged against other policies in the development plan. We can see that weighting and the question of reasonableness are starting to become important.

3 The need for information

A presumption against development clearly cannot be enough. Apart from explaining reasons for the presumption there is the more important need for authorities to spell out where development can go, the constraints operating on development and the ways in which archaeology is to be tackled. Initially this will require additional information to be submitted.

If the effects of development on archaeology are to be investigated, local authorities are likely to require information which enables them to:

- assess the archaeological importance of a site;
- assess the effect of development on those resources.

The extent to which these objectives are pursued will depend on the importance of archaeology in the area relative to other land use considerations. In historic towns and cities we can expect to see more weight given to archaeology than in other areas with variations made according to local considerations about encouraging development and protecting the heritage. Frequently these will encompass a range of other matters such as design, appearance, conservation, levels of unemployment and local politics. The need for extra information will be to enable the authority to make better judgements about archaeology in relation to these other considerations.

4. The impact of mineral operations

One area where different considerations will apply is mineral extraction. By its very nature, it is liable to cause irretrievable damage to the archaeological resource, yet frequently the problem is compounded by the fact that the archaeological importance of a site is not always fully known. The archaeologist's understanding is often based on only partial historical evidence with the result that mineral planning authorities can find it difficult to make informed judgements.

In response to this potential problem these authorities are likely to do two things:

1. Identify preferred areas for mineral extraction.
2. Set up procedures to ensure that decisions affecting archaeology are based on adequate information.

When seeking to identify areas suitable for extraction we should assume that authorities will have taken archaeological considerations into account. But if this information is limited it would also be prudent to assume that procedures will exist for an archaeological evaluation to be made, as in the following example from Berkshire:

> In order to allow an informed judgement to be made on the archaeological implications of an application for mineral extraction, the county council will, in appropriate cases, require the results of an archaeological evaluation of the site to be submitted before the application is determined. The brief for such an evaluation must be agreed with the county council before the evaluation takes place.
>
> *Berkshire County Council, 1993b*

The use of the words 'in appropriate cases' indicates that an evaluation will not automatically be required in every case and that the decision will rest on the information that is available. How it is interpreted and how it is acted upon will then be the next consideration where Berkshire's subsequent policy provides an answer:

> The county council will seek to ensure that archaeological sites and monuments meriting permanent preservation are left undisturbed and appropriately managed, and that elsewhere provision is made where necessary for an appropriate level of archaeological investigation prior to damage or destruction. Where appropriate the requirement for this provision will be safeguarded by planning conditions. Conditions may be imposed, or planning obligations may be sought, to ensure that access, time and financial resources are available to allow essential archaeological investigation and recording to take place.
>
> *Berkshire County Council, 1993b*

From this we can see that access, time and finance will be important local considerations which will have to be taken into account where archaeological investigation has been deemed necessary.

5 Exceptional circumstances

The use of presumptions in the planning process acknowledges that uncertainty is ever present. It also implies that exceptions can be made in the determination of development proposals. Indeed, this flexibility in decision-making is built into the British planning system, making it both acceptable and a nuisance depending on one's viewpoint. But this flexibility should have its own guidelines. If exceptions are to be made against the presumption to protect archaeological sites they ought to be stated. But what are they?

Several possibilities exist depending on local circumstances. Most important will be those relating to the development of communications, new housing and other basic human needs. Exceptions policies covering these and other matters can be found in structure and local plans. In Cheshire, for example, the essential needs of local people and agriculture are given high priority where sites of archaeological importance will be considered against these needs. Frequently, however, the exceptions are not specific, making it difficult for us to know where we stand. But that's the beauty of the flexible system!

6 Changing circumstances

Another important point about planning policies is that they can change over time. As archaeology becomes more widely recognized in the planning process and accepted as a material planning consideration, so we can expect to see policies change. They may, for instance, lead to a greater use of management agreements similar to those operating in the Environmentally Sensitive Areas (ESAs). In these areas the aim is to protect specific landscapes in accordance with requirements laid down by the Ministry of Agriculture, Fisheries and Food.

A similar approach appears to be taking place in planning circles. Berkshire County Council, for example, in its structure plan, approved by the Secretary of State in 1988, stated:

> In considering proposals for development, the County and District Councils will seek to ensure that:
>
> i) scheduled Ancient Monuments, their settings, and the most important non-scheduled archaeological sites, are preserved intact;
> ii) conflicts between the preservation of archaeological deposits and other land uses will be resolved by means of management agreements;
> iii) in the case of archaeological sites and monuments of unknown importance and areas of high potential, consideration will be given to the need, and provision will be made, as appropriate, for archaeological investigations;
> iv) archaeological sites and monuments not meriting permanent preservation have provision made for an appropriate level of archaeological investigation prior to damage or destruction.

In the revised draft structure plan (Policy EN6) the emphasis changes towards a requirement for information, that is, an archaeological evaluation. Thus:

> Scheduled Ancient Monuments and the most important non-scheduled remains, together with their settings, will be protected and managed to ensure that they are not damaged or destroyed. Where a lack of information precludes the proper assessment of a site or sites with archaeological potential, this information will have to be provided in advance of any decision to affect that site or area. In certain instances, destruction of a site or area may be acceptable if accompanied by archaeological recording.   *Berkshire County Council, 1993a*

We can see that previously the emphasis was on protection but that the need for information is now aimed, post-PPG 16, at protecting and managing archaeological sites by stating, in general terms, how the protection is to be pursued.

Detailed planning policies

At the local level policies become more specific, aimed at assessing the impact of development and how this impact should be controlled. The setting of local as opposed to national standards against which development proposals can be judged becomes important where nine broad areas of policy can be identified.

1 A requirement to protect

The general presumption against development referred to earlier will often be repeated in local and unitary plans but with more precision and clarity. For example, at Westminster, the City Council has adopted the following policy:

> The City Council will seek to ensure that the most important archaeo-logical remains and their settings are permanently preserved *in situ* and where appropriate are given statutory protection. In such cases, if preservation *in situ* is both desirable and feasible, the City Council will require the development design to accommodate this objective.
> *Unitary Development Plan, Policy DES 18 (iv), Westminster City Council*

In a very different context, Glyndwr District Council in North Wales puts forward the following policy for inclusion in its local plan:

> Permission for development will normally be refused on sites of archaeological interest where it is considered that the site of interest should be retained and where development and the retention of the monument cannot be reconciled.
> *Local plan, Policy C13, Glyndwr District Council*

From these two examples we can see that the developer is expected to design his project around archaeological remains although this need not always be the case because both authorities recognize the need to qualify their requirements. By referring to the appropriateness of the occasion with the words: 'if preservation . . . is both desirable and feasible' and 'where it is considered . . . the site . . . should be retained', they indicate that protection will rest on the importance given by the authority to the archaeology of individual sites.

These examples are typical of many areas and may seem inconsequential but they raise a point which developers should be aware of. Irrespective of the importance of a site, local considerations and criteria could be deciding factors in the determination of applications. For example, in Glyndwr, 44% of scheduled sites are of prehistoric funerary and ritual sites, but there are no Roman sites recorded. In the neighbouring district of Wrexham Mealor, on the other hand, prehistoric funerary sites account for only 15% of scheduled monuments while linear earthworks account for the largest number. Admittedly these figures relate to scheduled sites in one particular area but they show that different authorities could adopt different attitudes and put a different emphasis to protection based on local rarity value and uniqueness of sites. This may not be great but it is in addition to political and other planning considerations.

2 The designation of archaeological areas

In many towns and cities it is possible to identify districts and areas of land which are important for their archaeological content. They are where planning authorities are likely to give extra prominence to archaeology in the formulation of policy and where archaeological investigation will be required.

Varying in shape and size according to historic importance, they tend to be identified in supplementary guidance or development plans where a policy on lines similar to the following prepared by Gwynedd County Council may be used:

> Areas of archaeological significance as shown on the proposal maps will be recorded as planning constraints on development, and applications for planning consent to develop such sites will be referred to the Gwynedd Archaeological Trust for their observations.
>
> *Ardudwy District Plan, Policy 9, Gwynnedd County Council*

In Somerset, areas of high archaeological potential have been identified which have been further divided into two groups: the historic cores of settlements and landscape areas. They vary in size from a few hectares to several square kilometres.

In both examples different names have been given to these archaeological areas mainly to emphasize local importance but more significantly to distinguish them from the Areas of Archaeological Importance (AAIs) designated under the Ancient Monuments legislation of 1979 (this is looked at in the next Chapter). Within these AAIs located solely in the cities of Canterbury, Chester, Exeter, Hereford and York, special additional provisions relating to archaeological excavation apply.

Other descriptions, in addition to the two mentioned above, are used elsewhere: Table 6.3 lists some examples. They all serve the same purpose, that is, they indicate the concern of the local planning authority about archaeology and where policies relating to archaeological investigation are likely to be found.

In addition, we may find authorities grading archaeological areas. Just as historic buildings are graded according to their importance, it is possible for archaeological areas to be graded according to their importance. In York, for example, outside the AAIs the city council has decided to grade the remainder of the city as an area of archaeological significance. This is a second tier based on the knowledge that archaeological deposits are known to exist outside the AAI.

Table 6.3 Examples of designations given to archaeologically important areas by local planning authorities

- archaeological priority zones
- areas of archaeological significance
- areas of high archaeological potential
- local areas of archaeological importance
- archaeological alert areas
- zone of archaeological potential
- areas of special archaeological priority

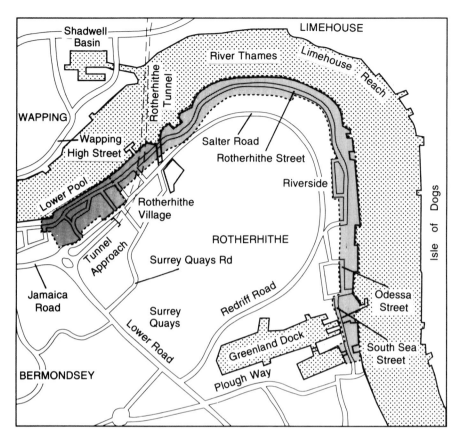

Figure 6.1 Rotherhithe Village and Riverside Archaeological Priority Zones, London. London. (Source: Southwark Council.)

Examples of locally important archaeological areas are shown in Figures 6.1, 6.2 and 6.3. The first, alongside the River Thames in Southwark, reflects the historical importance of the river and to the fact that the subsoils in this area are likely to preserve deposits in relatively good condition. Indeed, the authority believes that excavation in this area could be particularly worthwhile for the advancement of knowledge. The second example, also in Southwark, relates to what was once an important highway out of London to the village of Walworth. The third example, covering part of the centre of Leicester, signifies the importance of the historic core of the city – it is where local archives and the SMR show substantial past human activity. Note how the shapes and sizes of these areas reflect different local archaeological circumstances.

3 Controls on development within designated archaeological areas

Where archaeological areas have been identified the initial objective of planning authorities is likely to be one of requiring archaeological information to be submitted. Records will have shown that the area is important but

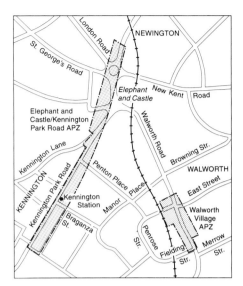

Figure 6.2 Walworth Village and Elephant and Castle/Kennington Park Road Archaeological Priority Zones, London. (Source: Southwark Council.)

the significance of individual sites will not necessarily be known, leading the authority to pursue a sequence of events.

The first policy in this sequence is likely to be on the following lines:

> AA1. A written assessment of the likely archaeological impact of a development shall be submitted with any planning application for development within the locally designated area.

In seeking to gauge the threat to archaeology at a site, the authority may ask for a written statement indicating the archaeological background, information on present and past development showing basements and old foundations where relevant, details of what is proposed, including foundations, and a conclusion highlighting the likely effect on surviving archaeological remains from the proposed development.

The assessment will not at this stage involve on-site activity such as trial trenching or the obtaining of soil samples from boreholes. It will simply be a desk-top study to enable the authority's archaeologist or archaeological adviser to assess the likely impact of development at the site. It would show to all concerned the possible effects this could have and hint at ways of mitigation. It would be particularly helpful to householders and small businesses where small-scale works are proposed, such as house or shop extensions. It might give an indication of the time and expense involved.

Following the submission of a written assessment three outcomes are possible:

1. It indicates that there is no threat to archaeology. This can arise where the proposed groundworks pose no threat or because previous disturbances to the ground, such as the construction of earlier structures, have already destroyed any remains that may have been on the site. If this is the case then there would be no need for further archaeological investigation.

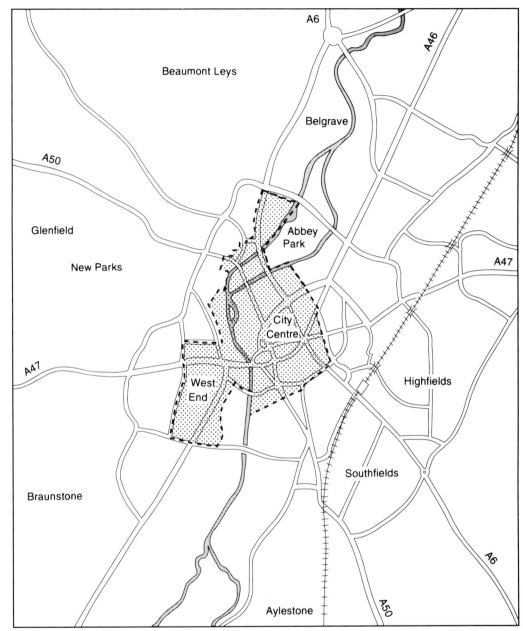

Figure 6.3 The Archaeological Alert Area at Leicester. (Source: Leicester City Council.)

2. It reveals that important archaeological remains are likely to be threatened by the proposed development, in which case preservation *in situ* would be required. This would normally require a field evaluation to be undertaken so that more detailed information can be obtained for the siting and placing of foundations and other groundworks.

3. It shows that archaeological remains of uncertain importance may be affected by the proposed development.

The second and third outcomes are likely to lead to a field evaluation where the second policy in this sequence applies:

> AA2. An archaeological field evaluation shall be undertaken to establish the importance and level of survival of the archaeological resource.

Unlike the written statement, a field evaluation involves a limited amount of on-site investigative work. This could involve the use of non-penetrating techniques of investigation such as the use of a magnetometer and by boreholes, although more accurate results are often achieved by small-scale non-destructive trial trenching. It is quite distinct from a full archaeological excavation.

Some authorities may approach the issue of assessment by asking for a field evaluation at the outset thereby avoiding the need for an earlier and separate written statement. This can be advantageous where archaeological deposits are known to exist at a site (possibly because of an earlier investigation) but could be a disadvantage for some developers such as small builders or householders who may be deterred from undertaking building work. Clearly much will depend on the importance of the archaeological resource within the designated area (and site), the objectives of the authority and how they are applied to different developers.

If we bear in mind that the aim of a field evaluation is to assess the nature, extent and significance of any remains, there will be three possible outcomes:

1. that no archaeologically significant remains exist at the site, in which case no further investigation is necessary and the development can proceed, assuming other matters are satisfactory;
2. that important remains are revealed which merit preservation *in situ*;
3. that archaeological remains are discovered which do not merit preservation *in situ* but which should be excavated and recorded prior to the commencement of development.

In order that the appropriate outcome can be properly assessed the authority is likely to require the evaluation to be submitted prior to or at the time of a planning application. If it is not the authority could ask for more information (the GDO makes provision for this) and delay the application.

For sites which merit preservation *in situ* the following policy may apply:

> AA3. The development shall be designed and constructed in such a way as to preserve the remains *in situ*.

The presumption in favour of preservation *in situ* is likely to be a major policy objective of many authorities, especially in view of PPG 16. Many may interpret this to mean total preservation with development or projects designed to achieve this either by reducing the area of ground disturbance or by the careful siting of buildings or by the careful design of foundations. Basements would probably be unacceptable and have to be removed or at least substantially reduced in size.

Alternatively, if the remains are extensive or if other circumstances are present it may prove difficult to retain them untouched. Some destruction may be unavoidable in which case, if refusal is not contemplated, then greater care and attention would have to be given to the siting of buildings and foundation design. The evaluation should reveal where the minimum impact is likely to occur although an authority may stipulate the maximum amount of destruction it is willing to accept. In York, for example, the council has adopted the following policy:

> AA4. Developments which disturb or destroy more than 5% of the archaeological deposits contained within the boundaries of an application site will normally be refused.

This can be seen as an admirable objective in several ways. It sets down a limit for destruction whilst at the same time acknowledging that some loss is acceptable and almost inevitable. It does, however, raise questions about why 5% and how it should be calculated.

Part of the answer to the first question relates to project design. A key factor will be the volume of ground required for foundations where Ove Arup, in their study for York City Council, found that the loss of more than 5% of deposits will only occur in exceptional circumstances and will not apply to most buildings (Ove Arup, 1991).

The second question poses several more. Assuming the calculation is based on volume, to what depth should it be taken? Should it start at ground level or should earlier destruction be taken into account and should all areas or parts of a site be treated equally? It would appear that different and opposing arguments on all of these matters can be put with equal force and yet sound reasonable. The underlying test, however, ought to relate to the expected importance of a site based on site evaluation.

If this shows that retention is not feasible then excavation and preservation by record would be the next step. This would be in line with the following policy:

> AA5. Where the retention of archaeological remains is not feasible they shall be excavated and recorded prior to development.

Large-scale developments covering large tracts of urban and rural land where archaeological remains are thought to exist will almost inevitably involve some destruction. The construction of a power station or a new trunk road in the countryside are good examples of this. Being limited in where they can go they will clearly raise questions about priorities and the weighting of conflicting factors. Excavation will probably not be one of them although it will frequently be a prerequisite to development.

Urban redevelopment sites in known historic areas are also likely to result in destruction, making it almost inevitable that the planning authority or government department will expect the developer to make provision for the excavation and recording of remains. This would be achieved by condition or obligation as we shall see in Chapter 10.

4 Archaeological investigation in undesignated areas

One of the problems with designating areas of archaeological importance is that it presupposes the areas to be appropriate for the protection of sites and advancement of knowledge. Where they exist it has to be assumed that this is where important archaeological discoveries are most likely to be made and where evaluation and excavation will produce the best results. Archaeologists, however, know that other areas can be equally if not more important and that significant finds can be found at other sites, whether or not they are near scheduled sites.

There is also the point that policy, once adopted, is intended to be in place for 10 years and that without this policy safeguard by the planning authority it could be too late to avoid destruction. The presumption in favour of the development plan when determining applications will reinforce this, indicating that policy concerning site investigation is not likely to be restricted solely to known important archaeological areas but will be directed more widely to cover unexpected finds at other sites. A policy the same or similar to the following might therefore be found:

> Where development proposals are submitted which are likely to affect sites of archaeological interest or their settings, an archaeological evaluation of the impact may be required.
>
> *Deposited Structure Plan, Gwent County Council, 1993*

One significant variation to this policy would be where an authority uses the word 'shall' instead of 'may'. In both cases, however, the emphasis will be on requiring archaeological information to be assessed before development proposals are determined.

5 Supplementary guidance

Where development is considered desirable or likely in areas of known archaeological importance, planning authorities may produce supplementary guidance for the benefit of potential developers. This could be in the form of a development brief or specification for individual sites or relate to a number of sites.

A development brief would state the planning authority's requirements for a particular site. It would specify all relevant policies in the development plan and other planning criteria considered relevant. Land use, the amount of development, design and other standards would be stated alongside any archaeological requirements. It would tell prospective developers what they will have to do if they wish to develop the site. Archaeological evaluation or excavation could be among the requirements set out in the brief.

Separate from this, an authority may produce an archaeological specification where the aim is to summarize the archaeological importance of a site and to inform developers what they will have to do to satisfy the authority's requirements concerning archaeology. Matters raised in a specification would normally include:

- a description of the site;
- a description of the known archaeology at the site;
- a summary of previous archaeological work at the site and in the vicinity;
- academic objectives;
- an indication of the types of development considered appropriate for the site;
- the ways in which the archaeological resource is to be further investigated;
- where trial trenching would be most appropriate;
- the requirements for the deposit of information;
- publication requirements.

The third type of guidance relating to a number of sites would be similar to a specification, the main difference being that it would establish the archaeological data base for a series of sites which the authority thought important. This could be in respect of anticipating development or where the local or unitary development plan sought to channel development. It would, in fact, be similar to the study produced for York City Council by Ove Arup (1991) where 35 sites were identified for investigation (Figure 6.4). Ranging in area from 0.1 to 27 hectares, the study covered the following matters:

- a review of archaeological data;
- a review of geotechnical data;
- a review of documentary sources;
- site inspections;
- specific site assessments indicating the required evaluation and mitigation strategy.

6 Funding archaeological investigation

One of the most crucial policy considerations concerning archaeology and development centres on who should pay for archaeological investigation. Should it be the developer who is about to destroy archaeological remains or should the money come from the taxpayer? Both have their proponents but equally both have their problems.

One of the strongest arguments appears to be that the developer should pay based on the 'polluter-pays' principle. If the archaeological resource is about to be destroyed the argument is that the cost of recording what is there should fall fairly and squarely on the shoulders of the developer. The view is taken that whatever the cost of investigation at a particular site the brunt of this should be borne by the developer.

Whilst sensible in many ways this will not always be straightforward and can present problems. First, the full extent or importance of archaeology at a site cannot always be known in advance. An evaluation, as we saw in Chapter 2, can miss important elements at a site which may turn out to be more important than originally envisaged. The original sum may be insufficient to meet unexpected additional costs. Conversely an expensive excavation could be mounted and reveal nothing.

Second, all sites are different. Irrespective of what may or may not be expected, some sites will inevitably contain more information than others and

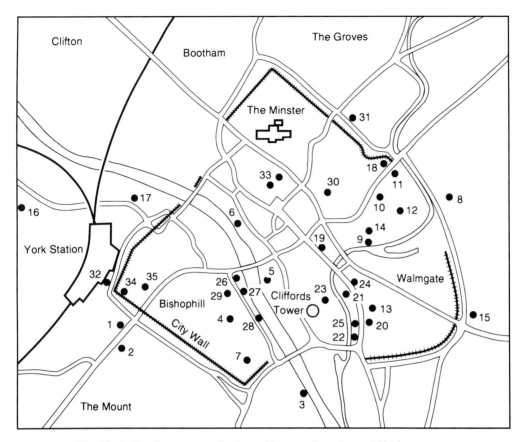

Figure 6.4 The York development study sites. (Source: Ove Arup, 1991.)

require a more thorough examination. This could penalize some developers at the expense of others and a developer unfortunate enough to end up in this situation could be placed in the unenviable position of having to pay far more for archaeological investigation than, say, a competitor at another site with a similar proposal.

Third, not all developers are equally capable of affording an archaeological investigation. As we shall see in Part Three, the developer can be a local authority or householder instead of a property development company; ability to pay can differ enormously not only between sectors but also between companies. The competence, experience and financial standing of one company can differ substantially from another, making it more difficult for some companies to make ends meet.

What these differences and uncertainties suggest is that the 'polluter-pays' principle ought to be adapted to suit individual circumstances. It suggests that the perceived importance of the archaeology of a site should be matched against the performance of the developer. This, however, has its own problems.

First, it equates investigation with ability to pay, thereby placing the advancement of knowledge second to market forces. If the ability is not there (and in many cases it is not) then the advancement of knowledge is impeded and destruction with more limited recording may be the result.

Second, human nature being what it is, it is likely that inequities will still occur; a landowner may refuse to sell below a certain price; the archaeological costs may be seen as excessive or the development appraisal may be inaccurate.

What these problems suggest is that a more equitable approach ought to be adopted. Indeed, Ove Arup hinted at such when they reported to York City Council in 1991 on the possibility of raising a 'heritage tax'. They considered that many of these problems would be removed if a general levy was imposed on all development in a designated area. The idea was put forward that a levy could be used to fund archaeological investigation and, if necessary, compensate developers for any loss suffered. They acknowledged, however, that this would not be without its problems and that its attractions are mainly theoretical.

One problem is that if money is to be channelled directly into archaeological investigation such a levy would need new legislation. This, however, would have to be worded so that the money was reserved solely for this purpose and not for any other, a proposal that the Treasury Department would presumably object to in the same way that it objects to other hypothecated taxes. There could also be political difficulties in trying to introduce such a levy.

In the meantime and without a more equitable system it is necessary to look at the practicalities of the situation and at the policies currently adopted by planning authorities. Here we find a varied response varying from a requirement on the developer to fund excavation by way of a planning agreement to the opposite view that it is of no concern to the authority.

Two examples can be used to illustrate these views. In the first, at York, developers are encouraged to enter into planning obligations to cover all aspects of a mitigation strategy including funding. That is 'as a condition of the grant of planning permission'. At Southampton, in contrast, planning agreements are no longer used in relation to archaeology. In the words of the development control officer:

> We take the view that PPG 16 makes this unnecessary. PPG 16 clearly gives archaeology the status of a material planning consideration and this can be controlled by condition. Accordingly, the sums of money involved in investigation are not a planning consideration. They are an economic matter for the developer themselves who should consider it in exactly the same light as he would any special infrastructure costs such as special foundations.

Planning authorities are allowed leeway in how they regulate the use and development of land. The funding of archaeological investigations is one example of where this flexibility is used to achieve different objectives. Politics and bias cannot be far removed and no doubt will be reflected in the views and motives of the authority, not so much about who should pay but how the funding should be controlled. Less apparent will be the implications of these motives.

7 Design of development to minimize destruction

In view of the above difficulties which archaeologists and developers face, one possible solution is to design a project so that it minimizes destruction or tries to avoid archaeological remains altogether. Both can be difficult, especially the latter, but they could leave open the question of whether an excavation is necessary. If preservation *in situ* is a possibility it could mean that costs are defrayed to a future time when more advanced techniques of investigation may be available.

In order to assess the effect of a project on archaeology, design solutions will have to be studied. Principally this would be in respect of foundation design where the authority and its archaeological advisers will need to be able to study these details and assess the impact. This means that foundation designs will have to be submitted as part of the planning application process where the power to ask for these details comes from the development plan. This would state that foundation designs must be submitted where archaeology is relevant to the development. The basis for this requirement would stem from the fact that archaeology is a material planning consideration.

8 Close proximity

Development in close proximity to a scheduled monument can affect its setting. Similarly the drawing of a boundary around an archaeological area, whilst based on careful assessment of all available information, will not necessarily cover every eventuality or discovery. There will be times when the setting of monuments or buildings will need to be considered as a matter of policy. Here, two proposals taken from Wrexham and York are considered pertinent. In the case of the former the following is to be found:

> Any development in close proximity to an ancient monument shown on the proposal map will be carefully controlled to protect the setting and character of the monument. *Wrexham Maelor Borough Council*

The situation in York is slightly different. Whilst there are seven Areas of Archaeological Importance within the city-limits the authority has found that sites outside, but close to, these AAIs have been found to be important archaeologically. So much so that it has deemed it necessary to include a 100 metre zone around these areas where assessments of the impact on archaeology are now required. As in the Wrexham case it emphasizes the importance of setting. In the former it is in respect of ancient monuments whilst in the latter it relates to archaeological areas.

9 Obtaining appropriate advice

It goes without saying that archaeological investigations will need to be carried out by archaeologists approved by the planning authority as can be seen from the following policy used by some authorities:

> Archaeological investigations shall be undertaken by a recognised archaeological unit approved by the planning authority.

Local units are often recommended because of their in-depth local knowledge and proven track record, although with the advent of competitive tendering, and as expertise grows and expands to other units over a wider sphere, more units will probably get involved. No doubt this would be similar to the situation where architects compete against each other for business.

REFERENCES

Berkshire County Council (1993a) *Berkshire Structure Plan 1991–2006: Deposit Draft*, Berkshire County Council, Reading.

Berkshire County Council (1993b) *Draft Replacement Minerals Local Plan for Berkshire*, Berkshire County Council, Reading.

Department of the Environment (1990) *PPG 16 Archaeology and Planning*, HMSO, London.

English Heritage (1991a) *Exploring our Past: Strategies for the Archaeology of England*, English Heritage, London.

English Heritage (1991c) Rescue archaeology funding: a policy statement. *Conservation Bulletin*, Issue 14, June 1991, English Heritage, London.

Glyndwr District Council, Local Plan.

Gwent County Council, Deposited Structure Plan.

Gwynedd Councy Council, Ardudwy District Plan.

HM Government (1990) *This Common Inheritance: Britain's Environmental Strategy*, HMSO, London.

Leicester City Council (1988) *A Policy for Archaeology and Planning*, City Planning Office, Leicester.

Ove Arup (Ove Arup & Partners and the Department of Archaeology, University of York in association with Bernard Thorpe) (1991) *York Archaeology and Development Study*, Ove Arup, Manchester.

Scottish Office Environment Department (1992a) *National Planning Policy Guideline: Archaeology and Planning*, Scottish Office, Edinburgh.

Scottish Office Environment Department (1992b) *Planning Advice Note: Archaeology and Planning*, Scottish Office, Edinburgh.

Southwark, London Borough of (1993) *Planning Policy for Archaeology and Development*, Planning and Economic Development Division, Southwark Council, London.

Wainwright, G.J. (1992) Archaeology and planning. *Conservation Bulletin*, Issue 17, English Heritage, London.

Westminster City Council, Unitary Development Plan.

Wrexham Maelor Borough Council, Local Plan.

York City Council (undated) *Conservation Policies of York: Archaeology*, Directorate of Development Services, York.

FURTHER READING

Department of the Environment (1992) *PPG 1 General Policy and Principles*, HMSO, London.

Department of the Environment (1992) *PPG 12 Development Plans and Regional Planning Guidance*, HMSO, London.

English Heritage (1991b) *Management of Archaeological Projects* (2nd edn), English Heritage, London.

English Heritage (1992) *Managing the Urban Archaeological Resource*, English Heritage, London.

Lane, J. and Vaughan, S. (1992) *An evaluation of the impact of PPG 16 on archaeology and planning*, Pagoda Projects, London.

Manly, J. (1987) Archaeology and planning: a Welsh perspective. *Journal of Planning and Environment Law*, pp. 466–484 and 552–563, Sweet and Maxwell, London.

Pugh-Smith, J. and Samuels, J. (1993) PPG 16: two years on. *Journal of Planning and Environment Law*, March 1993, pp. 203–210, Sweet and Maxwell, London.

Redman, M. (1990) Archaeology and development. *Journal of Planning and Environmental Law*, February 1990, pp. 87–98, Sweet and Maxwell, London.

Royal Town Planning Institute (1990) *Memorandum of observations to the Department of the Environment on its draft PPG 16*, Royal Town Planning Institute, London.

Wainwright, G.J. (1989) Archaeology in towns. *Conservation Bulletin*, Issue 9, English Heritage, London.

Wainwright, G.J. (1990) *Archaeology Review 1989–90*, English Heritage, London.

Wainwright, G.J. (1991) *Archaeology Review 1990–91*, English Heritage, London.

Wainwright, G.J. (1993) *Archaeological Review 1992–93*, English Heritage, London.

7 | The protection of archaeological sites

Archaeological sites come in many shapes and sizes but whenever development is proposed they all have one thing in common. They are, in theory, capable of being protected in some way. Notwithstanding that some planning authorities may not wish to intervene or that landowners may refuse access, legislative powers exist for their protection. How they are used will depend on the location, nature and importance of the site and the objectives of those responsible for their protection. Different circumstances will bring different protective measures into play.

As a general rule the greater the importance of a site the greater the degree of protection. Nationally important sites where archaeological remains are known to exist are extensively protected. Where the archaeological content is not certain, sites may be protected in order to allow an investigation to be carried out. Circumstances, however, can change. Unknown remains, upon discovery, may be recognized as important and be given comprehensive protection. Conversely archaeological sites can become less important for various reasons with protective measures lifted from them as a result.

There are two main ways in which archaeological sites may be protected. This can be either by protecting what is there or by controlling or restricting development proposals which might adversely affect a site. Sometimes the two overlap and it becomes difficult to distinguish between them. In this Chapter we focus on those legislative controls aimed primarily at protecting archaeological sites. Three sets of legislation are important.

The first and most significant deals with known nationally important sites and areas. These are protected under the ancient monuments legislation which at present consists of the Ancient Monuments and Archaeological Areas Act 1979 and the National Heritage Act 1983. Additionally, special attention is given in this Chapter to World Heritage Sites and Areas of Archaeological Importance.

The second area of legislation relates to submerged wrecks which lie in tidal waters. The relevant Act of Parliament here is the Protection of Wrecks Act 1973.

Finally, where the remains are human remains, such as can be found in old but forgotten burial grounds, The Burial Act 1857 and The Disused Burial Grounds Acts of 1884 and 1981 make provision for the reinterment of human remains provided certain rights and procedures are followed.

Those areas of legislation aimed principally at controlling development proposals are looked at in later Chapters. Chief among them are the controls exercised under the Town and Country Planning Acts. Also relevant are various aspects of countryside legislation and controls over the operation of statutory undertakers, most notably the privatized water and electricity companies.

7.1 THE ANCIENT MONUMENTS LEGISLATION

History of the ancient monuments legislation

This is the main area of legislation protecting archaeological remains. It dates back to the campaign to statutorily protect and preserve ancient monuments in the 1870s but more especially to 1882 when the first Ancient Monuments Act entered the statute book. The immediate effect of this Act was to protect a total of 29 monuments in England and Wales and a further 21 in Scotland. These were identified in a schedule attached to the Act.

Further Acts of Parliament were passed in 1900 and 1913, the effect of which was to establish an Ancient Monuments Board and inspectors whose purpose it was to inspect sites and prepare a list of monuments. As time passed so the list grew bigger. By 1931 there were approximately 3000 ancient monuments on the schedule.

Subsequent legislation gradually increased the powers of the government. In 1931 an Act was passed which was designed to preserve the character and setting of ancient monuments by making reference to their amenities. This was followed in 1953 by the Historic Buildings and Ancient Monuments Act which extended the control to cover not only the monuments themselves but also the acts or omissions of their owners.

Finally the law was again updated by the passing of the Ancient Monuments and Archaeological Areas Act 1979, the principal Act in operation today. The National Heritage Act 1983 makes a number of relatively minor amendments to the Act of 1979.

Throughout this period the number of monuments on the schedule has grown so that there are now approximately 15 000 monuments in England, 5300 in Scotland and a further 2700 on the schedule in Wales. It is envisaged, however, that the number of monuments will be greatly increased when the Monuments Protection Programme is completed towards the end of the 1990s. Some 700 000 sites are being investigated and it is estimated that around 50 000–60 000 monuments may be recommended for statutory protection.

Broadly speaking, what the 1979 Act seeks to achieve is to protect archaeological remains which are considered to be of national importance by including them on a list drawn up by the government. Once on the list, or schedule as it is called, then special consent must be obtained for any works which might affect these remains. The Act also conveys certain rights to excavate and record in designated archaeological areas where remains are likely to be found, but are not known at the outset.

The scheduling of monuments

The Secretary of State for the Environment and the Secretaries of State for Scotland and Wales are empowerd for their respective countries to compile a list of ancient monuments. The lists, or schedules, describe and identify those archaeological remains considered to be of national importance and the process of adding to or removing from the list is called scheduling.

This follows the original procedure adopted under the Act of 1882. What that Act and the present Act of 1979 require is that the Secretaries of State identify those remains which, by virtue of their historic, architectural, traditional or archaeological interest, are considered to be of national importance. If they are thought to be nationally important they may be included on the schedule. The Secretaries of State can decide whether to add them or not.

The meaning of national importance

Questions are sometimes asked as to what constitutes national importance. Here the advice of the Scottish Ancient Monuments Board to the Secretary of State for Scotland as reported in the Planning Advice Note *Archaeology and Planning* is particularly relevant:

> A monument is of national importance if, in the view of informed opinion, it contributes or appears likely to contribute significantly to the understanding of the past. Such significance may be assessed from individual or group qualities, and may include structural or decorative features, or value as an archaeological resource. *SOEnD, Para. 42, 1992b*

For professional advisory staff the following is used as a working definition:

> For a monument to be regarded as of national importance it is necessary and sufficient –
>
> (1) that it belong or pertain to a group or subject of study which has acknowledged importance in terms of archaeology, architectural history or history; and
> (2) that it can be recognised as part of the national consciousness or as retaining the structural, decorative or field characteristics of its kind to a marked degree, or as offering or being likely to offer a significant archaeological resource within a group or subject of study of acknowledged importance. *SOEnD, Para. 42, 1992b*

Defining monuments

Once an archaeological site is scheduled under the 1979 Act it becomes known as a monument. But there are different types of monument with different meanings and different levels of protection. To appreciate how they are protected we need to know what is meant by the word 'monument'. This is not in the everyday sense of the word, but how it is defined in the Act.

There are four different types of monument as far as the Act is concerned. They are:

1. monument;
2. scheduled monument;
3. ancient monument;
4. protected monument.

1 Monument

The word **monument** is important because it forms the basis for the other definitions that follow. It is a complex definition which is difficult to shorten without losing some of its meaning. Section 61(7) of the 1979 Act defines a monument as being:

(a) any building, structure or work, whether above or below the surface of the land, and any cave or excavation;

(b) any site comprising the remains of any such building, structure or work or any cave or excavation; and

(c) any site comprising, or comprising the remains of, any vehicle, vessel, aircraft, or other moveable structure or part thereof which neither constitutes nor forms part of any work which is a monument with paragraph (a) above; and any machinery attached to a monument shall be regarded as part of the monument if it could not be detached without being dismantled.

This definition is wide ranging. It means that it is not just the monument itself that is included in the definition, but also its site. This implies that the surrounding land or curtilage of the monument can also be included. In addition monument can refer simply to any part of the monument or to a group of monuments.

There are, however, exceptions to the definition. Three are important: ecclesiastical buildings used for ecclesiastical purposes; sites which are not a matter of public interest; and any vessel which is protected under the Protection of Wrecks Act 1973.

The definition can be important when building work is proposed in the vicinity of a monument. For instance, if scaffolding has to be erected around a building or site it might encroach on to the site of a monument. Alternatively site huts may need to be placed within the curtilage of a monument. If they do, it will be necessary to find out if the site is protected in any way and that it is in order to proceed.

2 Scheduled monument

In the words of the Act a **scheduled monument** is simply defined as any monument which is for the time being included in the schedule to the Act. Nothing else is mentioned in the definition which means, when works likely to affect a monument are proposed, that the protection is afforded simply because it is included in the schedule. This means that it is important to understand what a 'monument' means. In addition, to be included in the schedule the monument needs to be of national importance. We also need to remember that it is the Secretary of State who determines whether a monument is of national importance.

3 Ancient monument

An **ancient monument** has a wider meaning than a scheduled monument because it includes any scheduled monument and any other monument which the Secretaries of State consider to be of public interest. This is interpreted (Section 61(12)) to mean that it must have historic, architectural, traditional, artistic or archaeological interest attached to it.

Two points are worth mentioning here. First, it appears that a distinction can be drawn between national importance and public interest. Whereas a monument considered to be of national importance would be a scheduled monument, a monument considered to be of public interest would be an ancient monument. But in the case of the latter it can be both. An ancient monument which is of public interest can also be included in a schedule if it is of national importance as well. Thus we can expect to see some ancient monuments given the added protection as a result of scheduling while others will not have this protection. Clearly this point will need clarifying if development is proposed in the vicinity of an ancient monument.

Second, there is the question of what is meant by public interest. Here the Act gives some guidance by stating that an ancient monument should have historic, architectural, traditional, artistic or archaeological interest. Presumably, therefore, these are the criteria for determining public interest.

4 Protected monument

Finally, there is the **protected monument**, which is any scheduled monument and any other monument which is in the ownership or guardianship of the government, heritage agency or local planning authority. In other words it needs to be publicly owned and not privately owned. Figure 7.1 shows how the different monuments relate to each other.

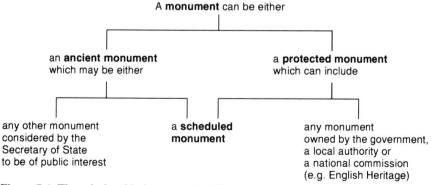

Figure 7.1 The relationship between the different types of monument. (Adapted from Suddards, 1988.)

How monuments are chosen for the schedule

The process of scheduling archaeological sites is carried out by government appointed inspectors. In England they are employed by the Historic Buildings and Monuments Commission (English Heritage), in Wales the responsible authority is Cadw, an executive agency of the Welsh Office, and in Scotland this work is done by inspectors at Historic Scotland which comes under the wing of the Scottish Office Environment Department.

The inspectors collect whatever information they can. This will include written documents, drawings, maps and photographs which are carefully analysed. A recommendation is made to the appropriate Secretary of State: either to include the site on the schedule or not to include it, depending on the prevailing circumstances.

In theory anyone can ask to have a site scheduled. All they have to do is approach English Heritage, Cadw or Historic Scotland with information supporting a case for scheduling. More commonly, archaeologists, local authorities and universities tend to get in touch with the appropriate authority. The matter is then taken up by the inspectors and a recommendation made. The final decision, however, is made by the Secretary of State who can decide not to include a site despite a positive recommendation.

An important aspect of this decision-making process is trying to decide what to include on the schedule. Not every proposal is accepted and much will depend on the circumstances in each case: the type of monument or site that is put forward; its location; the number of similar monuments already on the schedule; their location and so on.

Monuments tend to be classified by type of site. This is partly because the site can help to assess their rarity value particularly where location is concerned. If there are a number of monuments of one type in a particular part of the country then a further monument of the same type in the same area may be of less importance than a similar proposal in another part of the country where there are fewer monuments of that type. The type and location of monuments can therefore be important although a word of caution is necessary. With archaeological considerations growing in importance and with the current review which is likely to result in an increase of monuments we can expect to see far more sites included in future. Rarity value may become less important.

Monuments are classified in different ways according to national requirements, historic period and the type and class of monument. In England, Scotland and Wales different methods are used making it difficult to compare like with like. In Scotland, for example, monuments are classified into seven broad periods incorporating over 80 types as shown in Table 7.1.

In Wales monuments are grouped into ten historic periods (Table 7.2), whereas in England a more detailed and computerized approach is used – scheduled monuments can be identified by period, form or class. The number within each of these three groups is respectively 14, 15 and over 390. Tables 7.3 and 7.4 identify the periods and forms used. As far as classes are concerned these cover all manner of descriptions, a few examples being an anti-aircraft battery, coal mines, ice houses, railways and vineyards.

Table 7.1 The categories of monument in Scotland

PREHISTORIC RITUAL AND FUNERARY includes cairns, chambered cairns, long cairns, ring cairns, barrows, chambered barrows, long barrows, mounds, ring enclosures, henges, stone circles and rows, standing stones and cup-marked stones

PREHISTORIC DOMESTIC AND DEFENSIVE includes forts, duns, brochs, galleried dwellings, souterrains, houses, hut circles, homesteads, settlements, platform settlements, enclosures, palisaded enclosures, crannogs, fields systems, cairn fields and cultivation terraces

ROMAN includes military works, civil settlements and roads

CROSSES AND CARVED STONES includes crosses, cross slabs, market crosses and cross-incised stones. This category also includes Pictish symbol stones, inscribed stones, tombstones and a few miscellaneous sculptured stones

ECCLESIASTICAL includes churches and chapels (both sometimes prefixed by 'old' where there is likelihood of confusion between adjacent sites), monasteries, nunneries and priories, burial grounds and enclosures. It should be noted that churches and graveyards still in use are excluded from the schedule

SECULAR includes non-prehistoric works which are basically military or defensive such as castles, forts and mottes; works which are basically domestic such as houses and settlements; earthworks, homestead moats and towers which fall between the military and the domestic; and a host of other works such as barracks, artillery mounds, roads, bridges, tollbooths, dovecots, martello towers, prisons, hospitals and sundials

INDUSTRIAL includes canals and associated structures such as graving docks, tunnels, bridges and signal lamps; mills of various kinds, pottery kilns, engine houses, engines and railway stations. It also includes some iron bridges. This category includes monuments particularly characteristic of the Industrial Revolution as well as earlier sites representing the processing and manufacturing side of Medieval life

---

Source: Historic Scotland

Table 7.2 The monuments of Wales identified by type

Caves
Prehistoric funerary and ritual sites
Prehistoric domestic and defensive sites
Roman remains
Linear earthworks
Crosses and inscribed stones
Ecclesiastical sites and wells
Medieval and post-medieval secular sites
Bridges
Industrial sites

Source: Cadw

Buildings in use for ecclesiastical purposes and those used as occupied dwellings cannot be included in a schedule of monuments, although they could be listed for their architectural or historic interest. Instead of being scheduled for their archaeological interest they would be **listed** for their special historic or architectural interest under the planning Acts of 1972 and 1990 listed on p. 95. Thus, at a glance, a distinction can be made between the schedule and the list: it shows which legislative control applies. Another way of remembering the difference, although it is not always reliable, is to think of

Table 7.3 The monuments in England identified by period

Bronze Age
Early Medieval
Iron Age
Lower Palaeolithic
Medieval
Mesolithic
Modern
Middle Palaeolithic
Neolithic
Post Medieval
Prehistoric
Roman
Unknown
Upper Palaeolithic

Source: English Heritage

Table 7.4 The monuments in England identified by form

Building – bonded
Building – other
Enhanced natural feature
Earthwork
Flat – accumulated
Flat – unaccumulated
Inhabited building
Ruined structure – bonded
Ruined structure – unbonded
Submerged
Standing structure – bonded
Standing structure – unbonded
Subterranean
Uninhabited building

Source: English Heritage

scheduled monuments as structures which are normally unoccupied or incapable of being occupied whereas listed buildings would normally be used in some way. There are a few exceptions, but this is under review and in the future the distinction may become more clear.

Criteria for choosing monuments

The characteristics which make a monument nationally important are not always readily apparent. Legal judgements sometimes have to be made and following the exercise of the judgement guidelines have been adopted by the government to assist in assessing their importance. In England eight criteria have been produced by the Department of National Heritage. Similar criteria exist in Wales although they vary slightly in Scotland. In all, ten considerations can be identified as follows:

1. **Period**: It is important to consider all types of monuments that characterize a particular period and history. Monuments of different contemporary types will complement each other and provide broader evidence for the period.

2. **Rarity**: There are some types of monument which are now so scarce that all surviving examples, no matter how poor, ought to be preserved. Selection, however, may be necessary depending on distribution, both nationally and regionally.

3. **Group value**: The value of a single monument can be greatly enhanced by its association with other monuments in the vicinity either of a contemporary nature or of different periods. In some cases it will be preferable to protect the whole, including adjacent land, rather than to protect individual monuments within a group.

4. **Situation**: Certain types of monuments may be abundant in one topographical area but rare in others. Where this occurs special regard should be had to the extra potential archaeological value in the areas where they are scarce.

5. **Survival/condition**: The condition and degree of survival of a monument both above and below ground are important factors to be taken into account.

6. **Multi-period**: Sites which cover a number of periods with well-preserved components can be of special value and indicate a delicate or interesting phasing of development worthy of protection.

7. **Fragility/vulnerability**: Important archaeological evidence from monuments can be severely reduced by even slight mistreatment. The value of standing structures of particular form or complexity can be reduced by neglect or careless treatment while ploughing can damage some field monuments lying just beneath the surface.

8. **Diversity**: Some monuments may be selected for scheduling because they possess a variety of high quality features, others because they contain just one important attribute. Similar types of remains can be very diverse in their detail and interpretation.

9. **Potential**: Sometimes it may not be possible to specify the importance of a site but to anticipate its importance. The SMR of the local planning authority or other archive information might suggest that a site is important which could give sufficient reason to justify scheduling.

10. **Documentation**: The importance of a monument can be enhanced by the existence of earlier records and documentation. This does not have to be previous excavation but can include early estate records, annals, charters and contemporary written records. They can highlight a special feature or point about a monument thereby giving it added importance.

These considerations are not definitive. Rather, the government has stated that they will contribute towards a case for scheduling a monument.

The consequences of scheduling

The most important consequence of scheduling is that there is no automatic right of appeal against the inclusion of any monument on a schedule. If an owner of a monument or archaeological site finds that it has been included on a schedule of monuments he or she can ask the Secretary of State to remove it. The Secretary of State has the power to do this; or leave it on the schedule;

or amend it. However, the decision of the Secretary of State is final. The owner cannot appeal against this decision.

There is an alternative course of action available to an owner. If the owner is keen to get a monument removed from the schedule he or she can apply for scheduled monument consent to do some form of works to the monument and then, if the application is refused, appeal against this refusal. One of the grounds of appeal that is acceptable is to argue that the monument ought not to have been included in the schedule and that it should be removed. Again the Secretary of State's decision will be final.

The need for scheduled monument consent

Once a site is included on a Schedule of Monuments it is a requirement of the 1979 Act that **scheduled monument consent** be obtained for any works which materially affect the monument. As to what may materially affect it, the Act states (Section 2) that consent will be required for the following:

1. any works which result in the demolition, destruction or any damage to a scheduled monument;
2. any works which involve the removal or repair of any part of a scheduled monument;
3. any works involving the making of any alterations or additions to a scheduled monument;
4. where any flooding or tipping operations are proposed in, on or under land where there is a scheduled monument.

As we can see, the need for consent is wide-ranging. Virtually anything which affects a scheduled monument will require consent.

The procedure for obtaining scheduled movement consent requires an application to be submitted to the appropriate Secretary of State. It must be made using a prescribed form and accompanied by plans and drawings sufficient to show what is involved and how the monument may be affected. There is no provision for submitting or granting outline consent and drawings will have to be detailed. This means that it would generally help to discuss proposals with the inspectors at the earliest opportunity and before submitting an application. If insufficient detail is submitted the Secretary of State can request additional information before the application is determined.

A certificate of ownership must also be submitted with the application. On it the applicant must indicate that he or she is either the owner of the site ('owner' is defined as owner of the fee simple or of a tenancy of which not less than seven years remain unexpired); or that the owner has been notified; or notification has been attempted. There are prescribed ways in which this must be done.

Circumstances when scheduled monument consent is not required

A limited number of works on land in rural areas and on land owned by British Coal, the British Waterways Board and the respective heritage departments of the government are exempt from the above requirements. As a result of the Ancient Monuments (Class Consents) Order 1994 the following classes of works do not require scheduled monument consent:

1. Works of an agricultural, horticultural or forestry nature, being works of the same kind in the same location and spot as have previously been executed in the same location or spot in the last six years provided such works do not include:

   - any works other than in the case of ploughed land likely to disturb the soil below a depth of 300 mm;
   - drainage works;
   - the planting or uprooting of trees, hedge or shrubs;
   - the demolition, extension, alteration or disturbance of any building or structure;
   - the erection of a building or structure;
   - the laying of paths and hardstandings other than domestic garden works;
   - the erection of fences;
   - any works likely to disturb the soil below the depth at which ploughing has previously been carried out.

2. Any works by British Coal which are deeper than 10 metres below ground.
3. Works carried out on land owned or occupied by the British Waterways Board which do not materially alter a monument or which are essential to ensure the functioning of a canal.
4. Works for the repair or maintenance of machinery and which do not involve any material alteration to a monument.
5. Works essential for the purposes of health and safety.
6. Works carried out by English Heritage.
7. Certain works of archaeological evaluation undertaken by or on behalf of an applicant for scheduled monument consent.
8. Works carried out for the maintenance and repair of a scheduled monument or its amenities in accordance with an agreement between the occupier of the scheduled monument and the Secretary of State or English Heritage.
9. Works for the preservation, maintenance or management of a scheduled monument being grant aided by the Secretary of State or English Heritage.
10. Certain survey work being carried out by the RCHME or the RCAHMW.

In Scotland, under the Ancient Monuments (Class Consents) (Scotland) Order 1981, classes 7 to 10 above do not apply although changes in line with these classes are in the pipeline. As part of the consultation process some conservationists have argued that ploughing operations ought to have been removed from the Order because of the damage caused to archaeological remains. The department, however, stated that the earlier Order achieved a reasonable balance between the need to preserve nationally important monuments and the legitimate interests of farmers and did not need amending. The paper added:

Consideration was given to imposing a limit of 300 mm for ploughing (in line with that proposed for works to land other than ploughed land) instead of the present wording that consent is not permitted for works likely to disturb the soil 'below the normal ploughing depth'. However, the Department believes that divergent practices in different regions make it impracticable to define an absolute depth to which ploughing may be permitted. Nevertheless, if a particular site is threatened by repeated normal ploughing under the class consent, there is provision in the 1979 Act which enables the Department to revoke it.   *DNH, Para. 8, 1993*

Consideration of applications for scheduled monument consent

All applications for scheduled monument consent are determined by the appropriate Secretary of State, who can grant consent with or without conditions or refuse permission. Conditions can require site excavation for archaeological investigation. They can also require a watching brief to be maintained to allow an inspector to make sure the monument is not unnecessarily damaged as work proceeds.

Where building or rebuilding works are proposed the scope for conditions can extend to a requirement that work be phased or carried out in stages, so that one part of a project cannot proceed until another part has been completed. This could be required in order to allow more time for excavation on part of a site or to ensure that reinstatement, repair or improvement are properly carried out. Where the Secretary of State finds a proposal unacceptable the application may be refused, with reasons listed for the decision.

In the consideration of an application, matters relating to the criteria for scheduling will be relevant with one or more of the following factors applying:

- the importance, nationally and regionally, of the monument;
- the special features of the monument together with its rarity or group value;
- the vulnerability of the monument to alteration, repair or improvement;
- the nature of the proposed works and how they might affect the character of the monument;
- the setting of the monument.

There is no formal provision for the Secretary of State to consult the local planning authority on applications for scheduled monument consent, although informal links do exist. Where the development also requires planning permission the inspectors would normally discuss the proposal with the local planning authority and ascertain the views of the officers before making any recommendation to the Secretary of State.

As a rule the applicant is notified of the recommended decision before it is issued so that the applicant can exercise the right to ask for a hearing or local inquiry. The Secretary of State can also decide to hold a public inquiry if thought appropriate. If the proposal is also subject to a planning inquiry following a refusal of planning permission, the two hearings would normally be held at the same time.

The consent, once granted, is valid for five years unless the Secretary of State decides to vary this time period. This might be done to coincide with a time limit imposed on a planning permission or if the site is a particularly sensitive one. In the case of the latter it might be expedient to reduce the period in the interests of amenity or increase it in the interests of archaeological investigation.

Management agreements

Under the provisions of Section 17 of the 1979 Act the occupier of an ancient monument or of any land adjoining or in the vicinity of an ancient monument may enter into an agreement with the Secretary of State. The aim of such an agreement would be to cover one or more of the following matters:

- the maintenance and preservation of a monument and its amenities;
- the provision of public access, facilities, information or other services for the public;
- restricting the use of the monument or land, such as restrictions on stock grazing;
- the erection of fences or other means of enclosure;
- the eradication of pests;
- the carrying out of other works as may be specified in an agreement;
- compliance with any other restrictions of an agreement.

Terms can normally be negotiated between the owner, occupier and the government and grant aid may be available depending on the size and importance of the monument and the nature of the problem which is to be overcome. The extent to which improvements are possible will be an important consideration as grants tend to be restricted to those sites where significant improvements can be made.

Independently of the 1979 Act, it is possible to enter into management agreements under Section 39 of the Wildlife and Countryside Act 1981. This Act, which is designed to give protection to the natural beauty and amenity of any land including any historic components of the landscape, is aimed at conserving and enhancing the landscape. Thus the way in which land is cultivated for agricultural purposes could be restricted. It could also impose other obligations relating to agricultural or forestry operations, which, unless it provides otherwise, are binding on successors in title. If archaeological remains are present the agreement could seek to protect such sites.

The carrying out of unauthorized works to a scheduled monument

If any person undertakes or allows works to be done to a scheduled monument without obtaining scheduled monument consent he or she shall be guilty of an offence. The ways in which this can arise are if works result in:

- the demolition, destruction or damage of a scheduled monument;
- the removal or repair of any part;
- the making of any alteration or addition;
- the flooding or tipping in, on or under a scheduled monument.

A defence can be made under Section 2 of the 1979 Act against the claim that an offence has been committed in the following four circumstances:

1. Where it is alleged that the defendant has failed to comply with the conditions of a scheduled monument consent, that all reasonable precautions and all due diligence have been taken to avoid contravening the conditions.
2. If the allegation relates to demolition, destruction or damage, that all reasonable precautions and all due diligence have been taken to avoid or prevent damage to the monument.
3. Where demolition, damage, destruction, flooding or tipping is alleged, that the defendant can prove ignorance and had no reason to believe that the monument was a scheduled monument or that it was within the area affected by the work.
4. Where the works were necessary as a matter of urgency in the interests of health or safety and that the defendant had given written notice to the Secretary of State as soon as reasonably practical.

Rights to compensation

When an application for scheduled monument consent has been refused it is possible, within narrowly defined limits, to claim compensation. These limits arise when:

1. the refused works are reasonably necessary to carry out development that was granted planning permission before the monument was scheduled, and permission was still effective when the application for scheduled monument consent was made;
2. the works do not constitute 'development' as defined in the Town and Country Planning Acts or are granted permission by a General Development Order (e.g. Town and Country Planning General Development Order 1988);
3. the works are reasonably necessary to enable the monument to continue to be used for the same purpose immediately before the date of application for scheduled monument consent.

An important point to bear in mind with the above is that there must be an outstanding and unimplemented planning permission or deemed permission before any claim for compensation can be made. If planning permission is granted after the monument has been scheduled then there can be no claim for compensation.

The exception to this rule is where development may be granted permission by a General Development Order. Under such an order various extensions and works to different types of buildings are expressly allowed without the need for planning permission. If compensation is an issue, therefore, it will be important to establish whether planning permission was required or whether it was automatically granted permission by a development order.

Before compensation can be awarded there are, in addition, three other requirements whch must be satisfied. They are:

1. the claimant must have an interest in the monument;
2. the claimant must have incurred expenditure or a loss or damage;
3. the expenditure or loss or damage must have been as a result of the refusal or conditional consent of an application for scheduled monument consent.

All three requirements must apply before compensation can be paid although in special cases compensation may be payable for abortive expenditure and for depreciation.

7.2 WORLD HERITAGE SITES

So far we have looked at national legislation concerning the protection of ancient monuments but not at international controls. These do not, at present, make any significant difference as the national legislation is not altered. The World Heritage Convention, however, has recognized that some national heritage sites are considered to be of world-wide importance and ought to be recognized as such. Accordingly the British government has nominated a number of **World Heritage Sites** as identified in Table 7.5. More are being considered for inclusion in the list.

No additional restrictions apply as a result of the inclusion of a site in the list although it does highlight their outstanding national and international importance. It means that when local authorities formulate policies for these sites and their surroundings, we can expect to find policies in their development plans reflecting their presence. Great weight will be put on the need to protect them and this will no doubt be an important material consideration when determining planning applications, applications for listed building consent and applications for scheduled monument consent.

Table 7.5 World Heritage Sites in Britain

England
Durham Cathedral and Castle
Fountains Abbey and St Mary's, Studley Royal
Ironbridge Gorge
Stonehenge, Avebury and associated sites
Blenheim Palace
Palace of Westminster and Westminster Abbey
City of Bath
Hadrian's Wall Military Zone
The Tower of London
Canterbury Cathedral (with St Augustine's Abbey and St Martin's Church)

Scotland
The island of St Kilda

Wales
The Edwardian castles at Caernarfon, Harlech, Conwy and Beaumaris

Source: English Heritage, Cadw and Historic Scotland

7.3 AREAS OF ARCHAEOLOGICAL IMPORTANCE

An important feature of the Ancient Monuments and Archaeological Areas Act 1979 is that it conveys rights to excavate and record sites in certain designated archaeological areas. Known as **Areas of Archaeological Importance** (AAIs), they can be expected to reveal important archaeological remains. What is not known is how important they may be prior to any investigation. What the Act does is make provision for an investigation in order to find out.

The first step in this process is to designate Areas of Archaeological Importance. This is done by the Secretary of State who has designated areas in the five historic cities of Canterbury, Chester, Exeter, Hereford and York.

No other towns or cities have been selected for this special treatment and the Department of National Heritage has indicated that there are no proposals to designate any more. Thus whilst these AAIs form an important part of the 1979 legislation they are few in number.

Elsewhere, local planning authorities can make similar designations. Terms such as 'Areas of Archaeological Significance' or 'Areas of Special Archaeological Priority' can be expected with different titles deliberately used, although they can add to the confusion especially if 'area of archaeological importance' is used elsewhere. Such areas, however, should not be confused with the AAIs, designated under the 1979 Act. When used by local authorities they do not carry the same weight or rights as exist in the designated areas within the five cities chosen by the Secretary of State.

Operations notices

Within the designated AAIs the process of allowing sites to be excavated commences when a developer gives notice of intention to develop anywhere within the designated area. The Act requires (Section 35) that before commencing development the developer must notify the **investigating authority** in writing of the intention to develop.

The investigating authority in each case is determined by the Secretary of State. It can be the local planning authority or an independent archaeological unit. In York, for example, it is the York Archaeological Trust. In Exeter the Archaeological Field Unit of the Royal Albert Memorial Museum is the investigating authority.

The written notice is called an **operations notice**. It must be served on the investigating authority not less than six weeks before the commencement of any operations designed to disturb the ground. These can include flooding operations where land is proposed to be covered with water (or any other liquid) and all types of tipping operations. Operations in, on, under or over land can also be included, which means that removing topsoil from one site to another can involve operational development. The site from where it is removed and the one where it is deposited can both be important as far as archaeology is concerned. More importantly, it brings the work of the utility companies under control which elsewhere would be outside the control of the local planning authority.

Matters to be considered in the operations notice

Four important issues must be addressed in an operations notice:

1. **The address or location of the proposed operations**
   It is important for an accurate description to be given. Past information within a designated area will have been built up over the years indicating the relative importance of each site. In some cases this will be based on a wealth of local facts unearthed nearby. At other locations it will be no more than an approximation based on guestimate and experience. If the site is not accurately identified misleading information could be given which could be to the disadvantage of all concerned. By clearly stating the address or location of a proposed development the investigating authority should be able to make an initial assessment of the likely importance of the site and indicate whether a watching brief or a full scale excavation is necessary.

2. **Description of proposed operations**
   What is required is information about the operations which disturb the ground. The investigating authority will want to know what types of foundations are proposed, the depth of disturbance, whether a basement floor is proposed and the position or location of all of these elements. If topsoil is to be moved or building materials stored on site the authority may also want to know the exact location.

   In practice plans showing details of the proposed works and especially where the foundations are to be located should suffice. Drawings would normally be to a scale of not less than 1:500, obtainable from the architect or engineer engaged in the development project.

3. **The date of commencement of operations**
   The date on which operations are proposed to commence must be not less than six weeks from the serving of the operations notice. If works commence before the expiry of six weeks the developer may be guilty of an offence. On the other hand, if more than six weeks notice can be given, this may allow the archaeologists to enter the site at an earlier date. And if they can enter the site at an earlier date the developer may be able to negotiate an earlier date for their departure. The key word is 'may'. There can be no guarantee that this will happen as much will depend on the archaeological significance of the site. The more important it is, the more time that may be required for its investigation. Conversely if it is that important the policy may simply be one of preserving intact what is there with new development built around it.

4. **Certificate accompanying operations notice**
   When submitting an operations notice the developer must prove an interest in the site where the operations are to take place or prove a right to enter the site. The developer must certify to this effect in order to

comply with the operations notice procedure. Failure to do so, or provision of false or misleading information, can make the developer guilty of an offence.

Operations exempt from the operations notice procedure

The Secretaries of State are empowered to make orders exempting certain operations from the operations notice requirements. Under the Areas of Archaeological Importance (Notification of Operations) (Exemption) Order 1984, a limited range of operations relating to agriculture, forestry, landscaping, mining, tunnelling, the maintenance, repair and installation of highways, waterways and mains services may be carried out without having to comply with Section 35 of the Act. Where operations comply with the order no offence will be committed if an operations notice is not served.

Action by the investigating authority

On receipt of an operations notice the investigating authority will have to decide what it wants to do about the site. It has four options:

- to excavate the whole of the site;
- to excavate it in part;
- to carry out a watching brief as development proceeds;
- to do nothing.

Before making any decision on whether to excavate a site a number of factors will need to be taken into account. They are likely to include one or more of the following:

- the size and nature of the proposed development;
- an assessment of the archaeological importance of the site;
- the location of the site;
- the extent of destruction envisaged by the development;
- the number of excavations currently being carried out elsewhere;
- the resources available to the investigating authority;
- other commitments;
- the financial situation.

If the proposed development involves nothing more than erecting an extension to a building in a relatively unimportant part of an AAI the authority may decide to do nothing. To proceed with such an investigation would not be a good use of time and resources and it would not normally be appropriate to get involved. Alternatively if the site of the extension is close to a previously excavated site which revealed important finds, the authority might decide to carry out a watching brief or excavate the site (or part of it) prior to development.

Where a much larger development proposal is contemplated the investigating authority is likely to want to get involved in a comprehensive excavation of the site. However, much will depend on the perceived or known archaeological importance of the site and the resources available to the investigating authority at the time. It is possible that resources might be transferred from elsewhere.

Where the authority wishes to excavate a site it will have to notify the developer of its intention to excavate within four weeks of receipt of the operations notice. Failure to respond within this time limit means that it will lose the right to excavate the site and the developer wil be able to proceed with the development project without interference by the archaeologists and without committing an offence under the 1979 Act.

If the authority responds positively within the four week period its right to excavate will be protected. Under Section 38 of the 1979 Act it will be allowed to excavate the site for a period of up to four months and two weeks commencing after the expiry of the six week notification period referred to earlier. This means that from the time of the initial serving of the notice there will be a period of up to six months during which time the investigating authority will be able to exercise a right to excavate. Whether it chooses to do so in full will depend on local circumstances. Certainly it cannot be extended (except by agreement with the developer) although it can be reduced if thought necessary or desirable.

7.4 THE PROTECTION OF WRECKS

Wrecks can provide unique historic evidence. By remaining underwater they suffer little from erosion or infestation and in British waters, which are cool enough to deter the deadly shipworm, they tend to be well-preserved. They are capable of providing a wealth of reasonably intact objects and information.

The realization that wrecks can provide all sorts of treasure trove has been known for many years. In the 1960s and early 1970s, when Henry VIII's warship the *Mary Rose* was being investigated in the Solent, the fear of pilfering was a constant worry. So much so that by 1973, partly as a result of this concern, the Protection of Wrecks Act 1973 was passed by parliament. Henceforth historic underwater 'sites' such as the *Mary Rose* could be protected. Indeed it was one of the very first ships to be given protection by the Act. 'Sites', however, refer only to wrecks and their surroundings where cargo and other objects from the wreck might be found. It does not include other types of site such as submerged villages or forests which are not protected under the legislation. Such sites are protected under the 1979 Act although by 1993 none had been scheduled (DoE, 1993).

The designation of sites

The 1973 Act allows the appropriate Secretary of State to designate an area around a wreck site as a **restricted area**. In England this is done by the Secretary of State for National Heritage. In Scottish and Welsh waters authority is vested respectively in the Secretaries of State for Scotland and Wales.

If the Secretary of State is satisfied that a wreck site ought to be protected from unauthorized interference, he can make a **designation order**. This has the effect of restricting access within a specified area of water unless a licence to investigate the wreck has first been obtained. Without such a licence it becomes an offence to tamper with it in any way. Section 1(3) of the Act states that an offence is committed if a person:

(1) tampers with, damages or removes any part of a vessel lying wrecked on the sea bed or any object formerly contained in the vessel; or

(2) carries out diving or salvage operations directed to the exploration of any wreck or to removing any objects from it or from the sea bed or uses equipment constructed or adapted for any purpose of diving or salvage operations; or

(3) deposits, so as to fall or lie abandoned on the sea bed, anything which, if it were to fall on the site of the wreck, would wholly or partly obliterate the site or destruct access to it or damage any part of the wreck; or

(4) causes or permits any of these things to be done by others, other than under a licence.

These wide-ranging restrictions can affect navigation and fishing rights. They prevent anchoring or fishing with nets on the seabed in the vicinity of a wreck site. The exception is when the safe passage of a vessel is endangered. If there is any threat to life safety at sea must come first.

It is therefore important that the site and restricted area are properly designated and accurately recorded. This is achieved by the Secretary of State first taking advice from the Advisory Committee on Historic Wreck Sites (sometimes referred to as the Runciman Committee after its first chairman). In turn the Committee will be assisted by the Archaeological Diving Unit based at the Scottish Institute of Maritime Studies at St Andrews University.

The unit will normally visit the wreck and report on its condition. Age will be taken into account together with any historic, archaeological and artistic evidence of the wreck or its contents or cargo. The degree of preservation, known historical association and the extent of any threat to the wreck would also be considered.

In considering whether to designate a wreck account has to be taken of its historic, archaeological or artistic importance. This will be in respect of the vessel or any object contained or formerly contained in it. These could be lying on the seabed in or near the wreck, which is why an area of sea bed around the wreck is normally included in the designation. The latitude and longitude of the vessel is specified in degrees, minutes and seconds of arc and a circle is then drawn around the identified site to designate the restricted area. The radius is given in metres.

In Scottish waters, where four sites have been designated, the distances from the charted position of the wreck range from 50 to 250 m, reflecting the nature of the wreck, the locality and strength of tide. Where the shore line lies within this limit the area of designation extends up to the mean high water mark of spring tides.

A designation order can apply to any site in UK waters. These extend from the seaward limit of UK territorial waters up to the high water mark of ordinary spring tides. It can lie in areas where land reclamation, marina development or other projects might be proposed. They could pose a threat to an historic wreck.

The possibility of such a threat leads to the final point about designation. It is that anyone can ask to have a wreck protected under the Act. By submitting an application to have a site designation the Secretary of State will consider it, although in practice it is often the investigating archaeologists who apply to have a wreck protected.

The investigation of wrecks

Anyone who wants to investigate a wreck site must first obtain a licence from the Secretary of State. There are two types known as a survey licence and an excavation licence.

A survey licence allows the successful applicant, together with other named individuals, to carry out a survey and other non-destructive work within the designated area. The licence would normally require that the work be undertaken with appropriate archaeological advice.

An excavation licence is necessary if any salvage operations are proposed. These would be in respect of any part of the wreck or any objects from it. The licence would normally be issued only after a good pre-disturbance survey had been appraised. Other considerations would relate to:

1. the competence of the excavators;
2. the excavators being properly equipped to carry out the salvage operations in a manner appropriate to the historical, archaeological or artistic importance of the wreck;
3. the case for excavation being well founded;
4. sufficient resources being available to the archaeologists for the proper conservation of the objects raised;
5. the available resources being sufficient to see the project through to completion and publication.

These procedures are designed to ensure that the wreck and associated objects and cargo are not unwittingly damaged. Conditions and restrictions can also be imposed on a licence and if there is any doubt about the outcome of the investigation the Secretary of State can vary or revoke a licence at any time. This must, however, be done after not less than one week's notice has been given to the licensee. When something is recovered, whether historical or not, the recovery must be reported without delay to the Receiver of Wrecks at the nearest Customs House.

7.5 LEGISLATION CONCERNING BURIAL GROUNDS

The legislation relating to burial grounds can impose restrictions on archaeologists and developers if they wish respectively to investigate or develop a site where there are human remains. There are two legal requirements: one concerns the removal of bodies, the other the erection of buildings.

Under the provisions of the Burial Act 1857 it is unlawful to remove any body, or the remains of any body, which has been interred in any place of burial, without first obtaining a licence. Section 25 of the Act makes provision for application to the Home Office for a licence which can be granted or rejected depending on the circumstances. A grant can be subject to precautions and/or conditions as deemed appropriate. Additionally it is a requirement that the Bishop of the Diocese must give his authority.

Where development is proposed the provisions of the Disused Burial Grounds Act 1884 as amended by the Disused Burial Grounds (Amendment) Act 1981 come into play. They are designed to enable building to take place provided certain safeguards can be met.

One of these safeguards must be that the burial ground must be disused and no longer required for burial purposes. Such a ground can include any churchyard, cemetery or other ground, whether consecrated or not, which has been set aside for the purposes of interment. It applies irrespective of whether the burial ground has been partially or wholly closed for burials.

Buildings may be erected on a disused burial ground provided that there have never been any interments or that no personal representative or relative of any deceased person has objected to the building. It is also a requirement of the Act that if there are any human remains these must be reinterred or cremated in accordance with the Schedule of the 1981 Act. This stipulates that:

1. adequate notice must be given both at the site and in a local newspaper;
2. where the deceased has been buried for less than 25 years relatives of the deceased must be notified.

Any such notice must contain the following information:

1. the name and address of the burial ground where the remains are proposed to be removed so that the site may be inspected;
2. a statement indicating the rights available to representatives and relatives and how they may exercise those rights;
3. any directions or precautions that may have been issued by the Secretary of State;
4. the time limit for the reinterment of any human remains;
5. that any tombstones or memorials may be removed;
6. where any tombstones etc. are not proposed to be removed to another site that details including any inscriptions be recorded.

The exception to the above requirements is when the building is for the purposes of enlarging a church, chapel, meeting-house or other place of worship.

REFERENCES

Cadw: Welsh Historic Monuments (1993) *Schedule of Ancient Monuments of National Importance in Wales*, Cadw, Cardiff.

Department of National Heritage (1993) Consultation Paper on *Proposed Changes to Ancient Monuments (Class Consents) Orders*, DNH, London.

Department of the Environment, Welsh Office (1993) *Managing the Coast – A Review of Coastal Management Plans in England and Wales and the Powers Supporting Them*, HMSO, London and Cardiff.

Historic Scotland (1990) *A List of Ancient Monuments in Scotland, 1990*, Historic Buildings and Monuments, Edinburgh.

Suddards, R.W. (1988) *Listed Buildings: The Law and Practice of Historic Buildings, Ancient Monuments and Conservation Areas*, Sweet and Maxwell, London.

Scottish Office Environment Department (1992a) *National Planning Policy Guideline: Archaeology and Planning* (draft) SOEnD, Edinburgh.

Scottish Office Environment Department (1992b) Planning Advice Note: Archaeology and Planning, SOEnD, Edinburgh.

FURTHER READING

Chadwick, P. (1992) *Archaeology and the Planning System*. Paper presented at RIBA Seminar, 25 November, 1992, London.

Davrill, T. (1987) *Ancient Monuments in the Countryside: an Archaeological Management Review*, English Heritage, London.

Department of National Heritage (1992) *Notes for the Guidance of Finders of Historic Wrecks*, DNH, London.

Scrase, T. (1991) Archaeology and planning – A case for full integration. *Journal of Planning and Environment Law*, pp. 1103–1112, Sweet and Maxwell, London.

The need for planning permission

8

The planning Acts state that 'development' needs planning permission, the implication being that if operations or works are not development they do not need permission. And if they do not need permission the developer can proceed with proposals thereby avoiding any delay caused by the planning process. It means that conditions relating to an archaeological investigation cannot be attached to a developer's proposals who can proceed unencumbered by planning restrictions requiring an excavation to be undertaken. Not surprisingly it is an area important to many developers.

To fall outside the scope of the planning Acts a development project must satisfy one of two requirements. Either it must fall outside the definition of 'development', as defined in the planning Acts, or it must be granted permission in advance in some way.

8.1 THE DEFINITION OF DEVELOPMENT

Development is defined in Section 55(1) of the Town and Country Planning Act 1990 (Section 19(1) of the Town and Country Planning (Scotland) Act 1972) as:

> the carrying out of building, engineering, mining or other operations in, on, over of under land or the making of any material change in the use of any building or other land.

Two separate matters can be identified in this definition – operations and material change of use.

Operational development

Operational development means that some physical alteration to the land must occur. Thus the digging of a trench in preparation for building foundations is operational development. So too is pile driving and excavating for minerals. Less clear is whether the excavation of a site for archaeological purposes amounts to development. Digging into the ground clearly involves operations in the land and it could be argued that excavating consists of engineering operations and should require planning permission in the same way that mineral extraction requires permission. It is, however, possible to draw a distinction between the two.

When foundations are dug for new buildings or when minerals are extracted from the ground they are needed as part of the development. Archaeological excavations, on the other hand, are normally undertaken as a consequence of development. They do not form part of the development itself but are one of the matters affected by it. In the same way that a development proposal might affect surrounding properties so archaeological remains might also be affected. It is a matter that would be taken into consideration in the determination of a development project. Conversely, if excavations form part of research archaeology where no other development is proposed it could be argued that this type of archaeological investigation constitutes development in its own right for which planning permission would be required.

Included within the definition of building operations is the demolition of buildings. Applicable to dwellings but not other buildings, although a notification procedure does allow certain demolition controls to be exercised elsewhere, the aim is to prevent the unnecessary demolition of property outside conservation areas. If an applicant or landowner wants to demolish a dwelling it will be necessary to apply for permission. If the aim is to demolish other buildings, such as offices or industrial premises, or if an application for the construction of a building is submitted, then, with two exceptions, it will not be necessary to submit a separate application to demolish. The exceptions are in respect of listed buildings and buildings in conservation areas. In both cases if demolition is proposed a separate application to demolish must be submitted.

For archaeological purposes the demolition of dwellings outside conservation areas is likely to be less important than demolition within such areas as there is likely to be a greater chance of encountering historic or archaeological remains in these areas.

Material change of use

The second part of the definition of development refers to **material change of use**. Where a change of use is not material it does not fall within the definition of development and planning permission is not required.

The word 'material' is not defined in the planning Acts and it is not therefore surprising that disputes can and do arise around the question of materiality. At first this may not appear to be a concern for archaeology. However, whilst the concern is about activities that are proposed either on the land or within buildings there are uses of land which can have a substantial impact on archaeology. The main ones, however, fall outside the definition of development.

8.2 WORKS AND ACTIVITIES FALLING OUTSIDE THE DEFINITION OF DEVELOPMENT

The definition of development is wide ranging, suggesting that virtually any physical alteration or activities on land can fall within the scope of planning control. This, however, is not the case because the Acts qualify the definition in a number of ways.

Section 55(2) of the Town and Country Planning Act 1990 (and Section 19(2) in the Town and Country Planning (Scotland) Act 1972) state that six operations or uses of land shall not involve development. Four can have implications for archaeological investigation.

Internal alterations to buildings

The removal of internal walls, the breaking open of the ground floor, the construction of new internal walls, or the digging of trenches for services within buildings, or for archaeological investigation, can fall into this category and not be classified as development. Provided the external appearance of a building is not materially altered such works can, with one exception, proceed without hindrance from the local planning authority. The exception is when a building is listed for its special architectural of historic interest. If it is listed then any works, either internal or external, which affect its character will need listed building consent.

The need for listed building consent may be seen by some as an opportunity to control operations in the interests of archaeology. Such an argument, however, would be difficult to sustain. The only interest a planning authority can have is in respect of the character of a listed building and how its character might be affected. This would not include a concern for archaeology unless this could be shown to form part of the character of the building.

The maintenance or improvement of a highway within the boundaries of the highway

Where a highway is proposed to be improved by a highway authority, this can involve the realignment of a carriageway. The improvement might be to remove a sharp bend or to straighten out a winding stretch of road. In both cases the road could follow a new alignment not previously prescribed, thereby affecting what might be the archaeological remains of early habitation alongside the old alignment.

When this occurs much will depend on where the existing boundaries of the road are situated. If it is breached then planning permission will be required thereby opening the opportunity for an archaeological investigation to take place if thought necessary or desirable. Where the boundary is not breached then it is difficult to see how planning powers could be used to secure such an investigation. If there is a grass verge alongside the highway it could be argued that this forms part of the highway and the works would not require planning permission. The difficulty would be in trying to identify the boundary. Sometimes this is marked by a fence or hedge although in urban areas difficulties can be experienced in trying to find out where the boundary lies.

Difficulties can also be experienced in trying to establish the depth of this boundary beneath the highway. It is not unknown for highway authorities to say that their jurisdiction ends where the base course ends and that the land beneath the bottom layer of the highway belongs to the respective frontages. It is an argument that is sometimes used when improvements are required or proposed and the question arises as to who is to pay. But if that is the case does this mean that planning permission would be required? Probably not.

The use of any land for the purposes of agriculture of forestry

The use of land for agricultural or forestry purposes has been widely interpreted to mean that the ploughing or re-ploughing of fields for growing food and the preparation of land for the growing of forest trees do not constitute development. The general interpretation is that such activity falls outside the scope of planning control, although some might argue that there is inconsistency in this interpretation. The ploughing of fields, whilst being an activity on the land, nevertheless must involve some physical alteration of it. If archaeological remains can be churned up by the plough it could be argued that ploughing must involve operational development on the land rather than be simply a use of land. That, however, is not the accepted wisdom and ploughing generally falls outside the scope of planning control.

The carrying out of works by a local authority or statutory undertaker

Local authorities and statutory undertakers are employed to inspect, repair or renew any sewers, mains, pipes, cables or other apparatus, including the breaking open of any street or other land for that purpose, without requiring permission. Inspection and repair would normally involve the breaking open of land which has previously been broken and where any archaeological remains will have already been destroyed. Renewal, on the other hand, could involve breaking into new ground and could result in damage to buried remains or archaeological evidence.

8.3 DEVELOPMENT PERMITTED BY STATUTE

Just as some operations and uses fall outside the definition of development so others are permitted by planning legislation. In both cases they are exempt from the need to obtain a specific planning permission. The principal planning Acts make provision for this either by a) allowing regulations to be made which direct that permission is not required for certain specified types of development or by b) allowing different types of development to go ahead in specially selected areas. Those most relevant to archaeology are operations allowed under the Town and Country Planning General Development Order 1989, an Interim Development Order, an Enterprise Zone Scheme and a Simplified Planning Zone Scheme.

Development permitted by a general development order

The main aim of a general development order is to specify a number of developments that may proceed without express consent. Most relate to extensions to different types of buildings such as dwellings and industrial premises. There are also substantial allowances available to statutory undertakers, privatized utilities and to certain changes of use, although as far as the GDO is concerned it is only operational development that is relevant to archaeology. In some case operations are subject to extensive qualifications and restrictions covering size, siting and, less frequently, location. There is no reference to restrictions over foundation size or design nor to exceptions in archaeologically sensitive sites or areas, although those most likely to have an impact on archaeology are shown in Table 8.1. It does not include all of the allowances and restrictions (to do so would be impossible within the confines of this book) although as can be seen there are quite a few that can affect archaeology.

One important point about these permitted development rights is that they give exemption solely to the need for planning permission. They do not relate to other consents that may be required, such as listed building consent, conservation area consent or scheduled monument consent. These other

Table 8.1 Operations not requiring planning permission but which may have implications for archaeology

- the extension of a dwelling house
- the erection of walls and other means of enclosure
- the formation of certain vehicular accesses
- the construction of certain agricultural buildings
- certain mineral operations in connection with the use of land for agriculture
- a number of forestry operations including the erection and extension of buildings and the formation of private ways
- extensions to industrial buildings and warehouses
- the repair and renewal of sewers, mains pipes and other apparatus (where it disturbs new ground)
- the deposit of waste by a local authority
- minor works by local authorities (e.g. erection of shelters)
- improvements to watercourses or works by drainage boards
- provision of works, sewers, pipes and other apparatus below ground level by a water authority
- improvements, maintenance or repair in, on or under any watercourse or land drainage works by a water authority
- development on operational land by dock, pier, harbour, water transport, canal or inland navigation undertakings
- use of land by statutory undertakings for the spreading of any dredged material
- the laying underground of pipes and other apparatus by gas, electricity and road transport undertakings
- the construction or extension of runways and passenger terminals
- building and other operations on land used for mining purposes
- prospecting for coal by British Coal
- exploring for minerals
- the demolition of certain buildings

Warning: In every case listed above there are restrictions and/or conditions limiting the extent or the way in which the development may proceed. Some are quite severe. For further information check the relevant Town and Country Planning General Development Order and its amendments.
Source: interpreted from data in General Development Orders.

consent procedures are not affected by the GDO and would have to be applied for in the normal way when relevant.

Withdawal of permitted development rights

Notwithstanding that permitted development rights exist under the GDO, local planning authorities are empowered to withdraw these rights at any time. By making what is known as an **Article 4 direction** (this stems from Article 4 of the GDO and is the same Article in the Scottish Order 1992) an authority may issue a direction which has the effect of preventing development as specified in the direction from automatically proceeding. Planning permission, therefore, has to be obtained before the development can proceed.

The Article 4 procedure requires the planning authority to be satisfied that it is expedient to make a direction, that the action is necessary in the interests of the proper planning of the area taking into account planning policies of the authority, the character of the area and the perceived threat to it. Where an authority is concerned about the impact of a proposal the process enables it to give full attention to the details. Effects on archaeology could arguably fall into this category and if the planning authority thought a development proposed might pose a serious threat to archaeological remains, the authority could prevent that development from proceeding. The problem is that the authority would need to know of the threat in advance because the direction can only apply to a proposed development and not to something that has already occurred or is currently taking place.

Other limitations and safeguards are built into this process of removing permitted development rights. One is that the direction must, in most cases, be approved by the Secretary of State. The exceptions are:

1. when development needs to be undertaken as a matter of urgency;
2. where development has been allowed under a local or private Act of Parliament;
3. where the development relates to telecomunications work such as the installation of certain types of apparatus and antennae.

Article 4 directions are often seen as an imposition on personal liberty and for this reason are not lightly accepted by the government. There has to be a strong planning case for their introduction.

Development permitted under an interim development order

Certain developments are permissible under an interim development order (IDO). This stems from legislation relating to mining and mineral workings introduced before nationwide planning controls were brought into effect in July 1948. At the end of the Second World War the government recognized the importance of estabishing a balance between the needs for minerals for reconstruction purposes and the need to protect the countryside. In order to achieve this balance the Town and Country Planning (General Interim Development) Order 1946 was passed withdrawing permitted development rights for most surface mineral workings. Working in conjunction with the

Town and Country Planning Act 1947 they had the effect of terminating all permissions granted before 22 July 1943 but keeping alive permissions granted after 21 July 1943 and before 1 July 1948, but not implemented by the latter date. Thus mineral workings granted permission by an IDO between 1943 and 1948 were kept alive.

In 1991, however, the Planning and Compensation Act introduced new measures designed to limit these earlier permissions. As a result of Section 22, holders of IDOs who wished to rely on outstanding permissions had to apply to the mineral planning authorities to have them registered (the county councils in England and Wales, the regional and islands councils in Scotland and the metropolitan district councils in England). The deadline was 25 March 1992, after which date any outstanding IDOs ceased to have effect.

The reason for registration was that, unlike other planning decisions, no requirement existed to record publicly IDO permissions. Records proved sparse and imprecise with the result that planning authorities could not be sure where IDO permissions existed. With the requirement to register within a deadline the situation could be made clear. As part of the registration process the authority, if satisfied that the application was valid, could register it and impose conditions as considered appropriate. These could vary from the original and overrule those set out in any earlier permission. The new permission would have effect in the manner determined by the authority or, on appeal, by the Secretary of State for the Environment in England or the Secretary of State of Scotland or Wales.

The current situation, therefore, depends on the IDOs that have been registered with local authorities and the conditions attached to them. If mineral operations commence, apparently without consent, it is possible that they have been registered under the IDO procedures. Alternatively, the operations may relate to a planning permission kept alive by earlier operations.

Development permitted under an enterprise zone scheme

Enterprise zones were first introduced in 1981 as a result of the passing of the Local Government, Planning and Land Act 1980. This Act related to the whole of Britain but the provisions relating to England and Wales have since been incorporated into the Town and Country Planning Act 1990. In Scotland the 1972 and 1980 Acts both still apply. These have the effect of enabling the Secretary of State to designate areas as enterprise zones (EZs) and to incorporate for each zone an **enterprise zone scheme** granting planning permission for development as prescribed in the scheme. Only commercial and industrial development is possible although the former does include retail and hotel development. Granted life for a period of 10 years, the intention was to encourage commercial and industrial activity at a number of run-down urban areas experiencing the worst effects of economic recession: for example, where coal mines have been closed down, or where there are high levels of unemployment. This encouragement was to be achieved by freeing businesses from the need to obtain planning permission and from certain

Table 8.2 Benefits to be obtained by developing in an enterprise zone

- Exemption from rates on industrial and commercial properties
- 100% allowances for corporation and income tax purposes for capital expenditure on industrial and commercial buildings
- Employers exempt from industrial training levies
- Certain schemes would not require planning permission
- The speeding up of administrative controls
- A reduction in the need to supply statistical information
- Certain customs facilities would be processed as a matter of priority

Note: enterprise zones have a specified 'life' of 10 years and the above benefits would be limited to that period unless it is extended by the Secretary of State.

financial constraints. The list of benefits is shown in Table 8.2, from which it can be seen that there are considerable advantages to businesses which wish to develop in these areas.

It is not clear to what extent archaeological remains may have been affected by the designation of enterprise zones. In practice, probably not a lot, although by locating them in run-down areas where much dereliction exists it could perhaps be argued that these older areas are where archaeological remains are more likely to be found. The main threat would probably be to industrial archaeology although if sites are scheduled there will still be a need for scheduled monument consent. Enterprise zone designation cannot overule the consent procedures affecting scheduled monuments so that sites which have been identified in this way would still be protected. Elsewhere it is likely that many industrial processes, Victorian buildings and canal and railway developments will have destroyed many older archaeological remains.

Development permitted under a simplified planning zone scheme

A **simplified planning zone scheme** is very similar in concept to an enterprise zone scheme. In the same way that a local planning authority can restrict the scope of planning legislation by removing permitted development rights with an Article 4 direction it can also extend these rights to allow development of its own choosing in a **simplified planning zone**. First introduced by the government under the Housing and Planning Act 1986, a simplified planning zone scheme, unlike an enterprise zone scheme, can be set up by a local planning authority independent of the government. In other words, the power to introduce this relaxation of planning control is delegated to the local level where an authority, by designating an area of land as a simplified planning zone (SPZ), can grant planning permission for development the authority deems appropriate to the area. Made in advance of developer interest the aim is to encourage new development.

In the first four years after its introduction only a handful of SPZ schemes were introduced in Britain, although following a simplification of the procedures in 1992 they may get more popular. The current procedures are shown in Figure 8.1. This shows that if objections are lodged to a proposal a public local inquiry may be held. Previously the procedures made it necessary for an inquiry. What Figure 8.1 also shows is that any individual can request a

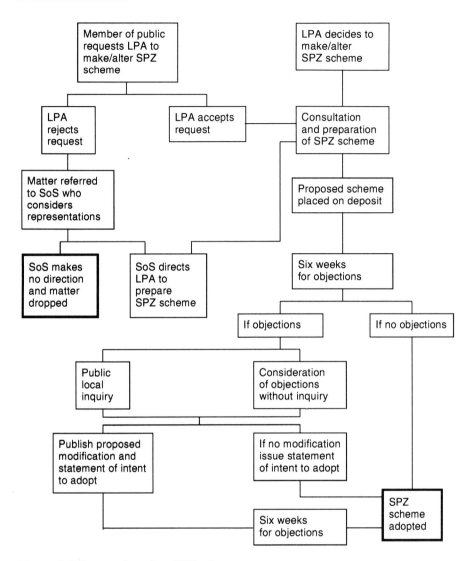

Figure 8.1 Preparation of an SPZ scheme.

local planning authority to prepare an SPZ scheme. Upon receipt of such a request an authority must consider it and can designate an area as they think appropriate incorporating such conditions or reserved matters as they deem necessary. The scheme would then remain in force for 10 years, similar to an enterprise zone scheme.

Another distinctive feature of the SPZ scheme is that the relaxation of control does not have to relate solely to industrial or commercial development. It can relate to whatever categories of development the planning authority think necessary and desirable. Thus housing development can be included. Alternatively a scheme can relate to a development brief setting out development and planning objectives for an area. In every case the main aim will be to regenerate the local economy and to create employment opportunities. An SPZ cannot, however, be set up in a conservation area, a national park, an area of outstanding natural beauty, a green belt, a site of special scientific interest or the Broads, although it can be very close: for example, at Grangemouth the SPZ at one point almost abuts an SSSI.

No mention is made in the permitting regulations of archaeological sites or areas, indicating that archaeology is generally seen as being less important and perhaps more likely to be outweighed by other considerations. The exception will be when remains are of national importance and form part of a scheduled monument, when scheduled monument consent will be required for any works affecting the monument.

8.4 DEVELOPMENT REQUIRING PLANNING PERMISSION

When development is not automatically granted permission and the steps shown in Figure 8.2 have been exhausted, a planning application has to be submitted. In many cases this is a straightforward exercise although complex proposals often present difficulties and so too can archaeology. The procedure usually involves the submission of a full application where all details of a proposal including its siting, design and external appearance are submitted. Where archaeology is relevant details may have to show how remains are to be protected with detailed drawings showing what is involved.

The alternative for a full planning application is to submit an outline application. If a developer is uncertain about the acceptability of proposals or simply wishes to establish the principle of development, the legislation allows for the submission of an outline application. This requires a description of the proposed development and the site to be identified. Details of the proposal are not required, the idea being that if the proposal is acceptable in principle the details can be submitted at a later date for subsequent approval by the planning authority.

One of the problems with all applications and especially outline applications is that further information may be required. If archaeology is likely to be an issue three things will need to be considered prior to submission. These are:

1. to establish the importance of any archaeological remains that may be present at a site;
2. to ascertain the extent to which development proposals will need to take those remains into account;
3. to decide how best to proceed with the submission of any application.

Assessing the importance of archaeological remains

As part of any investigations into the feasibility of a development project the developer or the developer's agent is strongly advised to assess the likely archaeological implications. The county archaeological officer or equivalent would be a good starting point. There is a county archaeologist appointed by all the shire counties in England. In London, English Heritage is the authority

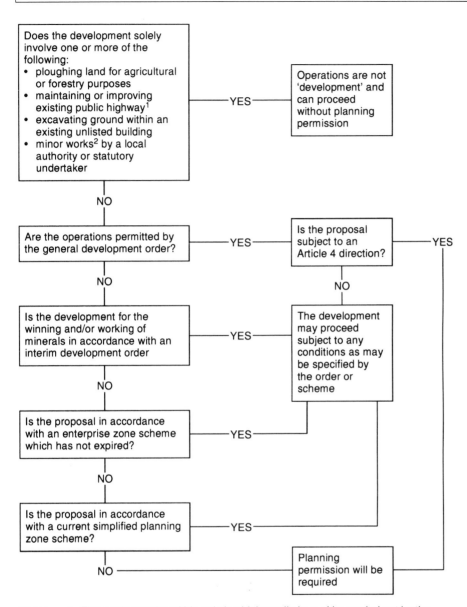

Figure 8.2 Assessing the need for planning permission for operations affecting land.

Notes:
1. This work must be within existing highway limits and be carried out by the highway authority.
2. These works relate to the repair and maintenance of sewers and other underground apparatus in accordance with Section 55.

to approach and in the six metropolitan areas (the large urban areas of Tyneside and Wearside, West Yorkshire, South Yorkshire, Greater Manchester, Merseyside and the West Midlands), archaeological information is provided jointly by the metropolitan districts within each metropolitan area. In Scotland the equivalent in most cases is the regional or islands archaeologist but where there is no local archaeologist (in Lothian and Tayside regions and the Western Isles), Historic Scotland should be approached. In Wales four archaeological trusts, namely the Clwyd-Powys Archaeological Trust, the Gwynedd Archaeological Trust Ltd, the Dyfed Archaeological Trust Ltd and the Glamorgan-Gwent Archaeological Trust Ltd, take on the county archaeologists' role for the whole of the country. If developers discuss their proposals with the archaeological officer at an early stage this can avoid expensive work later. Local authority archaeological officers, the Welsh archaeological trusts, English Heritage, Historic Scotland or Cadw can, for their respective areas, provide information about the location and details of known or anticipated archaeological remains. If these are thought to be important or are likely to prove important, additional expert advice can then be sought.

From this information it should be possible to assess the sensitivity of a site and whether an assessment or field evaluation will be necessary. An assessment would normally involve a desk-based study of available information from the SMR, historic maps held in the county archive and information from other sources such as a local museum, record office or archaeological unit. Sometimes this might be referred to separately as documentary research as opposed to a desk-top assessment.

A field evaluation, where necessary, would normally involve a ground survey making use of trial trenching, augering and/or boreholes and the examination of soil content. Geophysical prospecting using ground-penetrating radar, resistivity or magnetic techniques might also be used. Being quite distinct from a full archaeological excavation, the evaluation will nevertheless help to define the extent and character of any archaeological remains. The use of non-penetrating techniques and trial trenches should provide the investigator with enough information to establish the position and extent of major structures beneath the ground although, as stated in Chapter 2, care must be taken in any interpretation.

Soil samples might reveal important information about the chemical composition of matter and provide clues as to the activities that have taken place and where they were located. It could reinforce or supplement information about any substructures and lead the investigating archaeologist to assess the relative importance of a site within its neighbourhood or of those parts of a site considered more important than other parts of the same site. This assessment would indicate where development could proceed with minimal damage and where buildings or foundations should or should not be located. It ought to provide the developer with enough information to identify the potential options available, although great care needs to be exercised. Such information cannot be absolute and professional judgement and experience will be needed.

Armed with this information the developer would add it to other constraints identified as being applicable to the site. These might include physical, legal, economic, financial and planning varying in accordance with local circumstances. They would show what the site can reasonably accommodate. At the same time the developer would identify the opportunities for development in order to assess the site's potential.

The submission of a planning application

In the process of investigation by the developer and his advisors, the planning authority should be kept informed of what is happening. The needs of archaeology and development cannot always be reconciled but if the authority is kept informed of progress and of important matters this should reduce the potential for conflict. As ideas are formulated, so early discussion with the planning officer can help to smooth the passage for any subsequent application.

Where prior discussion is lacking, problems and delay can occur later particularly if the authority becomes aware that archaeology is a relevant factor. The proposal could pose a possible threat to archaeology leading an authority to ask for further information to be submitted. Regulation 4 of the Town and Country Planning (Applications) Regulations 1988 allows authorities to do this, provided it is done within one month of receipt of the application. These regulations apply to England and Wales only. In Scotland the appropriate order is the Town and Country Planning (General Development Procedure) (Scotland) Order 1992 (SI 1992/224). Failure to submit this information could lead to considerable delay. Alternatively the authority could refuse the application on the basis that insufficient and inadequate information has been received. Prior discussion should avoid this.

Two other questions arise as to the type of application and amount of information to be submitted. They depend on the location of the site, the type of development proposed, whether the applicant owns the site and how speculative the development is. Bearing in mind that planning permission runs with the land so that present and future owners can obtain the full benefit of any planning permission, it cannot always be in the interest of an applicant to submit a full application. If the applicant is not the owner he or she may not want to go to the trouble and expense of preparing detailed drawings if there is a risk of not being able to obtain the site or obtain planning permission. Any detailed work could be a waste of time and money and yet in some cases there will be no alternative.

Many urban areas are designated as conservation areas where local planning authorities have a duty to preserve or enhance the character or appearance of these areas. As part of this duty there will be a requirement for details to be submitted sufficient to show what is involved and how a proposal is to fit into the surrounding built environment. If a similar argument were adopted for archaeology, this could help tackle the problem of how much information to submit. If archaeological areas were designated in the same way that conservation areas are designated would this be the answer?

Another matter of concern in conservation areas is urban design. As a key factor in determining what can be built, it suggests that archaeology would carry less weight. But if archaeological remains are known to be present this knowledge could influence what is built on top and have an impact on urban design. It is conceivable that archaeological considerations could conflict with design principles and add to the architect's difficulties in trying to satisfy both requirements.

At greenfield sites the situation will largely depend on what is known about a site. If the Sites and Monuments Record shows a site to be important archaeologically, then some form of evaluation would most probably be required. In some instances an environmental assessment might also be necessary.

Archaeological evaluation

Where initial research and discussion indicate that archaeological remains are likely to be present it would be advisable, indeed necessary, to obtain an **archaeological evaluation**: advisable because it will save time, money and avoid problems later; necessary because the planning authority is likely to require it. In either case the aim must be to show how potential damage to any remains can be avoided or kept to a minimum. The evaluation should provide sufficient information to judge the impact on known or expected remains from a proposed development project.

Essentially the evaluation should do two things. First it should review the site's archaeological content to reveal the historic importance of a site, which period or periods of history are significant (e.g. Roman, Anglian, Medieval), and whether there has been any previous investigation at the site. An examination of the SMR would normally identify if there had been any earlier investigations, such as trial trenching, and the results of those investigations. In addition soil samples from the site and the use of non-penetrating investigative techniques would be advisable. Boreholes at carefully chosen positions should reveal the nature of the subsoil and its stratigraphic sequence and indicate the total depth and quality of human deposits and the natural underlying profile of the site.

If this information is used in conjuction with historical maps and other sources it may be possible to predict the depth of deposits over the entire site and thereby assess the likely foundation depths of recent or previous buildings of different periods. If the site is then traversed with, say, a magnetometer it should be possible to locate the more prominent hidden structures. Judgement and experience would then be used to interpret the findings.

Second, as part of an assessment, the authority wil probably want to receive exact details of levels, depths, borehole positions, the siting of trenches, if any, and what was found at the site. It will certainly want to know how and where new buildings or structures will fit into the site. They will want to examine the foundation details to ascertain the area of ground disturbance. The type and size of foundations and the extent of drainage and other underground works will be scrutinized to see what impact the proposals will have on known and expected archaeological remains.

As part of this analysis the authority may require detailed elevational drawings of foundations and accurate plans of where buildings are to be located. Associated engineering and drainage works may also have to be shown together with information about the methods to be used in the setting of the foundations. If pile foundations are to be used the authority may want to know if they are to be hammer driven or bored into the ground. With the

Table 8.3 Checklist of matters for inclusion in an archaeological evaluation

Pre-investigative matters
- Approval for the specification or works
- Approval for the suitability of the archaeological contractor
- The county archaeologist (or equivalent) to be consulted regarding sampling strategy
- Standards for conservation work to be agreed
- Arrangements for long-term storage and curation of site archive and finds to be agreed
- Arrangements for the analysis and publication of archaeological discoveries to be approved
- Agreement as to how work is to be implemented
- A method of site-coding to be agreed
- A timetable of works

Matters to be considered prior to or during investigative works
- Consent to be required if human remains are to be disturbed
- The appropriate museum or SMR to be consulted in respect of ceramic dating and analysis
- Recovery and analysis of finds to be in accordance with approved plan
- County archaeologist and/or other representatives to be allowed reasonable access
- CAO to be advised of any changes to timetable of works

Matters for consideration after site works have been completed
- Evaluation report to be sent to LPA/CAO
- Schedule of proposed works for further treatment of any remains (a mitigation strategy) to be submitted with planning application
- A summary of the results of works to be prepared to meet minimum requirements to LPA/CAO
- The archive to be completed and submitted to the recipient museum or agreed archivist within specified period of completion of fieldwork

former, vibration can be a problem whereas with the latter, a larger hole may cause more localized destruction.

The aim of the authority will be to see how the different sets of information compare and to assess the development option likely to be the least damaging. To make this assessment an evaluation will be needed; Table 8.3 provides a checklist of the matters that may have to be considered. More information is available from the model brief prepared by the Association of County Archaeological Officers (1993).

8.5 APPLICATIONS FOR CONSERVATION AREA CONSENT

One of the requirements of the Planning (Listed Buildings and Conservation Areas) Act 1990 is the need to obtain consent for the demolition of buildings in conservation areas. Virtually every building over 115 cubic metres in volume and not individually listed for its special architectural or historic interest in these areas requires **conservation area consent**. It overrides demolition requirements outlined previously and is designed to prevent premature demolition which might affect the character or appearance of the conservation area. It could also have implications for archaeological investigation and development.

The relevance to archaeology is that a planning authority can delay the timing of demolition until a contract to build has been settled, which could have the effect of either hindering or helping an archaeological investigation.

If buildings cannot be demolished until the last minute before development commences, archaeologists could have less time to investigate, less freedom of movement and may not be able to investigate in the most rewarding parts of a site. Alternatively there could be problems of cutting through ground floors of existing rooms and the need to avoid undermining of any existing foundations when digging into the ground. From the archaeologist's point of view, the suitability of buildings, the position of walls, the depth of excavation envisaged and the time of year will be important factors in determining whether to work within an existing building.

For the developer the main concern must be to ensure that demolition consent will be forthcoming and that any excavation can be undertaken as quickly as possible and with the minimum of delay to a project. If a dig has to be undetaken in the winter months there could be advantages in allowing the excavators to dig under the shelter of existing buildings to avoid adverse weather conditions. The exception would be if ground conditions required the excavation to extend deeper than would be safe for the stability of the building. If archaeological expectations thought this likely, earlier demolition would have to be requested by the developer where different authorities could have different views depending on how certain they were about the redevelopment going ahead.

8.6 APPLICATIONS FOR LISTED BUILDING CONSENT

Many buildings listed for their special architectural or historic interest will have been built on or be close to sites of earlier occupation. As such, alterations or extensions to these buildings could have an impact on archaeological remains because many have shallow foundations. If it is proposed to extend an historic building then, under the current building regulations, new foundations may have to extend far deeper than those of the existing structure. If archaeological remains are present it is possible that they would be destroyed and yet, ironically, it may not be possible to protect them.

If an extension falls within permitted development rights and does not need planning permission it is only possible, under the listed buildings legislation, for consideration to be given to the architecture or historic character of the building. This, however, raises the question of whether an archaeological investigation can be required under the listing procedures. One argument is that it would have to rely on the need for planning permission. Another is that archaeology could be seen as part of the setting of a listed building thereby affecting its character.

8.7 DEVELOPMENT BY LOCAL AUTHORITIES ON THEIR OWN LAND

Development on land owned by local authorities can be of considerable benefit to archaeological investigation, as witnessed by the development of the Coppergate site in York. A large part of it was owned by the city council which enabled extensive excavations to be undertaken, although it should be noted that this could have been just as possible had the site been in private ownership. It was the co-operation of the landowner which enabled the excavation to take place, not the fact that it was in a particular ownership. As such, we can see that the motives and objectives of the authority will be important factors.

Bearing in mind that authorities have many responsibilities concerning a number of matters it should not be surprising for a clash of interests to arise sometimes. Some, no doubt, will be interested in promoting development at the expense of archaeology although in the case of York the excavation ultimately contributed to the formation and setting up of the Yorvik Viking Centre. In effect, the city council was able to promote development and heritage at the same time. They were giving due consideration to both matters which clearly cannot always be easy.

REFERENCE

Association of County Archaeological Officers (1993) *Model Briefs and Specifications for Archaeological Assessments and Field Evaluations*, ACAO, Bedford.

FURTHER READING

Falkirk District Council (1992) *Granemouth Simplified Planning Zone Written Statement*, Falkirk.

Lomnicki, A.J. (1991) *Law of Town and Country Planning*, HLT Publications, London.

Moore, V. (1992) *A Practical Approach to Planning Law* (3rd edn), Blackstone, London.

Telling, A.E. (1990) *Planning Law and Procedure* (8th edn), Butterworths, London.

Young, E. and Rowan-Robinson, J. (1985) *Scottish Planning Law and Procedure*, William Hodge, Glasgow.

9 Environmental assessment

Environmental assessment is a term used to describe a technique for examining the likely effects of new development on the environment. Originating from a Directive of the European Commission in June 1985 (85,337,EEC) the process is essentially a technique for bringing expert quantitative analysis and qualitative assessment of the environmental effects of a project together, and presenting the results in a way which enables the importance of the predicted effects to be properly evaluate before a decision is made (DoE, 1988a). It can include an examination of the effect of new development on archaeology.

The passing of the European Directive imposed a requirement on the British and other EC governments to introduce the necessary legislation within three years. This was achieved with the issue, in July 1988, of regulations requiring environmental assessment to be undertaken before consent to develop certain projects can proceed. The idea is that the environmental effects of a project are fully taken into account in the decision-making process in a manner that is similar to the planning controls outlined in the last Chapter. The main difference is that the environmental assessment goes much further than planning requirements and can have wider reaching implications for archaeology and development, which is why we need to look at it now.

9.1 THE MEANING OF ENVIRONMENTAL ASSESSMENT

Planning, as we have seen, is primarily policy led by means of the development plan. If proposals are in accordance with policies contained in the development plan there is a general presumption in favour of granting planning permission. Environmental assessment, on the other hand, is geared to protecting the environment. Instead of a presumption in favour of development, there is a presumption that development proposals should not proceed unless it can be shown that they will not significantly harm the environment.

This difference of emphasis has produced a varied pattern of response. Some argue that one of the main aims of planning is to protect the environment, quoting Schedules 4 and 13 of the Planning and Compensation

Act 1991 to support their case. These state that development plans must include policies aimed at conserving the natural beauty and amenity of the land and improving the physical environment. The amendments introduced by this Act are sometimes used to reinforce the view that there is very little difference between planning controls and environmental assessment. They see environmental assessment as part of the planning process.

In one sense this is true. Environmental assessment, in the way that it operates in Britain today, focuses exclusively on the impacts of individual projects and pays no attention to the cumulative effects of different proposals nor to policies, plans or programmes for protecting the environment. It can, therefore, be deduced that planning takes on the role of devising policy for protecting the environment while environmental assessment operates as a tool to measure the impact of development proposals against these policies.

There is, however, a strong and growing counter-argument which archaeologists and developers need to be aware of. It focuses on the fundamental aims of planning and environmental assessment. There is an important difference between the two which does not always appear to be appreciated. However, it will probably become clearer as time goes by. It may also become more important.

The key difference between planning and environmental assessment is that planning is primarily concerned with the development and use of land whereas environmental assessment is principally concerned with the environment and how it might be affected by human activity. It is concerned with all aspects of the environment and not just the land. The effects of projects on air, water, soil, plants, animal life and people are also important. Furthermore it is concerned about the interaction between each of these elements, both short and long term, temporary and permanent, positive and negative. Planning, therefore, is more limited in scope when it comes to the environment. Its primary function is to look at development, that is operations in, on, over or under land or the making of a material change in the use of land or any buildings and to see if it is acceptable.

In other words, planning is concerned about change in the environment. Once that change has been implemented, planning is no longer involved except in so far as conditions, restrictions or obligations have been imposed to control or regulate the change. Environmental assessment, by showing a concern for the long term effects on the environment must, of necessity, remain an issue long after the change has taken place. Indeed, instead of it being part of the planning process it could be argued that planning should form part of the environmental assessment process! A radical view which, if it materializes, could have a significant effect on development.

There are, in addition, two other reasons why it is important to understand what environmental assessment is all about. The first is because some developments fall outside the scope of planning control but not environmental assessment and the second relates to the fact that environmental controls are still in their infancy and may change in future years.

In connection with the first of these two points, we saw in Chapter 8 that some activities and operations are exempt from the need to obtain planning permission. One example quoted was the use of land for agriculture where fields can be ploughed at will without any planning involvement. Such action can affect archaeological remains and, depending on the effect of ploughing or other operations, have quite an impact on our heritage and hence archaeology. Similarly, if fertilizers are used on the land they could cause harm not just to animal life or water but to archaeological remains as well. They could contribute towards a chemical reaction and adversely affect remains.

These actions suggest that a case for intervention can be made although much will depend on the scale of operations and the effects on the environment. The point is that such actions could have a significant environmental impact, but they cannot fall within the scope of current planning controls.

The second point is that in the absence of any other organization it is local government that has taken on the primary role of monitoring environmental change. In many cases the planning authority has to deal with environmental assessment, which has led some planners to state that because the authority also deals with planning applications there is very little or no difference between the two regulatory processes. This, however, is precisely why developers and archaeologists need to proceed with caution.

Partly because environmental assessment is still in its infancy it would appear that many people in local government do not have the technical expertise to critically analyse assessments submitted with planning applications. They have yet to be trained in assessing the full environmental impact of development proposals, which has led to criticism (Johnston, 1992) of the aims, methods and quality of the whole process. However, if improvements are to be made or if alterations are to be put forward it would be advisable to understand or appreciate how the regulations currently operate.

9.2 WHAT THE REGULATIONS REQUIRE

The process of assessing the affect of a development proposal on the environment is known as **environmental assessment**. Sometimes it is referred to as **environmental impact assessment** although the use of the word impact does give it a more restrictive meaning. Whereas for practical purposes the two phrases are synonymous, the word impact specifically means the effects from a particular cause. However, as far as environmental assessment is concerned it is the overall change in the environment that is important. The term environmental assessment incorporates the idea of change as well as the idea of effect. It is not as restrictive as an impact assessment and can take into account not only the impact of a development proposal but both positive and negative effects as well.

To distinguish between these positive and negative aspects of change several things have to be done. They include:

- the collection of information from different sources about a project;
- the analysis of that information;
- an assessment of the likely effects of a project on the environment;
- an appraisal of how to minimize or remove any adverse effects.

To appreciate how this is done there are two terms that need to be understood. They are **environmental information** and **environmental statement**.

Environmental information

The process of assessment requires information about a project and the environment to be obtained and considered. This is information from all sources and not just from the developer or an applicant if planning permission is sought. It includes information from statutory consultees such as the nature conservancy councils and other sources such as objectors. Information from all of these sources, whether they support or object to a proposal, make up the environmental information that has to be taken into account. It can be very wide-ranging.

One consequence of this breadth of coverage is that it can be difficult to know where to draw the line on the collection of information. Unlike planning applications where there are statutory procedures and generally recognized limits of intervention (although these too can present difficulties), no such limits have yet been identified for environmental assessment. There is insufficient case law which means that all manner of topics can and are being raised, as witnessed by the objections that have come forward on different occasions. The construction of an extension to the M3 motorway at Twyford Down in Hampshire and the felling of trees at Oxleas Wood in South-East London are two examples where strong differences of opinion emerged. They signify a new more vociferous approach to challenging decision-making with, as it happens, varied results.

Environmental statement

This is the document or series of documents which have to be submitted with a development proposal. Where planning permission is required the environmental statement would normally be submitted to the planning authority at the same time as the planning application for the development.

There is no prescribed form to an environmental statement although it must contain the information set out in Schedule 3 of the Town and Country Planning (Assessment of Environmental Effects) Regulations 1988. This is known as the specified information and comprises:

1. A description of the proposed development, including information about the siting, design, size and scale of the development.
2. The data necessary to identify and assess the likely effects on the environment.
3. A description of the likely significant effects on the environment (both direct and indirect) by reference to the possible impact on human beings, flora, fauna, soil, water, air, climate, the landscape, the interaction between any of the foregoing, material assets, and the cultural heritage.
4. Where significant adverse effects are identified a description of the measures to avoid, reduce or remedy those effects.
5. A summary in non-technical language of the information specified above.

Archaeology is not specifically mentioned in (3) above but is generally understood to form part of the cultural heritage. It is also worth noting that the regulations define effects in connection with the above requirements as including secondary, cumulative, short-, medium- and long-term, permanent, temporary, positive and negative effects. Thus, as far as archaeological considerations are concerned all of these effects, provided they are significant, and how they might be tackled, fall within the assessment regulations. This is far more comprehensive than the planning requirements.

9.3 THE NEED FOR ENVIRONMENTAL ASSESSMENT

There are many different types of development projects that are subject to environmental assessment. The majority are subject to planning control where planning permission is required, but there are a number of other occasions when the assessment regulations apply and the planning regulations do not.

Development projects subject to planning control

Where environmental assessment and planning controls do come together is through the 1988 Regulations (SI No. 1199). In Scotland the equivalent regulations are the Environmental Assessment (Scotland) Regulations 1988 (SI No. 1221). These stipulate that certain developments, before they can be considered by the local planning authority, must first be subject to scrutiny by the same authority under the environmental assessment regulations. There are two categories of development projects where environmental assessment is applicable. They are:

1. projects which must be subject to environmental assessment in every case (known as Schedule 1 projects);
2. projects which will be subject to Environmental Assessment when they are judged to have a significant effect on the environment (known as Schedule 2 projects).

Schedule 1 projects

There are ten types of development which come within the umbrella of Schedule 1. Nine relate to major developments such as oil refineries, power stations or inland waterways and one relates to the deposit of waste. All can be relevant to archaeology.

Schedule 2 projects

Schedule 2 is by far the more important of the two schedules as far as archaeology is concerned. It relates to a wide range of development projects of more common occurrence (examples are given in Table 9.1), where archaeological matters could frequently arise. The difficulty, particularly for

Table 9.1 Examples of development projects falling within Schedule 2 of the environmental assessment regulations

Extracting peat
An industrial estate development
An urban development project
Construction of a road
Flood relief works
Oil or gas pipeline installations
A yacht marina
Holiday village
Hotel complex
Waste water treatment plant
Modifications to aerodromes (with runways over 2100 m long)
Modifications to waste disposal sites
Mineral extraction
A number of metal processing operations
Many manufacturing processes relating to the chemical, food, textile, leather, wood and paper industries

the developer, is in knowing when this is likely to happen and when this schedule becomes operative.

The regulations require an environment assessment to be made if a project is 'likely to have a significant effect on the environment'. The problem is in trying to work out what is significant. It is not defined in the regulations although size, nature and location of a project must be key components in trying to establish this. Guidance is also available from the government in Circular 15/88 entitled *Environmental Assessment* (and its Scottish, Circular 13/88, and Welsh, Circular 23/88, equivalents). It indicates that there are three types of project where an assessment may be necessary. They are:

1. Projects of more than local importance

These are projects which, by virtue of their scale or where they depart from approved development plans, may be subject to environmental assessment. By being of more than local importance it has been thought that this was sufficient to require a statement, but this need not be the case. For example, a proposal to construct a motorway service station alongside the M40 was deemed not to require an assessment. Despite the fact that it could reasonably be argued to be of more than local importance, the key issue was whether it would have a significant effect on the environment. In that case it was thought that the service station would not.

2. Projects in sensitive locations

The more environmentally sensitive an area, the more likely it is that an environmental assessment will be required for development in that area. As to what is a sensitive location, areas such as a national park, a site of special scientific interest (SSSI), an area of outstanding natural beauty or an ancient monument are obvious examples. Other known archaeological sites could be included although projects affecting lesser-known archaeological sites could be excluded and not require to be assessed. Much will depend on the importance and rarity value of the site, its remains, and the locality.

3. Projects with particularly complex and potentially adverse effects

For a project to have potentially adverse effects, one of the most relevant factors that will have to be taken into account is pollution. The circular indicates that a number of industrial projects involving potentially hazardous emissions might fall into this category. The effect of acid rain is perhaps one example where upstanding archaeological remains have been affected although the difficulty would be in assessing the likely impact of a new project. The fact that it may be potentially adverse will add to this difficulty.

Despite the guidance that is available, one of the problems is that it is not always clear when, or if, an assessment will have to be made. As Paragraph 30 of Circular 15/88 states, it is not possible to formulate criteria or thresholds which will provide a simple test in all cases of whether environmental assessment is or is not required (DoE, 1988). The circular adds that the most such criteria can offer is a broad indication of the type or scale of project which may need to be subject to assessment.

Situation in a simplified planning zone or enterprise zone

Where development is proposed in an SPZ or an EZ the date of designation of the zone is important in deciding if an assessment is required. If the zone was designated before July 1988, a development project does not have to be subject to environmental assessment. If the zone was designated after July 1988 different procedures apply. Schedule 1 projects will automatically be subject to environmental assessment while projects which fall within Schedule 2 can be subject to one of two alternative requirements. Either the planning authority (in the case of SPZs) or the government (in respect of EZs) can exclude all Schedule 2 type developments from the zone or alternatively, the authority or government minister can exclude developments thought to give rise to significant environmental effects from the automatic grant of permission. In other words they would be subject to normal planning procedures.

Projects not subject to planning control

Whilst planning controls will apply to most development proposals, there are a number of projects which are exempt from the need for planning permission but which can nevertheless require to be assessed for their environmental effects. There are six main types of development projects that fall into this category and which could affect archaeological remains.

1. Motorways and trunk roads

Motorways and trunk roads are controlled by the government and not by the local highway authority. Under procedures set out in the Highways Acts the Department of Transport takes responsibility for deciding which routes to adopt (e.g. for a by-pass) and the procedures that must be followed to secure their construction. They do not require planning permission from the local planning authority and are determined by the government.

The first stage in this process is to decide the preferred route. Public consultation and a public inquiry can be involved but it is only once the preferred route has been chosen that environmental assessment falls to be considered. At the time when a draft order is published the Highways (Assessment of Environmental Effects) Regulations 1988 require the Secretary of State to publish an environmental statement on the likely environmental effects. Some would argue that environmental assessment should be brought in at an earlier stage.

This procedure applies to all new motorways and to trunk roads over 10 km in length. It also applies to shorter lengths of trunk road (over 1 km) where the proposed route passes through or within 100 m of a sensitive area. These are defined as a national park, an SSSI, a conservation area, a national nature reserve or an urban area consisting of 1500 or more dwellings, that is, where this number of dwellings lie within 100 m of the proposed road. Archaeological sites are not mentioned.

Where trunk road improvements such as road widening and realignment are proposed, an assessment will be required if the improvements are likely to have a significant effect on the environment. Other roads, whether they are developed by local authorities or private developers, would be treated in the same way. They would be subject to planning controls and require planning permission in the normal way with archaeological considerations, where applicable and deemed necessary, taken into account.

2. Afforestation

In the case of forestry proposals, if the Forestry Commission is of the opinion that they are likely to have a significant effect on the environment, they must be subject to environmental assessment. Here such factors as ecological change, the area and where new planting is thought to be potentially damaging appear to be the main criteria. If a proposed area for planting exceeds 100 hectares an environmental assessment will be required.

In the Environmental Assessment (Afforestation) Regulations 1988 four areas of environmental importance are identified where particular attention to the effects of forestry proposals are required: they are national parks, national scenic areas (these are located solely in Scotland), areas of outstanding natural beauty, and environmentally sensitive areas. No reference is made to sites of architectural importance, which suggests that archaeological remains will not have to be considered although this need not be the case.

If an ancient monument is affected there could be a requirement to assess the effects on it. Where it is suspected that there may be archaeological remains but no proof exists to support this, it is more likely than an assessment would not be required, provided, of course, there are no other considerations which could have an impact on the environment and which would need to be taken into account. Further guidance on the preparation of an environmental statement, the arrangements for consultancy, procedures for dealing with the statement and rights of appeal are available in a leaflet from the Forestry Commission (1988).

3. Land drainage proposals

Improvements to existing land drainage works are permitted developments and do not require planning permission if carried out by drainage boards or the National Rivers Authority. The improvement works could, however, have an effect on the environment to the extent that an environmental assessment becomes necessary. The problem is that it will not always be clear if an assessment is required. Under the Land Drainage Improvement Works (Assessment of Environmental Effects) Regulations 1988 the responsibility for deciding whether an environmental assessment is necessary rests with the drainage board. In other words the authority which wishes to undertake the improvement works is the same authority which decides if an environmental assessment has to be undertaken. It will have to decide on the submission and rule on its contents. In other words it is both judge and jury.

This could raise questions about double standards although in practice it may not matter. This is because the concept of environmental assessment hinges on likely known effects. The whole idea is based on taking steps to minimize any adverse effects on the environment, which means that there has to be advance knowledge of what is there. If archaeological remains are known to exist an assessment on the effects on those remains can be estimated. If they are not known, difficulties could arise. If, in the course of improvement works, remains are uncovered it is possible that they will be well preserved because of the lack of air and they will be an excellent source of archaeological information. The environmental assessment process, however, does not appear to guarantee the protection of this resource. It would appear that it is designed to protect what is already known, such as an existing ancient monument, rather than a potential ancient monument.

4. Ports and harbours

The construction of a harbour or the modification of an existing harbour, when carried out under the requirements of the Harbours Act 1964, can be exempt from the need for planning permission. The Harbour Works (Assessment of Environmental Effects) Regulations 1988, on the other hand, make provision for certain of these works – below the low water mark of medium tides – to be subject to environmental assessment. A second set of regulations was issued in 1989 designed to deal with proposals under the Coastal Protection Act 1949 which were not covered in the 1988 regulations. When the relevant minister considers they will have a significant effect on the environment a statement will have to be prepared. In England this could be the Minister for Agriculture, Fisheries and Food or the Secretary of State for Transport, depending on the nature of the works. In Scotland and Wales it would be the Secretaries of State for Scotland and Wales respectively. This must describe what is proposed indicating the measures to be taken to avoid or minimize the effect on the environment. Details will then have to be published in a local newspaper in a prescribed manner inviting comments from the public. In addition the relevant local authority, nature conservancy council, countryside commission and Her Majesty's Inspectorate of Pollution must be invited to comment on the proposals.

Representations received in response to these consultations and publicity will be considered by the minister when deciding whether the proposed works should proceed or not. All those who made representations would be notified of the decision, the considerations involved and the reasons for the decision.

5. Marine salmon farming

Onshore fish farming facilities normally require planning permission but offshore facilities do not. They require a lease from the Crown Estates Commissioners but before such a lease can be granted, if a proposal is likely to have a significant effect on the environment, an environmental statement must be prepared and submitted to the commissioners for consideration.

Guidance has been issued (Crown Estates Commissioners, 1988) indicating the criteria to be used in determining whether an environmental statement will be required. These show that all but one of the matters do not relate to archaeology. The exception depends on whether there is a wreck in the vicinity of the proposed salmon farm, in which case the provision of the Protection of Wrecks Act 1973 mentioned in Chapter 7 will apply.

6. Oil and gas

Certain electricity and gas proposals do not need planning permission from the local planning authority, not because they are too small but because they are too big! Under present electricity legislation, nuclear power stations and non-nuclear generating stations with a heat output of 300 megawatts or more require the authorization of the Secretary of State for Trade and Industry. Certain other works including oil and gas pipelines of more than 10 miles in length also fall into this category. The procedures simply require the local planning authority to be consulted.

Proposals such as these which fall within the Electricity and Pipeline Works (Assessment of Environmental Effects) Regulations 1990 (these revoke regulations made in 1989) must be subject to environmental assessment. An environmental statement must be submitted to the Secretary of State for Trade and Industry and advertised locally in the area or areas concerned.

Projects approved by a private Act of Parliament

When the environmental assessment regulations came into being in 1988 it was decreed in the EC Directive that they would not apply to projects approved by a private Act of Parliament. However, in the autumn of that year the Joint Select Committee recommended that each House of Parliament amend its standing orders to require an environmental statement to be deposited for projects which would otherwise normally be subject to assessment. This was subsequently authorized for all private bills although the Transport and Works Act 1992 replaced the need for many of these.

Part 1 of the 1992 Act introduced a procedure to replace private bills for schemes relating to the construction of railways, tramways, other guided transport systems, inland waterways, roads, watercourses, and ancillary works and buildings. Under the Act the minister concerned can direct that planning permission be deemed to be granted, although procedure rules will require an environmental statement unless the Secretary of State considers that the works do not have any significant environmental effects. Where a private bill is still needed an environmental statement will have to be submitted on a similar basis.

9.4 CHALLENGING THE NEED FOR ENVIRONMENTAL ASSESSMENT

One of the criticisms about environmental assessment is that it is not always clear whether a particular development should be subject to it or not. It is sometimes not clear if the effects of a development project on the environment will be significant.

The regulations accept that this is an area of uncertainty and accordingly make provision for a developer or applicant for planning permission to challenge the need for environmental assessment. There are, however, several points which must be considered if this course of action is to be pursued.

Prior to the submission of a planning application a developer can ask the planning authority if the proposals are likely to fall within one of the two schedules in the assessment regulations. In making this request enough information must be submitted for the authority to give an opinion within three weeks. A longer period is possible provided this is agreed with the developer. If there is no response within the three week or agreed longer period the developer can apply to the appropriate Secretary of State for a ruling on the matter. The information sent to the Secretary of State must be the same as that submitted to the planning authority.

Upon receipt of this information the Secretary of State is required to issue a direction within three weeks although the regulations allow this period to be extended if necessary. If the Secretary of State directs that an environmental assessment must be made clear and precise reasons must be given. The developer will then have to comply with the direction. Alternatively, if the Secretary of State directs that an environmental assessment is not necessary then the planning authority must observe the direction.

Sometimes a planning application is submitted without an environmental statement but the authority will still have to consider whether one is necessary. This, however, can be difficult particularly when it only has three weeks from receipt of application to notify the applicant in writing that a statement must be submitted. In addition, as part of this notification the authority should inform the applicant that it requires details of the applicant's intentions within the following three weeks. The choice is to either submit an environmental statement or to ask the Secretary of State for a direction on the matter.

This three week period is crucial to the applicant. If the applicant does not agree to its extension and fails to notify the planning authority of his or her intentions within the three week or longer agreed period, the application will be **deemed to be refused** at the end of this period. Equally important, the applicant will forgo a rights of appeal. The applicant will not be able to appeal against such a refusal.

In addition, a further point arises. Where the authority has notified the applicant that it considers an environmental statement necessary, the time to appeal against a failure to determine the application does not begin until either an environmental statement is submitted or the Secretary of State gives a direction that such a statement is not required. Thus, if the applicant has not submitted an environmental statement and has not received a ruling from the Secretary of State there can be no right of appeal.

Clearly in these situations it is important for an applicant to keep the planning authority informed of his or her intentions. It is also important to consider the need for environmental assessment at the outset. The late submission of a statement, particularly after the submission of a planning application, will make it look like an afterthought. If it merely endorses the planning application there will be the suspicion that environmental matters have not properly been taken into account.

9.5 PREPARATION OF AN ENVIRONMENTAL STATEMENT

In the preparation of an environmental statement there are several preliminaries to consider in addition to its contents.

Making use of consultants

Where an environmental statement has to be prepared it is the responsibility of the developer to see that it is done. Normally a firm of environmental consultants would be appointed to do this and if archaeology is a relevant factor it would be advisable to ensure that an archaeologist is one of the team.

The reasons why an archaeologist should be used are several. Apart from being able to give professional and objective advice on the archaeological importance of a site, he or she would also be able to advise on its importance relative to other sites. This can be more important than it seems. Whilst a site may appear significant, if it is one of several in an area its relative importance may be reduced. Conversely it could be regarded as being more important but this will depend on the type of site it is, the size and history of the geographical area investigated, the type, nature and location of other sites and the relative importance of each one. Only the archaeologist could properly supply this information.

Another reason why an archaeological consultant should be used, and which may be related to the importance of a site, is that advice could be given on what to preserve, on the identification of the least important parts of a site or how best to minimize any adverse environmental effects. Obviously much will depend on the nature of the site and its surroundings, the type of development that is proposed and the way in which the professional team approaches the subject.

An important factor as far as environmental assessment is concerned is that the existence of archaeological remains should be known in advance or be reasonably expected. If they are not known or are thought not to exist archaeology would not be an issue in the assessment. But how is this to be ascertained and at what stage should the archaeologist become involved?

Before any environmental consultants are appointed it will be important for the developer to think about the likely impact on the environment, including any impact on archaeology if this is thought to be a possibility. The developer should ask questions about it at any interview or, if competent to do so and able to spare the time, to carry out an investigation into the site personally. A key part of this would be to check the SMR lodged, in most cases, with the local authority. The alternative would be to make sure that the environmental consultants do this and are fully aware of how to tackle any archaeological matters. It could save a great deal of time and money in the long run.

Preliminary consultations

One of the problems associated with environmental assessment is who the developer or consultants should approach for advice. Whilst mention has already been made of the archaeologist, the chances are that the development will affect other aspects of the environment. It is equally possible that by overcoming one problem it could create another or pose a different environmental threat. For example, by repositioning a road to avoid archaeological remains, a new siting might affect, say, a sensitive area such as an SSSI. Archaeology, whilst important, cannot be seen in isolation from other factors. The overall effects of a development proposal will have to be taken into account which means that it will be important to consult the right people as soon as possible.

The environmental assessment regulations give some help on this point. They indicate, for instance, whom the planning authority must consult when a statement is received. They are:

1. any principal council if not the planning authority;
2. the Countryside Commission (or the Scottish or Welsh equivalents);
3. the national nature conservancy councils (English Nature, the Nature Conservancy Council for Scotland and the Countryside Council for Wales);
4. Her Majesty's Inspectorate of Pollution where the proposed development involves:

   (a) mining operations;
   (b) manufacturing industry;

(c) disposal of waste and other discharges where a licence or consent of the NRA is required;

(d) certain atmospheric emissions (as fall within Schedule 1 of the Health and Safety (Emissions to the Atmosphere) Regulations 1983).

5. any body which the local planning authority would have to consult under Article 18 of the Town and Country Planning General Development Order 1988 (in Scotland, Article 15 of the Town and Country Planning (General Development) Procedure (Scotland) Order 1992).

Table 9.2 lists the consultees involved. In many cases the planning authority may have to rely heavily on the advice obtained from these statutory consultees. The technical expertise required to assess the effects on the environment will rarely be readily available internally to the authority, which means that it can often pay the developer to approach the statutory consultees first. Apart from saving time it should be possible to obtain direct information from the technical experts and discuss how to minimize any possible adverse effects. This work should, of course, be done prior to the preparation of a planning application.

Table 9.2 Organizations required to be consulted by a local planning authority when an environmental statement is received

Organization	Development with possible archaeological implication
British Coal	Buildings/pipelines in area of coal mining
British Railways	–
Cadw	Development affecting a scheduled monument
Countryside Council for Wales	Development affecting a site of special scientific interest (SSSI)
English Heritage	Development affecting a scheduled monument
Health and Safety Executive	Development involving hazardous substances
Historic Scotland	Development affecting a scheduled monument
Local highway authority	Formation/alteration/improvement to certain roads and accesses
	Construction of certain highways
Local planning authority[1]	–
Ministry of Agriculture, Fisheries and Food	Certain non-agricultural development on agricultural land
National Rivers Authority	Fish farming, mining operations, use of land as cemetery
	Development at banks of rivers or streams or in river bed
Nature Conservancy Council	Development affecting SSSI
Nature Conservancy Council for Scotland	Development affecting SSSI
Sec. of State for Trade and Industry	Opencast coal mining
Sec. of State for the Environment	Development close to Royal palaces or parks
Sec. of State for Scotland	As applies to Secretary of State in England elsewhere in this table
Sec. of State for Transport	–
Sec. of State for Wales	As applies to Secretary of State in England elsewhere in this table
Theatres Trust	Development where there is a theatre
Waste disposal authority	Development close to land used for the deposit of waste

[1]This would be any other LPA for the same area (e.g. county council where application submitted to district council)

Preliminary discussion with the planning authority and statutory consultees, therefore, is very important. It would also be advisable to keep the planning authority informed if statutory consultees are approached early in the process. By letting the planning officer know what is happening it will keep him or her informed of the issues and how they are being tackled. It should also put the officer in a better position to explain to the planning committee what has happened and how the matters have been or will be dealt with.

Content of an environmental statement

Whilst there can be many matters needing attention in an environmental statement, how they are presented and how they might be affected will depend very much on what is proposed and the nature of the local environment. No two situations will be the same and the interaction of different factors will mean that statements will vary considerably in their content.

This scope for diversity has resulted in statements ranging enormously in quality from those which are scientifically suspect and sterile products hardly worth the paper they are written on, to those which positively assist in rational decision-making on important environmental matters (Clark, 1992). Part of the problem is that there is no prescribed way in which an environmental statement should be prepared. The only requirement is that it complies with the regulations which state that it must:

1. describe the development;
2. indicate the data used to identify and assess the main effects on the environment;
3. describe the likely significant effects;
4. describe the measures to avoid, reduce or remedy the environmental effects;
5. summarize the above in non-technical language.

These requirements, whilst broad in nature, do provide a guide for the preparation of a statement. A good starting point, however, is to ensure that all those involved know their responsibilities and duties in advance. It makes good sense to spell out the terms of reference to the consultants and later in the statement so that all concerned can see what is required of them and how the environmental matters to be investigated have been brought together. Where archaeology is involved this could include reference to the searching of records, whether a field evaluation is to be carried out and what this may involve in the way of boreholes, test trenches and so on. Reference should also be made to the procedure and timing of events in the preparation of the statement.

Where the statement has to refer to archaeological considerations one approach would be to incorporate relevant matters under the following headings:

1. Background data

As part of the background to a statement it would be useful to state, not just for the applicant and planning authority, but for third parties and consultees as well, sources of information. If a statement is to be assessed by an archaeologist it will be important to know where the information has come from so that the facts can be verified and conclusions drawn about the likely effect of the development on any archaeological remains.

Sources for this information could include the following:

- title deeds, site records and other information from the owner of the site concerning earlier operations or activities. Earlier landowners might be able to supply additional information;
- the SMR at the county council offices or elsewhere. These are likely to include old maps and records of antiquity, whether there had been any previous archaeological investigations at a site and what the findings, if any, were and aerial photographs;
- information from a local archaeological society or museum;
- information from a local archaeologist or historian who may have some specific local knowledge;
- published and other professional literature relating to the site or area.

An appendix listing sources of information and published references would give an indication of the thoroughness of the search.

2. Description of the development

Where the proposed development covers a large area of land, such as may be involved in mineral extraction or the construction of a motorway, it would be good practice to describe in detail those aspects of the development likely to have a direct bearing upon any known or anticipated archaeological remains.

At or in the vicinity of an archaeological site boreholes can provide information about the type of topsoil and subsoils (clay, gravel, limestone and their water contents etc.), which can then be used to assess the potential archaeological context. Depending on the water content it may also be possible to assess the degree of preservation of any remains. Soils can also be mapped to show the general overburden of textures and whether any change or erosion is apparent. This could signify a source for chemical analysis which might reveal important information.

If large amounts of earth have to be moved and finished levels of intended groundworks are known (even approximately) this can be used to assess the depth of excavation for the development. Coupled with detail of the subsoil, soil stripping, earth works, screening bunds and the exact positioning of any of these works, it could give an indication of the extent of destruction of any archaeological remains.

Design information about a development proposal including the size and position of buildings, access roads, landscaping and, of course, the extraction area, can also help to clarify the extent to which archaeological remains might be affected. Coupled with knowledge of existing ground conditions they could be used to work out not only the extent of any impact but also how best to minimize any such impact. The bringing together or analysis of these two sets of information might show where the development should be positioned or located so as to avoid or reduce any destruction. Later, when the mitigating steps to minimize the affects on the environment have to be stated, the earlier reporting of this relevant information would provide conclusive information. The statement would be more thorough.

3. Planning background

In the same way that detail of a proposed development will be essential background material for an assessment, so the planning situation can be important, especially for third parties. By including the planning policies relevant to a development proposal in the statement the assessors can weigh up the arguments for and against different migrating steps. If other background information about where the policies are to be found and the date of approval of the relevant plan (there can be more than one) are included then it can show to the developer, the planning authority and others how far the developer should proceed with these steps.

4. Archaeological constraints

Background archaeological data will give an indication of where archaeological remains are to be found and what to expect. The bulk of this information will relate to land within the proposed development area but it would also be worth looking in the vicinity of a site. If nearby features such as crop marks, burial mounds, linear features (e.g. ditches), earthworks or monuments and other specified remains and sites are carefully classified and shown on a plan (preferably with grid references) this can provide an overall picture of the archaeology of a site and its surroundings and enable the relative importance of a site or area to be assessed. If this is followed by a wider assessment it might be possible to compare the representation of the archaeological potential and importance of a site within this wider context. It could, for example, show that some historical periods are under-represented and others over-represented. Alternatively, it might show that a proposed development will result in the destruction of relatively unimportant archaeological remains. This wider knowledge could also be used to evaluate alternative sites for buildings or different alignments for other structures or engineering works. It could show how minor alterations might save something important and avoid unnecessary destruction. More controversially it could perhaps be used to show that a development project as proposed, whilst causing some damage, will cause less harm to archaeological interests within the area as a whole. It might be the most appropriate location compared with all possible alternatives.

5. Assessment of the effects

It has been said that archaeological remains occur, on average, once every 4 hectares. Of course, they do not occur at such regularity and there are wide differences in the frequency of archaeological sites. It is pertinent, however, to realize that on a very large development site there is a chance that archaeological remains could lie in the direct path of a proposed development and occur in more than one area. If a site is not thoroughly investigated for remains throughout its area after remains are found in one part of it, disastrous consequences could follow. A wider investigation is generally advisable.

In any assessment of the effects, consideration should be given to monitoring, the siting of waste material, planting proposals and design:

- **Monitoring the effects**

  Where operations involve the removal of deposits by extraction, trenching, stripping or channel cutting, a system of monitoring can be of benefit to all concerned. If referred to in the statement it lets the parties know how environmental effects are to be assessed – a matter which could be of substantial importance at large sites or those which are waterlogged or under water. A monitoring programme should also be considered in respect of off-site works such as the diversion of watercourses and the provision of infrastructure.

- **The stacking of material**

  If operations involve the stacking of material, such as topsoil from a site or the storing of building materials, care should be taken to ensure that they do not have a damaging effect and destroy any archaeological remains lying near the surface. The weight from extra material, which could be many tons, could have a substantial impact.

- **Planting**

  Tree and shrub planting can affect archaeological material. If a landscaping scheme is proposed, perhaps to soften the impact of a development project, operations associated with their planting such as earth-moulding and, later, growing root systems, can all involve further damage or destruction of archaeological material in the immediate vicinity. Consideration should be given to any possible adverse impact this might have.

- **Design**

  Elements of a development design can adversely affect archaeological material. If ground levels are to be substantially lowered, as in the case of mineral extraction and to a lesser extent at sloping sites, it could interfere with the local water table and threaten organic archaeological material by de-watering. Diverting watercourses or the pumping out of water from development sites could have a similar effect. They could be relevant to the assessment and their possible effects may have to be considered.

6. Measures designed to minimize adverse effects

If planning policies indicate that archaeological sites are to be protected and an assessment of the effects of development reveal that remains could be adversely affected, it will be necessary to examine how those effects might be minimized. There are several possibilities.

First, the siting of the proposed development should be carefully considered. What are the parameters governing location and what alternatives are available or possible? Do remains indicate that the proposed building works ought to be repositioned and what effect will any relocation have on the development? Alternatively if constraints dictate that other locations are impracticable would it be feasible to design a project around archaeological remains? Can the shape of the structure or foundations be such as to avoid destruction?

Questions like these need to be asked where important remains are known to exist. If any possible effects on an archaeological site are to be minimized, siting and design become fundamental to resolving any conflict. They could strike at the heart of a development project but if considered early enough in the development process it may be possible to devise a scheme that is acceptable to all parties.

Equally important for archaeology are matters of detail once a particular design or location has been chosen. Mitigating measures may still be necessary to ensure protection of the resource. Where to stack topsoil and project materials, the type and extent of any landscaping scheme, the possible effects of earth-mounding, the siting of car parks and roads and the construction of sewers, land drains and other underground services all become important. Mitigation may require a detailed recording being made of the archaeological resource.

7. Non-technical summary

The summary must be such that the ordinary layperson can understand what is involved without being confused by technical jargon and unnecessary detail. It is a requirement that any person must be able to make sense of anticipated adverse effects, in our case on archaeology, and of the actions proposed to remove or minimize those adverse effects.

9.6 SUBMISSION AND HANDLING OF A STATEMENT

As most development projects will be subject to planning controls the appropriate time to submit an environmental statement will be at the same time as the planning application. In the cases where planning permission is not required the timing of the submission will depend on the requirements of the individual government department or public agency concerned, which should be consulted as early as possible.

In connection with planning applications a difficulty can arise when the applicant is not the owner of the application site and where only the principle of development is being sought. In this situation an outline application which identifies the site and what is proposed would be the most appropriate application but the problem is that an environmental statement, where it is deemed necessary, will still have to be submitted.

This means that the applicant will have to consider more than just the principle of developing the site. If there are likely to be significant effects on the environment thought will have to be given to those effects and how they might be minimized. They could have an important bearing on how the outline application is determined and on the matters that an authority may wish to reserve by condition.

Where a full application is submitted the matter will normally be more straightforward. Full details of the proposed development and the likely effects on the environment would be considered at the same time. Note too that all applications in England and Wales will be publicized by the local planning authority. As a result of changes made to the General Development Order by the Town and Country Planning General Development (Amendment) (No. 4) Order 1992, it is the responsibility of the local planning authority to see that applications subject to environmental assessment are given adequate publicity. Where an environmental assessment is required this publicity must include a notice displayed at or near the site of the proposed development and a notice in a local newspaper. This is the minimum legal requirement. Some authorities may go further and extend the consultation process to people who live in the vicinity.

In addition, the planning authority will also have to notify statutory consultees of the application and invite them to comment on the environmental statement. If the applicant has already done this the authority does not have to repeat the exercise although in practice it is likely to do so, if only to let the consultees know when the application is received and at what stage they are in the decision-making process. It may also want to ensure that there has been no change of circumstances.

Where the authority considers the information contained in an environmental statement to be insufficient, it can require further information to be submitted. It could also seek to discuss a proposal with the applicant, particularly if the statement does not fully address matters which have been raised subsequently by consultees.

Once outstanding matters have been resolved the planning authority will proceed to determine the planning application. It will not determine the environmental statement which, in effect, is supplementary information to the planning application. It is used simply to help come to a decision on the application.

9.7 THE PROSPECTS FOR CHANGE

Finally, a few words about change. One of the growing criticisms of current environmental assessment practice is that it pays insufficient attention to the environment. Since its introduction in Britain in 1988 a number of weaknesses have appeared in the operation and purpose of environmental assessment which suggest that things may change.

The first of these weaknesses is that environmental assessment, by focusing on the impact of individual projects, cannot address the strategic environmental questions concerning overall environmental policy and its implementation. The existing system merely allows local planning authorities to react to each development proposal separately from all others. It does not allow them to anticipate what could happen nor to concentrate on the cumulative and secondary effects on the environment. Despite the change of name from environmental impact assessment, environmental assessment appears to concentrate on the impact of development projects. Without a strategic or anticipatory input a more positive approach to the environment cannot be made. Similarly it makes it difficult to consider or give scope to mitigation measures linked to the objectives of sustainability.

A second weakness concerns the quality of environmental assessment and particularly the quality of environmental statements in Britain. A research study prepared by Wood and Jones (1991) for the DoE highlighted, among other things, a number of problems concerning the quality of environmental statements, stating that they were very variable in quality with many being poor and unsuitable. The study showed that there was no uniform pattern to the statements and that they ranged from very good to totally inadequate. In another report (Clark, 1992) many are stated as being 'no more than a collection of information on individual topics – air, water, noise, ecological and social impacts – shoved between glossy covers and masquerading as scientifically valid investigation.'

At the other extreme some statements contain more than what is needed to satisfy the regulations, although even here commentators have argued that very few allow proper comparisons to be made between disparate factors (Johnston, 1992). There is a tendency, possibly due to lack of co-ordination, not to make predictions thereby making it difficult for decision-makers to make informed choices. The arguments suggest that in addition to a lack of overall assessment of the effects on the environment, there is also a lack of attention paid to the detail of some statements.

This lack of attention, where it occurs, leads to a third weakness that has been identified, which focuses on the role of the local planning authority. We have already seen that many planning officers lack sufficient technical expertise and are unable to critically assess statements submitted with planning applications. What this reveals is a problem in knowing how to proceed. Some planning authorities have found it difficult to deal with the technicalities of environmental statements whilst others have sought to negotiate with developers to obtain further information. This has sometimes resulted in improvements to statements and improvements to development proposals, but more importantly, with varying degrees of success. A lack of consistency exists because few authorities are in a position properly to deal with the situation.

Time constraints imposed by the regulations can add to this difficulty. With only three weeks to ask for an environmental statement, when one has not been submitted with a planning application, it is perhaps not surprising that difficulties occur. What is less surprising is that, given these difficulties and lack of knowledge, change towards a more thorough approach seems almost inevitable.

One area of change that is already emerging is the involvement of the public. A principal aim of environmental assessment is to ensure that the concerns of the public are properly addressed: in so doing it has strengthened the position of third parties. It has also provided the public with a new basis for consultation, which in turn has led to increased demands for protection of the environment. The actions of protestors to the extension of the M3 motorway at Twyford Down is one well-known example of these increasing demands.

What these actions show is that it is up to the planners to decide what is necessary but that their decisions can be based on inadequate information or an inability to adequately appreciate the circumstances or information that is presented. Decisions will inevitably continue to be challenged in the courts and lead to increasing demands and responses for more attention to be paid to the environmental effects of development proposals. This may include the effects on archaeology.

These weaknesses are one reason why change is likely. Another is the increasing concern expressed about the environment, stemming, not least, from the Earth Summit held in Rio de Janiero in June 1992. Heralded as the most important global meeting in history and attended by delegates from 178 nations and 116 heads of government, it focused on a great many issues including the interaction between the environment and economic activity, protection of the world's forests, biological diversity, climate changes, toxic wastes, unsustainable consumption and exponential population growth. Whilst going far beyond the realms of archaeology the summit raised issues that go far beyond current environmental assessment practices in Britain. They suggest that assessments in the future will become more thorough and more far reaching than at present. The question is, how will this affect the development process and what are the implications for archaeology?

These questions are difficult to answer because they rely on a great number of variables, not all of which can be predicted with any confidence. Politics, vested interests, natural disasters, a need for economic growth and other factors will all have an impact and a part to play. There are, however, two things which will probably emerge over the next few years. The first is that environmental assessment will become more strategic in nature, concentrating on the wider policy implications of human activity and development projects. We should expect to see greater attention paid to monitoring and possible alternatives and how they might be implemented. Archaeology could become more important. Second, as the scope of assessment widens, so we can expect to see more attention paid to pro-environment pressure, that is, the interaction between people and other living things and their environment. Archaeology may or may not form part of this environmental concern.

REFERENCES

Clark, B. (1992) A varied pattern in response, in *Environmental Assessment and Audit: A User's Guide 1992–1993*, Ambit Publications, Gloucester.

Council of the European Communities (1985) Directive 85/337/EEC *On the Assessment of the Effects of Certain Public and Private Projects on the Environment.*

Crown Estates Commissioners (1988) *Environmental Assessment of Marine Salmon Farms*, Crown Estates Office, Edinburgh.

Department of the Environment (1988) Circular 15/88 *Environmental Assessment*, HMSO, London.

Forestry Commission (1988) *Environmental Assessment of Afforestation Projects*, Forestry Commission, Edinburgh.

Johnston, B. (ed.) (1992) *Environmental Assessment and Audit. A User's Guide 1992–1993*, Ambit Publications, Gloucester.

Wood, C. and Jones, C. (1991) *Monitoring Environmental Assessment and Planning*, HMSO, London.

FURTHER READING

Clark, B. (1988) Environmental impact assessment: on the eve of legal proceedings. *The Planner*, February, Volume 74, No. 2, London.

Coles, T.F. and Tarling, J.P. (1991) *Environmental Assessment: Experience to Date*, Institution of Environmental Assessment, Horncastle.

College of Estate Management (1992) A CPD Study Pack on *Green Issues including Environmental Impact Assessment*, College of Estate Management, Reading.

Department of the Environment (1988), Circular 24/88 *Environmental Assessment of Projects in Simplified Planning Zones and Enterprise Zones*, HMSO, London.

Department of the Environment (1989) *Environmental Assessment: A Guide to the Procedures*, HMSO, London.

Department of the Environment (1991) *Policy Appraisal and the Environment*, HMSO, London.

Essex Planning Officers' Association (1993) *The Essex Guide to Environmental Assessment*, Essex County Council, Chelmsford.

HM Government (1990) *This Common Inheritance: Britain's Environmental Strategy*, HMSO, London.

HM Government (1992) *This Common Inheritance: 2nd Year Report*, HMSO, London.

Lee, N. (1992) Improving quality in the assessment process, in *Environmental Assessment and Audit: a User's Guide 1992–1993*, Ambit Publications, Gloucester.

Lichfield, N. (1989) Environmental assessment. *Journal of Planning and Environmental Law*, Occasional Paper No. 16, September, 1989.

Slater, J.R. (1992) Environmental assessment: the challenge from Brussels. *Journal of Planning and Environment Law*, London.

Therivel, R., Glasson, J. and Wilson, E. (1992) Sea change puts assessment on a higher and earlier plane, in *Environmental Assessment and Audit: a User's Guide 1992–1993*, Ambit Publications, Gloucester.

The determination of development proposals $\boxed{\textbf{10}}$

Before a development project can proceed it will need permission. In most cases this will involve the need for planning permission although other consents may also be required. Approval under the building regulations, scheduled monument consent, conservation area consent or listed building consent could all be required. Each will be concerned about different aspects of a proposal.

Building regulations will be concerned with the safety of a structure and the health and safety of its occupants. There will be a concern about foundations but this will not be directly related to archaeology. It will simply be a concern that foundations are adequate to support the required load. Scheduled monument consent, as we have seen, is designed to protect nationally important monuments and listed building and conservation area consent relate to the character and appearance of historic buildings and areas.

As far as threats to archaeological remains from development are concerned the most important and most significant decision-making process is that relating to planning applications. How they are determined, the factors likely to be taken into account and the weight to be given to them are what is important. How conditions are used and the implications arising from them also need to be understood together with the vexed problem of planning gain, or planning obligations as it is officially called. These and the appeal process form the main topics of concern in this Chapter.

10.1 MATTERS TO BE TAKEN INTO ACCOUNT

When determining a planning application the local planning authority is required by Section 70 of the 1990 Act (Section 26 of the Scottish Act) to have regard to just two factors, namely the development plan, in so far as it is relevant to an application, and any other material consideration. The legislation requires nothing else but when these two factors are applied we find that it is not easy. Both have complications which can affect the final decision.

The development plan

The development plan is now the most important factor in the determination of planning applications. The principal planning Acts, as amended by the Planning and Compensation Act 1991, state:

> where, in making any determination under the planning Acts, regard is to be had to the development plan, the determination shall be made in accordance with that plan unless material considerations indicate otherwise.
>
> *Section 54A, England & Wales*
> *Section 18A, Scotland*

This sounds fairly innocuous but is nevertheless very significant. It signifies a presumption in favour of development which accords with planning policy and a presumption against if it does not. A key opt-out clause nevertheless remains. The other material considerations could outweigh and overrule the development plan, particularly if it is out of date.

Planning policy, therefore, provides the essential framework for decision-making although in practice it is not that simple. Many areas lack detailed planning policy, making it difficult to know what the outcome for an individual project will be. Whilst structure plans have all been approved these, as we saw in Chapter 8, provide only a broad picture of what will be acceptable. They indicate in general terms the amount of development to be allowed and the main principles to be applied. For archaeology they tend to be aimed at protection without being specific.

The lack of policy is at the local or detailed level. Many urban and rural areas do not at the present time have local plan coverage, although this will improve substantially over the next five years as government requirements which statutorily require local plans to be in place take effect. In such areas we may find that authorities make use of supplementary guidance – a development brief for example – to fill part of the policy gap. This, however, does not carry the same weight as the development plan. It is simply one of the other material considerations to be taken into account.

Other material considerations

Every single matter that is not in the development plan but which is relevant to planning can be classed as any other **material consideration**. The term, however, is not defined in any way and interpretations differ as to what should or should not be included. Not surprisingly it has often led to arguments and litigation and, with the lack of a development plan in many areas, this has often added to the difficulty.

As a result of this lack of policy, attention has turned to government guidance and other relevant sources. PPG 16 is particularly important, especially when it states that: 'The desirability of preserving a monument is a material planning consideration.' (Para. 18).

This is the clearest statement of all about the role of archaeology in the planning process but it is only part of the answer. Whilst it informs us that archaeology is a relevant factor it does not tell us what weight to attach to it.

But then how can it? With decision-making fundamentally devolved to the local level and where flexibility is built into the planning system this is hardly surprising. And yet, lack of guidance can and does prove difficult for planning authorities. It means that greater reliance has to be placed on factors which may or may not be relevant. Even among planning officers there are differences of opinion. For others it is often more difficult. In some areas developers are required to pay significant attention to archaeology but in others very little or none at all. Much depends on where they wish to develop and which authority they have to deal with. There is no overall consistency.

Another important point about PPG 16 is its relative newness. Having opened the case for archaeology in the planning process it would appear that its impact will be increasingly recognized. Indeed, objections on archaeological grounds have became more common relating to a number of factors, including the following:

1. that development will destroy known archaeological remains;
2. that it will result in the destruction of as yet unknown remains which should be investigated;
3. that the development provides insufficient protection to the archaeological resource of a site;
4. that insufficient time has been allowed to investigate a site;
5. that inadequate resources have been provided to enable a proper archaeological investigation to be undertaken.

What these and other objections highlight is a number of archaeological considerations that can be relevant in the consideration of a planning application. But there are many other factors which a planning authority will have to consider, as Cook J in *Stringer v. Minister for Housing and Local Government* (1971) has stated:

> In principle . . . any consideration which relates to the use and development of land is capable of being a material consideration.

From such a wide interpretation it is clear that the range of matters will be great. Indeed it is not possible to provide a complete list although the following are considered to be the more important ones:

- siting and design;
- density, mass and height of buildings;
- means of access;
- attraction of vehicles and traffic generation;
- highway safety;
- effects on surrounding property;
- residential amenity (for new and existing occupiers);
- visual intrusion;
- character of the area (important in a conservation area);
- noise;
- character of a listed building;
- landscaping and open space;
- protection of trees;

- green belt;
- quality of agricultural land;
- protection of open countryside;
- protection of nature reserves, sites of special scientific interest, etc.;
- sites of archaeological importance;
- drainage and flooding implications;
- adequate supply of housing;
- planning history of a site;
- planning policy for a site (other than in the development plan);
- government policies;
- the need for economic regeneration;
- the creation of jobs.

It is emphasized that this list is not conclusive nor in any order of priority but indicative of the issues that can apply. Those relevant to a particular application would have to be extracted from the list.

10.2 WEIGHTING OF THE FACTORS

The question of how much weight to attach to different planning considerations when trying to decide how to determine a planning application is not an easy one to answer. Many issues can arise concerning the number and range of matters that are present, the importance the planning authority attaches to each factor and the way in which a balance may be struck between competing or conflicting objectives. Yet if we are to get a better understanding of the way decisions are made we need to look at these matters.

One way is to start by breaking them down into the main areas of concern relating to the importance of the development plan, the importance of the archaeological resource, the need for development and the details of the development.

The contents and importance of the development plan

For land uses such as housing, retailing, industrial, commercial and recreational use the development plan will contain policies directly relevant to that use. They are likely to relate to:

- the importance of the use in a particular locality;
- the amount of land required for that use;
- the locations where it will be acceptable;
- the type of areas where it will be unacceptable;
- the criteria by which to judge the proposal.

Less common uses tend to be judged against environmental standards aimed at safeguarding the character of the area, residential amenity and so on. Similarly some areas will be more sensitive to change than others and will accordingly be afforded greater protection. National parks, areas of outstanding natural beauty, conservation areas and ancient monuments are examples which fall into this category. They will be special in their respective ways and this will be recognized in the development plans.

The problem, however, is that this importance will be given different recognition by different authorities. Some will attach great weight to the development plan, others less so, each according to environmental, social, economic and other local considerations. The type of area, the thoroughness of the development plan, the characteristics of the local population, 'nimbyism', the year when the plan was approved, changes since then and many other factors will all influence the degree to which authorities will rely on their development plans. The flexibility works both ways.

The importance of the archaeological resource

A key factor in deciding what to do with any archaeological remains at a site will be its archaeological importance and its likely contribution to the advancement of knowledge. This highlights the need for prior evaluation although this may not always be available. For most applications it will not be relevant and the difficulty for some authorities could be in deciding when to require one. If areas are identified as being of archaeological importance we would not expect any problem – an evaluation would have to be submitted – but elsewhere the planning authority might be less sure and have to rely on external advice such as from the county archaeological officer.

Various factors should be considered. The likely significance of a site, investigations in the area (if any), the depth of remains, the time-scale involved for investigation and whether an excavation is thought necessary or desirable. Knowledge of these and related matters would be of assistance to the planning authority before making a decision.

The need for development at a particular site or location

Some types of developments have little choice in where they can be located. Minerals and water related activities are good examples where the scope for resiting will be limited. Communication links and pipelines can also present problems although if a strategic overview is taken it may be possible to position routes such as motorways and trunk roads in a way that will avoid many, if not all, archaeological remains. On the other hand, it may be cheaper to carry out an excavation and then carve through a site rather than pick another alignment; not necessarily a satisfactory solution, but one that nevertheless appears to be adopted from time to time.

Other developments will not be so limited in where they can go. Offices, shops, dwellings and other uses can generally be located in a number of places although these will not all carry the same benefits. Location, as we shall see in Chapter 15, is a key determinant in the viability of a project and can make all the difference between profit and loss. This, of course, will not be significant as far as the planning authority is concerned but the suitability of a site for a particular use, taking into account local policies and the character of the area, will be very important to the developer. The need for development will have to be judged against local policies and other land use considerations including archaeology.

Different viewpoints about the suitability of a site often stem from a difference between public and private interests. Local need, sustainability, the need (or lack of) for development in a particular area must be balanced against private motives concerned with profit and loss, ownership and land availability. Negotiations may centre on location, re-routeing, the principle of developing a site or the details of what is proposed.

Details of the development

Apart from other planning concerns the planning authority, when it comes to archaeology, will want to know what impact a project is likely to have. Where archaeological remains are known to exist and an evaluation has been submitted it should be possible to ascertain this. The proposals would normally show how the project has been designed to minimize any impact or damage from which a reasoned judgement can be made. Other things being equal, either the development is acceptable and can proceed or it will need to be regulated by condition. This could require an excavation or merely a watching brief.

Where an evaluation has not been submitted and a site is thought to be archaeologically important the planning authority may wish to receive more information before coming to a decision. Obtained from an independent source such as the county archaeologist or from the applicant who may wish to appoint an archaeological consultant, the information would indicate what ought to be done and may suggest ways of amending a project. The planning authority could require this on the grounds that archaeology is an important material consideration.

In this situation discussion will again focus on the issues important to the parties concerned relating to the likely extent of destruction, how potential damage can be reduced, and the feasibility and practicability of making amendments. The nature and importance of a site and whether it is in a conservation area or a sensitive part of the countryside will also be important considerations likely to influence the planning officers recommendation. The extent of this influence will depend on all of these factors measured against all other material considerations. They may tip the balance towards approval or refusal but unfortunately there is no easy way of knowing in advance. There is no simple technique and the final weighting of the factors will be based on information, experience and judgement.

10.3 WHO MAKES THE DECISION

Planning authorities normally delegate their functions to committees and officers of the authority. With planning applications it is usual for a planning committee to have full delegated powers to determine all applications. Sometimes this committee may itself delegate some of its powers, either to a subcommittee, or area committee, or to the chief planning officer. A subcommittee would tend to deal with certain types of development proposals or report on major schemes. An area committee would tend to deal with all applications for development within part of the authority's area.

Delegation to the planning officer is normally undertaken where there are no objections to a proposal or where there is a prescribed list of uncontentious matters which he or she is authorized to deal with. Examples of these would relate to house extensions and minor changes of use.

Where authority is delegated the decision of the committee, subcommittee, area committee or officer is the decision of the authority. It is not possible to delegate decisions to an individual member of an authority although the chair of a planning committee may sit in with the chief planning officer to inspect applications delegated to the chief officer. Where archaeology is concerned the majority of decisions are likely to be taken by the planning committee, although where matters are not contentious the chief officer might be delegated to prescribe, say, a watching brief.

Each authority can devise its own system of delegation as it thinks appropriate. Where councillors are making the decision they would normally be advised by the planning officer, who would point out the matters considered relevant to an application and the weight to be given to those matters. It would then be up to the committee to decide how to determine the application. They do not have to accept the officer's advice although they would have to show good planning reasons for not doing so. If they decide to refuse permission the reasons must be stated on the decision notice. If the decision is to approve an application it is likely that conditions would be attached to reflect concern over certain aspects of a proposal, depending on what is proposed and where it is located.

An outline of the planning application process is shown in Figure 10.1. This highlights the basic procedures applicable to all applications for planning permission with the decision-making options open to the authority and the applicant shown at the bottom. A more detailed chart which brings in archaeological considerations is shown in Figure 10.2. What these figures do not show is the influences that may bear on councillors where local politics will be a major factor. In some cases this can also have an impact on the planning officers' views, which again highlights the importance of early consultation.

10.4 TYPES OF DECISION

The planning Acts state that a planning authority can do one of three things when determining a planning application. It can either grant permission unconditionally, grant it with conditions or refuse planning permission. In addition there are two other things that an authority might do although both are infrequent. One is to fail to determine an application and the other is to seek some form of planning gain. It is the latter which has important implications for archaeology.

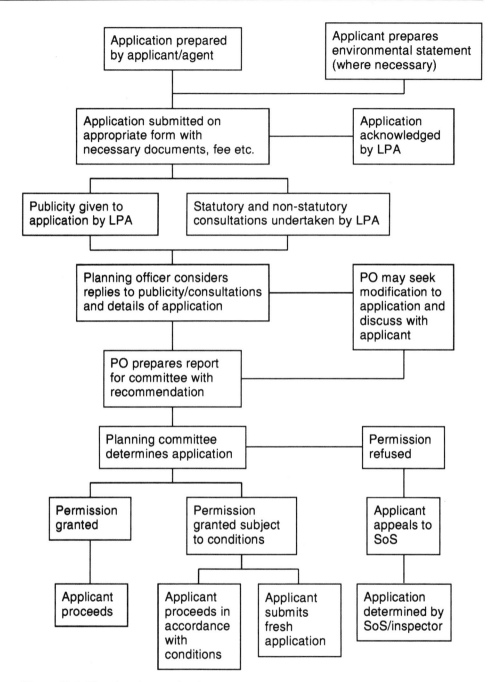

Figure 10.1 The planning application process.

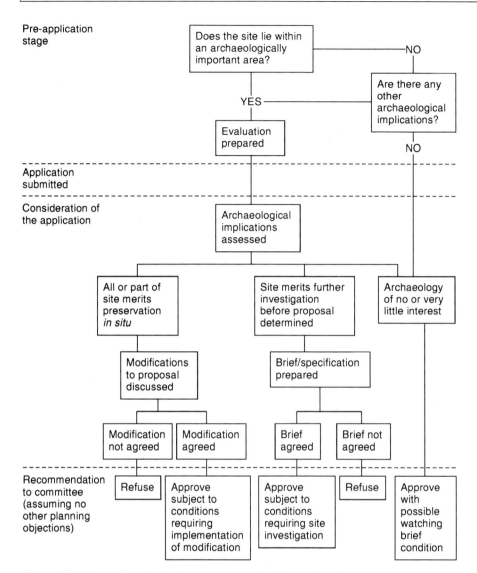

Figure 10.2 An archaeological response to planning applications.

10.5 THE USE OF CONDITIONS

Under Section 70 of the Act (Section 26 in Scotland) authorities and the Secretaries of State have wide powers to impose 'such conditions as they think fit'. In addition they may specifically attach conditions:

1. to regulate the development of land under the control of an applicant even if it lies outside an application site;
2. require the removal of buildings or works authorized by a planning permission at the end of specified period;
3. require development approved by a planning permission to be commenced not later than a specified date.

These statutory requirements have been interpreted in different ways. A local planning authority cannot do just as it pleases despite the above. Conditions which are thought to be fit must fulfil a planning purpose. They must fairly and reasonably relate to the proposed development and planning authorities cannot use their planning powers for some ulterior motive. This is irrespective of how desirable that motive may be.

If an authority makes a mistake or misuses its power the legality of a decision can be challenged in court. Indeed this has happened on many occasions to the extent that the House of Lords, in the case of *Newbury District Council v. Secretary of State for the Environment* (1980), set down four broad principles on the use of conditions, namely:

- a condition must not be so totally unreasonable that no reasonable authority would impose it;
- it must relate to the permitted development;
- it must serve a planning purpose and not some other ulterior motive;
- it must not be uncertain as to meaning.

Government Circular 1/85 on the use of conditions (the Scottish equivalent is SDD Circular 18/86) sets out further guidance. It states that conditions should only be imposed where they are:

1. **Necessary**. When considering the need for a condition the authority should ask itself if the permission should be refused if the condition is not attached. If not, then clear and precise justification for the condition becomes necessary.
2. **Relevant to planning**. Any condition which is not relevant to planning is *ultra vires*. If a condition is considered desirable but is not a planning matter it should not be imposed on a planning permission.
3. **Relevant to the development to be permitted**. It is not sufficient that a condition must relate to planning: it must also relate to the development that is proposed. It can be applied in a negative way to prevent certain things from happening at a site and it can apply to other land under the control of an applicant provided it is relevant to the development.
4. **Enforceable**. A condition should not be imposed if there is no way of enforcing it. If it is poorly worded and vague in content so that a different interpretation can reasonably be applied to its meaning then it should not be used.
5. **Precise**. It is necessary for an applicant to be able to ascertain how to comply with a condition. One which states that a site 'shall be kept in a tidy state' will not provide sufficient clarity and would not be suitable.
6. **Reasonable**. It is insufficient for a condition to meet the above requirements. In addition it must be reasonable and not unduly restrictive. It would be unreasonable, for instance, to impose a condition which could only be complied with by a third party and not by the developer. Similarly an unreasonable condition cannot become reasonable simply because an applicant agrees to it.

This guidance shows that conditions can allow development proposals to proceed which might otherwise be refused permission. It also shows that the careful use of conditions can make an unacceptable proposal acceptable. When applied to archaeology it means that development can be accepted if conditions relating to archaeology are imposed. It all depends on what those conditions are and what is proposed.

Conditions relating to archaeology

With archaeology recognized as a material planning consideration we can reasonably expect to see archaeological conditions attached to planning permissions when the need arises. What they require will depend on the prevailing circumstances where the issues could include the following:

- a requirement for an investigation to establish (as far as possible) the archaeological importance of a site;
- the setting of a time period for such investigation;
- the phasing of development to allow a more thorough investigation on part of a site;
- the protection of remains or part(s) of a site during the construction period;
- the siting and design of a project incuding foundation design in order to safeguard the archaeological resource following an investigation.

The above list is indicative of the types of issues that may be involved. How they are implemented will depend on the type of application that is submitted and the importance of the archaeological resource.

Development proposals submitted in outline

Where an applicant does not own a site or where there is uncertainty about obtaining planning permission, the planning Acts make provision for the submission of an **outline application**. Instead of submitting full details of what is proposed the planning Acts allow an applicant to apply solely for the principle of developing a site. All that is needed is a description of what is proposed and its location. Usually this would be shown on an Ordnance Survey map with the application site shown edged red.

If the planning authority is of the opinion that more information should be supplied it can ask for further details to be submitted. When it deems this necessary, and has written to say so, it can decline to entertain an application if these details are not forthcoming.

When the principle of developing a site is acceptable to an authority detailed information would be reserved by condition. Frequently the following standard condition is used:

> C1 No development shall take place without the prior written approval of the local planning authority of all details of the siting, design and external appearance of each building including a schedule of external materials to be used; the means of access thereto and the landscaping of the site.

The aim of this condition is to check detailed proposals against planning standards and planning criteria. This would enable siting and design to be judged, amongst other things, against known or anticipated archaeological remains. In addition an authority, if it thought that archaeological deposits could reasonably be expected to exist, might impose conditions specifically asking for:

1. an archaeological evaluation:

> C2 No development shall take place until a scheme specifying the methods of recording or preserving any archaeological deposits which may be affected by the approved works and including a timetable for such recording has been submitted and approved in writing by the local planning authority. The development shall be carried out in accordance with the agreed scheme.

2. for details of foundations to be submitted for approval:

> C3 the drawings required by (*standard outline condition as in C1 above*) shall include details of the foundations of the proposed (buildings/structures) hereby approved.

Often, but not always, planning authorities will impose a condition requiring compliance with the details such as in the following:

> C4 The development hereby permitted shall only be carried out in accordance with plans, drawings and particulars which shall have been approved by the local planning authority before the development is commenced and which define (*the details of the siting and type of foundations to be used*) (*the layout of the development including the siting of buildings, roads, paved areas, drains and other underground services*).

Detailed applications

Detailed planning applications can be either full applications when all relevant information about a proposal is submitted for consideration, or **reserved matters** applications when all or part of the details reserved by an outline permission are submitted for approval. In either situation several possibilities exist regarding the imposition of conditions, depending largely on the relative importance of the archaeological remains at a site.

Sites of little archaeological importance

Where remains are thought to be unimportant or where they are known to be unimportant, conditions will probably emphasize the need for a watching brief and no more. In this situation the following or similar conditions can be expected:

> C5 Before any works of excavation (*for building foundations*), setting out or any other associated works take place the (*name of archaeological organization to carry out watching brief*) are to be formally notified. *Westminster City Council*

C6 A nominated archaeologist from (*name of organization*) shall be afforded access to the development site at all reasonable times to conduct a watching brief to observe and record items of archaeological interest.

Occasionally the requirement may be more specific particularly in respect of giving advance notice of works. The following example has been used in York:

C7 The applicant shall
a) give a minimum of two weeks notice in writing of the commencement of works to the local planning authority and no works shall commence on site until the two weeks notice period has expired; and
b) shall afford access to an archaeologist or representative of an archaeological organization nominated by the local planning authority at all reasonable times and allow the archaeologist to observe the groundworks and record items of interest and finds.

A condition which requires work to be held up while an archaeological investigation takes place should not be imposed even if a developer is willing to support it.

Sites of archaeological importance but not of national importance

Many archaeological sites will fall into ths category and because of the recognized importance of archaeology in the planning process it is increasingly likely that a planning authority will ask for an archaeological evaluation from an applicant. In some cases this will have been submitted with the corresponding planning application indicating the likely or anticipated nature, position and importance of the archaeological resource at the site. It would have been used to assess the importance of the remains and to judge the extent of destruction by the proposed development. From this an assessment would be made as to whether the development should be altered to safeguard more of the archaeological resource or whether the destruction, as proposed, can go ahead.

If the planning authority decides that destruction is acceptable it is possible that some form of archaeological excavation will be required depending on the perceived importance of the remains. Subsequent recording of any remains might also be required with a condition aimed at prohibiting development until such time as an investigation had been carried out. The model condition set out by the government states:

C8 No development shall take place within the area indicated (*this would be the area of archaeological interest*) until the applicant has secured the implementation of a programme of archaeological work in accordance with a written schedule of investigations which has been submitted by the applicant and approved in writing by the local planning authority.

Any programme of archaeological works would include, as necessary, details of the areas and depth of excavation, a timetable of works and the duration of the investigation. There may also be information about how the site and remains are to be recorded, conserved and subsequently made available for publication.

If the development is to be amended to protect the resource there would normally be little point in requiring an archaeological investigation. The purpose would be to preserve what lies beneath the ground and any conditions would be aimed at ensuring that the development proceeds in accordance with amended drawings. Conditions such as the following might be appropriate:

C9 The (*enter description of development*) shall be carried out in accordance with the revised drawings (*enter drawing number if applicable*) submitted to the local planning authority on (*enter date*) and illustrating (*enter details of changes*).

C10 The foundations to be used to support the building shall be constructed in accordance with the details as shown in the submitted drawings (*dates and drawing numbers to be included*) and no variation to the details of these foundations shall take place except as necessary to preserve archaeological remains and as may be agreed in writing by the local planning authority.

Where details of foundations have not been agreed but are required to be altered the following condition, or words to its effect, might be used:

C11 No development shall take place until a detailed scheme for foundation design and all new groundworks has been submitted to and approved in writing by the local planning authority and that scheme will be monitored by the council.

Nationally important archaeological sites

Most nationally important sites will be included in a schedule of monuments, but as the schedule is subject to review, we can expect some sites to be of national importance but not scheduled. However, whether such sites are scheduled or not, the presumption will be one of preservation *in situ*. This means, in the main, that restrictions would be imposed on development proposals either by refusing planning permission or by allowing development whilst ensuring that it has no or minimal adverse effects on any archaeological remains. Conditions in line with (C6), (C9) and (C10) above can be expected. In addition futher protective conditions may be attached. Examples are:

C12 No development shall take place until fencing has been erected, in a manner to be agreed with the local planning authority, about (*insert name of monument*); and no works shall take place within the area inside that fencing without the consent of the local planning authority. *Para. 37, Appendix A, Circular 1/85 and Para. 31, PAN, SOEnD*

C13 The scheduled (*or unscheduled*) section of (*name of monument*) lying within the application site and outlined in red on the plan attached to this decision notice, shall remain intact and undisturbed by the development hereby approved.

Occasionally, circumstances may warrant the investigation of a site. If the case for development is overwhelming and destruction of all or part of any archaeological deposits is inevitable it is likely that an authority will grant consent subject to a condition requiring a detailed excavation to be undertaken. It is even possible for an authority to require details of foundations and other groundworks to be approved prior to the commencement of development. The reason for such a condition would ostensibly be to preserve the archaeological remains, an impossibility in the circumstances. If the remains are to be destroyed why amend the proposals?

A counter-argument might be that any excavation would itself lead to destruction and that the presumption in favour of presevation should prevail. This, however, will not always be appropriate. There will be occasions when circumstances dictate otherwise. Furthermore there can be benefits from excavation especially if it leads to the advancement of archaeological knowledge. If consent is granted subject to a requirement that a full and thorough excavation be carried out prior to development commencing this may well be preferable. Certainly this is what some authorities may think where conditions such as the following could be expected:

C14 A full archaeological excavation of the application site (*this would relate to the whole of the archaeological area affected by the development*) shall be carried out prior to the commencement of development in accordance with a research programme approved by the local planning authority (*or Secretary of State*) on the advice of (*the appropriate archaeological organization*).

C15 The excavation shall be undertaken under the direction of a person approved by the local planning authority (*Secretary of State*) as advised by (*the same organization as in (C14) above*).

10.6 THE USE OF INFORMATIVES

Some planning authorities add **informatives** to their decision notices. These are not part of the formal decision – they are not conditions – but are simply aimed at making applicants aware of other consents or licences that may be required before development can proceed. The more common ones relate to building regulations, food hygiene licences, protected trees, scaffolding requirements and similar controls. With regard to archaeology an authority may add an informative in order to draw an applicant's attention to the archaeological significance of a site and indicating a need for further investigation. Examples of informatives include:

Informative 1
Your attention is drawn to the need to liaise with the (*name of*

archaeological organization) and to allow adequate time for site investigation and/or excavation of the site prior to this development/ redevelopment; and for the need to accommodate the operations in the general building programme.

Informative 2

This site lies within an area designated under the Ancient Monuments and Archaeological Areas Act 1979 as an Area of Archaeological Importance and you will be required to submit a written notice (an Operations Notice) to (*the investigating authority*) at least six weeks before you undertake operations which disturb the ground or flooding or tipping operations.

10.7 THE REFUSAL OF PERMISSION

Government policy states that where important archaeological remains, whether scheduled or not, are affected by proposed development, there should be a presumption in favour of their physical preservation *in situ*. Where this is not possible and proposals are likely to have a significant impact on the setting of such remains, this policy adds that there should be a presumption against allowing the development.

Many local planning authorities have policies to this effect. Either in the development plan or in supplementary planning guidance they state that planning permission will normally be refused where development will destroy or substantially affect important archaeological remains. Each case, however, must be assessed on its merits taking all considerations into account, which means that the intrinsic importance of any remains will be a key consideration. On occasions there will be no doubt that permission should be refused. Either the destruction is too great or insufficient evidence is available to fully assess the extent of destruction. On other occasions it will be less clear and judgements will have to be made taking into account and carefully weighing all relevant material considerations previously outlined.

When refusing planning permission, local planning authorities are required to give reasons for their decisions. The decision notice refusing planning pemission must state why a development is unacceptable and make it clear to the applicant precisely why the proposal has been refused.

For this reason there should be no standard reason for refusal as each proposal will have its own individual problems which should be individually addressed. Some idea of what may be involved, however, can be obtained from the following examples:

R1 The proposed development is contrary to the provisions of (*insert policy number and name of development plan*) which seeks to preserve sites of archaeological interest and/or importance.

R2 The local planning authority is of the opinion that insufficient information regarding the effects on the archaeology of the site has been submitted to enable them to properly determine the proposal.

R3 The local planning authority, having regard to the archaeological importance of the site (*reference may be made to the details or significance of the site*), is of the opinion that the proposed development, by reason of its (*size, siting, depth of excavation, type of foundation either individually or collectively could be used*) would result in the loss of the archaeological resource to such an extent as to warrant a refusal of planning permission.

R4 The site lies within an area of archaeological significance (*or similar designation*) where insufficient information has been provided to enable the impact of the proposed development to be fully assessed.

R5 Notwithstanding that an archaeological evaluation has been submitted with the application the local planning authority is of the opinion that the proposed development by reason of its (*state reason relating to impact of siting, size, depth of building operations etc.*), would destroy the (*archaeological remains*) (*scheduled monument*) to an unacceptable degree.

10.8 PLANNING OBLIGATIONS

Planning obligations is the term used to describe an agreement between a local planning authority and anyone with an interest in land in the area of that authority. It can be important for archaeology for four reasons:

- it is a power available to a planning authority in addition to the ability to attach conditions to a planning permission;
- it can include matters that cannot be covered by conditions;
- it can be used more widely to regulate or restrict development or require specified things to be done;
- the remedies for breach are contractual and generally easier to enforce.

Another feature of planning obligations is that they are becoming more popular with planning authorities. First introduced in 1909 as planning agreements, they were originally not very restrictive in scope and there was very little planning authorities could achieve by their use. They also had to be approved by the Secretary of State, although this requirement was lifted in 1968. Since then, with the lifting of government controls and a growing awareness of what can be achieved, authorities have increasingly sought to make use of planning agreements.

Many have used, and continue to use, these powers both wisely and reasonably although some may be less constrained. For various reasons, not least the lack of clear-cut guidance, authorities have not always exercised this power to the same extent. Some have sought to persuade developers to enter into agreements they would not otherwise have done if they had the choice whilst others have made virtually no use of these powers (Healey, Purdue and Ennis, 1993). Similarly, some developers have sought to offer benefits in return for planning permission.

Such actions have led to criticism and brought the system of planning bargaining into disrepute. Many still refer to this as planning gain (there was a circular with this title), although today it does not have any statutory recognition and there is no definition of this. Others have been less charitable, but what they agree on is the lack of consensus as to what it means. Some argue that planning obligations should include not only the legitimate demands of a planning authority to overcome the adverse effects of a particular development, but also to secure wider community benefits as well. Archaeology would normally come under the former.

Statutory basis for planning obligations

The statutory requirements for entering and making planning obligations is set out in Section 106 of the Town and Country Planning Act 1990 and Section 50 of the Town and Country Planning (Scotland) Act 1972. In 1991 amendments to the English and Welsh legislation were made with the effect that any person interested in land in the area of a local planning authority may, by agreement or otherwise, enter into an obligation. Known as a planning obligation it can be used to:

1. restrict the development or use of land in any specified way;
2. require specified operations or activities to be carried out in, on, over or under land;
3. require land to be used in any specified way;
4. require a sum or sums of money to be paid to the authority on a specified date or dates or periodically.

The 1991 Planning and Compensation Act also made provision for the modification or discharge of a planning obligation. A person against whom it is enforceable may, after the expiry of five years from the coming into effect of a new Section 106A, apply to the local planning authority to have the obligation modified or discharged with a right of appeal to the Secretary of State if dissatisfied with the decision. Note, however, that these powers relating to planning obligations were not extended to Scotland, where the official terminology still pre-dates the 1990 legislation. They are still simply planning agreements.

Three important points arise from planning obligations. The first is that an obligation may be entered into by agreement or otherwise: both parties do not have to agree! A developer can put forward alternative proposals but in so doing is bound by them. The obligation or unilateral undertaking given is binding in law and the developer is obliged to see it through in the same way that a planning authority and developer are obliged to comply with the terms of an agreement. Hence the name planning obligations.

When a developer gives an undertaking the planning authority is not bound by it and does not have to accept it although it can require the person giving the undertaking to satisfactorily complete it. If necessary it can enforce it by serving an enforcement notice or injunction.

A developer, therefore, needs to ensure that any undertaking made in accordance with Section 106 is conditional to the granting of planning permission for development. If it is not the developer could be in the unfortunate position of having to complete a planning obligation whilst being refused planning permission or giving up on a development. In practice these eventualities are unlikely but it does highlight the need for obligations to be carefully drafted.

The second point is that planning obligations contain both positive and negative covenants. Before 1991 they were primarily negative in character, allowing agreements to be entered into 'for the purpose of restricting or regulating the development or use' of land. Positive requirements could only be included if they were 'incidental and consequential' to the main purpose of the agreement of if they were required under another Act of Parliament such as Section 33 of the Local Government (Miscellaneous Provisions) Act 1982. This was frequently used and its comparable still is in Scotland. In England and Wales financial considerations do not have to be incidental or consequential upon other matters and can be the primary or sole feature of a planning obligation. Thus a planning authority could, if it thought it appropriate, simply seek to obtain funds from a developer to help finance an archaeological investigation.

The third point relates to the ability to include positive and negative covenants. By reason of Section 106A it will be possible, after the expiry of five years, for the person on whom an obligation is enforceable to apply to the authority to have it altered or discharged. The ability to do this, however, will only apply to new obligations made solely under the 1990 Act. It does not apply to any agreements or obligations made under other provisions such as Section 33 of the 1982 Act nor, presumably, Section 52 of the 1971 Planning Act. Accordingly, if any agreement both now and in the future recites other statutory provisions, an application to the planning authority to modify or discharge an obligation cannot be entirely successful. The other statutory requirements would remain in force indicating that two quite separate regimes could be in force.

Policy considerations

Government policy concerning planning obligations is contained in Circular 16/91. It states that planning obligations, like conditions, should only be sought where they are necessary to the grant of planning permission, relevant to planning, and relevant to the development to be permitted. Five alternatives are outlined in the circular. They are:

1. that it is needed to enable development to go ahead;
2. that in the case of financial payment, it will contribute to meeting the cost of providing facilities;
3. that it is otherwise so directly related to the proposed development and to the use of land after its completion that the development ought not to be permitted without it;
4. that in the case of mixed uses, it is designed to secure an acceptable balance of uses or to secure the implementation of local plan policies for a particular area or type of development;
5. that it is intended to offset the loss of or impact on any amenity or resource present at a site prior to development.

Local planning policy on the use of planning obligations seems to vary more widely, especially when it comes to archaeology. Some authorities such as Southampton City Council and the City of London do not use planning obligations to obtain additional archaeological benefits, relying instead on the use of conditions. Others, such as York, sometimes require developers to enter into detailed planning agreements incorporating a mitigation strategy designed to protect or record as much as is practically possible of the archaeological resource. With such diverging approaches to archaeology the question arises as to how appropriate they are and how they compare with government policy. In short, how reasonable are they?

Tests of appropriateness

In any attempt to answer this question it is worth considering three things, namely, the Department of the Environment tests, the aims of the planning authority and recent case law.

The Department of Environment tests

In 1992 the Department of Environment published a research report on the use of planning agreements where three tests aimed at assessing the reasonableness of such agreements were put forward. Two are considered relevant to archaeology. Of these, one requires a comparison to be made between local policy and the five government principles mentioned above; the other requires a comparison to be made between what is necessary for archeological purposes and the scale and nature of the proposed development.

Test 1: comparison between national and local policy
In trying to compare local policy with government objectives it is possible to come to different conclusions, depending on viewpoint and personal interests.

In connection with the first principle, that an obligation is necessary to enable development to proceed, some might argue that an archaeological evaluation is necessary. Others, however, will point to the fact that whilst such an investigation may be desirable it is not needed to enable development of proceed. They will contend that development is capable of proceeding with or without an archaeological evaluation and that the issue is one of motive rather than substance.

The second principle relating to the financing of facilities rests to some extent on the first. At first glance it appears to ask the question – if an archaeological investigation is needed will financial support be of assistance? The answer, of course, must be that it will, but that is not really the point. The principle of finance in Circular 16/91 (from the Planning and Compensation Act 1991: Planning Objectives) rests on the provision of facilities needed for a development such as the provision of adequate car parking space. It is not clear how archaeological facilities can be provided unless they relate to important remains which are to be retained and incorporated into the proposed development.

The third principle must undisputably relate to archaeological sites and monuments of national importance. It is possible to envisage development in the vicinity of a national monument being designed so that it protects or incorporates it in some way within the overall development proposals. Other than this, it is hard to contemplate how this principle should apply.

A similar argument would apply to the fourth principle. An acceptable balance of uses does not appear to have any bearing on archaeological remains. It is geared to different types of development at a site irrespective of its archaeological content.

This leaves us with the fifth and last principle, which appears to be directly relevant. Archaeology is clearly an existing resource but what is initially less clear is how any loss or damage may be offset. The circular makes reference to the provision of nature conservation benefits such as planting trees and the establishment of wildlife ponds. Archaeology, however, is something different. It cannot be replaced, which suggests that to offset the loss of archaeological remains there should be some form of mitigation strategy. Either it should be aimed at reducing the loss by recording what is there or alternatively it should seek to ensure that there is no or little loss by making sure that development is designed to preserve any remains *in situ*.

Test 2: comparison between the archaeological resource and proposed development

In trying to make any comparison between archaeology and development, one conclusion can be that there ought to be a relationship between the extent of an archaeological investigation and the scale and amount of development proposed at a site. This would suggest that the larger the development, the bigger the archaeological investigation and *vice versa*.

This approach, however, ignores the importance of the archaeological resource. There can be no point in mounting a costly and time consuming excavation if there is little return at the end of the day. A more appropriate course of action would probably be to secure preservation *in situ*. On the other hand, important remains could be anticipated at a site where relatively minor operations are proposed. A proposed house extension, for example, could be on the site of known archaeological importance. Yet how reasonable would it be to expect the house owner to enter into a planning obligation which may or may not require a financial contribution towards an archaeological investigation?

It is clear that the question of reasonableness must vary from site to site and authority to authority. But this variation itself suggests that it would be unreasonable to allow such variety. It means that some developers, whatever they propose, will be less fairly treated than others and that some archaeologists and archaeological considerations may be disadvantaged in comparison to others. For both, a key factor will be the site chosen for development and the policies pertaining to it. Clarity of purpose by the planning authority will be all-important.

Aims of the planning authority

According to Healey, Purdue and Ennis (1992), there are three rationales which planning authorities can use to justify their position regarding planning agreements.

- Rationale 1 is concerned with the implementation of development. Under this approach agreements are seen as necessary to enable proposals to proceed, such as when the provision of off-site drainage works or highway improvements are required to make the development work.
- Rationale 2 concentrates on the impact of a project. Instead of making the development work as is the case with Rationale 1, this rationale is concerned with the adverse effects of a proposal on the environment and how they might be mitigated. Thus it could focus on the impact of development on archaeological remains and how they might be protected.
- Rationale 3 focuses on wider public issues making use of the 'polluter-pays' principle. Here the developer is seen as having a duty to pay back some of the profits from a project to the local community. As a sort of local tax or charge on development it is where an authority might require a developer to provide, among other things, money for archaeological investigation or for wider community benefits.

Two important differences can be identified between these rationales. The first is that whereas Rationales 1 and 2 can reasonably be used to support a refusal of planning permission, the third ought to be used to support the grant of permission. The second difference is between Rationales 1 and 2: whereas the first is concerned with making a scheme acceptable and therefore focuses on the relationship between the development and the obligation, the second is concerned about the relationship between the development and the impact it will have on the environment. As such it appears that it would be possible, in theory, to separate the issues of preservation from funding.

Recent case law

An important factor influencing the decisions of many local authorities is case law. How the courts interpret planning legislation has always been important and this applies equally to planning obligations. The Court of Appeal's decision in *Plymouth City Council and others ex parte Plymouth v. South Devon Co-operative Society Limited* (1993) is one such case, in that it provided guidance on the consideration of planning benefits (Department of Environment, 1992).

The Plymouth case
The facts of the Plymouth case are straightforward. Sainsbury, Tesco and the Co-op sought planning permission for superstores in the Plymouth area. The local plan included a policy requiring planning benefits to be provided by superstores and the city council also had the benefit of a restrictive covenant relating to the Tesco site. They expected to receive a reward for its release.

Tesco, after considering the local plan, offered a five point planning benefit package which included:

- provision of necessary highway works costing approximately £1 million;
- funds for an art competition;
- £100 000 towards the provision of a creche for use, in part, by employees working on the site;
- approximately £25 000 for landscaping works;
- making land available for a park-and-ride scheme if requested (it was not).

Sainsbury, who viewed the council's position as one of assessing competing bids, put forward a 10-point package incorporating:

- a tourist information centre;
- an art gallery display;
- an art feature;
- a bird-watching hide;
- a river enhancement scheme;
- £250 000 for highway improvements;
- funds towards the provision of a creche for use by residents;
- £1 million for infrastructure purposes;
- £800 000 for a park-and-ride scheme
- nearby road enhancements.

The council resolved to grant planning permission to Tesco and Sainsbury and, and a later meeting, the Co-op scheme. The Co-op, however, challenged the decision principally on the grounds that the benefits offered were not material consideration. The High Court and the Court of Appeal thought otherwise.

Lord Justice Hutchinson, in the former, concluded 'without hesitation' that the planning benefits were all legitimate. Lord Justice Hoffman in the latter stated, in respect of the bird-watching hide and other on-site benefits:

> I do not see how it can possibly be said that such embellishments did not fairly and reasonably relate to the development.

In relation to the off-site benefits, their lordships also found a clear relationship. For example, the offer to pay towards the servicing of industrial land was seen as contributing towards restoring the balance caused by the planning permission.

When the Plymouth decision was announced it was initially thought by some that totally unrelated matters had somehow become valid material planning considerations and that the permissions were tantamount to the purchase of planning permission. On reflection, and a careful examination of the proposals, what emerged was that many of the benefits formed part of the applications and were therefore clearly material.

What appears to be more significant for the archaeological point of view is the offer towards the cost of off-site benefits in order to offset the impact of the development proposals. This would appear to confirm two if not all three of the rationales identified by Healey, Purdue and Ennis. Is the servicing of industrial land a duty or obligation on the developer or simply a means of mitigating adverse effects? No doubt, the debate will continue.

Practical considerations

Nationally, the impact of planning agreements upon developers is very limited because only a few planning decisions (0.5%) are accompanied by agreements (DoE, 1992). However, when they do apply they can have quite an impact. Furthermore there is evidence, as we have seen, that this practice will grow. This could well be the case as far as archaeological considerations are concerned.

The study by Healey, Purdue and Ennis (1993) suggests that developers are prepared to enter into obligations dealing with the impacts of development (this could include the impact on archaeology) provided there is a profitable development at the end of the day. Two problems, however, can be identified. The first focuses on the range of benefits that may be sought. Whilst archaeology can be recognized as being directly relevant – falling within Rationale 2 – and perhaps justify financial support on that basis, what if an authority wishes to pursue other benefits at the same time? Should archaeology take precedence over other matters such as social or infrastructure provision?

The second problem lies in assessing the scale of obligations. If a developer is to be expected to make a financial contribution towards an archaeological investigation how is the contribution to be assessed? Should it relate to the known or anticipated importance of the archaeological resource at a site or should it relate to the size, cost or profitability of the project? If it is the former and the remains are not scheduled and lie underneath the ground waiting to be excavated what would be a reasonable assessment of the costs involved? Should they be based simply on the site evaluation which could prove inadequate (Chapter 2), or would the authority wish to see a further contingency set aside?

Another argument might be to base funding on 'ability to pay' although, as we shall see in Chapter 16, this can vary enormously from developer to developer and from scheme to scheme? Some developments will always be more profitable than others, some are better managed that others and some are more affected by the state of the economy. Many are also prone to the vagaries of the development cycle. Retailing is an example of one that is currently more profitable as witnessed by the Plymouth case, although this could change.

By raising these questions we can see that there is no simple answer. If funding is to be provided solely by the developer and not out of public funds (how reasonable is this?) it would seem that the form and content of planning obligations will have to vary, suggesting that the matter ought to be subject to public debate. In a sense it comes back to a wider consideration of the issues including those relating to the introduction of a levy as discussed in Chapter 6.

Finally, there is evidence (DoE, 1992) to show that some authorities duplicate conditions of a planning permission in planning agreements. No doubt this is to increase their powers of control although additional enforcement powers introduced by the Planning and Compensation Act 1991 largely supersede this. Clearly some authorities will make more use of enforcement powers, others less so. Again it will depend on local circumstance, resources and policy objectives of the authority concerned, all of which can vary so much. It is, and is likely to remain in the forseeable future, a complex and controversial subject.

10.9 CHALLENGING PLANNING DECISIONS

Both applicants and third parties can challenge planning decisions although they do not have the same rights and cannot always appeal on the same grounds or at the same time.

Appeal by the applicant

The rights of an applicant are the most extensive and have statutory recognition. Section 78 (Sections 33 and 34 in Scotland) allows the applicant to appeal to the Secretary of State, in practice the Planning Inspectorate (or Reporters in Scotland), where the planning authority has:

- refused planning permission;
- granted permission subject to conditions;
- refused an applicaton for matters required by condition;
- failed to give a decision;
- exercised powers to decline to determine an application.

This right of appeal applies only to the aggrieved applicant. It does not apply to any other person or party even if that person has an interest in the land. If the applicant is the prospective purchaser of a site and not the owner then only that particular prospective purchaser has a right to appeal and not the owner. This is despite the fact that planning permission runs with the land and not the person.

The appeal must be lodged with the Secretary of State's office within six months of receipt of the decision or, where there is no decision, within six months of the date by which a decision should have been made. This is either eight weeks after the planning authority receives the application or 16 weeks, when it is subject to environmental assessment.

When considering an appeal the applicant must give thought to the reasons for refusal and the planning merits of the case. The applicant should look to see if the reasons relate to matters of principle or to detail, although even here great care must be taken. In York, for example, a planning application for the construction of four dwellings on a backland site within the historic core and within the AAI was refused permission on grounds of overdevelopment, the effect on the character of the area and inadequate access and parking arrangements. Archaeological grounds were not included in the refusal notice but in the subsequent appeal the proposal was dismissed primarily on archaeological grounds. In paragraph 14 of the decision letter the inspector stated:

> Finally, part of the site is said to be located across the position of the bailee ditch of the castle of the Old Baile built by William I in 1068 or 1069. A Roman cemetery is known to lie close-by and may extend beneath the site. The York Archaeological Trust say that other Roman

Colonia remains may fall within the site. The Council have proposed that a Section 106 Agreement should be entered into for the protection of archaeological finds and your client indicated a willingness to adopt that course. However, no such Agreement had been formulated at the time of the hearing. While I am satisfied that there is no lack of goodwill on each side concerning archaeological finds and their preservation I have come to the conclusion that it would be premature to grant permission for the development until a full archaeological field evaluation has been carried out.

There is no doubt that archaeological considerations can be fundamental to both the principle and the detail of development. In the York case the issue appears to have been one of detail. It delays development rather than preventing it altogether. Another situation where great care needs to be exercised is when consent has been granted subject to conditions. If an applicant is aggrieved by a condition on a planning permission he or she may have been advised not to appeal against the decision. This is because an inspector, when determining a subsequent appeal, could dismiss the whole application. If the inspector considers the condition to be fundamental to the development and the permission should not be allowed without it, the whole permission can be refused. One day an applicant can have a conditional consent, the next, no consent at all!

The way applicants avoid this possibility from arising is by submitting a fresh application for the removal of the condition: by seeking permission for the same development without having to comply with the condition, if this second application is refused, an appeal can be lodged against this refusal whilst keeping the first permission intact. The original conditions are either complied with or the developer decides not to proceed with the earlier proposal.

The serving of a purchase notice

When planning permission has been refused or granted subject to conditions an aggrieved applicant, if an owner, may in certain circumstances require the local planning authority to purchase the interest in the land affected by the decision. The requirement would be by means of serving a **purchase notice** on the authority within 12 months of the decision. Similar to compulsory purchase, only in reverse, the applicant would need to show:

1. that the land, as a result of the decision, has become incapable of reasonably beneficial use in its existing state; or
2. where permission has been granted subject to conditions, that the land cannot be rendered capable of reasonably beneficial use by the carrying out of the conditional consent.

Within three months of receipt of the purchase notice the authority must serve a counter-notice stating:

1. that the notice is accepted; or
2. that it should be served on another authority; or

3. that the authority has rejected it and that a copy has been sent to the Secretary of State together with a copy of the original notice.

In this situation the Secretary of State may:

1. confirm the notice if satisfied that the requirements have been met;
2. grant planning permission for the development originally applied for; or
3. direct that planning permission be granted for another use, if applied for, which would render the land capable of reasonably beneficial use.

It is debatable whether a refusal of permission or a conditional consent based on archaeological considerations could render a site incapable of reasonably beneficial use. If a refusal states that existing archaeological remains should not be disturbed and they cover a large part of an application site it would appear that a good case could be made. If the remains are less extensive an alternative might be for part only of a site to be successful with the remainder receiving planning permission. Decisions of this nature have been made although much will depend on prevailing circumstances.

If a refusal is based on insufficient information being submitted with an application (e.g. where an evaluation has not been submitted), it would appear that a claim should be less successful if based on archaeological grounds. The authority would in effect be saying that they are unable to properly determine the application but that if additional information is received a more informed decision could be made. In such circumstances it would be expected that a claim would be more difficult to justify. It also suggests that the reasons for the decision and a knowledge of the extent and importance of the archaeological resource will be the determining factors when trying to assess whether or not a purchase notice will be successful.

Right of challenge

Planning decisions can have far reaching implications, particularly for objectors who have no right of appeal. There is, however, one way in which an objector may contest a planning authority's decision and that is by an application for judical review. An appeal to the High Court can be lodged by a third party on the grounds that:

- the decision was *ultra vires*, that is, it was taken outside the powers conveyed to the authority or Secretary of State; or
- the relevant statutory requirements were not complied with.

In either case the challenge or appeal is not against the merit of the case but against the way in which the decision was made. If the High Court finds a procedural irrgularity it can quash the planning decision which is then no longer valid.

The right to challenge must be by a 'person aggrieved'. He or she is not defined legally but case law has established that the person must be someone whose legal rights have been infringed, or who attended the public inquiry, or who made repesentations in respect of the application or appeal. The time-limit for making a challenge is six weeks from the date of decision, that is, the date the decision is sent and not the date it was received. There is, therefore, little time in which to prepare a case and apply to the High Court. There is also little time for second thoughts, opinions or professional advice.

Another way of objecting is to lodge a complaint to the ombudsman although this is generally far less effective. If the ombudsman accepts the complaint – there are prescribed procedures – attention would focus on the administration of the authority and how it reached its decision. Maladministration may be found but the remedy does not normally go to the heart of the planning objection. Once a decision has been made on a planning application it is extremely rare for a planning authority to change its mind.

REFERENCES

Department of the Environment, Welsh Office (1985) Circular 1/85 *The Use of Conditions in Planning Permissions*, HMSO, London.

Department of the Environment (1990) *PPG 16, Archaeology and Planning*, HMSO, London.

Department of the Environment (1992) Research Report on *The Use of Planning Agreements*, HMSO, London.

Department of the Environment (1991) Circular 16/91 *Planning and Compensation Act 1991: Planning Obligations*, HMSO, London.

Healey, P., Purdue, M. and Ennis, F. (1993) *Gains from Planning? Dealing with the Impacts of Development*, Joseph Rowntree Foundation, York.

Newbury District Council v. Secretary of State for the Environment (1980) 2 WLR 379; 1 AIIER 731; 40 P&CR 148.

R v. Plymouth City Council, J. Sainsbury plc, Estates and Agency Holdings plc, Tesco Stores Ltd, Vospers Motor House (Plymouth Ltd), ex p. Plymouth and South Devon Co-operative Society Ltd.

Scottish Development Department (1986) Circular 18/86.

Stringer v. Minister for Housing and Local Government (1971) 1 AIIER.

Westminster City Council, List of standard conditions.

FURTHER READING

Ashworth, S. (1993) Superstores – the Plymouth decision. *Property Review*, September 1993, pp. 350–352.

Department of the Environment (1983) Circular 22/83 *Planning Gain*, HMSO, London.

Heap, D. (1991) *An Outline of Planning Law*, (10th edn), Sweet and Maxwell, London.

Manley, J. (1987) Archaeology and planning: a Welsh perspective – Part II. *Journal of Planning and Environment Law*, pp. 552–56, Sweet and Maxwell, London.

Moore, V. (ed.) (1993) Notes of cases. *Journal of Planning and Environment Law*, pp. 538–565, Sweet and Maxwell, London.

Scottish Office Environment Department (1992) *Planning Advice Note: Archaeology and Planning*, SOEnD, Edinburgh.

Development Considerations

PART 3

The property development process $\boxed{\textbf{11}}$

Property development means different things to different people: for many in the building industry it is seen as an industrial process in which the market meets the demands of consumers by producing buildings and other structures; for others it is more socio-political in nature, aimed at providing society's property needs; and for some it is essentially a financial process, that is, it is a means of investing in the future.

For our purposes, property development may be defined as the process by which buildings and infrastructure are provided for occupation and use. It is a process which brings together the raw materials of land, labour, bricks and mortar, capital and professional expertise by a producer (developer) to produce a product (building or other structure) to meet the demands of a consumer (occupier or users). It requires the services of traditional skills in the trades and professions but occasionally has to rely on skills such as those of the archaeologist. The developer's task is to organize and control these and other inputs to produce what is required. It is not an easy task.

A number of external factors make the process a complex one. Politics, fiscal and monetary policies and market forces are just three which can have a tremendous impact. Government borrowing, the setting of interest rates and the international flow of money, for instance, can distort the flow of capital into property affecting property values, rental incomes and building costs. All can change dramatically during the life of a typical building period of two to three years. In comparison, archaeological considerations can appear relatively insignificant but this may be far from the case. Archaeology can have an impact on the development process, affecting timing and costs which may be very sensitive within the budget.

In the present economic climate where developers are expected to pay for archaeological investigation, and where public monies are severely restricted, it is all too easy to overlook the external factors and to say that the developer should pay for excavations. The property boom and subsequent recession, however, have shown that the ability of developers to pay for investigation can vary enormously. They show that there is a need to look at the development process more closely.

In this and subsequent Chapters the aim is to do just that. Initially it involves looking at the process itself and to see how and where archaeological considerations become involved. This is followed by looking at the management, design, contracts, finance and appraisal aspects of the process in more detail. All can be affected by archaeology.

11.1 THE DEVELOPER

In any consideration of the development process we should first consider the developer. Often seen as an opulent speculator seeking to make a quick profit from the provision of buildings, the reality is somewhat different. Whilst there will inevitably be speculators, the developer will typically be a hard-working entrepreneur frequently employed by one of a variety of organizations which can have very different motives. The full range, however, will be much wider where the following can all be classed as developers:

Occupiers

An occupier usually wants a building or an extension to a building to suit particular needs. These could be for domestic or business purposes where the profit from the development is taken indirectly from the benefit of occupation. Householders and many businesses fall into this category.

Landowners

A landowner's interest in development would normally be to maximize the return from the ownership of land by developing all or part of it in some way or seeking to establish development potential. Some may try to obtain planning permission and sell the land whilst others might wish to manage their estates more efficiently and more effectively.

Property companies

The prime objective of a property company is to make a profit from a development project. The company can be a sole trader or a multinational bringing together the factors of production to produce a building for sale at a profit or held as an investment to provide rental income. There will be those who wish to hold property as a long-term investment for raising income (a property investment company) and those who will be content to make a trading profit from the sale of a development and move on to the next project (a property trading company). Each will have different concepts of financial return.

Investors

An investor is interested in parting with money today in exchange for future income or capital gain. He or she is usually not interested in investing in a particular sector of the investment market such as property but merely in obtaining future income and/or capital gain appropriate to personal needs and circumstances. Those interested in property are primarily the institutions and pension funds. They are involved as financiers or purchasers of other people's schemes taking a share in or receiving income from the letting of property. They tend to have a long-term interest.

Government sponsored agencies

Organizations such as English Partnerships and the urban development corporations can engage in commercially and economically useful schemes although they are mainly aimed at providing employment and the regeneration of areas. In partnership with the private sector they may also get involved in the provision of infrastructure projects where a prime aim is to encourage further development.

Local authorities

These have in the past mainly been involved in the provision of housing and commercial and recreational facilities within their areas, although this role has diminished in recent years. They now act more as enablers rather than providers, or make partnership schemes with the private sector using their land banks, land acquisition and town planning powers to facilitate development. This tends to be funded and managed by the private sector.

Commercial organizations

Many commercial organizations lease space provided by others such as property companies and local authorities rather than develop for their own use. Some, however, because of special requirements or as a matter of policy, may develop their own property. Banks are a good example of commercial organizations which adopt this approach. So too are some of the major retailers such as Sainsbury, Tesco and Marks and Spencer who develop for their own purposes.

Builders

A builder is often employed as a building contractor taking profit from construction costs and time. For some, this contracting role is extended to include the promotion and risk of development. By combining building and development profit the return would reflect the risk of buying land, arranging finance and organizing sales or lettings. Housebuilders large and small usually fall into this category with some of the larger firms operating a property company subsidiary to undertake work in the commercial sector. There are also many smaller building firms.

11.2 CHARACTERISTICS OF PROPERTY

The second consideration in property. Containing almost unique characteristics which distinguish it from other commodities, an understanding of what they are will help to explain how the property market and development process works.

Limited supply

For all intents and purposes the supply of land is fixed. Apart from minor changes due to reclamation and erosion, the overall supply cannot change. This is a fact which is often emphasized but its significance should not be exaggerated because the stock of land for any particular use can vary. Depending on planning controls and how they are applied and the proportion of land currently used for a specific purpose, the supply of land for any individual use can vary. Change, however, takes time and in the short run the supply for any particular use is limited.

A similar situation applies where buildings and other structures have been built. A change of use may be possible, again subject to planning, but new buildings will first require existing structures to be demolished and the site prepared for redevelopment. Building construction on major projects can take five years to complete with the result that it will be some time before the change can be implemented. In the short run, property cannot easily adapt to change, making it limited in supply. Archaeology, if it adds to the delay, could have a short-term effect on this supply although it would normally be localized and very limited.

Location

By definition all property is fixed in location. For this reason, apart from any other, all properties are different and can command different values. This applies equally to similar properties in the same area as it does to identical properties in different locations. Relationships to other land and buildings both near and far will be different. No two sets of circumstances will be the same and neighbouring properties in the same terrace can even be different and command different values for a variety of reasons. They can be different in size, age, state of repair, be constructed differently or be used for different purposes.

Durability

Land is totally durable, buildings less so although they compare well with most other products. Eventually they will deteriorate but even when a property is old the value of the land can be such that this offsets the value of the depreciating building. Where land increases in value it can more than compensate for any deterioration in the quality and condition in a building. On the other hand, increased land cost can bring into question the viability of a project.

Forms of title

Although property cannot easily be divided physically it is possible to have different legal interests in it. A freeholder is vested with a perpetual right to use or dispose of property as he or she wishes, subject to statute and certain inalienable rights of others. Equally the freeholder can create lesser, leasehold interests over a property, conferring certain rights to possession and use for a specified period. This can be further subdivided so that there is a head lease and one or more subtenants. In theory there is no limit to the number of leasehold interests created in this way although the duration of any sublease cannot exceed the duration of the head lease.

Where different interests in property exist they can affect its value. Identical in every other respect (apart from location) property can command different values because of different interests. Thus the value of a freehold interest can be affected by the rent payable by a tenant and the duration of any leases remaining. If there is a subtenant, this will affect the value of the head lease which in turn will affect the value of the freehold interest. Not surprisingly, there is scope for considerable variation in properties which might otherwise be considered to be of similar value. This will be particularly important in historic areas where buildings are used for different purposes and where redevelopment may be contemplated.

Lack of standardization

Property cannot be a standardized investment. Unlike shares in a company, which are all the same, no two properties can be identical in terms of structure, tenant, lease and location. Attempts have been made to standardize legal interests in property through unitization, which divides a property into a number of units of ownership. Such attempts, however, have proved difficult to maintain. How do you value or tax a small part of a property at any time when different interests are held in it? Valuing a particular interest in part of a property at any one time is fraught with difficulty.

High capital value

Property is normally so expensive that it is not possible for a purchaser to buy it outright without raising funds or a mortgage. In some cases its cost is so great that even very large organizations have difficulty in purchasing it. It can also be of such a sum that it results in too great a proportion of an investment portfolio being put into one property. This can be unattractive to investors particularly if the market is depressed and a sale is needed quickly.

11.3 THE PROPERTY MARKET

The diversity of property and the legal interests that can be acquired mean that the property market is complex. But there are other factors which add to this complexity making it difficult to comprehend. Indeed, there is not one market but a conglomerate of many smaller markets.

We have seen that there are many different types of developer including those who build for themselves and those who build for others. In addition, there are many different types of property in all sorts of locations. The market for offices in Carlisle, for instance, is different from the market for shops in Dover. Add other types of property such as industrial, leisure and residential and we can see that there is a myriad of property markets and property players all over Britain.

With so many markets it is impossible for any one player to be aware of what is going on. This will apply even to the same type of development in one area. Admittedly some property agents will have a good idea of what is happening locally but as a rule there will always be an element of uncertainty. In the words of economists, it is an imperfect market. Imperfect knowledge makes it so.

This imperfection is crucial. It means that it is not always possible to assess accurately the demand for property, and, by implication, its value. Rental levels and capital value will be determined by the demand and supply of property at the time of completion and yet an investor will want to know what return is likely when investing in a development project. It means that the investor will be influenced by many factors and may not always be right.

The complexity of property interests and markets makes it essential for developers to employ professional experts when property development is proposed. The time factor makes this especially important although these imperfections probably help to make property prices more stable than share prices. The property market, by its very nature, is slower to react to change and if property prices are falling owners are usually unwilling to sell their properties and will retain them unsold. Paradoxically, such actions and the imperfections of the market help to maintain a semblance of price stability relative to other prices although this does not remove the uncertainty.

The demand for property

One of the most important roles of the property professional is to try and identify the demand for property. Generally described as market research, the aim is to find out what consumers want so that the development industry can meet those requirements profitably. Trying to assess demand, however, is not as easy as it may sound, as witnessed by the huge oversupply of offices in central London in the early 1990s.

For the market researcher there is a need to look at past and present demand in the relevant sub-markets from which estimates of future demand can be made. There are no set techniques by which the total demand for certain types of buildings in a town or region can be accurately forecast. Instead certain basic investigations have to be made to determine whether there is a reasonable chance of success. These focus on:

- **The potential user** Demands for some uses such as information technology or retailing can come from companies/organizations opening new premises in an area if they are expanding and developing. Decentralization from larger urban areas can appeal to some firms who want to set up in a more attractive working environment. Other firms already in an area may wish to expand or rationalize their space whilst a few may wish to move from older, out of date buildings. They could be encouraged by the setting up of an enterprise zone or a simplified planning zone or discouraged by an archaeological zone. Research would focus on who the potential users might be and the areas they might be interested in.

- **The balance of supply and demand** The total stock of property of whatever type can be quantified and current vacancy rates established. This can then be compared against past vacancy figures and past demand to get some idea of how the market is moving. The analysis will need to take into account the age, size, type and speciality of units together with their location. It will also be necessary in today's market to check against the take up of property. Simply comparing supply and demand is insufficient, and the real test in property growth and in identifying gaps in the market will be to see if there is positive net absorption of property and not a net loss of occupation. Developers would also be advised to find out which occupiers, both well known and less well known, are already represented in an area. This would be especially useful if targeting is intended.

- **Local economic and social conditions** The demand for space is, to some extent, a function of the strength of the local economy. Types of employment and levels of unemployment can help to show where gaps exist in the market or the manner in which the local economy might more easily be filled. They might also indicate how a planning authority will react to employment-generating proposals which possibly conflict with archaeo-logical interests. Other factors such as the type of area, the quality of housing and the adequacy of services can also help to indicate potential demand.

- **Estate agents' registers** Commercial estate agents are employed by firms to find accommodation. Agents are, therefore, a source of information on the assessment of unsatisfied demand relating to quantity and quality of space and preferred locations. In addition, as rents are a reflection of scarcity, rising rents will tend to indicate unsatisfied demand whilst static or falling rents are likely to indicate an oversupply of premises.

- **User requirements** Research here would focus on the design, layout, services and building specifications required by users. User survey techniques can be used to investigate requirements for different users or types of user although the cost of this type of research should not be underestimated. It is often labour intensive and would need to be carefully targeted to be of any real use.

- **Catchment areas** Aimed primarily at retail and leisure developments, space for these uses and particularly retail uses will largely reflect the spending power of the population. It is theoretically possible in relation to income and population to show if an area is lacking in shopping facilities. In practice, the difficulty is in trying to delineate the catchment area. Car ownership, personal preferences and insufficient or out of date data on incomes, expenditure patterns and existing facilities make it difficult to assess catchments accurately. In addition, the planning authority may be averse to proposals in retailers' desired locations on environmental grounds or because of the effect on existing shopping centres.

Market research can be used to refine the process of decision-making. It is about getting the right product in the right place at the right time. The employment of experts and sophisticated techniques can remove some of the risk although external influences such as the economic climate can have a considerable bearing on the level of demand at any one time, making it difficult to predict. When anyone buys or rents property a mix of motives will be present including personal preferences, market analysis, the availability of land, cost and gut feeling. All of these are important.

The choice of location

Another factor of considerable importance is location. Choosing a site is one of the first decisions which a developer must make. It may be determined by geographical area because that is where the developer is locally based or it may be as a matter of policy. A multinational corporation, for example, may look at a number of areas, even countries, before deciding where to locate. In addition, policy may be influenced by the presence of financial and other incentives. Development area status or the existence of an enterprise zone may influence the decision to choose a particular country, region or locality.

Ultimately the decision in the private sector will be influenced by the economics of the scheme with development proceeding where it is thought to be most economic and most profitable, having regard to the availability of land, planning controls, labour markets and other constraints such as archaeology. In the public sector, the primary concern will be to keep costs of development as low as practicably possible whilst minimizing adverse effects on the environment. Several factors will influence the choice of location depending, in part, on the type of development proposed, local politics, the locality and its ability to absorb the development.

As a rule, it is possible to identify three broad types of location for development projects, namely greenfield sites where no modern development has taken place, brownfield sites which consist principally of cleared sites in built-up areas and finally redevelopment sites where new buildings are proposed to replace existing structures.

All three types of site can be important to archaeology depending on the historical importance of the area and other environmental evidence. The most significant will be greenfield sites where new estate developments, trunk roads and pipelines are proposed and redevelopment sites in the historic parts of towns and cities. Significantly, each type of location has tended to attract different types of development although this could change. Greenfield sites are attractive for housing estates, business parks, leisure developments, out-of-town retailing and infrastructure projects. Historic town centre sites tend to attract residential and commercial developments, the latter consisting mainly of shops, offices and extensions to such buildings.

The practicability of developing in different locations has changed over the years and it is possible that we may see more change in the future. Environmental and economic considerations have become increasingly important factors in recent years, affecting the choice of location. It is likely that this will continue with environmentally sensitive areas increasing in number and becoming more restrictive in what may be allowed. We are already seeing this in conservation areas where tighter controls are being recommended for new development. It is possible that a similar approach might be applied to archaeological areas which could have the effect of encouraging developers to look elsewhere. Economic necessity will be a key factor in any drive to find the right location.

11.4 THE DEVELOPMENT CYCLE

In addition to the above vagaries of the property and construction market the developer also has a **development cycle** to contend with. We have already seen that the developer responds to demand or perceived demand with buildings supplied where the developer thinks they are most needed or will be needed by the time construction is completed. We have also seen that the property market operates in a very imperfect way indicating that supply is limited at any one time and cannot readily adapt to meet a change.

Supply and demand

Several implications stem from this and they are ones which archaeologists, planners and others should be aware of. The first is that the supply of property basically chases demand but rarely matches it. Whenever demand for property increases, supply cannot immediately meet that demand with the result that rents and land values are pushed up. This entices others to enter the property market to provide more buildings to meet the increased demand. Building costs, including labour costs, rise due to the short-term scarcity of resources.

As and when new buildings are completed so demand is gradually satisfied. More significantly, because of the imperfect and cyclical nature of the property market, supply may catch up with demand and even overtake it leaving an oversupply of property coming on stream. In between there is a brief spell when the upward-moving supply curve meets the downward-moving demand curve. This is when supply and demand are the same. Some time after this point is passed, building becomes uneconomic, new supply ceases and when demand picks up again there is a shortage of the right property in the right place at the right time. The cycle then repeats itself.

Causes of change

Important questions in all of this are what causes demand to change and how can it be anticipated? They are questions which tax many minds and organizations. Firms of accountants, chartered surveyors, investment consultants and others are all involved in this guessing game, some with considerable success, others less so. This is because there are so many players in the market and so many external factors which can influence demand. They make it difficult to predict with any degree of accuracy what is going to happen over a period of years. This is especially true regarding the property market, although for individual sectors such as office and retail development more information is available. Within these sectors a lot of time, effort and research has been spent in trying to predict future demand.

Broadly speaking there are three main external factors which can influence the demand for property. They are:

- **Government policy** According to market demand, political and international requirements, governments generally seek to encourage economic growth and/or prevent overheating of the economy. Thus taxation controls, bank rate and other regulatory or deregulatory measures are altered to suit social, economic and political considerations at the time.
- **Market forces** Property cannot be seen in isolation from other investments. An investor wishing to maximize the return on capital will not look solely at property but will be interested in the wider investment market including stocks and shares: resulting investment decisions will be influenced by the available and predicted rates of return indicating that property may not always be an attractive investment.
- **The system of land use controls** Although government sets out the machinery for land use controls, we saw in Part Two that it is principally local planning authorities which determine proposals for development. By adopting their own policies as thought appropriate and according to local democratic processes they can exercise their powers relatively freely. They are able to grant or refuse permission according to local circumstances, which, of course, can vary enormously and are not always predictable.

From the above it is clear that the amount of development must fluctuate through time. Indeed with so many external influences, coupled with the characteristics of property and the imperfections of the property market, fluctuation is inevitable. The problem for prospective developers is to determine at which stage in the cycle they are entering and what will be the position at and after the time of completion. The problem for archaeologists and planners is to know what the developer is thinking and how these factors will influence development decisions.

11.5 THE POST-WAR CYCLE OF DEVELOPMENT

If we look at how development has fared over recent decades it is possible to identify some of the causes for the boom and bust cycles. We have seen, for instance, that immediately after the Second World War there was an urgent need to replace much war-damaged property, but that the post-war building boom did not really get underway until there was a change of government. Public sector developments had proceeded but it was not until the 100% development charge on development value was abolished in 1953 and building licences were withdrawn in 1954 that private sector development started to flourish. Indeed it led to an unprecedented boom in land development which lasted until the 1960s.

One feature of much of this development was that many entrepreneurs held on to their property rather than sell it off. This was partly for taxation purposes as tax was payable on profits from sale but not on the surplus created before a development was sold. This encouraged developers to let their buildings on long leases and as a result they tended not to think seriously about the effects of inflation.

By the late 1950s, as living standards began to rise and consumer demands increased so inflation began to rise. At the same time the institutions which provided the long-term funds started to get interested in property. They could see that property was a good investment against inflation and began to cast an envious eye on development profits. They wanted a share. Interest rates were also rising which meant that developers were finding it more difficult to retain properties on completion. As the rate of interest rose (above the yield) so developers were forced towards profit-sharing with their financial backers. Thus the early to mid-1960s were characterized by profit-sharing schemes with the institutions playing a major part in this process. These years also witnessed a decrease in the profitability of property companies.

In 1964 a new Labour government came to power and shortly afterwards introduced strict controls on office development. Paradoxically, this helped to create a shortage of office building, particularly in central London. Inflation was also rising at this time, fuelled, in part, by shortages in accommodation, especially in London. As a result, rental values increased considerably. Property assets became more valuable with property company takeovers occurring more frequently. Rent review periods also fell, first to 14 years, then to seven and subsequently to five years. Together with rising inflation the cash flow into the institutions was such that they began to buy more property. Chiefly this was as a hedge against inflation. At the same time it also helped to finance an enormous development boom in the early 1970s.

The 1970s property boom

The period 1970–73 was characterized by a huge increase in land prices and a sharp upturn in development activity. Rising asset values encouraged developers to obtain short-term finance, relying on increased values to cover the cost of borrowing. Little attention was paid to the longer run and the importance of cashflow. Conservation also suffered although the interest at that time was in buildings and areas of historic interest rather than archaeology.

In 1973 the situation changed dramatically. The Arab–Israeli war in October of that year brought cheap oil and cheap everything else to an end. In its aftermath interest rates were raised to penal levels, killing demand at a stroke. Completed and unfinished buildings found no takers whilst their owners were having to pay prohibitively high loan charges. Sites which had been bought at excessive prices fuelled by the prevailing optimism and competition hung like millstones around the necks of their owners and the banks which had funded them. Property values plummeted, property shares collapsed and it became almost impossible to sell property or to obtain further borrowings against it.

For some years the demand for property stayed low. It was a period of retrenchment with a noticeable interest developing in techniques of viability and market research. The need for careful monitoring of supply and the rate of take-up was more clearly recognized. Meanwhile pension funds and insurance companies were helping distressed property companies and the banking sector by purchasing property investments.

By 1977–78 the downturn had run its course. Partly due to reflationary measures prior to the 1979 general election and partly due to radical changes introduced by the new Conservative government, the period up to 1981 saw a mini-boom in property development particularly in the south-east. Institutions were undertaken their own developments or financing developers, helped in part by the bargains picked up after the 1973 crash. By 1982, however, government measures to combat inflation were starting to take effect. Rising unemployment and recession began to hit tenant demand for property. At the same time yields increased, reflecting a lack of confidence in property which was to continue until 1986. The investment boom fuelled by the institutions was over.

Big bang

The late 1980s has been described as 'big bang'. Deregulation of the Stock Exchange and the opening up of the property markets to overseas investors led to a massive increase in investment in UK property. Bank lending for property increased enormously, fuelled in part by foreign competition which came mainly from the United States and Japan and later Scandinavia. In contrast, UK institutional investment in property saw a decline. From a total of around £2 bn invested annually in the early 1980s it fell to approximately £.14 bn by 1990.

The reasons for this decline are several. Investment performance in the early 1980s compared unfavourably with other investment opportunities. This was followed by a bull run on UK and overseas stock markets which attracted funds away from property. In addition the government's commitment to low inflation meant that property was not necessary as a hedge against inflation. Property, however, became far more popular following the worldwide stock market crash in 1987. The bulk of investment came from the banking sector as can be seen from Figure 11.1.

In 1989 the UK economy finished its expansionary phase and a year later it was becoming clear that the property market boom was ending. By the end of February 1991 outstanding debt to overseas banks was more than £17 bn or some 43% of total outstanding debt on property. Rental growth had ceased and lettings became difficult resulting in a rise in property yields. The banks were getting concerned about the mountain of debt which some commentators estimated to be a staggering £50 bn although this was probably an overestimate.

The 1990s

By 1993 the demand for well-let property investments had strengthened. Led by the main property companies, the property share price index started to outperform other share indexes enabling some companies to raise equity in order to reduce debt and fund new acquisitions. Banks, on the other hand, burdened by their overexposure to the property sector emphasized, and still

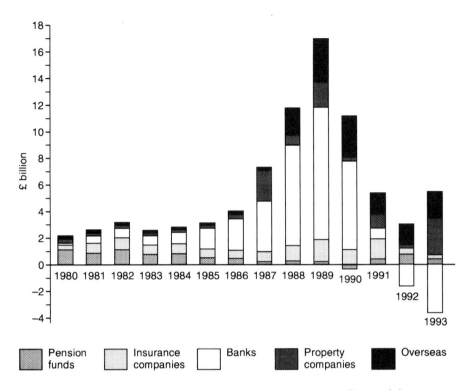

Figure 11.1 Money into property. (Source: Debenham Thorpe Research.)

do, debt-repayment rather than new lending. Overseas investment continued to decline although attention moved away from 'mega-deals' and developments of the late 1980s to a potentially more secure investment base. Central London has now become the main focus of attention whilst interest and acquisitions in other areas are very small and almost negligible (Debenham Thorpe Research, 1993).

Significantly, an important feature of the recovery of property has been the overwhelming need to acquire income-producing properties with secure tenants. Sophisticated financing techniques have also increased in popularity although they cannot remove the uncertainty. For many the level of borrowing or gearing has been too high, making it difficult to agree financial or refinancing packages. Income remains the key with very little being spent on new development. This means that there is little prospect for archaeological investigation funded by developers.

11.6 CONCLUSIONS ON THE DEVELOPMENT CYCLE

Given that property cannot quickly adjust to the demands of the market it is inevitable that there should be a natural cycle of development. What may be regarded as less natural is that external factors push this natural cycle to excess. Instead of a gradual change where supply and demand fluctuate gently we find that the supply of property can greatly exceed demand at one stage in the cycle to be followed by a severe shortage of accommodation at a later stage.

Market forces, government actions and the fact that it is such an imperfect market are the main reasons for this boom and bust. They make it virtually inevitable that the cycle of development will be excessive although it remains to be seen how future cycles will operate. After the collapse of the Exchange Rate Mechanism in 1992 property shares started to become more popular again with interest being shown by French, German and USA investors together with a large influx of money from Hong Kong. Perhaps a change of players may introduce new ideas and new motives. Perhaps they will make the same or similar mistakes.

As for previous cycles, it would seem that past booms were prompted by different motives. The 1950s and early 1960s appear to have been largely fuelled by pent-up demand which was unleashed when public controls were lifted to get the economy going. In the 1970s the motive appeared to be primarily one of investing as a hedge against inflation while in the 1980s it seemed to be motivated by a finance-led, 'get-rich-quick' mentality. In other words, history didn't quite repeat itself.

11.7 THE DEVELOPMENT PROCESS

The development process of finding a site, working out what to build on it and then constructing it has to operate within this cycle of development. Commencing at any time, it must work within the economics of supply and demand, acting vigorously when there is a shortage of accommodation and virtually coming to a stop when there is a glut. Where development has already commenced there is usually a need to complete it as quickly as possible in order to reduce building and borrowing costs. There may also be an increased possibility of a sale or letting if a building is completed early or on time. Contrary to what some archaeologists may think – that delay due to archaeological investigation is not significant – time, and timing, are of great importance to the developer. So much so that there will be times when it is better not to proceed.

Against this background, the development process in its simplest form works when a developer finds a site, employs an architect to design a scheme who then instructs a builder to undertake the work. The construction of a dwelling or similar one-off proposal (e.g. a golf club) would normally fall into this category. For much of modern property development, however, the process is not so simple. Sites are not easy to find or assemble and the financing and the provision of most buildings will depend on a number of factors. Uncertainty and risk are ever present and there is a need to evaluate carefully the proposal.

To overcome this complexity a useful technique is to break down the development process into recognizable stages. This can be done in a variety of ways but fundamentally there are four main areas of concern. They can be described as making development possible, preparation of the scheme, managing the construction and managing or disposing of the completed works. Archaeology will clearly be more involved with the first two of these stages although late discovery could affect the construction phase. The disposal state is the least important as far as archaeology is concerned although there are certain points that should not be overlooked.

Making development possible

Evaluation and preparation are the key to making a project viable. Indeed they are fundamental to its success, encompassing market analysis, financial assessment, planning considerations and detailed design. It is vital that a proper evaluation is made at the outset. Hunches and superficial knowledge of the market are totally unacceptable for many projects in the present economic climate. It is no good relying on the fact that someone else has carried out a similar project nearby and been successful. The chances are that it will not be repeated.

An understanding of the market is not enough. In order to evaluate a scheme properly the developer will also need to appreciate fully the practical aspects involved such as building costs, raising finance and so on. Short and long-term rates of interest and how they might fluctuate according to the cycle of development will also be crucial.

As part of this critical evaluation a number of preliminary investigations will be necessary and this is where archaeology can become important. Certain questions must be answered as soon as practicably possible so as to avoid abortive work. Matters such as land tenure, planning policy, legal encumbrances and, of course, archaeology should be investigated, according to local circumstances. The outcome of these investigations should enable the following question to be answered in the affirmative by a developer. Are you reasonably satisfied that the proposed development can proceed at the proposed site?

On occasions, some preparatory work will already have been done. Borehole samples may have been taken and a physical survey made of the site. Prudent developers may also have investigated the archaeological situation, but as a rule it is when the answer to the question is yes that preparatory work would proceed. Normally investigations would still continue as it is an ongoing exercise which does not cease until all the details of a scheme have been worked out.

Two aspects of preparatory work relevant to archaeology are planning control and a physical survey. As part of the planning process it is advisable, indeed necessary, to talk to the planning officer prior to submission of any planning application in order to establish what form the development can take and any archaeological or other implications that may exist. Sketch ideas can be of assistance at such a meeting and if archaeology is involved then an archaeological evaluation or an environmental statement will probably be required. The meeting would seek to find this out.

A physical survey would concentrate on site attributes and soil conditions. If redevelopment is involved the prospect of demolition and the existence of cellars would be relevant. They may indicate that all or part of the archaeological resource has already been destroyed, although on the other hand the presence of a building may prevent further site investigation where a site has not yet been acquired. An existing owner may not allow access or breaking into the ground for further examination. There could be sensitive equipment in use at the property, staff may be disturbed or the owner may simply be unwilling to allow access, in which case information will need to be obtained from other sources. The area planning officer and the authority's archaeological adviser would be a good bet. It might be advisable to notify them of any difficulties in obtaining access and information. They could suggest alternatives or at least provide other information about a site and its likely importance.

If listed buildings are involved or if the site is in a conservation area, restoration, conservation, limited new build or a combination of these would normally be expected. They might restrict access but allow phasing of development to proceed. This could suit both the developer and the archaeologist although care would need to be taken. Phasing may not suit both at the same time or in the same way and differences of opinion could create an impasse.

Preparation of the scheme

At this stage of the process the type of development appropriate to a site and to the developer will have been established. The principle would have been accepted by the planning authority, preferably with the grant of outline planning permission, and reports of surveys, market research and viability available for further analysis. They should enable the important work of detailed planning of the project to begin.

This will require a number of things. To start with, all available information should be examined to ensure nothing has been missed. A final check on viability would also be advisable with any development brief checked for technical and financial feasibility. A programme for the total project should be prepared with consideration given to the design team. This may or may not require the services of an archaeologist depending on the nature and importance of the archaeological resource. If in doubt it would be advisable to obtain archaeological advice. It could save time and money later.

During this period detailed drawings would be prepared for approval purposes and contractor selection. This may require the submission of applications under planning and health and safety legislation. The planning application would be either a full application incorporating all the details of the proposed development and how archaeological deposits may be affected or an application for approval of reserved matters, following the grant of outline planning permission. Care should be taken to ensure that all conditions attached to any permission were complied with. It might also be necessary to submit more than one application to cover all of the reserved matters.

Public health legislation requires that before building work can begin, the building regulations must be complied with. This involves either the submission of drawings for approval or the self-certification of drawings by the project architect. These drawings would normally form the basis for contract preparation and procedures. If the construction work is to be put out to tender, contract drawings showing plans, sections, elevations and details of the proposed works would normally form part of the documentation.

If the proposed development is large or complex it may be necessary to appoint a project manager, a matter which is looked at in the next Chapter. For smaller developments the developer or architect would probably be sufficient. Contracts would be entered into between the parties concerned and construction commenced.

Managing the construction

Once the building contract is agreed and exchanged by the parties involved there is no turning back. The parties are committed to the development which now starts in earnest. By this time archaeological excavations should have come to an end unless a phasing programme has been agreed allowing the archaeologists to continue occupying part of a site with the contractor commencing elsewhere. Great care needs to be taken if this arises, particularly in respect of health and safety requirements. If possible it ought to be avoided because it could lead to additional problems, particularly those relating to insurance.

One problem that could emerge after contracts have been exchanged is the discovery of important archaeological remains. This can and does happen, albeit infrequently, but it will almost inevitably result in delay to the contract particularly if there is a lot of adverse publicity. Public outcry can put the developer in an impossible position which means that the contract documents will need to safeguard against this eventually in some way. It is a matter which is referred to in the Chapter on contracts.

Assuming that archaeological excavations, if any, have been completed and the archaeologists have left the site, any remaining archaeological implications are likely to stem from restrictions attached to the planning permission. There could be conditions or planning obligations that still need satisfying.

Conditions attached to a planning permission may require protection of important archaeological remains at a site during the course of construction or that certain details of a development may need further approval. Protection of remains is likely to require some form of physical protection to prevent the contractor and subcontractors from entering the area. Further details for approval might relate to foundation design although this should already have been sorted out by this stage. More likely it may relate to the satisfactory implementation of the approved design with officers of the authority inspecting the site from time to time. This does not happen frequently although building inspectors, when checking groundworks under the building regulations, may report back to the planners on suspected infringements. Increased local authority enforcement powers introduced in 1991 and a reduced application workload may result in more of this happening.

The other most common planning requirement is for a watching brief to be maintained. This will involve an archaeologist occasionally inspecting a site and possibly taking photographs. He or she will be looking to see what turns up archaeologically speaking and noting what is there and what may be destroyed. It is very rare for it to develop into anything more than that. If important remains were thought likely the authority would normally have taken a greater interest at an earlier stage in the proceedings and determined the application accordingly.

One area where archaeologists may be particularly interested is ground-works associated with new buildings. At the early stages of design, attention often focuses on where buildings are to be erected, the type of foundations to be used and the likely impact of those foundations on archaeological remains. Where less attention is paid but which can be equally if not more important is the impact that drains, sewers, gas and water mains, electric cables, base courses for roads, car parking areas and the alteration of ground levels for landscaping purposes can have on archaeological remains. Depending on the suspected depth of deposits, these associated ground works could have a substantial effect on what lies beneath the ground. They should not be overlooked.

Disposal of the completed development

As stated earlier, this is the least important part of the development process as far as archaeology is concerned. With work completed, either an investigation has been made or remains have been destroyed or the design has been such as to leave virtually everything intact. Whichever, the records need to make it clear what has been done, that this is publicly acceptable and that this has been confirmed in writing. It would also be advisable to check all other planning requirements and public controls to ensure that they have been satisfied. The only matter likely to be outstanding will be the publication of finds following a site investigation. This could be a requirement of a planning agreement and would need to be checked.

REFERENCE

Debenham Thorpe Research (1993) *Money into Property*, DTZ Debenham Thorpe Ltd, London.

FURTHER READING

Darlow, C. (ed.) (1988) *Valuation and Development Appraisal* (2nd edn), Estates Gazette, London.

Fraser, W.D. (1984) *Principles of Property Investment and Pricing*, Macmillan, London.

Millington, A.F. (1989) *An Introduction to Property Valuation*, Estates Gazette, London.

Topping, R. and Avis, M. (eds) (1991) *David Cadman and Leslie Austin Crowe: Property Development* (3rd edn), E. & F.N. Spon, London.

Managing the project **12**

New building projects are hardly ever the same. Site factors and various constraints act to make each project different, requiring a lot of thinking about what to build and how to construct it. Concerns about size, appearance, methods and techniques of construction, funding and many more show that it is a not a standard product. Satisfactory completion must rely on the bringing together of many different ideas requiring interaction between the developer, a range of advisors and the builder. It requires team effort where the more a team puts into a project the more it will get out of it.

Many developers do not have the experience or the resources to get the right or best development from a site. Professional advice is often necessary which, traditionally, has been given by the architect. Other professionals, however, including the valuer, quantity surveyor, planner, structural engineer, electrical engineer, interior designer, accountant and solicitor can all be important. In our case we need to include the archaeologist as well.

The developer, whether an owner building for occupation, a commercial developer building speculatively or a government agency building for public use, has the problem of selecting a team and someone to co-ordinate their actions. Specialist property developers sometimes have an in-house team of experts or, more frequently, are able to select and lead a team of experts. Other organizations tend to rely on one or more of the professions, perhaps the architect, to perform the supervisory function. More recently, there has been a growing desire, especially with larger projects, to separate overall supervision from the design and build roles. A separate project manager is sometimes used, drawn from one of the property professions.

To be effective, a project manager must have a wide appreciation of all matters related to property and economic viability. Knowledge of building construction and aspects of design are very important but increasingly there is a need to understand the market, valuation techniques, finance, taxation, legislation and letting and disposal techniques. Many of these are pre-contract considerations which highlight the importance of controlling a project from inception to completion, from pre-contract to post-contract work.

It follows that the manager for a project should be appointed as soon as possible after the developer has decided in principle to proceed with a scheme. Initially the manager will need to interpret the client's or developer's requirements and advise on site identification and acquisition. This will bring valuation and planning skills to the fore, but it is also the time enquiries about archaeology should be made. The manager should ensure that there are no outstanding archaeological problems or, if the archaeological content of a site is not known but suspected to be significant, that steps to mitigate any problems are put in hand.

Once a scheme has been worked up and site, design, planning, financial and archaeological considerations have been taken into account, the procedure to commitment under a building contract can be followed. Decisions will then have to be made on which method of procurement to use, programming and budgetary controls. They are matters which can all be affected by archaeology particularly if remains are discovered after development commences.

In this Chapter the aim is to look at these matters, first by examining what we mean by project management and then to see how it can be used to satisfy the developer's requirements. This is followed by a brief examination of the different ways to secure the construction of a project, where the aim is to draw attention to the advantages and disadvantages of each procurement route. What they indicate is the need for a contract strategy which brings together the project team, design and evaluation, financial considerations, tendering and finally managing the construction.

12.1 DEFINING PROJECT MANAGEMENT

There are several ways in which project management can be defined. At its most simple it can be described as 'the management of the development process from start to finish' or more thoroughly as:

> the overall planning, controlling and co-ordination of a project from inception to completion aimed at meeting a client's requirements and ensuring that it is completed in time, to budget and to the required quality standard.
> *CIOB, 1982*

The parameters of the client's brief are all important. Physical and financial objectives should be clearly identified with procedures established and implemented to secure those objectives, updated and modified as and when necessary.

An important feature of project management implicit in this definition is that unlike general management, which is ongoing, it has a specified start time and completion date. Each development project requires its own plan of action which in some cases will require management only of the construction phase. In others it will be necessary to cover feasibility through to commissioning of the completed building where a team of professionals, with a project manager acting as leader, with a host of delegated powers will be needed. On such occasions it may be necessary to appoint an archaeologist to the team.

Whichever role is played the client will want to ensure that his or her objectives are obtained, wherein can lie a problem. The client is not always sufficiently informed of the relevant facts to make the best or most appropriate decisions. This could be so with archaeological matters where the client's judgement may suggest one course of action but not another which may be more appropriate. What the client needs is a project co-ordinator who can be relied upon to give the right advice, although this may not be easy. Differences of opinion can emerge with conflicting ideas about what to do or what is best. In the end, how people work together becomes important. Personalities and strength of character can often have an undue bearing on the final outcome. The ability to get on, therefore, can be crucial if a project is to be managed satifactorily.

12.2 THE DEVELOPER'S REQUIREMENTS

Different organizations will have different structures and requirements depending on their objectives and priorities. All will demand the quickest, cheapest, most valuable and best building possible but if time, cost, value, quality and function are to be assessed properly these objectives need to be identified. They can vary according to how we classify the developer.

Private or public

The aims of a private organization will differ considerably from those of a public body. From a preoccupation with profitability in the private sector to one of cost-effectiveness in the public, budgetary procedures, time-scales, cashflows and reporting mechanisms will all differ. Internal and external politics will also vary and require careful handling particularly where environmental concerns such as archaeology are present. Policy towards protection could differ enormously although this does not have to be so. If a public body takes on the role of the developer a different approach can sometimes be discerned.

Individual or corporate

The project management role can apply both to an individual or a corporate structure. If a scheme is large or where the individual lacks expertise, a project manager would probably be appointed although the role could differ. Different methods of working and reporting could mean that the project manager acts in an advisory capacity or as an important decision-maker. Depending on background the project manager could have to make decisions on a variety of matters including archaeology although it is likely that specialist advice would be sought.

Construction experience

Depending on the amount of previous experience a developer has, the level of confidence between the parties, the degree of involvement, the means of communicating between them and other relationships will vary. The less the experience, the greater the need to depend on the project manager although in practice this is not always the case. The desire for independence, a need to hide insecurity and a sense of bravado can lead to poor decision-making which could be crucial where public controls are involved, particularly those involved with archaeology.

Occupation or speculation

Timing, cost, quality and function can all vary according to whether or not the developer intends to occupy a building for personal use or whether it is to be sold to someone else. Sometimes a project manager will have to make the speculator more aware of users' requirements or the prospective owner–occupier more aware of the marketability of a project. Both will need to be kept aware of public interest and the concerns, among others, of archaeology.

Delegatory or hierarchical

Client organizations can operate in very different ways in terms of level of authority, degree of bureaucracy, method of approval, style of reporting and speed of response. An appreciation of the methods used will be important in devising the most effective way of communicating between the developer and project manager. Timing and conditions of contract could be crucial where difficult and unexpected decisions (archaeological discovery?) have to be made quickly.

12.3 THE ROLE OF THE PROJECT MANAGER

The first thing the project manager needs to do is establish his or her terms of reference and, more precisely, the degree of authority and responsibility to be exercised over the professional team and others engaged in a project. Ideally he or she should be the single point of reference representing the client. This can be important, particularly when the client is a corporate body or committee. Methods of communication and reporting must be agreed although this must be both ways. It is important that the project manager continually keeps the developer informed. Many developers will insist upon this and some will exercise their right to attend all meetings during the development. Others may assume part of the project manager's responsibilities themselves.

Where responsibilities are shared the attendance at meetings of both will be a necessity or there must be absolute certainty and confidence over responsibilities. It is a matter that should be discussed at the beginning of any appointment. If archaeology is a matter for consideration, as with other subjects, it is imperative that the developer and manager are both fully aware of their respective responsibilities.

A second initial consideration for the project manager will be an assessment of the developer's requirements for a site. Consideration should be given to the form of development, location, funds, time and environmental constraints. If a brief for a project has not been prepared the project manager ought to prepare one. If it has already been drawn up, now would be the time for the project manager to carefully scrutinize it. Things could have been missed out or insufficient attention given to some aspects of a development such as design or finishes whilst too much may have been given to others. Archaeology could be a factor not sufficiently catered for in a brief.

Where a developer or client intends to occupy completed premises attention will often be paid to operational needs as opposed to marketability. It would be unwise, however, to consider only the client's requirements without paying attention to market conditions. Personal preferences may not be generally acceptable and they could make a property more difficult to sell at a later date. Conversely, where cost is the overriding consideration great care should be paid to such matters as design and user-requirements. If too many savings are made it may be difficult to find an occupier willing to take possession at the required rent or price. These points are important because if archaeological considerations are present they could affect cost. They will make it necessary to ensure that the development will still satisfy operational needs and be a marketable proposition.

To ensure that these different possibilities or eventualities are not overlooked and are fully taken into account, the management structure must be designed around the project and fit in with local circumstances and conditions. These and other variables including complexity, degree of innovation, market forces and external factors will need to be built into the system if success is to be achieved. It will also be necessary to identify the main decision points in the development process and determine the consequences which may flow from events such as the grant of planning permission, the completion of site acquisition, the exchange of building contracts and the final certification of completion of a project. A programme of action should be prepared which identifies the critical path through the development. The management structure however will depend, in part, on the procurement route, which is one of the important considerations for the project manager and client to sort out.

12.4 THE PROCUREMENT PROCESS

When people in the construction industry talk about procurement they are talking about how to bring design, construction and management functions together to ensure satisfactory completion of a project. There is a need to make sure that it is completed as efficiently and as effectively as possible. Not surprisingly it is an area of considerable concern to developers.

In practice there are four main ways of organizing procurement. All require the developer to define the fundamental objectives of the project, how first-line responsibilities are to be carried out, who will have the ultimate responsibility and how finance is to be provided. Different emphasis will be placed on these requirements according to local circumstances. All can have a varying impact on archaeology and, when present, be affected by it, making it necessary to proceed with caution. Each procurement route has its advantages and disadvantages.

The four main procurement routes are usually referred to as the traditional route, the design and build approach, the management approach, and the design and manage system.

The traditional route

Traditionally, contracting in the construction industry was built on the need for a strong chain of command and the avoidance of divided responsibility at all stages of construction, from inception to completion.

In accordance with this route an intending owner, once the works had been designed, would place the responsibility for production in the hands of a contractor normally selected from a group of contractors tendering against each other in competition. This contractor would then be free to organize the construction of the works. The contractor's own labour force could be used or parts of the work could be sublet to other firms where the contractor's labour was inadequate or lacked sufficient skills.

Over the years the practice of subletting grew in popularity although it was recognized that this could act against the owner's interest. Having taken care to choose a contractor capable of producing work to a desired quality there was a need for the owner to ensure that this quality was maintained by all the subcontractors. It therefore became customary in construction contracts to require the main contractor to obtain the owner's permission for any subletting or assignment.

As construction projects became larger and more complex, fewer contractors were able to carry them out solely from their own resources and subletting became an acceptable practice. In addition, architects and engineers found it increasingly necessary to require certain aspects of a project to be undertaken by specialist firms. These were often selected by the architect or engineer because of their known ability in a particular field of work. Such subcontractors or suppliers were **nominated**, as opposed to those chosen by the main contractor who became **domestic** subcontractors or suppliers.

Over the years this traditional approach has been refined to take account of changing circumstances with contractual relationships now generally conforming to the pattern shown in Figure 12.1. More care is now taken at the feasibility stage to ensure that the project is viable. Preliminary designs undergo a process of cost-checking and a great deal of attention is paid to the final design and cost estimates by consultants who then prepare tender documents.

A key feature of the traditional approach is the sequencing of events. Consultants are appointed first to design and cost the project, with the main contractor generally appointed at a later date on the advice of the consultants. Complete or nearly complete information is supplied to the contractor from which a tender can be compiled. More recently, an accelerated approach has been developed where tenders are based on partially complete information and the successful contractor becomes part of the design team assisting with the completion of the design.

These traditional methods rely on the separate professional disciplines working within established and well-tried procedures. Standard forms of

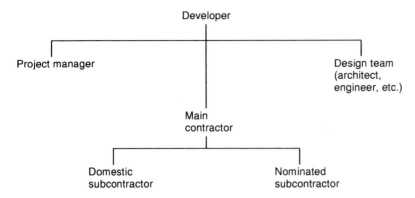

Figure 12.1 The traditional procurement route.

contract, standard methods of measurement and standard information are all essential to its smooth operation. There is a sequence of events which provides for effective construction but if the project has to be altered in any way for any reason, it can result in considerable delay to the project. Even with each professional's function being carried out in the correct sequence, the method is not always efficient, which is why it is not favoured by many developers.

For archaeology there can be distinct advantages in adopting this procurement route. If attention has to be paid to special design features or if archaeological remains are discovered after the commencement of development, the approach does allow for variations to be made. The disadvantage is that because of the inherent delays built into this method efficiency will be inhibited. It can leave the developer with a building that is delivered late and at a higher price than was originally expected or agreed.

If the design is inadequately prepared the quality of the scheme tends to suffer. Savings may have to be made in the types of materials used or in design solutions although this can cause unexpected problems. Urban archaeological sites tend to be located in conservation areas reflecting the historical character of these areas and where local planning authorities have a special duty to seek to preserve or enhance their character or appearance. This comes before any duty to consider the proposal against archaeological considerations, which means that if any savings have to be made they may have to come from archaeology rather than from design considerations.

If both are important there could be difficulties for the developer and project manager, although if time is important an accelerated method can be used. This relies on quicker decision-making procedures being established although, to be successful, the whole of the project team needs to be able to act quickly. Ideally they should be located at or near the site, which can be difficult. Without this accessibility, however, the process of decision-making and adjustment to the professional and contractual inputs for the most appropriate sequence becomes more difficult. Thus, whilst the traditional approach can accommodate archaeological considerations it is a matter that needs to be investigated at the earliest opportunity. If it is not there could be unacceptable delay and additional costs.

The design and build approach

As the name suggests, this type of arrangement is where one organization, generally the contractor, is appointed to design and construct the project. Illustrated in Figure 12.2, the process starts with a developer selecting a contractor who then proceeds with the project in accordance with given instructions. These will vary depending on the objectives of the developer and the approach that is adopted. Three are possible, namely the direct, the competitive and the develop and construct approaches.

Direct

Here a designer-contractor will be appointed after some appraisal but without competition. The contractor then provides the whole service of design and construction in accordance with a budget agreed by the developer, who will frequently appoint a project manager or representative to protect the developer's interests.

Competitive

With this approach a brief will be prepared outlining the developer's cost limits, space needs and building quality requirements, in what is sometimes referred to as a performance specification. A limited number of contractors will be approached, chosen for their expertise in the particular fields of design and build relevant to the project. They will then offer designs and prices in competition and in response to the initial brief. Each will develop a solution to the project which will almost inevitably provide the developer with a choice in design, price and time-scale. The chosen contractor will go on to complete the scheme, usually under the watchful eye of a developer's representative who will monitor progress and quality.

Develop and construct

This system is similar to the competitive approach above but varies to the extent that consultants are appointed to partially design the building with the contractor completing and guaranteeing the design in competition. The developer will still get a choice of final design as each contractor will produce a variation from the original, although there will be less variety because they will all spring from the initial partial design provided by the developer. The successful contractor will complete the scheme and again, a developer's representative or project manager will normally be appointed.

Whichever of the above three variants is adopted, the two main factors which will determine the success of the project are the developer's brief and quality control. It is essential that the developer knows and can make it clear what his or her requirements are before entering into a design and build

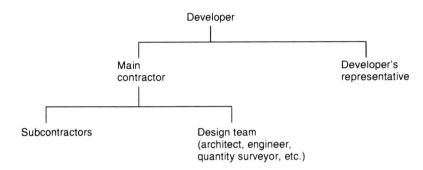

Figure 12.2 The design and build procurement route.

contract. The statement of need must be as detailed as necessary to reflect those matters which the developer considers important. At the same time the contractor should be provided with discretion so that the most effective design can be produced.

With regard to quality control, the overall performance will depend on the quality assurance procedures that are adopted. At each stage of the development process, the developer's advisers should check the proposals, components and completed construction work to ensure that they come up to the required standard. Sometimes this can be difficult to quantify and lead to disagreement and arbitration.

It follows from the two requirements for success that the design and build approach will be more appropriate where construction is to be a proprietary system or if a contractor has specialist knowledge and experience in a particular type of development. It is less likely to be suitable for complex or innovative projects where ideas or products have not been sufficiently tried and tested.

It also follows that the design of a scheme should not be varied once it has been agreed because the system provides no equitable basis for valuing alterations. Thus, if there is any likelihood of archaeological remains being discovered, which require changes to be made to the scheme, this approach would not be suitable. On the other hand if only a watching brief is required or if an archaeological investigation has already been carried out and no mitigating strategy is necessary this approach could be used. It would save time and could, other things being equal, be an efficient and cost-effective way of procuring a building.

The management approach

Under this approach the developer appoints design and cost consultants to prepare a building design and basic tender documents. Thereafter a manager is appointed to manage the construction process in one of two ways. Either a management contractor is appointed to deliver the project within an agreed time-scale and to a fixed price, as shown in Figure 12.3, or a professional firm is approached to provide the management service, as in Figure 12.4. The former is known as **management contracting**, the latter as **construction management**.

In both cases the design and initial tender documents are generally provided by consultants and the appointed management contractor or consultant only manages and controls the construction activities. This means that the developer must play a key role in the procurement process. Whereas the developer has to define the project objectives, select the procurement system, provide the finance and select the firms to carry out the first-line responsibilities in all procurement systems, under the management systems the developer must also act as chair or referee. Under the management approach a team of equals is created.

This equal status is a distinctive feature of the management approach. It means that the developer has to be involved fully in key decision-making mainly to ensure that the objectives of the project are met and remain paramount. It is a demanding task requiring careful thought and preparation. Frequently a specialist representative is appointed to help in this task but at the end of the day the resultant building will depend very much on the degree of control the developer retains over the various specialists who actually carry out the work.

Specialist contractors appointed under this route will have more responsibilities than in the traditional approach. Their selection, therefore, must be

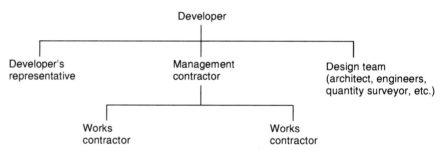

Figure 12.3 The management contracting procurement route.

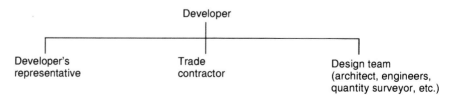

Figure 12.4 The construction management procurement route.

based on previous experience that is directly relevant to the project in hand. A 'can-do' attitude is often required when faced with potential problems, success depending on everyone pulling together to meet the project's objectives. Normally archaeological considerations should have been taken into account by the design consultants.

The design and manage system

This system combines many of the characteristics of the design and build and management routes. The developer appoints one firm to design and deliver the project with specialist contractors appointed to carry out the construction work. Two variations are possible. In the first, the firm taken on to design and manage the project takes a contractual risk in delivering it to an agreed price and an agreed time employing design consultants and specialist contractors as subcontractors. In the second, the project manager and designer is employed as the developer's agent and specialist contractors enter into direct contracts with the developer.

This approach is not widely used in the UK although it operates with some success elsewhere. It provides a synthesis of the design and build and management approaches which are themselves becoming more popular. The key to their success, however, depends on how well the developer's objectives are set out and how well quality assurance is built in. By combining single-point responsibility, it is attractive to many developers although it does require special contractual arrangements.

12.5 CHOICE OF PROCUREMENT ROUTE

The selection of the appropriate contract arrangements for any type of construction will depend on prevailing circumstances, which can vary and conflict. Vested interests, experience, prejudices and time and cost factors can all make the choice difficult. Conflicting opinions may be received and they may not necessarily always be in the developer's best interest. Sometimes advice may be more beneficial to the person or organization offering it or it may be given against a limited professional background. The planner or archaeologist, for instance, may be convinced that alterations should be made to a scheme but not be aware of the full time and cost implications to the developer of making those alterations. It highlights the need for a team of professionals working together for the benefit of the client. This is especially so where he or she is dependent on the professional advice received.

The client's main requirements are time, cost and quality, as shown in Table 12.1. Each can be satisfactorily accommodated within the procurement routes although different emphasis and different levels of risk and control apply. For example, a developer who wants speed and economy and is content with straightforward, reliable quality should consider the design and build route. If high performance, archaeology or individual design are important and time and money are less of a problem, the traditonal route should be considered.

Table 12.1 Main concerns of the developer about a project

	Importance of need as percentage of total	Total percentage
Quality		
Aesthetics	5	
Function	25	
Technology	15	
		45
Cost		
Initial	25	
Life cycle	10	
		35
Time	20	20
		100

Adapted from Walker (1989)

Within each method trade-offs between design, quality, innovation, speed of construction and cost are possible and developers must therefore consider what value to attach to cost, time and quality. This however, raises a number of issues.

Cost

It is generally believed that competitive open tendering produces the cheapest price from a contractor and that a negotiated tender is likely to add about 5% to the contract sum. Special requirements such as an unusually short contract period or the imposition of higher standards for the construction process are also believed to push up costs. However, of growing importance to many clients are cash flow projections and, depending on whether or not the developer is going to retain possession, life cycle costs. The different contractual arrangements will not treat these matters equally and it can be difficult to make fair and realistic comparisons even when similar projects are proposed. Evidence for one course of action in preference to another may not be clear.

In addition it is important to set a sound budget incorporating a realistic contingency sum to cover unforeseen circumstances. On all but the smallest projects expectation of a fixed price is totally unrealistic. Building projects are inevitably complex and not every eventuality can be planned and costed in advance. Variations occur for a variety of reasons and not just archaeology and the project manager must allow for this. The final cost will generally be above the original estimate and the developer must retain a reserve to cover this. The project manager would in effect be the guardian of this contingency.

Time

Developers of all types usually want their building 'yesterday'. Design and construction processes, however, are lengthy and can be longer if archaeology is involved. Time will impact on buildability and different methods of procurement and contractor selection must be carefully examined against the time factor. Note too that this can vary. For example, a superstore may need to be opened for the Christmas period whereas a new school may not be needed until the beginning of the next academic year. Public works are sometimes delayed until the existing infrastructure can no longer cope with the requirements placed on it so that the project then needs to be completed as quickly as possible in order to reduce complaints by the public. In every case a deadline will be imposed.

Design

It is sometimes argued that the best design structure will be produced by someone who is independent of the builder and who has a wide experience of the type of development that is proposed. Some designs, however, have lacked buildability and resulted in considerable defects in use. They have not always fulfilled the developer's broader needs with the result that many developers favour the design and build alternative because it transfers responsibility to the contractor. It is an approach that is becoming increasingly popular although it will not be suitable everywhere. Archaeology can be one of the factors making it less of a practical alternative. It can lead to one of the more traditional and conventional designs being preferred.

Quality

Linked to design is quality. The statement 'you get what you pay for' is particularly apt with quality reflected in the design, specification, supervision and capabilities and skill of the builder. Fast-track procedures and the lack of supervision can impair quality. Where subcontracting and privatization are involved they can add to problems of quality control, although firms which are known to complete on time to performance standards and who are reputable can go a long way towards satisfying quality objectives.

Quality, however, is often a problem. Trotman (1992), Head of Advisory Services at the BRE, for example, reported that some 28% of problems are caused by design faults, 17% by component failure with 37% caused by faulty execution. Pre-contract planning and quality control, therefore, are crucial making it vital that developers select the appropriate quality level for their projects. This will generally be more effective than allowing a greater contingency sum to cover problems later on.

Responsibility

Once the issues of cost, time and quality are resolved the next important factor for the developer is to decide on the level of personal involvement in the management of a project. Levels of involvement differ considerably according to the procurement route taken. Construction management involves a considerable input by the developer whilst the design and build system places responsibility on the contractor. This allows the developer to define requirements and merely monitor the actions of the contractor, although this may be insufficient if archaeology is relevant or where outstanding archaeological matters are not fully resolved.

Various options are available concerning the level of responsibility and much will depend on the knowledge and experience of the developer. Some will be more informed than others and will ensure that all essential specialist skills are brought into their projects as and when necessary. They will know when to employ an archaeologist and have a pretty good idea of what to do when things go wrong. For others the risks are likely to be greater.

Commitment

The next important decision the developer will have to make is when to enter into a firm contract for the construction work. The procurement routes allow this decision to be made at different stages in the process. The design and build route allows this to be made early in the development process which again could cause problems. There will be a need to ensure that archaeological matters are resolved through the evaluation process which may make the traditional route a more suitable alternative, especially if matters are still outstanding or where uncertainty exists. Under the management system, although the client will appoint a management contractor or consultant, individual construction contracts will not have to be signed until required, making this another alternative, although even here much can depend on the results of the archaeological evaluation.

Flexibility

Another important factor which will influence the choice of procurement route is the need for the developer to make changes as design and construction proceed. All the options make allowances for change but the important issue is the ease with which this can be done. Changes can be very expensive and different routes can have different effects on both cost and time.

Archaeology is a matter that would normally become apparent and be resolved at or before the design stage. Occasionally it will arise later suggesting that the traditional approach would be more appropriate. Change, as we have seen, is most difficult under the design and build approach.

Risk

There are risks for everyone involved in a development project. Problems can arise from a number of causes including:

- the late submission of design details, where information about archaeology has not been co-ordinated;
- misunderstandings between designers and contractors;
- uncertainty over construction method;
- the possible knock-on effect of delay caused by the discovery of archaeological remains or other environmental problems.

Contracts with consultants, contractors and specialists provide the developer with considerable control and influence but risks will still be present. Generally they will be shared between the parties involved although this can be to varying extents as we shall see in Chapter 14.

Conclusions on procurement route

The developer's final choice will depend on the developer's objectives in terms of function, value, time, cost, quality and certainty. Table 12.2 outlines what is involved in choosing between the alternatives although it should be noted that not all of the factors will be present with every project. Different developers will have different priorities and as no two schemes are the same there can be no simple or single solution. Whilst archaeological considerations would normally be best accommodated under the traditional route, if an investigation has already been undertaken and no further investigative work is required, on the face of it, there may be no reason why the design and build approach should not be adopted. The case against such a route would be if there were a strong possibility of unexpected and important finds being discovered. In other words, location and the known or expected historical importance of an area become important considerations.

12.6 SELECTION OF CONTRACTOR

There are several ways to choose the contractor for a project ranging from open competition with any number of firms to negotiation with a single contractor. All have their advantages and disadvantages and each will have its own implications for archaeology which, when relevant, should be considered as part of the selection process.

Open competition

This method allows any contractor who feels capable of carrying out a project to request the appropriate tender documents. In theory, any firm can submit a tender although in practice there will usually be limitations on the number who receive the documents and who return then completed. This is because the costs of preparation can be expensive. There is also the realization that each firm will not know the extent of the competition and competitors are unlikely to be vetted beforehand. Standards will vary and some applicants may be inappropriate for the job. A reputable firm may not find it worthwhile to compete in this situation with the result that standards may also be lowered. The standing of some contractors may be in doubt resulting in a reduced standard for the project at little difference in cost. The result could be inappropriate if archaeological considerations have to be taken into account. Insufficient attention might be given to such matters or insufficient allowances made for archaeological investigation in the pricing.

Table 12.2 Choosing the procurement route – strengths and weaknesses

Priorities	Procurement route								
	Traditional		Design and build			Management		Design and manage	
	Sequential	Accelerated	Direct	Competition	Develop and construct	Management contracting	Construction management	Contractor project manager	Consultant project manager
Time		●	●	●	●	●	●	●	●
Cost	●		●	●	●				
Flexibility		●				●	●		
Complexity		●				●	●		●
Quality	●	●				●	●		●
Certainty (completion/budget)	●		●	●	●	●	●	●	●
Responsibilities (single-point)	●		●	●	●			●	●
Risk avoidance				●				●	●

Dots denote where methods are likely to have advantages

Selective competition

This method can be used for almost any type of building or civil engineering project where there are enough suitable contractors to approach. It generally involves a code of procedures which, whilst not mandatory, provide useful guidance on the preparation and selection of tenders. Contractors know where they stand and will generally put more time and effort into their proposals. More care and attention will be given to detailing, which can include allowances for archaeology. The client does not have to accept the lowest tender price with the result that those firms selected to tender will know that they will have a reasonable chance of success: it will be far greater than in an open competition and is likely to result in a better quality of proposal.

Negotiation

This method involves the agreement of a tender price between a single contractor and the client. There is no competition, other than acceptability of price, which means that this procedure is likely to result in a higher tender sum than might be achieved using a form of selective competition. It is sometimes used, however, when a business relationship already exists between client and contractor, or where an early start on site is required or where the contractor has known special capabilities which the client considers to be important for the success of the project.

A negotiated contract should result in fewer errors in pricing and consequently there should be fewer claims to recover any losses. It could involve contractor participation in the design of the project and lead, as a result, to greater co-operation during the construction period. It would not, however, be appropriate for many public sector projects. Local authorities do not favour this method because of the increased costs and the need for public accountability. It could also lead to suggestions of possible favouritism. In the private sector it might be suitable where archaeology is important and the contractor is known to have experience in this field.

12.7 THE PROJECT TEAM

In order that a project is managed efficiently and effectively, there will usually be a need for someone who understands the development process to take charge. A project manager with a knowledge of building technology and construction methods in use today, and who can appreciate the effects they can have on the development process, is normally the best person. If employed in-house by the client the project manager may well have this knowledge. This is sometimes the case in the public sector and with some large private sector operators who have their own in-house departments. Elsewhere, if the developer does not feel confident to do the job, an outside consultant should be used.

Frequently developers will need to employ specialists to prepare briefs, co-ordinate consultants and oversee construction work. Decisions will have to be made about the range of professionals to appoint from the various disciplines, whether to appoint one firm for this work or to approach different firms for different aspects of the work. There may be the question of whether to appoint a team that has worked together previously or to assemble a new team especially for the job in hand. In every case the respective advantages and disadvantages of each alternative must be explored and weighed most carefully. The chemistry of individual personalities will also be important.

If archaeological matters are relevant there will usually be a need for specialist archaeological advice. Other consultants, too, will need to know more about the effects of archaeology and to advise on aspects of a project. The developer may need to know, for example, what the effects of archaeology will be upon structural design and how they can be tackled. There are several interrelationships which could be important as outlined in the following:

- **The client's representative** Ostensibly to represent, look after and maintain the client's interest, the client's representative will assist the developer in the formulation of a brief, establish cost and time parameters, advise on procurement routes, appoint consultants and generally fulfil a co-ordinating role for the project. It is debatable how conversant the representative may be with archaeological matters and how to deal with them, indicating that background and experience will be important.
- **Project manager** Increasingly the project manager takes on the role of client's representative but where this is not the case the project manager will manage the project either from inception to completion or during the construction phase on behalf of the client. When it is the former the project manager will normally be responsible for the administration, management, communication and co-ordination of a project and be required to provide a range of services, as shown in Table 12.3. Naturally, not every project will involve all of these services although the list does give a good indication of where the project manager may be involved. Again, background and experience will be important.
- **Architect** Traditionally the design team leader, the architect may or may not have responsibility for co-ordinating the efforts of other members of the team. Inevitably the architect will provide the basic design although structural engineers, heating engineers and others may be called upon to flesh out detailed aspects of the design. If archaeological remains are present the architect would be advised of any constraints they may impose on the design and layout of a project. Factors such as siting of buildings and type and position of foundations will be the most important.
- **Quantity surveyor** The primary role of the quantity surveyor is to act as financial adviser to the design team and often to propose the most appropriate procurement route and the contract most suited to the client's needs. The quantity surveyor will frequently produce many of the contractual documents, taking care when archaeological matters are involved. These could affect the costings and the procurement route and it

Table 12.3 Services that may be provided by a project manager

- Site selection
- Analysis
- Funding
- Valuation
- Appointment of consultants
- Project brief
- Design and quality control
- Reporting
- Programming
- Managing the budget
- Construction economics
- Cash flow forecasting
- Obtaining approvals
- Contract procedures
- Contract management
- Building management
- Fitting out
- Commissioning
- Tenancy arrangements

may be necessary for the final decision to be a team effort based on an evaluation of the alternative costs involved.

- **Structural engineers** The structural engineer is responsible for ensuring that the architect's design is capable of realization and that any foundation design and basic construction method, where required to avoid archaeological remains, will satisfactorily carry the necessary loads. If an innovative approach is adopted this could have cost implications.
- **The planning consultant** The planning consultant will usually be employed where planning difficulties are thought likely. This could be in respect of obtaining planning permission but, where archaeology is involved, an assessment of the conditions and other restrictions will probably be more important. The planning consultant's advice on the terms and reasonableness of a Section 106 agreement (Section 50 in Scotland) could be significant.
- **The archaeologist** Largely self-explanatory, the role of the archaeologist will be to advise the other members of the team of the importance of the archaeological resource and the degree to which it should be protected. He or she would advise on the most important parts of a site, the areas that might be acceptable for limited destruction and the consequences of not fully taking public controls into account. There may also be a need to give independent advice on any archaeological brief or specification prepared by or on behalf of the local planning authority.
- **Landscape architect** On many larger building sites landscaping is important. Hard landscaping (i.e. paved areas, etc.) and soft landscaping (planting, trees, mounding, etc.) are often seen as necessary to enhance a project although both can have implications for archaeology. The additional weight of earth mounds or the possible effects of tree roots may mean than different solutions will have to be found to avoid undue damage to archaeological remains. Alternatively, where they are exposed it may be

necessary to design them carefully into the landscaping. The landscape architect would give advice on these matters.

Comments on the team

The above are those professional advisers to a development project who are most likely to become involved in matters relating to archaeology. Other team members may be present but their concerns about archaeology will be secondary. The heating engineer, for instance, will not normally be involved although the marketing surveyor might wish to use archaeological remains as a marketing tool in the disposal of a property.

Where the project manager or co-ordinator has the opportunity to assemble and integrate a team this will provide a great advantage for proper management of the project although in many cases the client will want to approve the appointment of the members of the professional team. The actual selection, however, should be carefully assessed and acted up on at the outset if potential problems are to be avoided.

Increasingly, a choice has to be made between the different methods of procurement referred to. Therefore, it is often essential that the contractor is a member of the project team and plays a full part in the design process. The more the contractor knows about any archaeological considerations in advance the better.

12.8 DESIGN AND EVALUATION

As far as design is concerned the architect's role is fundamental to a project and should not be underestimated. He or she must know the accommodation and essential space requirement of the developer so that sketch layouts which will form the basis for approximate cost and financial viability can be prepared. The architect's brief should include special fitments and services, the standard of decoration and finishes required, servicing arrangements and, of course, any limitations that may be imposed by archaeology. In some cases the architect may be required or have to find this out personally.

With larger schemes or those in sensitive locations there may be a planning brief prepared by the planning authority setting out design and other parameters to work to. Such a brief will not have statutory force but will nevertheless be a material consideration and explain the authority's policy for a site. It cannot be ignored and will form an important factor influencing design and layout. Other constraints on a site such as legal encumbrances, an archaeological specification and the precise establishment of site boundaries will have to be taken into account in the design concept.

Once the architect has prepared detailed proposals they will require scrutiny and examination. Apart from initial cost, future maintenance and management points of view, the archaeological implications should also be studied where they are recognized as having an impact. There will be a need to ensure that the design not only minimizes any adverse effect on remains but that it is feasible and practical to construct in the circumstances. The last thing the developer and architect will want is to have to change the design after development commences.

Of course, unexpected archaeological discoveries can be made and it should be appreciated that alterations may be necessary and incorporated into plans for a project. This has happened on occasions in the past, admittedly infrequently. It does emphasize the need for a 'hands-on' approach and the ability to adapt to changing circumstances.

12.9 FINANCIAL MATTERS

Viability and funding

The architect's drawings will form the basis for the financial consideration. Initially this will focus on viability and how to fund the development to be followed by a more detailed cost analysis and cost-planning exercise. Viability will be assessed in terms of total costs against value. Gross and net floorspace figures will be used alongside comparative costs and rents per square metre to appraise the development. As we shall see in Chapter 16 the techniques for doing this are based on deducting total costs from estimated value (the residual valuation) or by discounting future costs (the discounted cash flow technique).

The resulting figures can be used to assess where the money is to come from. Several possibilities exist and the project manager should be aware of the alternatives available and advise accordingly. Discussed in Chapter 15 in more detail, they will principally involve internal self-financing, borrowing short-term or involving a longer-term equity partner to provide the finance. The aim of the project manager will be to see that there are no outstanding problems regarding the sources of finance and that matters such as archaeology will not result in additional money being sought.

Other financial aspects are grants and taxation. These should also be considered at this stage. The project manager's role will be to ensure that the necessary advice is sought and obtained with the options compared in relation to costs and client's preferences. The project manager will also need to ensure that any grants will be available as and when they are required. The client will be consulted on cost and expected income where appropriate.

Cost-planning

Cost-planning mainly consists of the quantity surveyor providing information on the cost of a project design or alternative designs as necessary. The initial financial appraisal may have assessed cost on a comparative cost per square metre basis. It will not have taken account of any variations such as the shape and detailing of external walling or unusual foundations that may be required to avoid archaeological remains. What is now needed is a more detailed cost-plan.

The cost-plan will usually provide estimates broken down into the scheme's different elements. These will be defined as the substructure, superstructure,

Table 12.4 Main elements of a project cost-plan

Substructure	Type and extent of foundations
Superstructure	Type of frame, roof structure, external walls, windows and external doors, stairs
Internal finishes	Wall, floor and ceiling finishes
Fittings and furnishings	Reception areas, office and catering fittings
Services	Sanitary appliances, disposal installations, water and heating systems, ventilation systems, electrical and gas installations, lift and conveyor services, communication and other special installations
External works	Site works, drainage, access ways, paving and car parking work, landscaping and other external works and services

finishes, fittings, services and external works where the aims will be to achieve a balanced expenditure and to control the design so that the client's financial commitments are met. Table 12.4 shows the elements involved. Those directly relevant to archaeology are, of course, the substructure and external works. The frame and external and internal walls in the superstructure could be indirectly affected.

The process of cost planning should achieve a balanced design solution. By covering all of the client's expenditure requirements it should be possible to:

- identify a realistic overall cost limit;
- assess a cost limit for each element of the project;
- identify where unusually large or expensive elements occur;
- ensure that money will be spent as intended.

The plan enables checks to be made and can help identify possible savings. In short, it will provide financial control over the design and help keep it within the bounds of economic viability.

As far as the impact of archaeology is concerned, a main area of concern will be foundation costs. If a project has to be designed to accommodate or preserve archaeological remains it may be necessary to locate piles further apart with additional strengthening. This could mean larger and deeper piles plus reinforced beams spanning the remaining but fewer piles. The cost-plan, however, should reveal any disproportionate amount for the substructure.

Another cost implication arising from archaeological considerations and which should be revealed by the cost-plan is the possible effect on superstructure. If the design has to straddle or go round archaeological remains it could affect walling and the above-ground framework. It may be necessary, for example, to use other design principles (Chapter 13 touches on this) in order to reduce project excavation works. Alternatively there may be scope for incorporating remains as a design feature of the development. Either way, the cost-plan should identify the cost implications, although if these are excessive it may be necessary to reassess the proposals. Viability could be affected especially when the development is small in scale and where the developer is working to a tight schedule and budget. Smaller schemes could be the hardest hit although, ironically, these are often the ones where less attention is given to archaeological matters.

12.10 TENDERING

Archaeology normally has few implications for tendering although two points are worth mentioning. These relate to maintaining control and examination of the submitted tenders.

First, the preparation of tender documents is normally the task of the quantity surveyor. Certainly that is the case for all major projects where detailed bills of quantities are prepared. It is the preferred option which, importantly, means that there is little room for subsequent manoeuvre by the contractor. In many cases this will not matter, especially when the contractor is known for experience, quality of work, financial soundness and capacity to undertake the work. The client will be able to rely on performance. On the other hand, where the contractor is not known or where cost is a critical factor in choosing the contractor, great care will need to be taken to maintain the standard of construction work. This will be particularly important where sensitive design and environmental conditions, including archaeology, are present.

Second, there will be a need to examine carefully the submitted tenders. It is well known that the lowest tender is not always the best. The contractor may constantly seek 'extras' for work that has not been clearly specified in the contract. Alternatively the contractor may seek to economize in the quality of work to the possible detriment to the client. In such situations the advice of consultants should be sought and clear objectives set regarding the standard, quality and performance of the work.

On the basis of the cost-plan the tendering packages can be examined. Checking and monitoring of the information will be necessary because it is at this point that potential problems need to be identified. Detailed design decisions will need to be finalized with those responsible for different aspects of the work clearly identified. The design team leader will need to ensure that the different aspects and specialisms are properly co-ordinated and that the design concept is not compromised. Once this has been achieved contracts can be determined.

12.11 MANAGING THE CONSTRUCTION

When all the pre-construction work has been sorted out and on-site operations are about to start, the project manager must ensure that the project is constructed according to the approved brief. The project manager will normally be required to accept the completed building on behalf of the client, which means that in conjunction with those superintending all levels and stages of the process, he or she will need to be assured that the structure and services are properly provided.

To do this requires a master programme: all stages of the construction, the ordering and delivery of materials, reporting procedures and monitoring systems must be devised. Schedules of meetings, ways of authorizing variations to a project and techniques of monitoring will all be important throughout the process.

The impact of archaeology will normally arise at the earlier stages of construction depending on when site works are carried out. For the building or structure itself the concern will be to ensure that foundations are properly located in accordance with the agreed foundation design. Where deposits and other archaeological features are located close to proposed structures, fences or sheet-piling may have to be put in place so that workers are kept away and accidents and unnecessary destruction avoided.

With many projects the building contractor will have freedom to decide on how to tackle things. When problems arise, as they invariably do, the contractor will normally have scope to vary specified aspects of the development. This could include foundations where awkward ground conditions might require deeper trenches or more concrete to be used. On the other hand, if this has implications for archaeology the constractor may, but not always, need to obtain prior approval.

Earthworks associated with a project could also have an impact on archaeology. The removal of topsoil from a site, if poorly deposited or wrongly located could possibly affect archaeological deposits. So too could landscaping works especially where earth-mounding is proposed. The bulldozing of soil or rubble cannot always be carried out sensitively or accurately, indicating that careful planning and monitoring will be necessary.

Another aspect of the development that will need careful monitoring is the provision of services. Privatized utilities, drainage boards and others involved in providing services may not be aware of the archaeological importance of a site. The position of underground pipes in relation to archaeological deposits may have been overlooked at the design stage only to present a problem once construction commences. Alternatively, services may have to be repositioned because of unforseen obstructions or difficulties of providing the right gradient. Particularly devastating for archaeological remains can be the provision of an on-site or off-site surface-water lake or reservoir. Where the rate of run-off needs to be strictly controlled, the removal of a large volume of soil for construction purposes could be particularly damaging. If the remains are important there could be a public outcry leading to delay or, at worst, costly rearrangements.

Careful monitoring, therefore, is vital. Techniques such as network analysis with or without the aid of computers can help forestall any problems. More important, however, is the need to ensure beforehand, that whenever earthworks and operational development are proposed, that no aspect of the groundworks and their possible effect on archaeology have been overlooked. Access roads, landscaping features, site-levelling, cuttings and embankments, the construction of car parks and all the services to be provided should be carefully examined beforehand.

REFERENCES

Chartered Institute of Building (1982) *Project Management in Building*, CIOB, Ascot.

Trotman, P.M. (1992) Paper presented at United Nations Seminar on *Building Pathology and Prevention of Disorders*, Prague, 17–20 November 1992.

Walker, A. (1989) *Project Management in Construction* (2nd edn), Blackwell Science Ltd, Oxford.

FURTHER READING

Building Economic Development Council (1985), *Thinking about Building*, National Economic Development Office, London.

Calvert, R.E. (1986) *Introduction to Building Management*, Butterworths, London.

Darlow, C. (ed.) (1988) *Valuation and Development Appraisal*, Estates Gazette, London.

Gabriel, E. (1992) Project management renaissance at the Sainsbury Wing. *Planning and Development Bulletin*, Volume 1, Issue 5, RICS, London.

Murdoch, J. and Hughes, W. (1992) *Construction Contracts: Law and Management*, E. & F.N. Spon, London.

Watkinson, M. (1992) Procurement alternatives – II. *Faculty of Building Journal*, Winter 1992, Nottingham.

13 Design considerations

When a site is to be developed and it contains archaeological deposits, public planning policy will normally require the scheme to be designed so that it minimizes any disturbance of those deposits. Frequently, development projects will have to be adapted to protect what is there but occasionally remains may be incorporated into the proposal as a design feature. A third alternative is to reconstruct the past which may be done to help the heritage economy or to promote a project.

These options present three main design solutions to consider: how to design a project around archaeological remains; how to incorporate remains into the design; and how to design a scheme aimed at reconstructing the past. For all three, site investigation, foundation design and type of construction become important factors. They form the basis of this Chapter.

13.1 SITE INVESTIGATION

The suitability of a site for development purposes will depend on a range of factors encompassing economic, planning, legal, financial, physical, archaeological and development considerations. Each will have an influence on the ultimate design although our concerns lie primarily with the physical qualities of a site. Assuming that the principle of development is accepted we need to see what can be built on a site where archaeology is a factor that has to be taken into account.

Ground conditions

Ground conditions will influence what can be built on a site although to support a particular load two things need to be known. They are the amount of load and strength of the ground. The former can be calculated and is simple to assess. The latter is more difficult and will depend on two aspects: natural ground and made-up ground.

Natural ground conditions

The main components of the ground will be soil and bedrock. Geological maps will show the underlying rock formation, but in many cases soils will be the important factor. Formed by the disintegration of rocks through weathering processes, they will vary in size from boulders to clays with a range of gravels, sands and silts in between. Strength will depend on two physical properties: cohesion, where small moist particles stick to one another; and friction, where the rougher the surface the more it prevents adjacent particles from sliding freely past each other. An example of the former is when clay sticks to your boots and of the latter when two pieces of sandpaper are rubbed against each other.

These properties of soil help to classify their strength of cohesion. Soils are said to be either cohesive or cohesionless. Cohesive soils such as clays and silts depend for their strength on particle size and surface tensions in the water between the particles which have the effect of drawing the particles together. Cohesionless soils, by comparison, depend on the frictional qualities of the particles which in turn depend on particle size and their resistance when being rubbed past each other. Table 13.1 gives an indication of their bearing capacities.

The two soil types behave differently. Clay strength, for instance, remains roughly constant at all depths except when weathering is present. Sands and gravels, on the other hand, gain strength when pressure is applied. Frictional strength will increase roughly in proportion to the pressure applied, with the result that sand and gravel tend to get stronger the deeper they are below the surface of the ground.

Made-up ground

This is the depth between present ground level and natural ground level. It is the stratum created by people's earlier building and demolition activities and

Table 13.1 Bearing capacity of soils

Safe bearing capacity for cohesive soils	
Type of soil	*Safe bearing capacity (kN/m^2)*
Very stiff clays and hard clays	*300–600*
Stiff clays	*150–300*
Firm clays	*70–150*
Soft clays and silts	*up to 75*
Very soft clays and silts	*NIL*

Safe bearing capacity for cohesionless soils		
Type of soil	*Safe bearing capacity (kN/m^2)*	
	Dry[1]	*Submerged*
Compact gravel and compact sandy gravel	600+	300+
Medium dense gravel and medium dense sandy gravel	200–600	100–300
Loose gravel	up to 200	up to 100
Compact sand	300+	150+
Medium dense sand	100–300	50–150
Loose sand	up to 100	up to 50

[1]Dry refers to ground above highest ground water level
Source: Faber and Johnson, (1979)

is where archaeological remains are to be found. Varying enormously in depth from 0 to 15 m, depending on the type and duration of human occupation and ground conditions, it will not normally be suitable for taking heavy concentrated loads because of its variable consistency and nature. It would only be suitable, as a rule, for smaller domestic scale development such as the construction of one- and two-storey buildings.

Desk-top study

An important part of site investigation is the desk-top study. Similar to an archaeological investigation outlined in Chapter 2, it is where an inspection would be made of Ordnance Survey maps, library archives, geological maps and aerial photographs. In addition, certain other matters should be investigated.

Planning requirements

Assuming that the principle of developing a site is acceptable to the planning authority, investigations should nevertheless be made of planning standards and site considerations. Design, bulk, size and siting of buildings, car parking and other standards set by the authority will affect what can be built on a site. This will be particularly so in conservation areas where archaeological remains may be found.

Building control requirements

The local building control officer will normally be familiar with difficult ground conditions and where they are likely to occur. He or she may have information about the proposed site and possible problems that may arise – the presence of basements, drains, etc. – and be able to offer preferred solutions for foundation design.

Nearby work

It is often useful to check with those working on nearby sites to see if there are any local problems concerning ground conditions, local authority require-ments, public utility interests, the nature and state of the local construction industry and archaeological considerations.

Access analysis

This will involve a detailed examination of where vehicular and pedestrian access into a site can be gained. Possible problems of entering and leaving a site must be identified, with the recognition that they could present different difficulties for archaeological investigation, construction and end-user purposes.

Legal restrictions

A variety of legal constraints may exist relating to restrictive covenants, rights of way (public and private), rights to light (for adjoining and nearby buildings), licenses, way-leave agreements, easements and other reservations such as rights to running water, the use of drains or existing cables. These could impose restrictions on the design although most can be resolved or diverted by the application of time and money.

Archaeological evaluation

An evaluation would be used to establish as far as practicably possible the extent, depth and significance of archaeological remains. As discussed earlier in Parts One and Two it would show, where relevant, what needs to be done in design terms to protect the archaeological resource.

Contamination

A relatively new but complicated subject related primarily to industrial sites but possibly to industrial archaeology as well, it could have a significant bearing on what is built. Part(s) of a site may have to be cleared or not built upon and the costs of clearance may be such as to restrict the design severely.

Underground services

In addition to mains belonging to the gas and electricity suppliers, water company, telecommunications suppliers and local authority sewers, other apparatus and private drains could be present at a site. There may also be a need to check with the transport authority, the waterways board and the railway company regarding tunnelled services. It is worth noting that some of these services may be provided above ground and need diverting.

Site survey

Armed with information from the above investigations, the next stage is to survey the site itself. For design purposes two areas of concern will be important, namely the initial site inspection and survey drawings.

Site inspection

This will involve a visual walkabout taking note of the shape of the site, slope, orientation, the position and state of the boundaries, existing buildings both on the site and at the boundary, vegetation, surface soil conditions, fly-tipping and general site condition. A photographic record should be made. Note that this is separate from a physical investigation which is discussed below.

Survey drawings

Precise knowledge of site boundaries and any monuments within the site is crucial to design. Inaccuracies can and do occur which later create problems for the siting of buildings. Permanent reference points are desirable and the survey should indicate ground levels and invert levels for drainage purposes. Details of adjoining buildings will also be important especially if new buildings are to abut or be close to them.

Physical investigation

Whereas the site survey looks closely at and measures what is there, the physical investigation will involve an examination of the site both at and below the surface. Fundamentally, it consists of an investigation into subsoil conditions with the intention of establishing:

- the level of ground water;
- a description and quantitative information about the soil at various depths;
- the possibility and extent of settlement;
- whether any harmful chemicals or contaminants are present (in the soil or ground water – and particularly sulphates);
- possible foundation solutions.

The above are standard investigations that will apply to most construction work although in our case it is assumed that archaeological conditions will also have to be established. Generally there will be two ways of checking subsoil conditions, either by the use of boreholes or trial pits.

Boreholes

These are created by hand auger or boring equipment. The former may be used in unconsolidated soils up to 5 m in depth although made-up ground may obstruct this. Normally it would be used where simple shallow foundations, in cohesive soils, are proposed.

Boring equipment would be used in other situations where two kinds of samples would normally be sought, one from disturbed ground – where archaeological remains might be found – the other from undisturbed ground. Like archaeologists, building contractors will be looking at colour and consistency but unlike archaeologists they will be looking at these properties above and below made-up ground and at the natural characteristics of the soil including structure, particle size, density and moisture content. Frequency of hole will be very important as conditions can vary enormously within a site. Testing for shear, compression, moisture and sulphur content would take place in the laboratory.

Trial pits

Either hand-dug or excavated by hydraulic digger for depths up to 3–4 m, these present a good way of looking at the underlying nature of a site and for establishing ground water levels. The presence of water can affect bearing pressures and the advantage of knowing the water level will be of assistance particularly if the site is to be subject to archaeological excavation. Opening up the ground can also reveal practical problems and difficulties that may arise although, as with boreholes, it will be dangerous to extrapolate too much information from this and certainly not far beyond the area tested.

13.2 TYPES OF FOUNDATION

The different types of foundations used in construction work which can have a relevance to archaeology may be broadly classed into shallow foundations, piled foundations and basement foundations.

Shallow foundations

Shallow foundations are those which either carry little weight or spread the load. There are three main types, although each has its variations.

Strip foundations

This is the traditional method used for buildings of normal loading of up to three storeys. As a continuous unreinforced concrete foundation its width and depth will vary according to the nature of the subsoil, where the minimum depth of the foundation (below the wall) will be 150 mm and the maximum in the region of 850 mm. Walls have to extend into the ground not less than 300 mm (for frost reasons) but the minimum overall depth into the ground of wall plus foundation should be 750 mm.

Occasionally, deeper strip foundations will be necessary, usually where excessive seasonal movements due to changes in the water content occur or where there is considerable made-up ground. This type of foundation, also known as **trench-fill**, will probably be between 450 and 600 mm in width and 900 mm deep. Ready-mixed concrete would be poured into the trench where a reinforced steel mesh might also be required.

Pad foundations

This is normally a square or rectangular slab of concrete carrying a single column. Reinforcement either in the form of steel rods in a grid form or, for very heavy loads, steel beams would be placed in both directions at the bottom to resist bending stresses. Generally the slab would be wide and set at a depth above the subsoil water table.

Raft foundations

A raft foundation is basically a large slab or pad foundation designed to cover the whole or a large part of a load. It may be used when soil is weak and columns are so closely spaced in both directions that individual pads would almost completely cover the site and be uneconomic. In these circumstances a raft may be more appropriate although much will depend on the depth of the weak soil (Foster and Harington, 1977).

The ideal raft would be a regular shape carrying columns symmetrically arranged and of equal load and where the load of the structure would be equally carried. There are three main types varying according to their design and construction: solid slab, beam and slab, and cellular. The type used would depend largely on loading and stresses and the way these are distributed.

As the natural ground can vary considerably in strength, its underlying strength, or weakness, will be a key factor when choosing the type of shallow foundation to be used. Normally it will be necessary to remove made-up ground so that the load-bearing subsoil can take the load. However, if this subsoil is weak it will significantly affect the amount of soil to be removed and could affect archaeological deposits. If a raft foundation is necessary virtually the whole of a site, perhaps to a depth of 1 m, will need to be excavated or disturbed. Strip foundations, on the other hand, will be dug along the route of proposed load-bearing walls and could have less of an impact on archaeology. It may even be possible to position them around archaeological remains.

Piled foundations

Piled foundations are, essentially, vertical supports in the ground placed at intervals under walls or piers used to transmit the weight of the structure to soil at a depth far in excess of what would be required for shallow foundations. Piles may be classified by reference to the way in which they transfer loads to the subsoil or by the way in which they are placed in the ground. Both can have implications for archaeology.

Methods of transferring loads to the ground

The way in which loads will be transferred to the ground will depend on the material used, the size or diameter of piles and their spacing:

- **Material** Before the twentieth century carefully selected timber was used for piling purposes. Today concrete, reinforced concrete and steel are the most common materials with the choice between them depending on the nature of the ground, what is to be supported and cost. The load will be transferred either by the bearing of the foot of a pile on firm substrata (known as a bearing pile); by friction between the surface along the length of a pile and the surrounding soil (known as a friction pile); or by the interlocking nature of steel sheets (sheet piling). Often they are used in combination with one type dominant, although sheet piling will only really be involved where there is a significant change in ground level. With compacted soils, friction piles are likely to be more common because they avoid excessive depth and are likely to be more economical. Concrete piles tend to be the most economic and used more frequently.
- **Size of pile** Length and diameter are the two key variables where site

conditions and load bearing requirements will be the main considerations. Broader piles increase both friction and end-bearing capacity thereby improving anchorage. Smaller diameter piles (300–600 mm) which would be suitable for loads up to 1000 kN would normally need to be longer. They could, however, be useful in avoiding archaeological remains although there may need to be more of them.

- **Spacing** The spaces between piles should be planned in relation to anticipated loads. This will determine where the piles may go and the maximum distances between them. For many buildings a grid system will be preferable, adjusted to avoid archaeological remains if possible. A six-metre grid is often used which, according to Ove Arup and Partners (1991), can preserve over 95% of the ground. Indicated in Table 13.2 this shows the area of ground occupied by piles of different diameter on a 6 m by 6 m grid where the maximum loss of deposit is 4.7%.

Method of placing piles in the ground

The way in which piles are placed in the ground can affect archaeological remains as well as have other impacts. Broadly, there are two techniques. Either piles can be driven into the ground or holes can be bored first. The selection of method will depend on:

- underlying soil conditions including the level of ground water;
- the nature and size of the load to be supported;
- the materials and installation equipment that are available;
- environmental constraints including archaeology;
- economic factors.

Both methods have their advantages and disadvantages which need to be assessed carefully before a decision is made.

Displacement piles

Formed by driving pre-cast concrete or steel piles into the ground, the main concerns are with the soil displacement and vibration. In a built-up environment the local planning authority may also be concerned about noise

Table 13.2 Site area affected by piles of different diameter

Pile diameter (mm)	Allowable load (kN)	Cross sectional area (m²)	% of grid (6 m × 6 m) area occupied by pile	% of grid area occupied by pile plus 50%
450	1300	0.16	0.5	0.75
600	2300	0.28	0.8	1.2
750	3600	0.44	1.2	1.8
900	5250	0.64	1.8	2.7
1050	7100	0.87	2.4	3.6
1200	9300	1.13	3.1	4.7

Source: Ove Arup, 1991

although techniques are available to reduce the sound from the drop-hammer. It is a temporary environmental issue separate from archaeology.

Soil displacement results in ground movement which can cause damage to adjacent buildings and adversely affect archaeological remains in the immediate vicinity. Where there is a substantial amount of made-up ground, archaeological remains such as old timber beams could be damaged or destroyed as the pile is forced down. If the obstruction is more solid it could cause the pile to deviate from the vertical or even damage it structurally. An additional problem for archaeology is the possibility of increased capillary action whereby the water-table is lowered, increasing the chances of decay.

The main impact of vibration is likely to be damage to buildings and, possibly, displacement. It will vary according to ground conditions and the sensitivity of nearby buildings to vibration. Older and historic buildings are more at risk due to their traditionally shallower foundations and chimneys are sometimes removed for this reason. The advantages of the driven pile are that it produces a stronger foundation and gives an indication of load-bearing capacity. The act of forcing piles into the ground tightens the soil particles, creating a wedging action thereby increasing strength. The force used to drive the pile into the ground will also give an indication of the resistance of the ground and thereby its load-bearing capacity.

Replacement piles

Replacement piles, or **bored piles** as they are generally called, are formed by boring or excavating a hole in the ground. Instead of displacing soil laterally it is removed altogether, normally to be followed by the lowering of a cage of reinforcement into the shaft which is then filled with concrete.

The main advantages of using this technique are that:

- there is minimal ground movement;
- vibration and noise levels are significantly reduced;
- a smaller rig is required making it easier to use at smaller sites where access may be restricted;
- the rig, if there is one, can normally be erected more easily;
- it makes the construction of larger diameter piles easier thereby carrying more weight and possibly advantageous to archaeological considerations;
- spoil excavated from the bore can be inspected by the archaeologists.

The main disadvantages of this technique are a) that it does not have the same strength as the driven pile and b) it could also cause damage to archaeological remains. For example, it may improve soil drainage and again lower the water-table. Generally, however, and for lighter loads, bored piles would be appropriate. For much larger buildings and structures the displacement pile would be preferred.

Basement foundations

The important thing about basement foundations is that they require a large volume of earth to be removed. A single-storey basement may require up to 4 m of excavation and if it is to be used for car parking purposes there will be sub-basement drainage works as well. It will not be possible to preserve archaeological remains *in situ* which means that preservation, where applicable, will need to be by record. Excavation for a basement also means that the sides of the hole will have to be supported and ground conditions may be such that water is present. Retaining walls will be necessary either as a temporary measure or constructed as part of the permanent structure. They could require sheet piling and it may be necessary to instal a water pump.

13.3 ADAPTING THE DESIGN TO PROTECT ARCHAEOLOGICAL REMAINS

There is no single or simple solution to designing projects around the archaeological resource. Much will depend on the type of development that is proposed, the prevailing ground conditions and the extent and importance of the archaeology. It is possible, however, to identify five main areas of concern which must be considered when tackling this problem. They focus on the type of development, technical preservation problems, foundations, the building frame and future access. Ideas for each are looked at, but it is stressed that they cannot present a complete picture and are indicative of what may be involved. There could be variations in each case.

The type of development

Different building types will have different space and support requirements. A few may require basements whereas all will require one or more of the three foundation types (Table 13.3). Most commercial and industrial buildings and some infrastructure projects will require pad or pile foundations whereas most dwellings will require strip footings. Not all will be the same and local conditions will dictate to a large extent what should be done: occasionally two-storey houses will require pile foundations and an office may have to be built on a raft. These, however, will be the exceptions.

Table 13.3 Types and characteristics of development projects

Type	Structural support grid	Minimum structural type	Normal foundation construction	Requirement for basement
Housing	Cross-walls	3.5 linear	Strip footing	None
Offices	Columns	6 × 4	Pads or piles	Car parking Lift pits
Individual shops	Columns	6 × 4	Pads or piles	Can be avoided
Shopping centres	Columns	12 × 6	Pads or piles	Car parking in city centre – none elsewhere
Institutional	Columns	6 × 6	Pads or piles	Some often required
Industrial	Columns	12 × 6	Pads or piles	Machine pits, etc.

Source: Ove Arup (1991)

Technical preservation problems

When building over or around archaeological remains there will sometimes be a need to protect those remains from further damage. This may be the case when organic matter is exposed, especially if it is deemed important. There will be a need to reduce oxygen at the excavated surface and to restore moisture content as closely as possible to pre-excavation conditions. At less sensitive sites where organic material is not present this need for protection will not be so great.

Various possibilities exist to protect such remains, mainly centred around the careful back-fill of material such as sand, peat or clay. These will not, however, always be appropriate. Peat, for example, might raise the acidity of soil water to an unacceptable level and cause damage to material particularly if it is organic in nature. Similarly if building work is proposed on top of peat this could be unsuitable because of the lack of support. Sands and clays could also cause problems, one of which could be the creation of air pockets thereby allowing further oxidization to occur. To be successful, new back-fill should be as similar as possible in its biological, chemical and physical make-up to previous conditions.

One site where these problems were encountered was the Rose Theatre site in London where a solution was needed quickly to avoid deterioration of the ancient timbers. Several suggestions were put forward but the one chosen after consultation was devised by English Heritage's Research and Technical Advisory Service and the Ancient Monuments laboratory (Ashurst, Balaam and Foley, 1989). This method required the wrapping of exposed timbers in 'cling-film' and an outer covering of heavier grade polythene. This was done after the remains had been carefully recorded and photographed. All surfaces were then covered with 'Terram', a form of permeable geo-textile sheeting, which was held in place by a lime-and-sand mortar which was covered to a minimum depth of 300 mm above any remains with Buckland sand. This was then saturated. The process subsequently incorporated water-monitoring points, a 'leaky-pipe' irrigation system, moisture monitors and further blinding, as shown as Figure 13.1. It remains to be seen how successful this will be in the long-term.

Foundations

All three foundation types identified as having an impact on archaeology can be adapted to protect archaeological remains although there may be complications.

Basements

Basements will have the greatest effect and destroy a great deal of what may lie beneath the ground. The exception will be when earlier structures on a site, such as Victorian buildings with basements, had already destroyed the archaeological resource. If basements were previously constructed there may now be little point in objecting on archaeological grounds to new basements

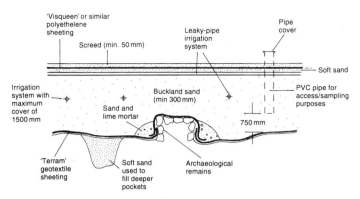

Figure 13.1 Example of preservation techniques. (Adapted from Ashurst, Balaam and Foley, 1989.)

in the same position. An evaluation will still be desirable, and in some cases necessary, to show what impact, if any, the development would have on archaeology. Where basements have not been constructed previously it is likely that archaeological considerations will increasingly restrict their use. This would normally be through the planning process.

Shallow foundations

The effect of strip and other shallow foundations will very much depend on the depth of the archaeological deposits. Where these lie close to the surface, perhaps because there has been very little or no previous development on a site, some form of mitigation may be necessary. Careful siting to avoid remains could be one solution or alternatively there may be scope for avoiding remains by varying the type or depth of foundations.

One technique might be to use a raft construction placed on raised ground made up of inert material. This could also be used for other site works where roads and services (gas, water, electricity and telephone) are proposed although buildings would have to be such that their weight and load distribution could be supported by the raft. This suggests that low-rise residential development or suburban or rural locations would be the most appropriate. The nature of the ground and the need for a flat site would be additional considerations and existing invert levels will generally dictate the level of on-site sewers. These could have a greater impact.

Pile foundations

Pile foundations will be the preferred solution for many development projects, although as far as archaeology is concerned, the main considerations will be in respect of the effects of the following:

- the number and spacing of piles;
- the effects of groups of piles;
- their diameter;

- the size and position of pile caps;
- the extent, size and position of ground beams.

An important initial consideration must be the loads to be transferred. Here building height and type of construction become important factors in determining size and spacings of pile foundations. Ove Arup (1991) for example have shown that a pile of 450 mm diameter can be used to support a two-storey building with 6 m by 6 m grid, but that if the number of storeys is increased to six the diameter of the pile would need to be enlarged to 600 mm. Various combinations are possible although a 6 m by 6 m piling grid would suit many buildings (Ove Arup, 1991). Occasionally a larger grid will be necessary where 7.2 m by 7.2 m is quoted as an example. This will suit some superstructures although it can raise the question of whether groups of piles in close proximity to each other might be preferable.

Larger pile grids may generally be thought to protect more of the archaeology although if ground beams are required for strengthening purposes, the combined effect could lead to more destruction. A smaller grid would normally avoid this problems although because there will be more piles, the cumulative effect could be just as damaging. Clearly much will depend on site conditions and the archaeological evaluation.

One example which is particularly instructive is in York. At Micklegate the position of archaeological remains discovered during the course of construction indicated that a revised foundation design making use of a larger grid with ground beams would have less of an impact. Figures 13.2 and 13.5 illustrate the before and after situation and how more of the

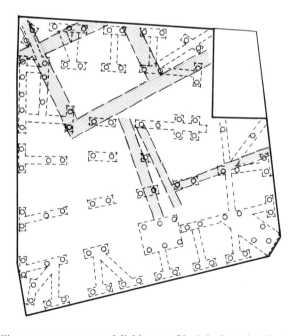

Figure 13.2 Piling arrangements at Micklegate, York before the discovery of Roman remains: the Roman remains are shown by shading. (Source: David Readman.)

Figure 13.3 Part of the Roman remains at the Micklegate site, York. (Source: York Archaeological Trust.)

Figure 13.4 Viking remains that were destroyed at the Micklegate site, York. (Source: York Archaeological Trust.)

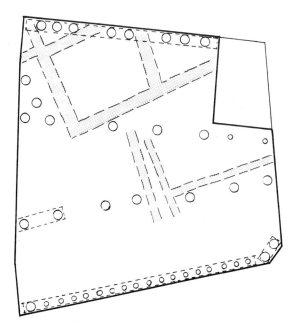

Figure 13.5 Revised scheme of pile foundations at Micklegate, York. (Source: David Readman.)

archaeological resource was preserved. Figures 13.3 and 13.4 show respectively part of the Roman remains that caused the problem and Viking remains that were destroyed. Work on the revised scheme is shown in Figure 13.6 where the limited access and change of levels do not appear to have presented any problem. Note the evidence of bored piles in the foreground.

Framed structures

For many buildings and virtually all those more than three-storeys in height, some form of framed structure will be the most suitable. In terms of economy, adaptability, ease and speed of construction and better use of internal space, it makes sense to build around a frame. Framed structures can also be good at helping to preserve archaeological remains.

Generally, a standard frame or 'cage' is used incorporating a grid system. There may, however, be times when it is necessary or desirable to adapt the building grid to suit local circumstances or to avoid archaeological remains. Two variations are possible. One is to reduce substantially the number of pile foundations by using longer-span girders, the other is to make use of the cantilever principle.

With regard to the reduction of pile foundations we have already seen in Figures 13.2 and 13.5 how a foundation scheme can be amended. In that particular case, speculation, adverse publicity and planning controls virtually dictated that the scheme be amended but the building had already been designed to satisfy severe planning restrictions. Amendments to foundations presented a major problem for the developer but the structural engineer was able to come up with a solution using much larger 'I' frames which protected

Figure 13.6 Development under construction at Micklegate, York. (Source: York Archaeological Trust.)

more of the archaeological resource whilst allowing the same building to proceed. In other circumstances this may not be possible.

The second approach, making use of the **cantilever principle**, is another way of reducing the number of pile foundations. Instead of trying to adapt them to an existing design, as mentioned above, it requires a different design concept by cantilevering the building over archaeological remains. Again, York provides us with a good example.

At Skeldergate, where an archaeological evaluation concluded that the bulk of the archaeological remains were located in one part of the site (away from the present river frontage because the River Ouse in Roman and Viking times ran further to the south-west), it was possible to devise a foundation design which located the pile foundations in the centre of the site away from the remains. As shown in Figures 13.7 and 13.8 the main part of the building is constructed around four central columns which rest on four large pile foundations. The building is cantilevered out from this central core which supports the roof which in turn supports the upper floors and external walls.

In devising such a scheme it must be remembered that it can impose tremendous weight and stresses on the central pillars and that great care and attention must be paid to loads in order to avoid excessive pressure and settlement. Construction costs must be carefully assessed especially if there are any changes in ground level across the site. If this is different on opposite sides, sufficient room must be allowed for settlement of the structure otherwise severe problems can occur.

Maintaining access to remains

If development is necessary and there is no prospect for excavation, an alternative, following an evaluation, would be to design a project so that an excavation can be carried out at some time in the future. Two possibilities exist. The most obvious is to locate buildings or other structures clear of known or expected remains provided certain precautions are made. If a site is

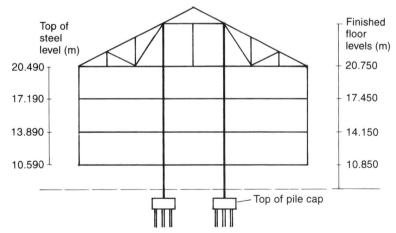

Figure 13.7 Design principles used at Skeldergate, York, showing cantilevered building. (Adapted from drawing produced by Terry Dudley and Partners.)

Figure 13.8 The Skeldergate building, York, under construction. (Source: Costas Georghiou.)

large and there is scope for locating buildings on different parts of it (e.g. a retail store), it might be possible to erect the building around the remains and utilize the sensitive area for perhaps landscaping or car parking purposes. Precautions, however, would have to be made in respect of site works for car parking, access vehicles, landscaping and associated drainage. These could be just as destructive of archaeology as new buildings.

One technique aimed at minimizing this destruction is to raise the ground level with inert material. If sand or gravel is laid across the areas concerned to a depth that ensures that the base courses of roads and parking areas will not penetrate into the archaeological strata (500 mm has been used), this would allow investigation at a later date. If the important areas could be landscaped with shallow root systems, so much the better. Drains, of course, will have to to be prescribed invert levels but it may be possible to carefully position drain runs clear of suspected archaeological areas.

Where there is no scope for siting buildings clear of the archaeological resource an alternative method would be to design the building or structure with removable floor sections. This could apply to, for example, a multi-storey car park or a warehouse where pre-cast concrete floor slabs resting on beams could be used, as shown in Figure 13.9. This technique, however, would not normally be suitable for buildings such as residential or office development.

13.4 INCORPORATING REMAINS INTO THE DESIGN

There are several reasons for incorporating archaeological remains into a project design. The main one will be to preserve what is there, but others can be to help educate the public, to enable people to enjoy the heritage, to help

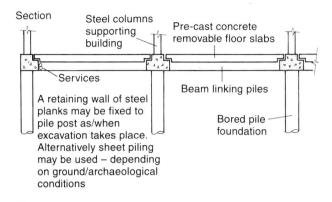

Section

Steel columns supporting building

Pre-cast concrete removable floor slabs

Services

Beam linking piles

A retaining wall of steel planks may be fixed to pile post as/when excavation takes place. Alternatively sheet piling may be used – depending on ground/archaeological conditions

Bored pile foundation

Plan

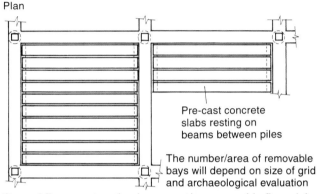

Pre-cast concrete slabs resting on beams between piles

The number/area of removable bays will depend on size of grid and archaeological evaluation

Figure 13.9 Ground floor construction incorporating removable floor slabs. (Adapted from Ove Arup, 1991.)

boost tourism and the local economy or to help promote a development project. Each will have its advocates according to the motives and objectives of those involved.

As with many things relating to archaeology, much will depend on the importance of the site and its visual attractions although other factors can be important. In general, the following would need to be considered:

- the importance of the archaeological resource;
- its physical size and geographical or site area;
- the fragility of the remains and their ability to withstand erosion;
- the extent and degree to which they need to be protected from overuse by the public;
- the extent to which they can or should be put on display;
- the ways in which they can be shown to best advantage visually, educationally and/or as a means of promoting development;
- the ways in which they might be incorporated into a design.

When considering and analysing these factors circumstances are likely to dictate the design options available to the architect. Either there will be little disruption or considerable efforts will have to be made as has been highlighted at Stonehenge. In York, for example, a scheduled monument – a Roman bath – has been incorporated into a public house and put on display. Refurbishment for commercial reasons dictated a larger open-plan sales area within the public house enabling the monument, albeit in a limited way, to be exposed to patrons through a glass panel. The design concepts at Stonehenge could not be more different, requiring solutions physically divorced from the monument itself.

One of the problems about display is that it is not just the past itself that is important, but the way we make use of it today. Invariably the context in which a monument exists will be altered radically by new development suggesting that preservation *per se* can only be part of the answer. Other motives such as education, employment-generation or enhancement of a development project may have to be considered. Indeed, without one or more of these benefits it would seem that this type of preservation would probably be limited to nationally or internationally important sites.

13.5 RECONSTRUCTING THE PAST

Reconstructing archaeology can theroetically take place anywhere although local historical and archaeological associations will be important influencing factors affecting where to locate. Another important consideration will be the extent to which the past should be recreated. As Lowenthal and Binney (1981) point out, all preservation alters the past and new techniques of display increasingly refashion old relics into modern artefacts. The pursuit of heritage, of reconstructing the past 'as it was' inevitably requires interpretation with its associated problems as outlined by Hodder (1993). Focusing on the archaeological aspects he draws attention to the difficulties of interpreting the past and the need for it to be made alive and more accessible to the public. Inevitably they pose questions for the designer. What is to be reconstructed? What emphasis is to be put on actively reliving the past? What opportunities present themselves and how can they be presented to the public?

There are just a few of the archaeological considerations that will need to be taken into account. Alongside them will be a variety of commercial considerations and questions. How much will the reconstruction cost? How much space will be required? How many people will it attract? How can they be catered for? What income will it produce? What will be the running costs and how might they affect other aspects of a project?

The designer will need to consider all these questions when working on a design solution. If it is a rural site the following may need to be considered:

- the location of the site in terms of accessibility, direction of arrival of visitors and the existence of public transport;
- site area together with ownership and boundary constraints;
- the shape and size of the site;
- town and country planning considerations regarding design, height of structures, landscaping, use of materials and other planning standards;
- the number of people to cater for;
- access into the site and car parking requirements together with associated kiosks, office and other facilities;
- servicing arrangements;

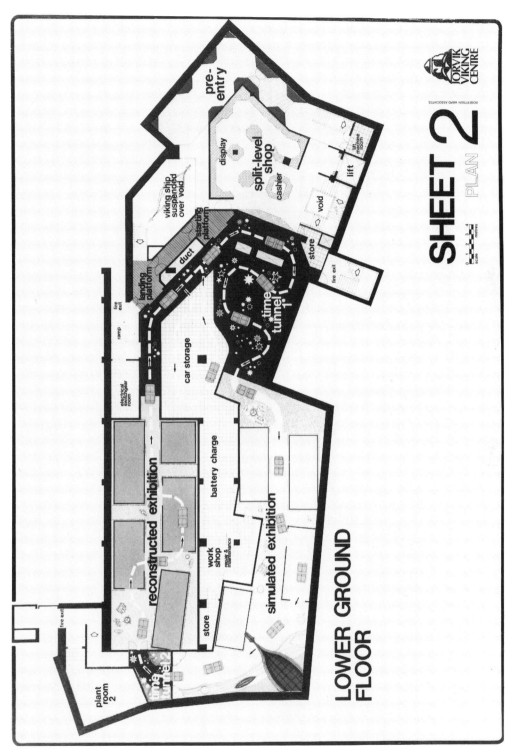

Figure 13.10 The original floor plan for the Yorvik Viking Centre, York. (Source: York Archaeological Trust.)

Figure 13.11 Inside the Yorvik Viking Centre, York. (Source: York Archaeological Trust.)

Figure 13.12 The Coppergate development, York, under construction. (Source: York Archaeological Trust.)

Figure 13.13 The Yorvik Viking Centre, York, under construction. (Source: York Archaeological Trust.)

- drainage and infrastructure requirements;
- the provision of ancillary facilities such as shops, refreshments, washrooms, etc.;
- movement within the site and the speed and direction of the throughput of people;
- health and safety requirements concerning means of escape and access for emergency vehicles;
- the finance available.

At urban sites the considerations will largely be the same, although car parking arrangements and the means of arrival are likely to be less important. On the other hand, greater emphasis will normally have to be placed on means of escape, servicing of the site, shape and size of the size together with the impact on and from adjoining property. A right to light of neighbouring buildings may inhibit design whilst a right or way could prove beneficial.

A good example of an urban reconstruction is the Yorvik Viking Centre in York. Based on extensive excavations at the site, a design solution was prepared (Figure 13.10) aimed at incorporating the exhibition into the Coppergate shopping centre. The final internal layout was later altered (the time tunnel was reduced in area (Figure 13.11) and the adjoining fire exit became the entrance) but the overall plan and extent of the basement remained the same. In short, the ground area allocation had been set within which the exhibition could be designed. The shopping and residential complex were built around it (Figure 13.12) and Figure 13.13 shows that part of the project which was subsequently to become the Viking Centre.

REFERENCES

Ashurst, J., Balaam, N. and Foley, K. (1989) The Rose Theatre overcoming the technical preservation problems. *Conservation Bulletin*, No. 9, English Heritage, London.

Faber, J. and Johnson, B. (1979) *Foundation Design Simply Explained*, Oxford University Press, Oxford.

Foster, J.S. and Harington, R. (1977) *Structure and Fabric Part 2: Michell's Building Construction*, Batsford, London.

Hodder, I. (1993) Changing configurations: the relationships between theory and practice, in *Archaeological Resource Management in the UK: An Introduction* (eds J. Hunter and I. Ralston), Alan Sutton Publishing, Stroud.

Lowenthal, D. and Binney, M. (eds) (1981) *Our Past Before Us. Why Do We Save It?* Temple Smith, London.

Ove Arup (Ove Arup & Partners and the Department of Archaeology, University of York in association with Bernard Thorpe) (1991) *York Archaeology and Development Study*, Ove Arup, Manchester.

14 Construction contracts

In one respect a construction contract is like an archaeological contract in that there is an agreement between two parties for a consideration. But in other respects there are important differences. Risk is far greater where construction is proposed and needs to be dealt with in more detail. The contract should cover all eventualities bestowing benefits where appropriate but also extracting penalties if one of the parties fails to observe the terms and conditions of the agreement.

Archaeology is one of the matters which can give rise to penalties. A requirement to excavate, in the worst scenario, can result in unexpected delay and lead to contractual problems. Even where evaluation and site inspection do not reveal anything of archaeological importance, the possibility of unexpected finds cannot be ignored. There will still be a need to look at the risks involved and at ways in which they may be tackled.

Similarly, choice of contract can also be important. Different sizes and types of construction project set different parameters and priorities suggesting that we should look at the types of contract that are available and the terms relating to archaeology. These, in fact, form the matters which are looked at in this Chapter.

14.1 CONTRACTUAL RISK

Risk is defined in the Oxford English Dictionary as 'hazard, chance of bad consequences, exposure to mischance'. Linked with uncertainty it is often thought of as indicating that a range of alternatives is possible, each of which has its own chance of occurring. Applied to construction, however, risk is something more than this. It means that there is more than mere chance and that it has to be associated with action of some sort. This can be both positive or negative, that is, a lack of action, where we can think of it, for example, as relating to building materials not arriving on time. Sometimes referred to as **economic risk**, it is where something is bound to happen and the risk is in the degree of probability of it happening.

The other risk is when the unexpected happens, which is where **contractual risk** becomes important. In this situation it will be hoped that things will not happen but, if they do, someone will have to pay for them. If unexpected archaeological remains are unearthed it will be necessary for the contract to

Table 14.1 Situations where risk can occur in a development project

Type of risk	Examples
Physical works	● ground conditions (ability to carry load) ● underground obstructions (drains, services, archaeology) ● site investigation and preparation ● defective work and materials ● weather
Delay and dispute	● late possession of site ● disputes over site layout and design ● delays due to other parties
Direction and supervision	● incompetence and inefficiency ● lack of communication ● lack of clarity in specifying requirments ● changes
Injury to persons	● accidents ● negligence ● matters beyond parties' control
Damage to property	● negligence ● accidents ● consequential losses ● inadequate insurance cover
External factors	● problems in obtaining planning permission ● health and safety requirements ● other environmental and building controls ● financial constraints ● discovery of archaeological remains ● theft and wilful damage ● labour relations
Payment	● disagreements over measurement and value ● delays in settling claims ● recovery of monies and/or interest ● effects of inflation/devaluation
Legal matters	● interpretation of the law ● delay in resolving disputes ● ambiguity of contract ● enforcement ● changes in law

apportion any costs arising from this between the parties concerned. Risk will be translated into cost terms where one or more of the parties becomes financially liable.

Situations where risk might arise

There are eight main areas of risk, all of which can affect or be affected by archaeology although not to the same extent. Identified in Table 14.1, we can see that there are many variations within each area, where archaeology can cause problems. These could arise from one or more of the following:

- the discovery of archaeological remains and obstructions;
- trying to lay out and design a development proposal so that there is minimal loss to floor space and archaeology;
- attempting to minimize delay whilst trying to accommodate different viewpoints;
- trying to resolve planning disputes amicably and with the minimum of fuss.

In respect of these matters it is important to think about their chances of happening and the extent to which they may affect pricing arrangements. The impact of archaeology will be rare but it is the unexpectedness that will be the problem. It suggests that there ought to be a strategy for how to respond to these and other potential risks.

Dealing with risk

When dealing with risk the wish will often be to try and avoid it altogether, although this will not normally be possible. The lifeblood of business is to make money by taking calculated risks where the aim must be to identify the risk at the outset. By making it explicit, objectives can be more clearly aimed at the completion of a project.

With this in mind the way to deal with risk can be identified as falling into three main stages:

1. **Identifying the risks** The list in Table 14.1 is a useful preliminary guide. By tabulating many of the main issues it can form a basis for identifying the risks although circumstances will differ from site to site. One of the developer's objectives will be to assess the degree to which one or more of the factors will be brought into the calculations. For example, if time is a critical factor the ways in which archaeology might delay a project will need to be considered carefully.
2. **Analysis of the risks** The chances of something happening and its likely effect will form the key elements in any analysis. Each risk should be assessed for its likely frequency and severity of impact on a project. Alternative scenarios can be studied so that overall and relative effects can be considered. Thus the chances of important remains being discovered and their possible effects, taking account of different delay periods, can be considered and judged against objectives and priorities. The judgement will inevitably contain an element of subjectivity but at the same time it will raise the level of awareness, which will be no bad thing.
3. **Response to the risk** How a developer responds to the risks of archaeology will depend on what has been learnt about a site. Where an evaluation has been undertaken it should be easier to identify possible responses although the unexpected can arise just as if the archaeological content was unknown beforehand. Location and size of development will clearly be important where historical towns or country areas can increase the chances of archaeological remains being discovered. The response must be to seek agreement on as much as possible beforehand.

Responses to risk

When responding to risk at a site, irrespective of any archaeological considerations, there are five possibilities for the developer to choose from. They are:

1. **To transfer the risk** Accepting that risks are always present at development sites the question arises as to how they may be transferred. This, of course, is a fundamental intention of contracts, although it would not be wise to transfer all risks inherent in a project, especially those which are difficult to assess. Conscientious and skilled contractors will increase their prices or insert qualifications in their bids in order to deal with them, whereas careless or unscrupulous contractors will disregard these risks. Subsequently, when they find themselves in difficulty they will try to pass the cost back to the developer. Failing that they may be forced into liquidation and walk away from a project, suggesting that some degree of risk-sharing would be more appropriate.

   A good example of risk-sharing would be the way in which a contract deals with exceptionally bad weather. If it provides for an extension of time to the contractor, without entitlement to financial compensation, the overall result will be a risk shared between developer and contractor.

   Difficulties, however, can arise. Suppose, in the above example, development is delayed because of poor initial advice about archaeology and, when work is about to start, it is further delayed by bad weather. If proper advice had been given about archaeology the project may not have been subsequently delayed by the bad weather or at least not to the same extent. Who is responsible in this situation? This shows how the simple sharing or transfer of risk can become complex when the combined effects of different factors are taken into account.

2. **To accept the risk** In the same way that it is unwise to transfer all risks, so it is unwise for a developer to impose undue or unbalanced risks onto a contractor. There may be short-term advantages in doing this but in the long run someone will have to pay. As Murphy's Law states, 'if a thing can go wrong, it will go wrong'. If too much risk is shifted onto a contractor who has to accept it to stay in business, in the long-term fewer contractors will be willing or able to tender for work.

   Some risk should remain with the developer. If no one can control or mitigate a particular risk, such as the late discovery of archaeological remains and all that entails, it makes little sense to assign this risk to contractors and others involved in a project. If it is transferred it will carry a huge premium yet what happens if archaeological remains do not turn up or are insignificant? The developer will have wasted money in paying such a premium. We know that all risks will have a certain probability attached to them but that those which are predictable become certainties and can be absorbed into the contract. Those that are highly unpredictable ought to be borne by the developer.

3. **To avoid the risk** When risks have been identified and considered it may be that some are unacceptable. If important archaeological remains are

likely to be unearthed when foundation work is undertaken the developer may be persuaded to redefine or even abandon a project. The implications on funding or the possible loss of a pre-let may be such that the feasibility of a scheme is in jeopardy and should not proceed in its original form. Either the scheme should be redefined or abandoned, depending on circumstances. Clearly good professional advice and clarity of purpose in advance will be paramount.

4. **To insure against risk** One of the primary functions of a construction contract is to allocate risks between the parties involved. One party would be identified as being liable to the other for a particular loss or damage and it follows that this party may wish to cover the risk by insurance. The risk would be against becoming legally liable to someone else or to be compensated for actual loss or damage suffered as a result of someone else's negligence. The former is referred to as **liability insurance**, the latter **loss insurance**. Archaeological consideration might apply in the case of the former.

5. **To do nothing about risk** There will be times when the parties to a development project are not concerned about risk. Such occasions can arise through poor advice and a failure to appreciate the risks involved or by deliberate choice. The balance of risk within a project may have been carefully weighed and the parties involved choose to do nothing.

One further possibility is that archaeological discovery may not have been thought about with the result that the contract makes no mention of it. It is therefore conceivable to believe that the contract does not apportion risk concerning such an event although this would be wrong. The fact that it is silent does not mean that it does not allocate risk. On the contrary the risk will be conveyed to one or other of the parties thereby leading to misunderstanding which is a risk in itself.

14.2 CHOICE OF CONTRACT

Construction contracts are based to a large extent on the use of drawings and specifications or bills of qualities. The precise nature of the contract documents will flow from these irrespective of whether the contract is for building or civil engineering works. The normal arrangements are shown in Table 14.2. Relatively small works such as the construction of a building extension or a dwelling would normally be let on the basis of drawings and a specification. Larger projects would be let on the basis of quantities, although size is not the only consideration. Complexity, innovative schemes, value and archaeology could also be relevant. No two projects will be the same.

When procuring a building or other structure it is common practice to use a standard form of building contract. Several are available having evolved from different parts of the construction industry to suit different needs. All have a role to play depending on the complexities and risks involved although they are rarely used as printed, for two main reasons. First, it is common in the industry for standard forms to be amended with clauses not liked being deleted and preferred ones added. Second, the industry encourages this

Table 14.2 Contract documents

Contracts based on	Building contracts	Civil engineering contracts
Drawings and specification	Articles of agreement Conditions of contract All extant drawings Specification	Articles of agreement Conditions of contract All extant drawings Specification
Bills of quantities	Articles of agreement Conditions of contract A limited selection of drawings Bill of quantities	Articles of agreement Conditions of contract All extant drawings Bill of quantities Form of tender

fragmentation because its structure encourages different sectors to concentrate on particular types of work. Builders and engineering contractors rarely meet, with the result that clauses will not always be the same.

Partly to overcome these differences and difficulties a number of forms are available.

JCT contracts

The Joint Contracts Tribunal (JCT) is the origin of the most widely used standard contractual documents. Formed by an affiliation of interest groups it operates as a forum for discussing and determining the content of clauses for a wide variety of contractual circumstances common in the construction industry. Membership of the tribunal, which covers all aspects of the industry, is shown in Table 14.3.

This membership is both the JCT's strength and weakness. With such a broad body of opinion it stays very much in touch with contractual problems within the industry and can respond to changing requirements. Its weakness is that by operating on a consensus basis where every member has the right of veto, agreement to urgent changes can sometimes be difficult to obtain. This means that new forms can take a long time to produce and may be one of the reasons why other systems have been introduced. It does, nevertheless, maintain a dominant market position.

The Tribunal has published a number of forms which are reviewed briefly.

Table 14.3 Membership of the Joint Contracts Tribunal

The Royal Institute of British Architects (RIBA)
Building Employers' Confederation (BEC)
Royal Institution of Chartered Surveyors (RICS)
Association of County Councils
Association of District Councils
British Property Federation (BPF)
Committee of Associations of Specialist Engineering Contractors (CASEC)
Federation of Associations of Specialists and Subcontractors (FASS)
Association of Consulting Engineers
Scottish Building Contract Committee

JCT 80: The Standard Form of Building Contract

This is the most widely used form of contract for major building works. It falls within the traditional form of procurement and is best used for specified work intended to be completed within a specified period. It is long and complicated and requires a good working knowledge to be used effectively. There are three versions – a form with quantities, one without quantities and a form with approximate quantities. Each has a local authority and private edition.

The standard form with quantities is for use where the developer provides a full set of drawings and bills of quantities specifying the quality and quantity of work. Variations can be made, the contract period can be extended and fluctuations in cost can be paid if the developer so chooses. It can, therefore, accommodate archaeological considerations.

The standard form without quantities likewise requires a full set of drawings which must be accompanied by a specification or schedules of work. In order to cover cost-fluctuations and variations in value, where applicable, a supporting document from the contractor in the form of a schedule of rates or a contract-sum analysis is required. Otherwise it is the same as the 'with quantities' form.

The standard form with approximate quantities is similar to the 'with quantities' form but is for use where the developer wants to make an early start and where adequate contract documents cannot be prepared before the tender stage. As work progresses it is completely remeasured and forms the basis for pricing the contract using rates set out in the bill of approximate quantities. The only difference between this and a firm bill of quantities is that it is prepared from less complete design information. It therefore saves time, although if a site is being excavated for archaeological purposes this could affect the design considerations, which in turn would affect the approximate costs. It could affect any saving in time although this would probably be to a limited extent. If time is of the essence there should be advantages but if it is not then the 'with quantities' form would be more appropriate.

JCT IFC 84: The Intermediate Form of Building Contract

Introduced in 1984, this form of contract is designed to cover middle-range jobs between those for which the standard JCT forms and the JCT Agreement for Minor Works are issued. It is suitable where the proposed building works are:

- of a simple content involving the usual basic trades and skills of the industry;
- where complex building service installations are not required;
- where the work is adequately specified prior to the invitation of tenders;
- where the contract period is not more than 12 months duration;
- where the value of the works (in 1987 prices) is not more than £280 000.

Notwithstanding this recommended limit on value about 20% of the use of the JCT Intermediate form has been on contracts between £1 million and

£5 million in value. The form reflects most of the provisions of the standard form in a simplified way, although it does not make provision for archaeological discovery. Any problems from this would need to be seen in the context of an extension to time (clauses 2.3, 2.4 and 2.5).

JCT MW80: Agreement for Minor Works

This form is designed for use only on small and simple works such as domestic extensions. Its main advantage is simplicity but because of its lack of detailed provision it can leave the employer exposed to risk. It is not suitable for specialist works so if archaeological remains were discovered and further investigation were necessary problems might arise.

JCT FF76: Fixed Fee Form of Prime Cost Contract

This form, which is now rather dated, is intended for use in situations where it is not possible to know in advance the full extent of the work involved. It is not particularly liked by contractors since it only allows for a 'fixed fee' as opposed to a more flexible arrangement which would take into account the value of the work done. There are, however situations where the true extent of the work to be done is not known, such as in extensive repair or renovation work. It may be suitable for conservation work as opposed to archaeology.

JCT CD81: Standard Form with Contractor's Design

Following the increasing practice of developers to obtain both design and constructon of their buildings from the contractor, this form was published in 1981. There are three versions:

- where the complete design is undertaken by the contractor;
- where certain parts of the work are contractor-designed with the remainder undertaken by the client;
- where the contractor's design incorporates optional provisions.

CD81 is primarily intended to be used where the contractor designs the complete works and where the contract is let on the basis of a document known as the **employer's requirements**. This specifies what the contractor has to do in a form of performance specification. It means that the developer will or should have researched all matters including those relating to archaeology so that the contractor fully takes them into account. It may be appropriate where an evaluation has been undertaken and the planning authority is satisfied that no further archaeological investigation in necessary.

JCT MC87: Management Contract

Introduced in 1987 to deal with the growing number of management-type contracts, the document envisages the appointment of a management contractor to oversee the pre-construction work of the professional team. Aimed at overcoming possible bias on the part of in-house consultants it concentrates on the ability to manage the work involved.

Project drawings and project specification are generally prepared by the professional consultants and, if necessary, can take archaeological considerations into account in the design. It must be remembered, however, that the management contractor will be under a contractual obligation to achieve completion on time, so if there is a strong possibility of delay due to archaeology this approach ought not to be used. The archaeological considerations would need to be resolved fully at the initial design stage.

Other forms of contract

In addition to the main JCT contracts outlined above, individual interest groups within the construction industry have produced building contract forms to suit their specific requirements.

The ACA Form of Building Agreement

The ACA (Association of Consulting Architects) form first appeared in 1982 and was radically revised in 1984. Its main feature is an attempt to be flexible by providing a range of alternative provisions or clauses aimed at dealing with such matters as:

- completion dates, where alternatives include for extensions of time, partial possession of finished parts or works and possible acceleration;
- extra costs, where the contractor is obliged to provide an estimate of the cost implications for agreement but before architect's instructions are issued;
- information, where an agreed schedule for the agreed supply of information is produced;
- design, where the extent of the architect's and contractor's resonsibilities for the design of a project is agreed.

A remarkable aspect of the ACA form is the use of standard alternative clauses which can be used in a range of combinations to satisfy different requirements. There is no restriction on size or type of job and it is appropriate where bills of quantities are used or where a specification and schedule of rates are adopted. It also allows for lump sum contracts with both fixed or fluctuating price versions making it suitable for parties to many projects.

These strengths are also its weakness. The flexibility afforded by alternative clauses means that great care must be taken to ensure that the appropriate clauses have been incorporated and the inappropriate ones deleted. Perhaps it is for this reason that it is not widely used although it is probably best suited to mid-range projects in terms of size and complexity.

The British Property Federation system

The BPF System for Building Design and Construction was first introduced in 1983 and immediately attracted a lot of attention because it formalized a new way of working and called for a change of attitude to working relationships on the part of designers and architects in the interests of profitability and efficiency.

The system divides projects into five stages, namely:

1. **Concept** The client develops the concept, prepares an outline cost-plan and examines feasibility and viability. If confident in the scheme, the client appoints a client's representative.
2. **Preparation of the brief** This is developed by the client's representative with input from the design team. It is a detailed statement of what is required including cost and time limits so that the team can design the project.
3. **Design development** The design team makes use of the information available to prepare drawings and specifications. Amendments are only possible with the approval of the client's representative.
4. **Tender documentation and tendering** Once detailed planning has been granted, tender documents are produced by the design team. Any parts of the design not specified in the documents must be specified for the contractor to design. The successful contractor will be invited to break down the tender into a more detailed schedule which will then be used as a basis for payments.
5. **Construction** The client's representative will retain control, co-ordinating as necessary, but with the contractor responsible for the work up to completion.

When it was introduced, the BPF system produced considerable hostility although some aspects such as fee-tendering now appear acceptable. Its main influence has been in the way the building industry perceives its clients and in moving much of the risk back onto the building team. For archaeology this should be no bad thing provided sufficient thought has been paid to archaeological matters at the concept and brief preparation stages.

The Institution of Civil Engineers Contract

First published in 1945 with the sixth edition appearing in 1991, the ICE Conditions of Contract is intended for use on major civil engineering projects. For use by private or public clients it is designed for works such as roads, railways, bridges, tunnels, canals, harbours and dams, all of which can, of course, have significant implications for archaeology.

An essential feature of the ICE contract is that it is made between a promoter and a contractor. The promoter becomes the employer with the engineer providing the technical aspects of design and specifications. The engineer is not a party to the contract and therefore has no legal rights or obligations under the contract. Conditions require **remeasurement** which means that the contractor is paid for actual work done, yet this has to be to the satisfaction of the engineer.

Government Contracts for Building and Civil Engineering

GC/Works contracts are split between Works/1 covering general works and Works/2, a simplified version aimed at minor works. Widely used by government departments the GC contracts contain features not found in other contracts. Special provisions for design responsibility, unique payment provision relating to cash flow 'S-curves' instead of measured work and the employer's right to determine a contract without having to give any reason are three examples. The wording is very clear but it is, of course, tailored to the specific requirements of central government.

A significant point for archaeological investigation is that a government department issuing a contract has absolute power in decision-making. Many contract conditions give binding force to decisions of the employer, who should weigh archaeological considerations against other factors of departmental and perhaps national or governmental importance. PPG 16 would be relevant here.

14.3 TERMS OF A CONTRACT

In order to secure the proper performance of obligations, a contract should spell out as clearly as possible what it is that has to be performed by the parties involved. Who is responsible for what, and what should happen if entirely unforseen circumstances occur, are just two of the considerations. The contract should state the manner in which a project is to be completed by reference to its terms and conditions. It should also state the price that is to be paid or the way it is to be calculated, and refer to all of the documents which describe the obligations of the parties. In particular it should refer to the specification, drawings, any special conditions and other technical and non-technical requirements. Cross-references should be established and it would also be expedient to state the order of priority of documents.

Table 14.4 lists the headings to be found in the JCT 80 Standard Form of Contract with Quantities, from which a wide range of matters can be observed. The bulk of these fall under 'general conditions' with a few supplementary conditions added. Special conditions may be necessary for some projects where the aim will be to make it quite clear who is to be responsible for certain matters such as:

- site inspection, access and security;
- compliance with law;
- insurance;
- health and safety;
- extension of time;
- damages for delay;
- inspection;
- supervision of work;
- contractor's rights to determine contract;
- guarantees and warranties.

Terms and Conditions can relate to many other matters governing the relationship between the parties. Archaeology can have a bearing in each of the above although conditions relating to archaeology are usually to be found under the heading of antiquities.

Table 14.4 List of headings in JCT Standard Form of Building Contract

Articles of Agreement
Recitals (First–Fourth)
Articles
Attestation

Conditions: Part 1: General

1. Interpretation, definitions, etc.
2. Contractor's obligations
3. Contract sum – additions or deductions – adjustment – Interim Certificates
4. Architect's instructions
5. Contract documents – other documents – issue of certificates
6. Statutory obligations, notices, fees and charges
7. Levels and setting out of the Works
8. Work, materials and goods
9. Royalties and patent rights
10. Person-in-charge
11. Access for Architect to the Works
12. Clerk of works
13. Variations and provisional sums
14. Contract sum
15. Value added tax – supplemental provisions
16. Materials and goods unfixed or off-site
17. Practical Completion and Defects Liability
18. Partial possession by Employer
19. Assignment and Sub-Contracts
20. Injury to persons and property and indemnity to Employer
21. Insurance against injury to persons or property
22. Insurance of the Works
22A. Erection of new building – All Risks Insurance of the Works by the Contractor
22B. Erection of new building – All Risks Insurance of the Works by the Engineer
22C. Insurance of existing structures – Insurance of Works in or extensions to existing structures
22D. Insurance for Employer's loss of liquidated damages – clause 25.4.3
23. Date of Possession, completion and postponement
24. Damages for non-completion
25. Extension of Time
26. Loss and expense caused by matters materially affecting regular progress of the Works
27. Determination by Employer
28. Determination by Contractor
28A. Determination by Employer or Contractor
29. Works by Employer or persons employed or engaged by Employer
30. Certificates and payments
31. Finance (No. 2) Act 1975 – statutory tax deduction scheme
32. Outbreak of hostilities
33. War damage
34. Antiquities

Conditions: Part 2: Nominated Sub-Contractors and Nominated Suppliers

35. Nominated sub-contractors
36. Nominated suppliers

Conditions: Part 3: Fluctuations

37. Choice of fluctuation provisions – entry in Appendix
38. Contributions, levy and tax fluctuations
39. Labour and materials cost and tax fluctuations
40. Use of Price Adjustment Formulae

Conditions: Part 4: Arbitration

41. Settlement of disputes – Arbitration

Code of Practice: Referred to in Clause 8.4.4

Appendix

Supplementary Provisions
(The VAT agreement)

Source: JCT (1980)

Conditions relating to archaeology

Within the broad context of contract type and terms, conditions relating to archaeology are dealt with either under **antiquities** (the word used to cover archaeological matters in the standard contract) or extensions of time. Archaeological considerations, therefore, are either specific or implied.

Antiquities

Contracts such as the JCT 80 Standard Form of Contract make provision for the effects of archaeology. Referred to as antiquities, there are three clauses that are stipulated.

Clause 34.1 The effect of a find of antiquities
The clause states:

> All fossils, antiquities and other objects of interest or value which may be found on the site or in excavating the same during the progress of the Works shall become the property of the Employer and upon discovery of such an object the Contractor shall forthwith:
>
> 34.1.1 use his best endeavours not to disturb the object and shall cease work if and insofar as the continuance of work would endanger the object or prevent or impede its excavation or its removal;
> 34.1.2. take all steps which may be necessary to preserve the object in the exact position and condition in which it was found; and
> 34.1.3. inform the Architect or the clerk of works of the discovery and precise location of the object.

The clause is designed to cover situations where objects are previously unknown but may be discovered during construction operations. Although fossils and antiquities are specifically referred to, finds do not have to be historic or prehistoric. 'Other objects' can include all sorts of archaeological artefacts and the words 'of interest or value' cater for a wide interpretation. When found, the aim is to ensure that objects are not damaged unnecessarily or through inexpert actions which may dislodge an object from its position in the ground.

If in any reasonable doubt about an object a contractor should observe the precautions of this clause rather than destroy or unnecessarily move it. Instead of acting capriciously or in an unreasonable manner it would be more appropriate to notify the architect or clerk of works immediately. By doing this the contractor would be entitled to any consequential reimbursement for direct loss and/or additional expense. It should be noted, however, that this applies solely to the late discovery of archaeological remains. Clause 34, which is followed in general terms by the ICE form of contract, only applies to objects found during construction works and does not apply to any statutory requirements under the town and country planning Acts or the ancient monuments legislation.

Clause 34.2 Architect's instructions on antiquities found
When archaeological remains of any description are discovered decisions have to be made about what to do. Clause 34.2 commences this process by stating:

> The Architect shall issue instructions in regard to what is to be done concerning an object reported by the Contractor under clause 34.1, and (without prejudice to the generality of his power) such instructions may require the Contractor to permit the examination, excavation or removal of the object by a third party. Any such third party shall for the purposes of clause 20 be deemed to be a person for whom the Employer is responsible and not to be a sub-contractor.

Before the architect gives instructions, consideration should be given to the nature of the discovery. If, for instance, substantial ancient remains are revealed it would be advisable to seek professional archaeological advice. Such a discovery may require further excavation, although this need not be the case. As at most sites the problem will be in assessing the degree of importance, which will not always be immediately apparent. At worst, the discovery, from the developer's viewpoint, could result in a lengthy and time-consuming excavation. At best, it may only be necessary to photograph or record remains relatively quickly (possibly the same day). Pre-contract enquiries would help to assess the likely significance of the site in historic and archaeological terms.

Clause 34.3 Direct loss and/or additional expense
Where work has to stop as a result of a discovery of antiquities, a contractor could be put to direct loss and/or additional expense. Clause 34.3 makes provision for this eventuality by stating:

34.3.1 If in the opinion of the Architect compliance with the provisions of clause 34.1 or with an instruction issued under clause 34.2 has involved the Contractor in direct loss and/or expense for which he would not be reimbursed by a payment made under any other provision of this Contract then the Architect shall himself ascertain or shall instruct the Quantity Surveyor to ascertain the amount of such loss and/or expense.

34.3.2 If and to the extent that it is necessary for the ascertainment of such loss and/or expense the Architect shall state in writing to the Contractor what extension of time, if any, has been made under clause 25 in respect of the Relevant Event referred to in clause 25.4.5.1 so far as that clause refers to clause 34.

34.3.3 Any amount from time to time so ascertained shall be added to the Contract Sum.

This clause provides for reimbursement to a contractor who incurs additional expense either by the cessation of work under clause 34.1 or as a result of the architect's instructions under clause 34.2. Expenditure that might arise from these can include:

- extra payment for time spent attending to the archaeologist;
- extra setting-out costs required as a result of any archaeological work;
- excavation and additional filling works undertaken by archaeologist;
- the preparation and implementation of foundations not originally planned for in the project;
- additional labour costs arising from delays, waiting time, resetting and so on and directly attributable to archaeological investigations.

It will be gathered from the above that circumstances will vary and that disputes could arise as to what is a relevant expense. The extent to which the critical path is affected will be significant and questions about payment will invariably arise. Payment for attendance, for instance, would be dealt with as daywork and could differ from the previously agreed method of payment. New setting-out could differ from the previously agreed method of payment. New setting-out costs could also be disputed particularly if finds are below the cleared level for operational development. Similarly judgements may have to be made by the quantity surveyor as to the amount and duration of work required to remedy the situation.

Difficulties in trying to ascertain the correct assessment in situations where there are no comparable data can easily occur. The bad news for the contractor is that there are no rules as to how this sum of money should be calculated. This means that some form of dispute resolution/arbitration will be required where the parties cannot reach agreement.

Extension of time

If there is no clause specifically relating to the effect of a find of antiquities attention should focus on what the contract provides by way of an extension of time. If archaeological remains are found during construction, apart from the notification procedures mentioned above, there will almost inevitably be a delay to the project. The question is how significant is this and what recourse is open to the parties concerned?

Under the JCT 84 Intermediate Form of Building Contract, Clause 2.1 requires the contractor, once in possession of a site, to 'thereupon begin and regularly and diligently proceed with the works' subject to the provisions for an extension of time under clause 2.3. The first two paragraphs of this clause state:

> Upon it becoming reasonably apparent that the progress of the Works is being or is likely to be delayed, the Contractor shall forthwith give written notice of the cause of the delay to the Architect/the Contract Administrator, and if in the opinion of the Architect/the Contract Administrator the completion of the Works is likely to be or has been delayed beyond the Date for Completion stated in the Appendix or beyond any extended time previously fixed under this clause, by any of the events in clause 2.4 then the Architect/the Contract Administrator shall so soon as he is able to estimate the length of delay beyond that date or time make in writing a fair and reasonable extension of time for completion of the Works.

If an event referred to in clause 2.4.5, 2.4.6, 2.4.7, 2.4.8, 2.4.9 or 2.4.12 occurs after the Date for Completion (or after the expiry of any extended time previously fixed under this clause) but before Practical Completion is achieved the Architect/the Contract Administrator shall so soon as he is able to estimate the length of the delay, if any, to the Works resulting from that event make in writing a fair and reasonable extension of the time for completion of the Works.

The events which clause 2.3 refers to are defined in clauses 2.4.1 to 2.4.13. They include matters such as *force majeure*, exceptionally adverse weather conditions, civil commotion and so on. Archaeology is not specifically mentioned and matters relating to it will have to be dealt with under instructions issued by the architect or contract administrator. The general provisions which could have archaeological implications are where:

- inconsistencies appear between different documents issued to the contractor (these could arise from errors and omissions);
- variations to the project are deemed necessary;
- provisional sums of money are to be spent in a specified way;
- where work is to be postponed;
- where the contractor is unable to enter into a subcontract with a named subcontractor (i.e. one named by the employer/developer) subject to certain limitations and conditions.

If archaeological matters have to be taken into account it is up to the developer's representative (usually the architect) to issue instructions to the contractor. Failure to do so does not automatically enable the contractor to claim for loss and/or expense although if work on-site has to stop for a period in excess of what may be allowed for in the contract the contractor could seek to determine the contract.

14.4 VARIATIONS TO A CONTRACT

The need for a variation

Variations to a development proposal can arise as a result of archaeology: either because the design has not been sufficiently prepared at the time of tender or because the complexities of the situation require changes to be made at a later date in the building project. With the first, lack of preparation will usually mean that not all the detailed working drawings have been prepared although basic design principles including foundation design would normally have been resolved. It is where variation due to archaeology is less likely to occur although it could arise if procurement is by the design and build route. If that is the preferred option it is conceivable that variations may have to be made to avoid or protect archaeological remains.

It is more likely that variations due to archaeology will have to be made as a result of late discovery. Here key factors influencing whether a variation is necessary will be the nature and importance of the discovery, the extent of public outcry and the way in which public statutory controls can be exercised over the development. In the aftermath of PPG 16 such variation should be rare but, if it is necessary, it can take some time to resolve and lead to a great deal of uncertainty. This has happened on occasion in London and elsewhere, where it was often found to be easier, quicker and cheaper to initiate a variation to the project. In the long run this may be the best way forward although much will depend on local circumstances and what is involved.

Provision for a variation

A wise precaution would be for the contract to make provision for this. Without it, any attempt by the developer to vary the work could, with one exception, simply be refused by the contractor. The lack of any provision for a variation could effectively enable the contractor to negotiate a new price for the contract although in practice this is unlikely to happen. For one thing the courts, if it got to that, would probably allow a minor change to be made. For another it would be unusual for a contractor to refuse to carry out small changes and a contractor would be unlikely to go to court in an attempt to refute them.

The insertion of a variation clause enables the developer to alter the works as and when necessary and to permit consequential changes to the contract sum. The variation cannot be so great as to 'go to the root of the contract'. It can, however, include any 'alteration or modification of the design, quality or quantity of the works' (JCT80, clause 13.1.1). This can include:

- alterations to the foundation design in order to execute the work in a specified way;
- limiting the work space (this could allow archaeologists to investigate elsewhere);
- restrict access to any part of a site;
- limit the hours of working (this could enable, very briefly, for other activities to proceed during the hours of cessation, such as taking photographs or perhaps extending the investigation).

Where the development is, for example, an infrastructure project, the ICE definition is more explicit. Variation can include additions, omissions, substitutions, alterations, changes in quality, form, character, kind, position, dimension, level or line, and changes in any specified sequence, method or timing of construction. It would appear that variations due to archaeological considerations could be incorporated into several of these factors.

Once a variation has been issued in writing by the architect (or contract administrator) the contractor has no authority to alter it. It is not possible for the contractor to substitute a better quality of work or new materials that are not specified. The contractor could not, for instance, install a revised scheme of shoring which would help archaeological excavation without authority. A more appropriate course of action would be to seek agreement with the architect to a revised scheme. This is possible because the architect can, in many cases, sanction minor variations put forward by a contractor. Shoring, if it applied, could be considered a minor variation although much will depend on the type of contract that is used. Their provision concerning variations do vary.

14.5 FRUSTRATION OF CONTRACT

Contracts can be affected by external events to the extent that they can no longer be complied with. Through no fault of the parties concerned conditions can make it impossible to proceed with the terms of a contract, freeing them from any further obligations under the contract. In the eyes of the law the contract can be treated as terminated under the doctrine of frustration.

When this happens losses can be allocated in accordance with the Law Reform (Frustrated Contracts) Act 1943, although this will not always be possible. If a contract makes provision for different eventualities for determination then the doctrine cannot be used to override those circumstances. Frustration of contract will normally only be possible where there has been *force majeure*, loss or damage by any one or more of the specified perils or by civil commotion. The specified perils are defined in JCT 80 as being fire, lighting, explosion, storm, tempest, flood, bursting or overflowing of water tanks, apparatus or pipes, earthquake, aircraft and other aerial devices or articles dropped therefrom, riot and civil commotion, but excluding excepted risks relating to contamination by radioactivity, combustion of nuclear fuel or other nuclear components and pressure waves from supersonic travel.

It is debatable if archaeological matters can lead to frustration of contract. If nationally important archaeological remains are discovered a lengthy detailed excavation might be necessary. Alternatively, if preservation *in situ* is the preferred option it could require radical change to a project design. Of course, neither of these need be the case and it is far more likely that other matters totally unrelated to archaeology would lead to frustration of contract. But it is conceivable that actions to accommodate archaeology could lead to a claim that a contract must be or has been suspended. If this happens the question arises as to the chances of such a claim being successful.

Two decisions of the House of Lords give some guidance. In the first case, *Davis Contractors v. Fareham UDC* (1956) AC 696, the contractor sought to terminate the contract and claim for work done. He contended that due to bad weather and labour shortages the fixed-priced contract took 22 months to complete instead of 8 months, leading to frustration of contract. It was held, however, that the risk was within the limits that should have been assumed by the contractor and accordingly no relief was given. In the other case, *Metropolitan Water Board v. Dick, Kerr & Co. Ltd* (1918) AC 119, the circumstances related to the construction of a reservoir at the onset of the First World War. Six years were allowed for completion but after 18 months the government ordered the contractors to stop work and sell their plant. This, it was held, was sufficient to bring the contract to an end. The action went far beyond what could reasonably be expected or accepted, fundamentally preventing what was originally envisaged and allowed for.

These two cases suggest that if there is some chance of archaeological remains being discovered this alone would be insufficient to support a claim for determination. The discovery would come within the risks to be expected. On the other hand, if the discovered remains are of such importance that they have to be protected and the contract cannot proceed as planned, it is possible this could lead to frustration of contract and subsequent termination. Clearly, local circumstances will be all important.

14.6 BREACH OF CONTRACT

In the normal course of events it is unlikely that archaeological factors would lead to a breach of contract. Clauses relating specifically to the discovery of antiquities or extension of time together with determination procedures would usually be sufficient to deal with late discovery of archaeological deposits. Occasionally, however, such discoveries, if linked to other events, and where the remains are of national importance, could create a situation that makes it impossible to proceed. One or both parties might seek to determine the contract or, in some cases, one might try to claim a breach of contract.

For breach of contract to occur either the work of the contractor must be incomplete or defective, or the contractor must suffer actual loss or be deprived of profit by actions of the developer. In either case one of the parties must be seen to have failed to complete or defectively perform contractual obligations without lawful excuse.

In order to support a breach of contract it is necessary to examine the terms of the contract, express and implied, to see what the contractual obligations are and then to look at what has happened to see if that party has failed to perform one or more of those obligations. If a breach occurs the party not in breach will be entitled to sue for damages. The aggrieved party will not automatically be able to terminate the contract.

The general principle is that a developer has no legal right to order the suspension of work and a contractor no legal right to stop work. Once a contract has commenced the contractor has an obligation to complete the work and the developer or employer has a duty not to hinder the contractor. The exception is when express terms in a contract indicate otherwise or where the breach constitutes a repudiatory breach, in which case the other party may terminate the contract altogether. Repudiation of a contract refers to a situation where the misconduct of one party is so serious that the other party is lawfully given the option of bringing the contract to an end. This is not as easy as it may seem.

Two cases indicate the difficulties involved. In the first, *Hill (J.M.) & Sons Ltd v. Camden LBC* (1980) 18 BLR 31, it was argued that a suspension of work by the withdrawal of labour and most of the plant from a site, whilst a presence by supervisory staff was retained, amounted to repudiation. The Court of Appeal, however, held that this did not amount to repudiation. In another case, *Treliving (F.) & Co. Ltd v. Simplex Time Recorder Co. (UK) Ltd* (1981), the matter rested on whether there was any intention to abandon the contract. The circumstances in that case suggested that for a case to be made for terminating a contract, it would be necessary to show that one of the parties not only abandoned the contract but intended, beyond reasonable doubt, to abandon the contract. It is difficult to see how this could be applied solely to the late discovery of archaeological deposits.

FURTHER READING

Ashworth, A. (1986) *Contractual Procedures in the Construction Industry*, Longman, London.

Chappell, D. (1991) Forms of contract: how to choose one. *Architects Journal*, 26 June 1991.

Murdoch, J. and Hughes, W. (1992) *Construction Contracts: Law and Management*, E. & F.N. Spon, London.

Ribiero, R. (1990) *Building and Engineering Contracts: Law and Practice*, Mitchell, London.

Turner, D.F. (1989) *Building Contract Disputes: Their Avoidance and Resolution*, Longman, London.

15 Development finance

In this Chapter the aim is to throw light onto the complexities of financing development projects where two broad matters need to be considered, the costs of development and the raising of finance. Archaeological costs, where relevant and connected with evaluation and excavation, are included under the former. They are, however, looked at within the wider context of project costs and development grants so that, hopefully, a better appreciation of the overall factors and cost elements can be obtained. This is followed by an examination of where money for development may come from. Here, sources of finance, the practical problems associated with obtaining finance and the concerns of the parties involved in providing or receiving money for development, form the main areas of concern.

15.1 DEVELOPMENT COSTS

For any project it is necessary to get as accurate an assessment as possible of development costs. A realistic budget is a prerequisite for obtaining finance indicating that even small changes such as may be caused by archaeological investigation must be carefully assessed. They make it imperative that the factors influencing costs are identified and taken into account. No two development projects are the same and costs will always differ. Nevertheless it is possible to identify the main factors where location, site characteristics and design requirements are important ingredients. They can also affect and be influenced by contractual arrangements and construction and market conditions.

Location

It is not always easy to recognize the ways in which location might affect development costs, but it can be significant in a number of ways and affect building, land and labour costs. To take the first, building costs, we can see from Table 15.1 how they vary from region to region. If building costs are £92 000 in the East Midlands, the same materials would cost around £109 000 in Scotland or £97 000 in East Anglia.

Local supply, size of load, distance from supplier, delivery cost and the general level of activity can all influence cost. Discounts or premiums on some materials, the contractor's credit rating, cash flow, and the cost of

Table 15.1 Regional variations in building rates, January 1994

National average	1.00
East Anglia	0.97
East Midlands	0.92
Greater London	1.11
Northern	0.97
North West	0.99
Scotland	1.09
South East	1.03
South West	0.94
Wales	0.94
West Midlands	0.94
Yorkshire and Humberside	0.96

Source: RICS Building Cost Information Service

borrowing will, in turn, affect what is purchased. Similarly, plant costs will be influenced by builders' expectations of future work which will determine whether plant is bought or hired, or, where it is already in use, whether it is replaced or has its life extended. Local, personal and planning requirements can increase these regional differences.

Location will also affect land prices. As an indicator of market demands and local supply it will vary according to many factors including the state of the market, future prospects, the level of opportunity and, of course, the nature of the proposed use. Residential land, for example, can vary enormously in price as can be seen from Figure 15.1. Compare 2 hectares in Mansfield at £185 000 with £750 000 in Newcastle upon Tyne, £390 000 in Eastbourne or £3 250 000 in West Central London (Maida Vale). These figures provided by the Valuation Office (1993) are illustrative and not definitive but they do highlight the importance of location. Furthermore, land for other uses can be even more volatile.

Labour costs, in comparison, are standard but their variations are important. Dependent upon the level of activity in an area, they will be lower when supply exceeds demand but if there is an upturn in construction activity skill shortages will often occur thereby substantially increasing labour costs.

Location, then, by affecting local levels of building investment, future prospects, commercial and social needs and factors of production will have an important bearing on development costs. It can influence the level of grants, the possibilities of tax relief and how planning and environmental controls may be exercised. It means that archaeological costs, where applicable, could possibly have a greater impact in some regions or locations rather than others. Clearly individual developers will be concerned about all of these factors and how to establish, maintain or exploit their position in a particular area. These in turn will affect tender prices and development strategies.

Site factors

Site characteristics will affect what can be built. Soil conditions, size and shape of site, the degree of slope, restrictions on site access, the presence of

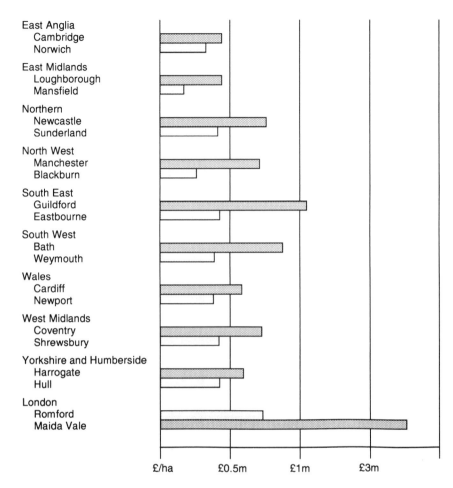

Figure 15.1 Regional variations in residential land values: the range of typical values for approximately 2 ha building land in April 1993. They should be regarded as illustrative rather than definitive. (Source: Valuation Office, 1993.)

ground water and archaeological remains are just some of the factors that will influence costs. Significantly they will interact so that siting and the type of foundations can be affected in different ways. Ground conditions might favour one siting, archaeology another and the level of ground water yet another. Each could require different foundations prompting a careful analysis of the alternatives to be undertaken.

Where ground conditions are good, shallow foundations would normally cost 4–7% of total building costs. Archaeological remains, on the other hand, could require pile foundations to be installed thereby increasing foundation costs to possibly more than 10% of building costs. Alternatively the size of building or ground conditions might require piling yet archaeological considerations require that the scheme of piling be altered. Fewer piles with larger spans requiring additional horizontal and vertical strengthening need not necessarily be cheaper and could, in fact, add to the cost.

From the archaeological point of view, attractive and historically significant areas may be tempered by additional planning and environmental controls aimed at protecting the built environment and the archaeological resource. In run-down urban areas a very different approach might be taken, although even here sites and areas may contain archaeological remains that are important. Old mills, canal basins and other examples of industrial archaeology may be present and have to be taken into account. They could have an impact on development costs and may also affect viability. Other factors such as contamination will probably be even more important.

Preparing a site for building can also be expensive. If redevelopment is proposed demolition, site clearance, removal or containment of contaminated ground and the diversion or removal of underground structures and services might all be required. Structures could include underground storage tanks, basements or archaeological remains. Each could present difficulties and add to the cost. In addition, the avoidance of one might add to the costs of dealing with another. Where several factors are involved at the same time they could make a scheme uneconomic.

Design requirements

Once a realistic budget is set the quantity surveyor should be able to advise the developer on how much to spend and how to allocate this money to different parts of a project. It will influence design objectives which in turn will affect the developer's plans. Within the funds that are available it will be necessary to establish design criteria relating to size, form, structure, external appearance, internal finishes and services. Design procedures will also have to be established to ensure that money is spent as intended.

Size, form and structure are where archaeology is likely to be most influential. Size will be influenced by planning requirements and the need for financial viability. Factors such as the funding of an archaeological excavation will act as constraints on development, almost inevitably increasing costs particularly for smaller schemes. The developer might argue that additional floor space and hence additional value is necessary to compensate for this. On the other hand, as the building gets larger, so more ducting may be necessary, circulation space may have to be increased, foundation costs are likely to rise and, with each additional floor, construc24on costs can also increase.

Tall city centre buildings, for example, become progressively more expensive to construct. If nothing else, construction workers will spend more time moving up and down the construction project in more restricted working conditions thereby adding to the cost. As Table 15.2 shows, costs for additional storeys increase when measured in terms of net lettable area as compared with gross area. It suggests that flexibility decreases as buildings become taller and no doubt this will frequently be a factor influencing what is built. This is in addition to the important factor of site value.

As an alternative, wider and deeper buildings are sometime put forward although these too are not straightforwad. If the floor space is to be subdivided this will have the effect of making capital and occupancy costs higher than shallower buildings. Despite the design advantages there can be

Table 15.2 Possible effects of building height on costs

No. of storeys	Circulation and plant %	Net lettable area %	Cost/m² gross floor area £	Cost/m² gross floor area Index	Cost/m² of mean net lettable floor area £	Cost/m² of mean net lettable floor area Index
2–4	14–18	86–82	750	100	893	100
5–9	18–24	82–76	850	113	1090	122
10–14	24–28	76–72	950	127	1284	144
15–19	28–32	72–68	1050	140	1500	168
20+	32–35	68–65	1200	160	1800	202

Source: adapted from Darlow (1988)

additional costs associated with air-conditioning, energy consumption and lighting. Additional ground cover could also be more damaging to the archaeological resource or, alternatively, make it more difficult to fit the building to the site satisfactorily.

The structure or framework of a building can also be significant for archaeology. Load-bearing brick structures are rarely suitable for buildings over three storeys and especially for commercial buildings where uninterrupted floor space is usually required. Steel or concrete frames provide a much better solution, but they require deeper foundations where much will depend on the grids and spans required for columns and beams. A common span of 6 m when increased to 7.5 m can increase the cost by 5%. Cantilevering, perhaps to avoid disturbing the ground, can increase costs by 8–10%, although if this relates to the external envelope costs can be significantly higher. Where frames are exposed or articulated as features, the cost of steelwork can increase by up to 80–90%.

Other elements of the design such as internal fittings and services will be less important as far as archaeological considerations are concerned although if prestigious finishes are required the additional cost might need to be offset elsewhere in the development costs. There is also the point that whilst some of the above matters may appear insignificant, the way they interact can have a substantial and cumulative effect on building costs. They are all crucial to the developer.

15.2 GRANT AID

Against this background of cost differentials it might be argued that grant aid could make up the difference and encourage development. Grants for development, however, vary enormously and are often only available in selected or targeted areas. Restrictions are regularly imposed on their availability making them unattractive to developers. Just as grants for archaeological investigation can be limited, as we saw in Chapter 6, so the same applies to development projects. The following provides an outline of the main types of grant that may be available.

The Urban Partnership Fund

Originally set up as the urban programme under the Inner Urban Areas Act 1978, the scheme was altered in 1993 and is now known as the Urban Partnership Fund. It remains an important vehicle through which a number of regeneration initiatives are pursued although it is not so dominant now as it was in the 1980s and early 1990s. The fund makes £20 million available for tackling economic, environmental, social and housing problems principally by giving support to local authorities although private sector support is encouraged. It is targeted at 57 urban areas listed in Table 15.3, where priority treatment for city grant and city challenge is also focused. A key aspect of the fund is support for capital projects including building, land, infrastructure and environmental improvements. Archaeology could conceivably be taken into account but it is far more likely that local authorities would seek to remove eyesores, preserve buildings, improve infrastructure and pursue environmental improvements. Financial constraints and the need to obtain value for money virtually dictate this.

The Assisted Areas

Originally set up by the government under the Distribution of Industry Act 1945, the Assisted Areas are designed to tackle unemployment and

Table 15.3 The Urban Partnership and City Challenge Areas

1. Barnsley*	30. Liverpool*
2. Birmingham*	31. Manchester*
3. Blackburn*	32. Middlesborough*
4. Bolton*	33. Newcastle*
5. Bradford*	34. Newham*
6. Brent*	35. North Tyneside*
7. Bristol	36. Nottingham*
8. Burnley	37. Oldham
9. Coventry	38. Plymouth
10. Derby*	39. Preston
11. Doncaster*	40. Rochdale
12. Dudley	41. Rotherham*
13. Gateshead	42. Salford
14. Greenwich	43. Sandwell*
15. Hackney*	44. Sefton*
16. Halton	45. Sheffield
17. Hammersmith and Fulham	46. South Tyneside
18. Haringey	47. Southwark
19. Hartlepool*	48. St Helens
20. Islington	49. Stockton on Tees*
21. Kensington and Chelsea*	50. Sunderland*
22. Kingston Upon Hull	51. The Wrekin
23. Kirklees*	52. Tower Hamlets*
24. Knowsley	53. Walsall*
25. Lambeth*	54. Wandsworth
26. Langbaurgh	55. Wigan*
27. Leeds	56. Wirral*
28. Leicester*	57. Wolverhampton*
29. Lewisham*	

*Denotes areas where City Challenge funds have been awarded

encourage new development on a regional basis. Through what are known as the Development Areas (DAs), Intermediate Areas (IAs) and the two split-level areas introduced in 1993 (Figure 15.2), the main types of assistance for the development of land in the Assisted Areas consists of:

- **Regional Enterprise Grants** Covering projects in the DAs, grants for innovation may be used to pay for feasibility studies and development specifications while grant aid for an investment project may be used for the purchase of land, site preparation and the cost of building. Archaeological costs could, therefore, be covered although the grants are limited respectively to £25 000 and £15 000 which suggests a preference for innovation rather than development. There is also a limit on the size of firm which may receive the grant which is not paid until expenditure has been incurred. In addition the grant is discretionary. Localities affected by colliery closure or certain ERDF programmes are also eligible.
- **Regional Selective Assistance** The grant, available in the DAs and IAs, can be either job-related or capital-related. Within the latter, site preparation, land purchase and building construction are all eligible and there is no stated limited to the amount that can be forthcoming. Certain criteria, relating to viability, need, regional/national benefit, employment and private section input, must be met and if more than £25 000 is being sought further information must be supplied and evaluated. It is not available in addition to Regional Enterprise Grant.

Derelict Land Grant

Land which is so damaged by industry or other development that it is incapable of beneficial use without treatment is eligible for derelict land grant (DLG). Made available to local authorities in the 57 priority areas and to developers elsewhere, it can be used to treat many kinds of problem sites: a closed power station, former docks, old steelworks and so on. Some may have few problems and be suitable for quick treatment, whilst others may present greater difficulties: contamination from chemical processes and the release of methane gas from rubbish tips are two examples. Archaeological remains could also cause a problem although it is probable that many archaeological sites will already have been destroyed at derelict industrial sites. On the other hand many may have industrial remains suitable for scheduling under the ancient monuments legislation or protection under the listed buildings Acts.

Enterprise Zones

EZs were set up initially as an experiment to see how far commercial and industrial development would be stimulated by 'lifting the burden' of certain taxes and certain planning restrictions. Rather than grant aid, the following financial benefits became available for a 10-year period to enterprises setting up in these zones:

- exemption from rates on industrial and commercial property;

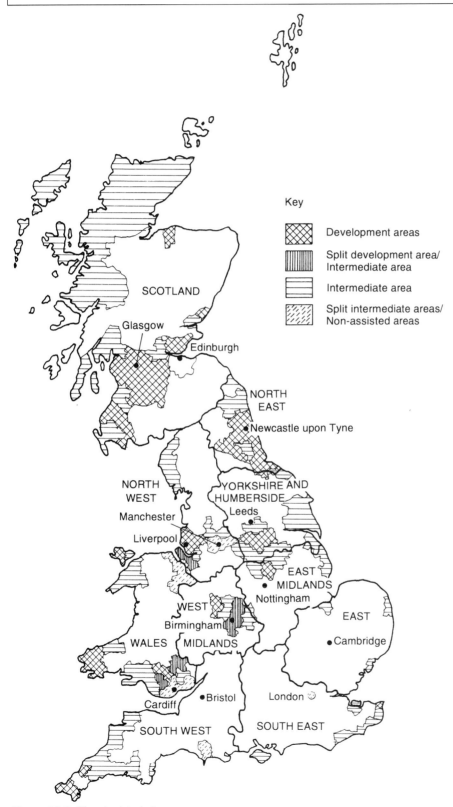

Figure 15.2 The Assisted Areas.

- 100% allowances for corporation and income tax purposes for capital expenditure on industrial and commercial buildings;
- exemption for employers from industrial training levies.

In addition to these financial gains other incentives such as exemptions from the need for planning permission, customs controls and the supply of statistical information were also established. Not surprisingly they attracted much interest and many have been successful in attracting new businesses. Many of these, however, relocated from elsewhere. It is unclear what effect EZs have had on archaeology because:

- many of these zones were set up before archaeology was recognized as a material planning consideration;
- without the need for planning permission there were no public checks on development (although scheduled monument consent still applies);
- the priority was to encourage development where archaeology, if relevant, would have taken lower priority;
- the archaeological content (apart from the possibility of some industrial archaeology) would not always have been apparent prior to the setting up of an EZ.

City Grant

Launched in 1988, City Grant is designed to support projects which are:

- undertaken by the private sector;
- capital investments;
- above £500 000 total project value (not project cost);
- in a priority inner-city area;
- unable to proceed without grant;
- expected to provide jobs or private housing at reasonable cost.

DoE, 1992

Available for industrial, commercial, leisure and private housing projects which create jobs or housing, a key factor affecting the receipt of City Grant is the assessment of value. Based on a calculation of development cost and value, it works on the assumption that a site cannot be developed without the grant. This means that applications will be carefully scrutinized for abnormal costs (e.g. extravagant costings) and the special effects of a site and its location.

Locational disadvantages including the physical character of an area can be taken into account. The need to clear existing structures, reclaim derelict land, re-route or supply infrastructure, protect listed buildings and adjacent properties are all identified in the guidance notes (DoE, 1992) as potentially eligible. There is no reference to archaeology although there does not appear to be any reason why this should not be included in the environmental appraisal.

The other point about City Grant is that it can be far more substantial than the grants already mentioned. Intended to bridge the gap between cost and value, the range of grant to individual projects has already varied enormously from around £40 000 to over £10 million. However, the areas where it is available and the conditions attached to the issue of City Grant mean that it will be far more restricted than might otherwise be expected. Note too that it is aimed at attracting further private sector development in the locality suggesting that archaeological interests are probably best achieved through the scheduled monument legislation.

City Challenge

Launched in 1991, the aim of City Challenge was to draw local authorities, business interests and community groups together to produce comprehensive action programmes for urban regeneration. Within the 57 priority areas a number were invited to submit action plans with the aim of prioritizing government finance to those schemes considered the most imaginative, innovative, realistic and practical at the same time. Plans which encouraged the clearance and reuse of derelict sites and the rehabilitation of buildings tended to be the most successful, while the 'losers' received no advantages within the overall programme. In all, 32 areas have been successful and are now eligible to receive £37.5 million each (spread over five years) from the inner cities and housing programmes. Table 15.3 identifies the successful areas.

Finance from Europe

Grants relating to land and development are available from three European funds, namely the European Social Fund (ESF), the European Regional Development Fund (ERDF) and the European Agricultural Guidance Fund (EAGGF). The aim of these funds is to combat regional disparities in economic prosperity with the ERDF being the most important for land development. Projects which involve infrastructure development, industrial investment and environmental protection are generally eligible where grant aid for the following may be available:

- for dealing with pollution problems particularly in coastal regions;
- for measures designed to promote tourism, environmental improvements and agricultural productivity, within border (between countries) areas;
- for assisting shipbuilding areas by improving run-down industrial areas;
- for improving communications, energy, water supplies and the development of local industry.

These are just a few of the schemes that are provided by the European Commission. They relate to the least favoured regions and those seriously affected by industrial decline. Interest may be shown in archaeology although grant aid will be more concerned with economic development. It will also be subject to limitations and will frequently have little effect on the costs of development.

15.3 COST-PLANNING

The factors influencing costs and the limitations on grant aid make it vital for total costs to be kept within an overall budget. If a scheme is to be viable and produce an acceptable return the resources must be used to their best advantage preferably in accordance with a cost-plan. This should not be solely for construction purposes but cover design and planning as well. The initial budget should be calculated with detailed designs prepared on the basis of the cost-plan. If control mechanisms are then installed it should ensure that development proceeds according to plan within the identified cost limits.

Calculation of the initial budget

The aim of an initial budget is to assess the likely financial requirements. It should be used to help the architect assess design requirements and what may be feasible in relation to the amount of money available. It should be as accurate as information will allow and not be over- or underinflated as the former may kill off a scheme whilst the latter may not adequately cover the cost of any alterations which have to be made at a later date.

In total there are four main ways of estimating initial costs ranging from a very basic approach of costs per unit to an assessment of the quantities involved, the most accurate and most reliable method. Between these extremes are two other possibilities referred to as the superficial method of calculating costs on a square metre basis and a more detailed elemental method where costs are broken down into figures for the main components of a structure such as foundations, building frame and so on. If archaeology is a factor that has to be included in the budget the superficial method should be the minimum used although the more detailed approaches, if time permits, would be better.

The superficial method

For many schemes the initial budget is often based on an overall cost/m^2 although this cannot sufficiently take account of irregular shape and overall height. Abnormal items such as specialized foundations can normally be catered for by using specialist lump sums or making an allowance which is added to the normal superficial price. With floor area, however, differently shaped areas can require substantially different amounts of walling, thereby affecting price, as can be seen from Figure 15.3. This shows that two buildings with the same floor area and height produce markedly different wall areas. It shows that simply calculating costs on a square footage basis can lead to substantial cost differences. It also shows that savings can be made by constructing rectangular buildings (square ones are the most economical) and yet archaeology could have been the factor requiring the irregular shape. If budget calculations are made on the basis of square footage alone and a building's shape is subsequently altered, this could lead to a serious cost underestimate and present the developer with a possible financial shortfall later.

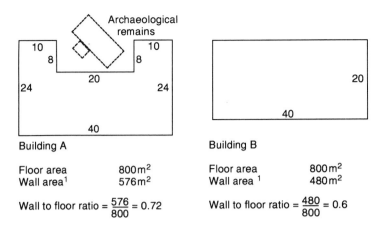

Building A

Floor area	800 m²
Wall area[1]	576 m²

Wall to floor ratio $= \dfrac{576}{800} = 0.72$

Building B

Floor area	800 m²
Wall area [1]	480 m²

Wall to floor ratio $= \dfrac{480}{800} = 0.6$

Note: 1 wall height is taken to be 4 m per floor.

Figure 15.3 Differences in wall area for differently shaped buildings.

The elemental method

Partly as a result of the disadvantage of the superficial method, but also because of the increasing popularity of cost-planning, the elemental method is now becoming more important. Using this method, each major component of a building or structure is estimated separately so that an early study can be made of the main cost elements. Table 15.4 shows what is involved. In it the six main components of substructure, superstructure, internal finishes, furnishings and fittings, services and external works are divided with costs attributed to each. Substructure and external works will be the most important as far as archaeology is concerned although it could also have an impact on superstructure costs depending on how the building is to be supported, its shape and where it is to be sited. If differences or discrepancies are likely or possible this method should make them obvious. Any cost alterations required to accommodate or protect archaeological remains can be incorporated relatively easily into the budget.

Approximate quantities method

This is the method most preferred by quantity surveyors as it uses ideas common to the preparation of a bill of quantities. It is the most reliable of all the forms of estimating and should be used whenever possible but especially when checking costs at the detailed design stage. The actual method of measurement will vary depending on the type of building and the purpose for the estimate. For example, a composite rate could be used for upper floors where ceiling finishes, floor construction, floor screed and other items such as skirting boards might be included. It does, however, take time to assemble and involves a number of calculations. Alternatively the different materials and fittings might be priced separately.

Table 15.4 Example of the elemental method: A single-storey warehouse building with total floor area of 7500m^2

	Element	Cost per m^2 of gross floor area £	Element totals £
1.	Substructure	29.45	29.45
2.	Superstructure		
	Frame	32.00	
	Upper floors	nil	
	Roof	45.20	
	External walls	22.50	
	Internal walls	0.35	
	Other (doors, windows, etc)	5.40	
	Group total		105.45
3.	Internal finishes		
	Walls, floor and ceiling		18.00
4.	Fittings and furnishings		nil
5.	Services		
	Toilet facilities	6.90	
	Heating	26.70	
	Electrical	24.00	
	Other	2.40	
	Group total		60.00
	Subtotal excluding external works		212.90
6.	External works		
	Site works	27.00	
	Drainage	6.95	
	External services	1.20	
	Minor works	3.85	
	Group total		39.00
	TOTAL (excluding contingencies)		251.90

NB. 1. Contract sum for above: £2 338 000
2. Elements such as substructure can be broken down into component parts which can be adjusted to suit site conditions, allowances for archaeology etc.

Cost control

The total costs derived from the preliminary estimates would normally be checked by the architect and quantity surveyor on an elemental basis. A cost-plan would be drawn up setting the budget limits for the project and providing an economic framework for the preparation of detailed drawings. It would also be used for checking and comparing tender prices, which would be judged against performance, financial soundness and capacity to undertake the work. These could show that the lowest tender price is not the most appropriate although the method of building procurement will affect choice and it will normally be for the project manager to decide how best to proceed, reconciling competitive cost with quality of work. A combination of tender and negotiation may be the best approach with performance bonds negotiated with the selected contractor.

It is also important for a master programme to be prepared. This should detail the steps to be taken; their proper sequencing; identify responsibilities; and provide a cash flow plan. All components must be planned, analysed, scheduled and controiled using whatever techniques best suit the occasion. Several software packages which use critical path analysis exist to facilitate monitoring. On site, bar charts are frequently used by supervisors or clerks of works for reference purposes coupled with regular meetings to ensure development proceeds according to time, cost and plan.

15.4 FINANCE FOR PROPERTY DEVELOPMENT

The availability of finance for property development is influenced by a number of factors and is a very complex area of study. In particular it will be influenced by the state of the economy, the level of inflation, prospects for rental growth, property investment yields, the availability of institutional funds, letting prospects, the supply of suitable sites for development, changes in building costs, future location and design requirements, the volatility of the stock market, levels of taxation and politically motivated discrimination. On top of all that it will be influenced by the attitudes and opinions of investors and their expectations for the future. This will apply to all sectors of the property market, but especially to the private commercial sector which is most frequently asked to contribute towards the cost of archaeological investigation.

In our consideration of finance, therefore, we need to pay special attention to the commercial sector where property will be provided by developers in one of two ways. Either it will be built for sale or it will be held as an investment and provide rental income. The two methods produce different developer interests and different financial requirements.

A company which builds to sell, often referred to as a **property trading company**, will usually sell to an investor or institution. Less frequently it will sell to an intending occupier. The aim will be to make a trading profit from the sale so that the company can move on to the next project. Profits are ploughed back into another development proposal and the company proceeds to make a living in this way. It is dependent on suitable sites coming forward for development.

The second approach is where a company is in business to let property once it is completed. Known as a **property investment company**, the aim will be to maximize growth in asset value and rental income. Different types of property in different locations will normally be the best mix to guarantee a regular flow of income although some companies specialize in particular types of development and others seek to manage and adjust their portfolio according to external circumstances and their own particular objectives.

Both types of property company will be concerned with the margins between cost and value, whether they be assessed in capital terms or converted into income. Profit will normally outweigh occupational requirements, which means that finance for property will frequently have to be seen in this light. In many instances, however, different considerations will apply to the two types of property company influencing the way they are financed. These could have implications for archaeological investigation.

Principles of property funding

There are many ways in which finance for property development can be obtained although basically they fall into two categories: either money can be borrowed from one or more sources and paid back with interest over a period of years or the lender can participate in the rewards and risks of a project. Sometimes both may be used at the same time depending on the circumstances of the borrower and the conditions deemed necessary by the lender. The two types of finance are referred to as **debt finance** and **equity finance.**

Debt finance

Borrowed money or debt finance has to be repaid at some point with interest paid on the amount borrowed until the loan is repaid. Repayment proceeds irrespective of what happens to a development proposal. If it is delayed because of an important archaeological discovery or for any other reason, the repayments will have to continue. Certain guarantees will have to be given aimed at recouping or rearranging a loan should something go wrong.

For this and other reasons a loan will be limited to a proportion of the total cost or total value. If **project cost** is the yardstick the maximum loan would be in the region of 75–80% of the cost of development. If **estimated end-value** is used any loans would normally be limited to 67–70% of value depending on the status and standing of the borrower. For example, if a project costs £20 m and the banks are prepared to provide 80% of the cost the developer will have to find 20%, or £4 m, from his or her own resources. This will be the developer's risk or equity contribution.

Equity finance

Participating in the risks and rewards – equity – depends on an assessment of the likely success or failure of a project by the person or organization providing the money. Concern will therefore focus on where the money is to be spent, usually a single project, and on the developer's ability to complete it according to plan. There will be an interest in trying to maximize profits to be shared between the parties involved.

The implication for archaeology is that there will be a strong interest to resolve as much as possible of any archaeological consideration before any finances are agreed. If preservation of archaeological remains is a planning requirement there may be a preference to achieve this by preservation *in situ* as opposed to preservation by record. There may be financial advantages in doing this as it could be the cheaper of the two options.

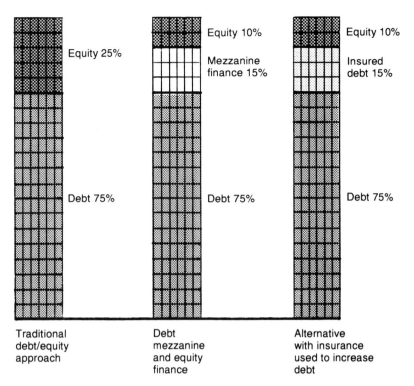

Figure 15.4 The principle of mezzanine finance.

If a developer wants to borrow a larger proportion of the total cost it is possible to do so but at extra expense. A lender would want a higher return than on the portion already lent to compensate for the additional risk no longer covered by the developer. The higher return would most likely include a share in the profits of the development and would contain an element of both debt and equity finance. Referred to as **mezzanine finance**, because of its intermediate status between these two types of finance, Figure 15.4 shows what is involved.

Debt and equity finance can both be incorporated into a project by various means with levels of each depending on whether the primary aim is to reduce the cost of debt or to reduce or increase the equity contribution. However, before addressing the criteria for funding, we ought to look at the two main types of finance for property development.

Types of finance for property development

Money for property development may take the form of either **project finance** or **corporate finance**. The first is an investment secured on a particular project and the second an investment in the company carrying it out.

Project finance

It is a condition for obtaining finance for development that it must be secured in some way although the ability of property companies to provide security will differ. A small or young company will probably have little to offer other than the development itself. Consequently it must obtain finance on the strength of the value of the development. For larger companies and especially those listed on the stock market the choice of sources of finance will be much greater. Ranging from project finance to raising equity in the stock market, a choice will be available where decisions will be frequently made against the impact it will have upon the balance sheet.

Where the aim is to seek project finance various methods are available including:

1. **Internal funds** In recent years property companies have rarely had sufficient funds to develop on this basis and this possibility mainly exists where the developer is a pension fund or insurance company with sufficient funds for property investment.

2. **Short-term borrowing** In this case the developer will borrow from a merchant or clearing bank where up to 75% of value might be borrowed although at the time of writing it is frequently less than this. Repayment of the loan will fall due on completion or letting when the developer will seek to sell or refinance the project.

3. **Mortgage** This is the traditional approach although other means have become more popular. Mortgages are more attractive when money is cheap and rents are able to cover loan repayments.

4. **Sale and leaseback** Not so popular in the 1990s, this method, at its simplest, involves the developer selling the project to an investor in return for a long lease. Rent is paid to the investor at an agreed rate calculated on an appropriate rate of return related to the purchase price, with the developer then subletting the project at a profit rent. There are several ways in which the rental income may be divided, not all of which suit the developer.

5. **Partnership** This is where a number of parties may become directly involved in a development scheme. Frequently it includes a landowner, developer and a funding institution who come together to carry out a property development and share the eventual income on an agreed basis. The landowner, rather than sell outright to the developer, participates in the income and, possibly, the design. The developer contributes experience and project management with the chance to build or enhance a reputation. The investor, apart from providing finance, will also share in the income.

6. **Forward-funding** A developer, having acquired a site and identified its potential, may seek to sell the land to an investor but continue with the scheme as project manager. The investor provides the finance, usually with an upper limit, and the developer's profit would be calculated on the basis of development value less total costs. The formula for deciding these is decided in advance.

7. **Forward sale** Here a development scheme is sold in advance at an agreed price or formula. For the developer it can make short-term finance easier to obtain or be agreed at a concessionary rate. From the purchaser's point of view it may lead to a better price.

8. **Joint ventures** Similar to a partnership a joint venture is where two (or more) parties join together on an equal basis to secure the completion of a development project. Previously, a joint venture company was established on a 50:50 deadlock basis so that it was not a subsidiary company, thereby creating taxation advantages. In 1993, however, the regulations were changed to close this loophole which means that future actions in this field, whilst continuing, will probably be at a reduced level.

9. **Revolving credit** Seen more as a technique than a source of finance, it is nevertheless important because it allows a property company to draw on funds and repay in stages at its own discretion. Within time limits and an upper ceiling specified by the bank, this type of facility is more useful when a development is completed and sold (or refinanced) in stages. It allows the amount of outstanding debt to the bank to fluctuate during the period.

10. **Syndicated project finance** Syndication arises where members of the banking sector wish to become involved in property financing. Some banks have in-depth knowledge of property lending, others may have played only a minor role and lack their own in-house expertise but wish to become more involved. Syndication allows these banks to do this with a lead bank managing the financial arrangements. It usually applies to large commercial development proposals.

11. **Mezzanine finance** This is a type of financial arrangement referred to earlier and aimed at reducing the equity contribution of the developer. Where banks will normally lend between 75–80% of project cost or 67–70% of final value, it is possible for the developer to borrow part of the remaining equity contribution in the form of mezzanine finance. However, it involves greater risk on the part of the lender who, therefore, requires a much higher return. There will also be a maximum percentage lenders will allow using this technique.

Corporate finance

Property companies wishing to expand their operations for acquisition or development purposes can raise capital on the stock market. By increasing their equity base to match the size of an investment or development to be undertaken they can overcome the problem of debt finance where 100% cannot normally be raised. Equity finance can be obtained in various ways:

1. **An offer for sale of shares** When a company is not listed on the stock market it can place an offer for sale on the Stock Exchange or the Unlisted Securities Market (USM). The latter was established in 1987 to provide a market for smaller and less secure companies. Securities to the USM are not officially listed for statutory purposes and accordingly there are restrictions on the extent to which they can be purchased by certain

investors. The requirements for companies, however, are less onerous than for listed companies on the Stock Exchange.

2. **Rights issue** Established companies listed on the stock market will often be able to raise further equity by offering new shares to their existing shareholders. Investment companies, however, must consider the consequences of this because the issue of further shares will dilute **net asset value** per share. They should only do this when they are trading at a premium to their **net asset value**. Trading companies do not have the same problem as their assets are valued on a profit-earning basis.

3. **Preference shares** Preference shares are another form of equity capital but have characteristics similar to debt finance. Normally paying a fixed dividend similar to that of a fixed rate of interest on a loan, they offer shareholders greater security than ordinary shares although they rank below debentures and loan stock. Their advantage to an investment company is that they are not normally taken into account when calculating net asset value per share and therefore do not dilute the shareholders' interest. Several forms of share are available, the most popular being the **convertible preference share**. In essence this is midway between debt and equity finance where securities are issued with fixed interest payments with a fixed redemption date for loan stock but with an additional right to convert on specified date(s) to a stated number of ordinary shares in the company.

5. **The commercial paper market** Commercial paper is essentially a short-term 'IOU'. Available to companies listed on the stock market, it is issued by the borrowing company to investors who require short-term investments for their money. Usually sold at a discount rather than paying interest, it can enable investors – usually institutions, banks and other companies – to gain a return in excess of the yield on bank deposit rates. The maximum amount that can be raised is £50 m with a minimum of £500 000. Maturity is between seven days and one year although further issues can extend this period. The key issue is one of financial standing and there must be a fall-back facility in case monies have to be repaid or if market conditions are unsuitable when repayments have to be made.

Other forms of corporate finance

Specialized forms of corporate funding also exist alongside those already mentioned. Aimed at the corporation these methods need not necessarily be for a specific development project but may be intended for the purchase of existing property. Sometimes a joint venture company might be set up to undertake a project, in which case the finance would be for the project, but sometimes the money is for wider use. Often it is unsecured making credit rating important. As such these methods will rarely be applicable to smaller developers and it will only be the largest international companies which can raise money by these specialized means.

Methods include the issuing of debentures, bonds of several kinds (eurobonds, deep-discount bonds) and multi-option financing facilities. Finance can be arranged for short, medium or long-term and can be at fixed or variable rates of return. Debentures, for example, are usually secured at a fixed rate of interest for the period of the loan which can vary between 15 and 35 years. This makes them more popular in periods of low inflation but unpopular in periods of high inflation.

Summary of financial options

Key elements in any consideration of project or corporate finance will be the size and standing of the property company, timing and the nature of what is proposed. As a rule, the larger and more established a company the more likely it will be to obtain money on its strength of trading rather than on an individual project. Small or new companies will be less able to offer security other than on the proposed development itself and even then there can be difficulties. The proportion and amount that may be borrowed will vary from company to company with those able to offer less security finding it more difficult.

The terms on which money may be borrowed will also differ. Larger companies may be able to negotiate a more favourable rate of interest whilst the smaller developer could be penalized for the shortest of overruns. Timing will be important especially in such an imperfect market. Problems can arise in bringing the developer and investor together at an opportune time to both parties. Timing within the development cycle will also be important.

Linked to the above is security for the money to be advanced. One of the

Table 15.5 Project and corporate finance by type of finance

	Type of finance
Project finance	
● Development in consortium with financial institution	Equity
– joint ventures	
– sale and leaseback	
– partnership	
– pre-funded projects (forward sale)	
● Revolving credit	Debt
● Other loans (these could include an element of profit-sharing i.e. equity)	Debt
– mezzanine finance	
– convertible mortgages	
– participating mortgages	
Corporate finance	
● Internal Fund	Equity
● Overdraft	Debt
● Debentures	Debt
● Mortgage	Debt
● Share issue	Equity
● Commercial paper	Debt
● Multi-option financing facets	Debt
● Bonds	Debt
● Term loans	Debt
● Non/limited recourse	Debt

main concerns of lenders is to ensure that guarantees are incorporated into any financial deal. If the advance is against a particular project, attention will be paid to the details of the development, development costs and the cost-plan together with rents to be received. Company details will also be important and some form of guarantee or recourse would normally be necessary. Banks frequently require a guarantee that the development will be completed so that they do not have the responsibility of sorting things out. They may also want guarantees against interest and cost overruns so that if a project is delayed because of, say, an archaeological discovery, the interest will be covered.

Three types of recourse are possible, namely **non-recourse lending**, **limited recourse lending** and **full recourse**. Non-recourse means that the bank has recourse solely to the project and no charge on other assets of the borrower. Limited recourse is where guarantees are given in respect of interest payments but do not extend to the repayment of the loan itself. Full recourse is where a company gives full guarantees for the borrowings on a project. Circumstances will dictate which method is adopted although it would not be advisable to opt for the last if there is a strong risk of substantial delay.

Rates of interest

There are two aspects of interest rates that are important to the developer. One is the actual rate or rates at which money can be borrowed, the other is the ability to fix or vary the rate of interest.

With regard to the first, the most common yardstick against which interest rates are judged is the London Interbank Offered Rate (LIBOR). This is the rate of interest at which the banks themselves lend to each other. Interest rates for development will be so many basis points above LIBOR where a basis point is one hundredth of a percentage point. Thus 25 basis points would be a quarter percent so that if LIBOR were 8% the rate of interest for the developer would be 8.25%. In practice the rate agreed between a developer and a lender will normally be 2–6% above LIBOR depending on the duration and size of loan, the guarantees or collateral available, whether interest will be paid periodically or 'rolled-up' and how much of the total cost is to be loaned.

Fluctuations in interest rates can cause more of a problem particularly when interest rates are volatile, as they were in the late 1980s and early 1990s. They create a desire on the part of borrowers to seek protection against the wildest swings. Fortunately this can now be done by using one of three advanced funding techniques. The first is where the rate can be agreed in advance and remain unchanged over the life of the loan. The second takes account of short-term movements in interest rates in the market as a whole, and the third allows the borrower to fix the interest rate at a later date in the loan period.

The simplest answer would usually be to borrow money at a fixed rate of interest. In the long run this often works out to be the cheapest method but of course the money may not be required for a long period. Finance for development will depend on how the property company operates. If a project is to be sold on completion, short-term finance would be required but this would most probably suit the second option, namely a floating rate of interest. It is long-term borrowing, such as debentures, where a fixed rate is more likely to be suitable and agreed. This would suit a revenue-producing development where a company intends to keep hold of a property as an investment. Long-term borrowing would match the long-term investment. The main drawback is that if the fixed rate is locked into a relatively high rate of interest to start with and interest rates fall, no benefit can be obtained from the reduction. The developer could be at a disadvantage compared to others who have borrowed at a floating rate of interest. It could mean that there is less room to manoeuvre especially if unexpected problems arise, such as the discovery of important archaeological remains, which delay completion.

The way round this would be to adopt the third alternative which enables the borrower to 'hedge' against interest rate rises. Several methods are possible although always at a price. In part these costs can be offset by agreeing to forego other benefits such as a reduction in interest rates, but the important thing for the developer will be to decide at the outset on what is the most appropriate alternative. Again it is a complex subject and it will not be easy to anticipate what is the optimum arrangement. And, of course, some developers will be in a better negotiating position than others and have access to more information.

The borrowing period

Money can be borrowed for as short a period as a year or up to 30 years. The choice will depend on the status of the borrower and the type of project. If the borrower is a trading company a loan would probably only be required for the development period to cover construction costs. The money would be repaid when the project is sold or if long-term refinancing has been arranged.

Loans for investment purposes would normally be repayble over a longer period indicating that the crucial factor will be the ability to service interest commitments from rental income. This would be helped, where necessary, by structuring the transactions to include fixed interest rates or the purchase of interest rate caps in a way that will equate income with interest during any period of shortfall and imbalance. The concern will be with possible long-term fluctuations and not with any immediate problems such as may arise from archaeological discovery.

Another factor affecting the borrowing period is complexity of the project. This can be brought about by a number of factors including the size and scale of a project, the development mix, the degree of innovation and the impact of archaeology. For example, an innovative design for a mixed residential, commercial, retail and leisure complex would, by its very nature, require a longer time period to be negotiated. Similar allowances may have to be made to cover archaeological excavation if this cannot be avoided.

Status of borrower and type of development, therefore, must be considered at the outset. Whereas the former may require the purchase of extra security the latter may require the purchase of extra time for repayment of the loan. In some cases both requirements will apply at the same time.

15.5 SOURCES OF FINANCE FOR PROPERTY DEVELOPMENT

The sources and types of finance are many and varied. As economic and financial conditions change so new sources of finance open up to deal with new situations. The globalization of capital markets in the late 1980s is one example which added to the complexity.

In practice the choice will often rest upon the status of the developer and the degree of risk attached to the project. It can almost be said that each transaction will dictate its own terms, irrespective of any special considerations, which can include archaeology. The main sources are discussed below although it is important to be aware that this list is neither exclusive nor exhaustive. Circumstances keep changing to meet new conditions and there will always be an element of confidentiality. Developers and financiers are reluctant to reveal the terms of individual agreements.

The institutions

Institutional investment in property is divided between the insurance companies and pension funds. The former consist of general insurance and life funds whose motivations for investment differ slightly. The general funds provide insurance for risks against accident, fire, car accidents and so on, where the need is to pay up as and when required. Timing is unpredictable but the amount is fixed necessitating the ability to meet liabilities with fixed-sum investments. Property tends to provide long-term income and together with other investments and premiums can meet most claims. In contrast, life funds of necessity take a longer-term view, being concerned with life assurance where policies are paid out on death or maturity. The liability and timing are known in advance, providing relative stability in the availability of funds.

The liabilities of pension funds are very similar to those of life assurance companies. Regular contributions are invested in property and other sources to provide pension money although in recent years their interest and that of the insurance companies in property has fluctuated. Low inflation, wider investment opportunities, poor performance of property and high management costs have all contributed to the decline in the allocation of new funds into property. Privatization and reductions in work forces have added to this decline reducing the flow of income to the pension funds. In contrast, the insurance sector has actually benefitted from pension fund changes (e.g. insuring against redundancy) and now appears to be paying greater attention to property investment.

The general effect of these requirements and changes means that the institutions are likely to take a cautious view of property. Their policies will be project based where tight control over land acquisition, design, construction and sale or letting programmes are likely to be exercised. There will be a strong desire to minimize uncertainty indicating a preference for good location, collateral guarantees and an absence of speculation. Archaeology could coincide with good location and lead to a desire to overcome any problems although the opposite could be the case. The uncertainty could be too great.

The banks

Traditionally the banks have adopted a different approach to property investment, being more concerned about the borrower than the project. The emphasis has been on the assets of those to whom they lend and the security that can be offered rather than on the type of property, although there has always been an interest in what the borrower intends to do with the money. As the business of the banks is to make a profit out of money they will be just as interested in the business of the borrower as in the project, if not more so. In this respect the clearing banks have tended, in the past, to be geared to small and medium-sized projects where they have looked for security connected with project finance. The merchant banks have generally been more enterprising especially where corporate finance and funding packages are required although they are still interested in project finance.

In recent years, however, we have seen dramatic changes. The property boom of the 1980s, for instance, led to excessive lending brought about chiefly by a wider client base and an imperfect market. The resultant debt, estimated by Debenham Thorpe Research (1993) from Bank of England figures to be £41 bn in 1991, has made them circumspect and wary of lending to property. When highly-borrowed companies began 'to go under' in the early 1990s, loans became non-performing as property values fell. They were also unable to rely on institutional long-term finance on unlet buildings which resulted in the problem of either forcing sales or extending or restructuring loans. Not surprisingly the effect was to dramatically change bank sentiment towards property.

Falling property values and a realization by the investment market that there will be times when the banks will want to offload unwanted property compounded the problem. If the banks' own loan portfolios have to be written down this reduces their capacity to lend. Conversely, when markets pick up they show a propensity to return quickly to the market, although they now appear to be taking more interest in the nature, type and location of property as well as the business activities of the borrower. There is now a keener interest in location, quality and the services being provided, and it is possible that these factors will affect lending policy. If there are constraints or uncertainties which will affect the viability of a project and the ability of the developer to repay outstanding financial commitments, the banks may well think twice about lending on such ventures. Archaeology could be one of these constraints.

Criteria for funding

Many developers will have well-established links with one or more financial backers. Where there is no link or where a developer wishes to approach a new source of finance, close scrutiny will invariably be given to the property company and to the proposed project. Both will be examined by reference to a set of criteria before any financial support is forthcoming. The following are likely to be important among these criteria.

Past performance

The track record of a developer will be the starting-point of any assessment. Levels of success, management skills, competency in all aspects of performance (particularly financial performance) and even levels of activity during the downturn in the property cycle will all be matters taken into account. If archaeology is thought to be relevant, past experience in overcoming archaeological problems would be a great help. Subjectivity and personal chemistry will be relevant, with the financier probably forming an opinion fairly quickly although references would be thoroughly checked. It is well known that where a developer sees opportunity the financier sees risk and the developer will have to show that all past experience will be fully applied to the project in question.

Company accounts

The accounts of a development company will tell their own story and will form an essential part of the application assessment. In appraising the assets of a company the financier will take note of any portfolio mix of properties owned by the company with special regard to quality, tenants, location and sectoral spread. The proposed development should not be too large in comparison to the overall resources of the company and not all of the assets of the company should be pledged. There should be a healthy balance between the company's equity and liabilities and between short- and long-term financial commitments. In particular, it will be important not to place undue reliance on short-term borrowing which could lead to pressure to refinance which could have repercussions on the security sought by the financier.

The project

Development projects must not only meet the objectives of the developer but they must also meet those of the financier. Size, value, sectoral balance and property portfolio will all be important factors where the fund will have its own criteria. It will also want to be assured that the location is such that the project can be properly and adequately managed. More specifically, the financier will want to be satisfied about local demand for space in the building, flexibility of use, facilities provided and comparables in the market. Design and layout standards will be important especially if the construction has to be designed around archaeological remains or if special foundations are required or innovative design solutions offered. In addition the fund will inevitably want to reserve the right to approve tenants for the scheme because this will be an important element of control over the project and the developer. All of these factors will be doubly important if the developer has not borrowed from them before.

Amounts to be borrowed

Most financiers will only lend a proportion of the total amount required to fund a project. We have already seen that this will usually be limited to 70–75% of cost although for quality development in a good location, with good covenants and a foreward sale already agreed, this may be increased to 80% or even 85%. At these higher percentages, however, borrowings will often be considered as equity, usually referred to as mezzanine finance, where the financiers will exact a higher price. If these conditions cannot be met the developer's contribution, as a matter of principle, will be 25–30% or more of cost.

Period of the loan

Banks will normally consider loans for periods up to five years and, in exceptional cases, up to 10 years. The institutions, on the other hand, because of their longer-term interests will consider periods up to 30 years, often with a minimum term of 10 years.

Interest rates

We have already seen how interest rates will be pitched above the LIBOR base rate and that a fixed rate, a floating rate and a mechanism which combines fixed and floating rates can be used. Increasingly, however, the rate of interest is likely to be traded against the amount of equity participation. Timing of interest payments will also be important indicating that the financial position of different developers can vary enormously. Whereas one developer may be able to contribute a relatively large sum of money towards archaeological investigation, another developer, who may appear to be on an equal footing, may have little or no money to spare and be in a very different position. The type of company, the way it is run, the nature of the project and how it is to be financed can create tremendous differences in the abilities of developers to perform and reach their financial targets. These factors can also make tremendous difference in the abilities of different companies to fund archaeological investigation.

REFERENCES

Brett, M. (1990) *Property and Money*, Estates Gazette, London.

Darlow, C. (ed.) (1988) *Valuation and Development Appraisal* (2nd edn) Estates Gazette, London.

Debenham Thorpe Research (1993) *Money Into Property*, DTZ Debenham Thorpe Ltd, London.

Department of the Environment (1992) *City Grant Guidance Notes*, DoE, London.

Royal Institution of Chartered Surveyors (1994) *Building Cost Information Service*, RICS, London.

Valuation Office (1993) *Property Market Report*, VO, London.

FURTHER READING

Barter, S. (ed.) (1988) *Real Estate Finance*, Butterworths, London.

Fraser W. (1984) *Principles of Property Investment and Pricing*, Macmillan, London.

Financial appraisal | **16**

In the present economic climate it is imperative that development projects are accurately appraised. Simple back-of-an-envelope calculations together with intuition are no longer sufficient to assess viability. Nowadays, whilst experience remains important, sophisticated techniques of market research, feasibility, estimating, appraisal and management are required. Financial appraisal will form a crucial part of this assessment: it will be needed to assess the price to pay for a site; the viability of a project; and expected costs and profit. In our case we are also interested in how archaeology may affect these matters.

Four things will be of prime concern to the developer: the value of the completed development; existing site value; total development costs; and the profit to be derived from the project. Each must be incorporated in one way or another into any financial appraisal. How they are pursued will depend on the information available and what is uppermost in the mind of the developer at the time of the appraisal. The developer may, for instance, be worried that the anticipated value may not be realized or, bringing archaeology into consideration, that total development costs will exceed expectations.

These concerns, for appraisal purposes, can be expressed in one of the following three equations:

1. to assess the value of the land, thus:

$$V - (C + P) = S$$

2. to establish total costs:

$$C = V - (S + P)$$

3. to estabilsh profitability:

$$P = V - (C + S)$$

where C = total developments costs
P = developer's profit
S = existing site value
V = value of the completed development

These three equations explain the basic concepts behind all valuations. They are used to assess the financial outcome of any situation where property development is concerned although it needs to be stressed that there are many variables which can influence the final outcome. For example, in a market economy such as ours the demand for buildings can change almost overnight. Financial deregulation or a change in interest rates can have a substantial effect on the demand for property and affect profitabilty. A change in public controls over the use or development of land can also have an effect as witnessed by the increasing importance of archaeology in the determination of planning applications. As far as the developer is concerned it adds to the uncertainty. The difficulty is in knowing what these changes might be, how they should be assessed and how they might affect viability.

It is because of this uncertainty that appraisals are necessary, not only at the initial stages of a project but throughout the development process. The developer will normally want to establish site value but will continually need to reassess profitability. The developer should, in effect, do to things: first, carry out a residual valuation to establish site value; second, use one of the cash flow techniques to assess not just land value but development costs and profit as well. They adopt a more refined approach aimed at tackling the same basic problems and can be particularly useful if archaeological considerations need to be taken into account. This will be especially so if remains are discovered during the course of construction.

In this Chapter we shall look at these two approaches to valuation. In the case of the residual method we shall assume that archaeology is a known factor prior to site purchase. The aim will be to take a hypothetical city centre site valued as if there were no archaeological considerations and then to add the costs of investigation to arrive at site value. The cash flow technique will be used to show how the late discovery of archaeological remains could affect profitabiltiy at a site already purchased for housing development. The site could be within an urban area or a greenfield site.

16.1 THE RESIDUAL METHOD OF VALUATION

The basic equation

The rationale of the **residual valuation** is very simple. It is based on the value of a development site being equal to the value of the completed development less costs including profit. It looks at property from the point of view of the entrepreneur who must decide on the surplus available to buy a site after all costs have been met.

The starting point of the valuation is to value the proposed development. Here, an experienced developer or surveyor with local knowledge should have a good idea of the demand for different types of development and the rents and values likely to be obtained. From these the gross development value can be estimated.

This is followed by calculating the costs of development. The main element will consist of building costs usually calculated at a rate per square metre of floor space. In addition any site preparation costs, borrowing costs and a sum for ancillary expenditure and emergencies would normally be added. If archaeological costs are expected additional money can be set aside for this purpose. The combined figure would represent total development costs.

If these costs are deducted from gross development value the remainder would be divided between the sum to be paid for the purchase of the land and the developer's own reward. Once the latter has been decided the residual amount would be the maximum that the developer would be prepared, in theory, to pay for the site. The way this valuation is worked up is shown in Example 1. This indicates in simplified form how a commercial development of shops and offices would be valued. Archaeological considerations are not yet included because the intention, at this stage, is to show the basic principles involved.

Example 1: Site for commercial development – no archaeological evaluation

In this example it is assumed that a developer wishes to demolish existing buildings at a city centre site and construct five shops with offices above. The completed development is expected to be worth £5.6 m, total building costs including demolition costs and all fees are expected to be £2.5 m, the building period is estimated to last 1 year and the total development period is 15 months. The developer wishes to estimate the price to pay for the site.

Expected Gross Value

	Notes		
Income	(1)	£ 476 160	
Yield @ 8.5%	(2)	11.76	
Capital value		£5 599 640	

Expected Development Costs

Construction costs (including demolition costs + fees)	(3)	£2 181 700	
Finance costs	(4)	£ 202 525	
Letting and contingencies		£ 147 350	
		£2 531 575	
Return to Cover Risk and Profit	(5)	£ 839 946	
			£3 371 119

Site Value

Residual site value	(6)		£2 228 521
Incidental costs	(7)		£ 362 939
Interest charges			£1 865 180
Maximum site value today		say,	£1 865 000

Notes on the valuation, Example 1

(1) **Income**

This is the amount of money expected to be obtained from the completed development. It is calculated on the basis that the buildings would be available to let today and not when the project is completed in two years time. Today's rents are used to avoid the difficulty of trying to predict what they might be on completion.

Rents are taken from the best available comparable evidence, adjusted to take account of location, the facilities available and the standards of design and space being provided. Net floor space is used to calculate net rental value on the basis that occupants pay solely for the usable space. This assumes two things. First, that non-usable space such as stairs and landings are not included in the floor space calculation. Second, that all outgoings such as repairs and insurance are born by the tenant and not included in the rental value. If there are a number of tenants (as in a shopping centre), management charges may be payable but these would normally be deducted separately. They are not incorporated in this exercise.

In a project where different uses are proposed the net floor space figures for each use can differ considerably. For example, the net floor space for shops would exclude partitions and toilets (these might amount to 10% of the gross floor space) whereas with office development the reduction to arrive at a net figure could be 20%. Space for lifts, stairs, landings, toilets, corridors and entrance halls (where these are shared with other tenants) would all be deducted from the gross figure.

(2) **Yield**

The yield on a property is the return an investor would expect to get on the money paid out for that property. The principle is the same as applies to other investment decisions and can be said to be the price for the money obtained. The idea is similar to the interest that would be received from a bank or building society deposit account.

To give an example, if an investor pays £1 m for an office building which will let at £70 000 a year, the initial return, or yield, on the money will be 7%. This is calculated as follows:

$$\text{yield} = \frac{income}{pricepaid} \times 100$$

Thus, for the above example:

$$\text{yield} = \frac{70\,000}{1\,000\,000} \times 100 = 7\%$$

The level of yield will depend on a number of factors including the security and regularity of the income, the security of the capital and the ability to sell the property. It will thus reflect the performance of the property in the economy, its strength of covenant, the potential for rental growth and other factors thought to be relevant.

The greater the certainty of capital and income the greater the security of the investment. And the greater the security the lower the yield. Where there is more risk, which could arise if archaeology is a factor, a higher yield would be expected. The skill is in assessing it at the right level.

(3) **Construction costs**

No two sites are the same and all will have unique qualities which will affect building costs. Projects will also vary depending on the size, nature and complexity of what is proposed. The major component will be the building costs although other costs will usually be present. Items such as demolition of existing buildings, possible salvage value, the diversion of underground services and the compensation for buying out private rights over a site (such as rights of light or easements) may be included. In this example it is assumed that buildings will have to be demolished. Professional fees would be included under this heading.

(4) **Short-term finance**

For most development projects money will be borrowed with interest paid on the outstanding amount of loan. A small builder will usually borrow money from a bank in the form of an overdraft or loan. For large development projects it is more likely that both equity and debt finance would be present, making use of one or more of the sources outlined in the last Chapter.

The rate at which short-term finance is obtained will vary according to the project, the size of the loan, the length of time it is required and the status of the borrower. It will relate to the cost of short-term loans generally, that is, LIBOR. A small development company with little experience and security may have to pay 6% or more above LIBOR. A major development company with a lot of experience in property development, might expect to pay as little as 1–2% above this rate. Exceptionally, if an institution intends to acquire a longer-term interest in a property, short-term finance might be arranged at a preferentially reduced rate in return for the reduced acquisition price. Normally the rate of interest will relate to LIBOR at the time of the calculation.

(5) **Return for risk and profit**
The time period from inception to completion can be as much as several years during which time rental values, interest rates and yield can fluctuate. It can be difficult to anticipate accurately the development period especially where major projects are proposed and where archaeological remains are discovered. A developer, therefore, will need to incorporate into the appraisal an allowance to cover these risks and to ensure that there is a profit or return for time and effort. How much will depend on the perceived level of risk, the nature and size of the project and the extent of the competition.

The allowance will be expressed as a percentage of the total development costs or as a percentage of the capital value. In the case of the former, figures around 10% are often quoted, and with the latter, 15%. A typical allowance would certainly be in the region of these figures, although a lower or higher percentage might be used depending on the size and duration of the project and the expected realization of the profit. Archaeology could possibly have some effect on the allowance.

(6) **Residual site value**
The difference between the development value and the total costs of the project including profit represents the sum available to spend on the land. In some cases the building and ancillary costs will exceed the net proceeds of sale. If this happens there is negative value and the land is not suitable for that particular development.

(7) **Incidental costs**
The land cost contains four elements. In addition to the price to be paid for the land itself there are professional fees, stamp duty and the interest on the money borrowed. All four relate to the actual price to be paid which in turn depends on the four elements. It will also depend on the profit sought from the development.

The effects of archaeology

Archaeology can affect the valuation in up to five ways. First, it can add to the time taken to complete a development thereby increasing the amount of interest to be paid on borrowed money. Second, it can adversely affect the value of the completed development. Third, it can add to the professional fees. Fourth, it can add to building costs and finally there are the costs of archaeological investigation.

The effects of time

The time factor will be influenced by the type and nature of the archaeological investigation to be undertaken. Evaluation costs would normally be incurred prior to acquisition although the evaluation might be undertaken after an option to buy has been made. If permission to enter a site is delayed it could hold up the preparation of drawings for the proposed development. On average, however, the effects of evaluation should be negligible.

The bulk of any delay will occur if a site has to be excavated. In Areas of Archaeological Importance the maximum statutory period for excavation is six months. Elsewhere, whilst there is no fixed statutory peirod, local planning authorities can stipulate any time period thought to be appropriate. It could be more or less than six months depending on the perceived archaeological importance of the site. Financially, additional costs will principally be as a result of interest charges on money borrowed.

The effect on value

It is possible for archaeological matters to affect the value of a completed development, leading in the worst scenario to reduced rents and possibly a lower capital value. For example, if on-site car parking provision has to be reduced in order to preserve archaeological remains it could have the effect of reducing rents occupiers are prepared to pay: without convenient on-site car parking the property could be less attractive to prospective tenants who might decide to go elsewhere. It could necessitate a reduction in anticipated rent in order to attract potential occupiers.

A counter-argument is that because planning authorities are increasingly demanding less or no car parking provision at city centre (and historic) sites, rents and values will have to be adjusted downwards to reflect this reduced standard. By applying it across the board, the argument is that in the long run any differences in rental income between properties will diminish. The problem, however, is that in the meantime different authorities will approach the matter with differing degrees of enthusiasm; some land and property owners may hold out for higher prices; and it will not apply to existing properties where no such restrictions exist.

Another factor affecting values is yield. If the prospect for rental growth at a site is not as good as it might otherwise be and not as good as other sites in the locality, the yield on that property is likely to reflect this reduced attractiveness. The change in yield will not appear significant (it may be less than a quarter per cent) but when it is used to capitalize rental income to produce site value the residue for risk and profit can be substantially reduced. For instance, if the anticipated rental income of an office building needs to be reduced by 10% from, say, £200 000 to £180 000 per annum, and the yield increased from 8% to 8¼%, the capitalized value would be reduced from £2 500 000 (200 000 × 12.5) to £2 181 600 (180 000 × 12.12), a reduction of £318 400 or 17%. This shows, and it is not uncommon, that a slight variation in rental income or yield can have a disproportionate affect on value and be crucial for viability.

The effect on fees

At first glance we could be forgiven for thinking that archaeology will not have any significant effect on fees. The presence of archaeological remains, however, could require the architect and structural engineer to work out additional structural calculations and design details. It could mean that an environmental statement has to be prepared by environmental consultants and it may be necessary to pay for additional legal advice concerning a planning obligation. This is apart from what the obligation may require in the way of funds. In addition, there could be extra accountants fees for insurance purposes together with additional costings to be estimated by the quantity surveyor. Fees for archaeological advice would be on top of this where the overall expense could run into many tens of thousands of pounds.

The effect on development costs

Archaeology can affect development costs in basically five ways. First, there could be additional site preparation costs relating to earthworks, shoring or delayed demolition. The last of these might help speed up archaeological excavation if the archaeologists can work under the shelter of an existing building, athough demolition costs could be higher if demolition is postponed. Secondly, the cost of building materials could be higher because of inflation. Either the materials are acquired at a later date at a higher price or they are bought earlier thereby increasing borrowing costs. Either way costs will increase. Thirdly, any delay to the project, irrespective of when materials are bought, will mean that money will be required for a longer period thereby adding to interest charges. Fourthly, the design solution to avoid archaeology could be more expensive to construct. Specialized foundations or siting could require additional expense which may not be necessary but for the archaeology at the site. Finally, there can be the costs of the archaeological investigation itself. Ranging from a few thousand pounds to six or seven figure sums in extreme cases, the effects of these costs can greatly affect viability.

A detailed residual valuation

To give some idea of what is involved, Example 2 looks at the same basic valuation problem as before but with archaeological factors included.

Example 2: Site for commercial development – incorporating archaeological evaluation

The site is assumed to be in a good shopping location in the centre of an historic town. It contains three-storey buildings which are to be demolished to make way for five shops with three floors of office above. The local planning authority has set a car parking standard of 1 car space per 150 m^2 of office floor space. There is no parking requirement relating to the shops. The authority requires an archaeological evaluation to be submitted with the planning application and it is expected that permission will be granted subject to a site excavation funded by the developer.

Preliminaries

1. *What is the optimum development?*
   a) Site area: 33 m × 30 m = 990 m^2
   b) Shops: 5 m × 6 m frontage
   plus 3.0 m for front and rear
   access to offices .... 33 m
   Maximum depth .... 20 m
   Gross Area 660 m^2

   c) Offices: 33 m frontage × depth 20 m = 660 m^2
   Number of floors 3
   Gross Area 1980 m^2

   d) Car parking: 1 space per 150 m^2 = 14 spaces
   Area per car 23 m^2 including circulation
   Area required 322 m^2

2. *Rental Values:*
   From recent comparable information, unfitted shops are expected to let at £800/m^2 per annum (Zone A) and offices at £140/m^2

3. *Building costs*
   From comparables:

Shops (shell units only)	£450/m^2
Offices	£800/m^2
Car parking	£25 000
Landscaping	£20 000

4. *Archaeological costs*

Archaeological evaluation	£25 000
Archaeological excavation	£80 000
Archaeological research and publication	£50 000

5. *Development period*
   Allow:
   3 months for archaeological investigation
   1 year for construction plus 3 months for letting void

6. *Borrowing costs*
   Current rate taken at 10% nominal, charged quarterly @ 2.5%
   APR = $(1 + 0.03)^4 - 1$ = 10.38% pa

VALUATION

A Gross Development Value
   Rental value of shops:

Zone A 183 m^2 @ £800	£	146 400
Zone B 183 m^2 @ £400	£	73 200
Remainder 234 m^2 @ £200	£	34 800
Offices (net space) 158 m^2 @ £140	£	221 760
	£	476 160
YP perp @ 8.5%	11.76	£5 599 640
Less costs on sale of completed scheme (legals, agents): say 2.5%		£ 139 990
		£5 459 650

B Development Costs
   Site preparation costs (see note 1)

Demolition	£	40 000	
Archaeological evaluation	£	25 000	
Archaeological excavation	£	80 000	
Archaeological research and publication	£	50 000	£ 195 000

Building costs (see note 2)

Shops 600 m² @ £450	£ 270 000	
Offices 2040 m² (1980 + 60) @ £800	£1 632 000	
Car Parking	£ 25 000	
Landscaping	£ 20 000	
	£1 947 000	
Fees excluding site preparation costs @ 10% (see note 3)	£ 194 700	£2 141 700

Finance (see note 5)

i)	Site preparation costs for 18 months @ 10.38%	£ 30 363	
ii)	Building costs £1 947 000 (÷2) @ 10.38% pa	£ 101 049	
iii)	Letting void @ 3%	£ 50 525	
iv)	On 75% of fees 18 months @ 10.38%	£ 23 306	
v)	Arrangement fee @ 1% of building loan	£ 21 417	£ 226 660

Letting costs (see note 6)

10% × FRV + promotion costs, say	£ 50 000
Contingencies 6% of building costs (see note 7)	£ 116 000
Total Costs	£2 729 360

C Developer's Profit	
15% GDV	£ 839 946

D Residual Amount For Land (£5 459 650 − £3 569 306)	£1 890 344
Interest on land costs: defer	
18 month @ 10.38%	
18 months to letting PV of £1 in 2 years @ 10.38%	.863
	£1 631 367
Incidental costs on purchase at 3%	£ 48 941
Residual Amount	£1 582 426
Site value	say, £1 580 000

Notes on the valuation, Example 2

(1) Site preparation costs

With redevelopment in a town centre demolition costs will be necessary. Other costs can also be expected: the removal of legal encumbrances, the shoring of adjoining buildings and the protection of the public highway, the last two being especially important if basement floors are proposed. Archaeological evaluation costs would be included in these preparatory costs.

One problem with site preparation costs is that they are not always easy to calculate and can differ considerably. Demolition costs will vary from site to site depending on what has to be demolished. The size, height and condition of existing buildings will all affect the cost, not to mention the materials used in their original construction. The removal of reinforced concrete will pose difficult problems requiring solutions different to those for buildings constructed in brick and timber. Sometimes material can be reused if carefully removed and can help pay towards the costs of demolition. This is especially so with handmade bricks and roofing slate which are often in demand.

As for archaeological excavation costs, these can vary from as much as £1.6 m to as little as £2500 on urban sites of similar size! In this example a figure of £80 000 has been chosen.

(2) Building costs

Building costs will depend on the size and complexity of the project. The major component will be the figure agreed with the builder and incorporated into the building contract. Traditionally, present day costs are used, as in the assessment of rents, thereby avoiding any difficulty in trying to predict future costs. A further justification for this approach is that any increases in building costs will be matched by increases in rental values, although this need not be the case. The normal method of calculating building costs is to apply the local rate per square metre to the gross internal area of the building, that is, the area of the building as measured to the inside of the external walls. Rates will vary from region to region, as we have seen, and on the finishes required. An historic city centre site may lie within a conservation area and require more to be spent on design and external finishes. Internal finishes and services will also be important. Central heating, air-conditioning and the level of prestige sought will all affect building costs.

Separate from these costs are the ancillary costs that may be present: car parking provision separate from buildings; hard and soft landscaping; on-and-off-site drainage works; and other engineering works are just a few examples. In some cases a local planning authority might want a developer to make a financial contribution over and above what might normally be expected. Apart from archaeology, a developer may need to contribute to off-site highway improvements or to alternative off-site car parking arrangements. Other elements linked to planning gain might also be required.

(3) Fees

Until the late 1980s most fees were based on a fixed scale of charges but with the abolition of fixed rates for most professionals, fee competition is the result. Instead of fees being based on a percentage of building costs it is now possible to negotiate an agreed fee. Hence variations will occur although savings can be made depending on the size and complexity of the job. A large multi-use development may require a large team of professionals including archaeologists and a considerable amount of expert advice and input. On the other hand, a simple residential estate development involving repetitive designs may require very little.

(4) Development period

The cost of construction has to be financed not just for the building period but also for the time it takes to sell or let the completed development. The duration of this period is therefore important as it will affect the overall cost of the scheme. Estimates of the time it takes to complete an archaeological investigation, the building period and the time to let or sell the property must be realistically set. This is especially so when environmental matters are becoming increasingly important and when uncertainty exists over the willingness of prospective purchasers and tenants to come forward.

(5) Finance costs

Within the developer's overall costs will be the cost of the money employed in the project. Once completed it will usually be disposed of either by sale or lease. If sold any loan can be repaid. If let, arrangements will need to be made for long-term financing but in any event the bridging loan can be repaid. The finance costs, therefore, relate to the short-term or bridging loan. What need to be calculated are the compound interest charges from the time costs are incurred until the property is sold or refinanced. There are four elements:

(i) *Interest on purchase price and incidental costs of land*

Once the land is bought interest will be payable on the land price plus the incidental costs of purchase. These will include stamp duty, agent's fees and legal costs. They amount to approximately 3% of the land price.

(ii) *Interest on site preparation costs*
This will be at the normal 'cost of money' rate from the time the costs are incurred until the project is completed and disposed of. It will be necessary to estimate the time involved, making allowances for the duration and cost of archaeological investigation.

(iii) *Interest on building costs*
Payments to a contractor are normally made monthly according to the work done so that a fraction of the cost is incurred every month during the contract period. This will continue until the end of the contract when all work will have been paid, apart from any retention monies which are paid later. Thus a small part of the cost is attracting interest over most of the building period with the bulk paid towards the end. There is a gradual build-up of costs which normally reach a peak after 60% of the contract period has elapsed with a tail-off towards the end.

A close approximation of interest on building costs can be made by halving the period for borrowing. Thus, for a 12 month construction period, if interest were payable at a rate of 15% per annum the interest on building costs would be calculated at 15% divided by two. Any void from completion to actual disposal would of course incur interest charges for the whole of the void period on the total sum borrowed. So too would any rent free period which may be offered. This sometimes happens in times of recession when it is more difficult to let or sell a property. Rent-free periods may be offered as an inducement especially if a 'fitting out' period is involved with rents adjusted later. All of this time would constitute a void and incur interest charges at the full rate for all of this period.

The halving of the construction period for interest charge calculations has been criticized for being inaccurate. It can, however, be fairly accurate
for simple schemes. For larger ones, one of the cash flow techniques would be more appropriate.

(iv) *Interest on fees*
A large proportion of fees (75%) is traditionally paid at the start of a project although in recent years and in times of recession it may be possible to agree on a later date for payment. When calculating the interest payable on fees it is common for this sum to be incorporated with building costs. The alternative is to calculate the charge separately on 75% of the fees, as used in Example 2.

(6) Letting and selling costs

For a developer building to sell, an allowance for sale costs must be made. Where property within a scheme is to be sold in phases it would be normal practice for fees to be negotiated, usually at a reduced rate. With commercial developments that are let and then sold, both letting and selling costs will have to be allowed for. Major institutions will deduct their own legal and surveyor's expenses so that gross development value is reduced. Deductions will reflect vendor's agent's fees on sale, vendor's legal fees on sale, purchaser's agent's and surveyor's fees on acquisition, purchaser's legal costs on acquisition and stamp duty.

(7) Contingencies

It is always advisable to put aside a sum of money for unforseen costs. Arising as extras over and above the contract sum, they would, for example, cover any additional costs associated with the discovery of unexpected underground services or other difficult site conditions. An allowance of 5% on construction costs is often used although the amount would vary depending on the anticipated degree of uncertainty. With the possibility of delay or extra costs arising from archaeological considerations a higher percentage could be expected. In this Example 6% has been used.

The two valuations compared

In Example 1, where there is no archaeological expense or involvement, the site value is estimated to be £1.865 m. In Example 2 we can see that expenses directly attributable to archaeology amount ot £155 000 and yet the sum available for the site is reduced to £1.58 m, a difference of £285 000 from the earlier figure. There is a shortfall of £130 000 and yet the value of the completed development is the same and there are no additional building costs. Admittedly some of the refinements are not included (e.g. costs for the sale of the completed development) but this omission does not make up for the shortage. What we find is that it is the knock-on effect of archaeological costs arising primarily from interest charges on the upfront archaeological costs.

16.2 THE CASH FLOW APPROACH TO APPRAISAL

The traditional residual method of valuation is most frequently used to value a site before it is purchased. However, with the advent of sophisticated and computerized techniques it is now common to see this method replaced, or at least supplemented, by one of the cash flow techniques that are available. This is particularly so where large projects are proposed and where larger property development companies and financial institutions are involved.

The cash flow technique is also useful after a development site has been bought. As proposals are firmed up and more is known about them and the site, so the costs can be ascertained with greater certainty. The receipt of tender prices from a builder and the signing of contracts will add to this certainty but there will still be a need for caution. It is when the cash flow approach can be of help by dividing costs and income into monthly, quarterly or yearly amounts. In addition, other information, as and when it becomes available, can be fed into the equation thereby enabling the developer to predict the outcome with greater certainty.

The key to a cash flow approach is the timing of outgoings and income. By recording events as and when they happen it is possible to analyse them to see when and how changes occur and make alterations to improve performance. It may be possible to delay a payment or alternatively to identify a potential problem in advance thereby overcoming that problem.

Apart from these benefits there are some types of development that virtually necessitate a cash flow approach. A residential estate development, a shopping centre development and a business park are three examples where the cash flow approach would be more appropriate. This is because in each of these cases the flow of cash will be complex with money coming in and going out at different times. While some houses on an estate are being sold others may still be under construction.

At business parks similar circumstances can apply. Some buildings will be completed before others but instead of being sold they may be let and produce income. Alternatively individual sites might be ground leased to provide a smaller but earlier income. In each of these situations a cash flow appraisal would be a more satisfactory way of appraising the development. Essentially, there are two methods, normally referred to as the **period by period cash flow approach** and the **discounted cash flow approach** (DCF). Both are described and illustrated below with examples although these have been kept simple in order to illustrate the basic methods involved. They relate to the development of a hypothetical site for residential development where archaeological remains of any significance are not expected when development commences.

The period by period cash flow approach

As the name implies, this method calculates accumulating debt on a period by period basis. It is a detailed form of cash flow which has the advantage of showing the amount of loan required in any period and the total outstanding debt at any one stage of the development.

Example 3: Site for development – no archaeological excavation

A site has permission for 12 houses where it is estimated they can be built and sold over a two-year period. It is assumed that two dwellings will be sold each quarter beginning after nine months on-site. The calculation is to establish the profitability of the development where the site was acquired for £250 000.

Assumptions

- land price fixed at £250 000 and costs of acquisition estimated at 3%;
- a quarterly time period is used;
- site preparation costs calculated at £40 000;
- site works (roads, drainage, etc.) calculated @ £75 000 carried out in three periods of £25 000 each;
- overall building costs estimated at £585 000;
- professional fees (including agent's selling fees) negotiated at £53 000 overall reflecting the repetitive nature of work;
- an interest rate of 3% per quarter;
- archaeological evaluation did not reveal any significant finds; no excavation required.

Example 3 appraisal

Period 3 months	Activity	Total costs (£) (a)	Income (£) (b)	Net flow (£) (c = a − b)	Capital outstanding previous period (£) (d)	Interest @ 3% (£) (e)	Capital outstanding (£) (f = c + d + e)
1	Land acquisition	250 000					
	Acquisition costs (3%)	7 500					
		(257 500)		(257 500)		(7 725)	(265 225)
2	Site preparation	40 000					
	Site works	25 000					
	Building costs	50 000					
	Fees	6 000					
		(121 000)		(121 000)	(265 225)	(11 587)	(397 812)
3	Building costs	80 000					
	Fees	6 000					
		(86 000)					
	2 houses sold		210 000	124 000	(397 812)	(8 214)	(282 026)
4	Building costs	95 000					
	Fees	8 400					
		(103 400)					
	2 houses sold		210 000	106 600	(282 026)	(5 263)	(180 689)
5	Site works	25 000					
	Building costs	95 000					
	Fees	8 400					
		(128 400)					
	2 houses sold		210 000	81 600	(180 689)	(2 973)	(102 062)
6	Building costs	95 000					
	Fees	8 400					
		(103 400)					
	2 houses sold		210 000	106 600	(102 062)	—	4 538
7	Site works	25 000					
	Building costs	95 000					
	Fees	8 400					
		(128 400)					
	2 houses sold		210 000	81 600	4 538	—	86 138
8	Building costs	75 000					
	Fees	7 400					
		(82 400)					
	2 houses sold		210 000	127 600	86 138	—	213 738 (profit)

NB Fees include both professional and agent's fees for convenience.

The discounted cash flow approach

This alternative cash flow technique is widely used to appraise investment decisions in various sectors of the economy. It is similar to the period by period cash flow method in that a timetable of expenditure and income is required. The key difference is that instead of adding interest at regular intervals to give a net surplus at the end of the project, all cash flows are discounted backwards at the borrowing rate to arrive at a **net present value**.

Example 4: Site for housing development – no archaeological excavation

Using the same example of 12 dwellings as before, the calculations are similar to the previous example except that different valuation tables are used (the present-value-of-£1 table is used rather than the amount-of-£1 table).

Appraisal

Period	Costs	Income	Net flow £	PV of £1 @ 3%	Discounted net cash flow
0	257 000	—	(257 500)	0	(257 500)
1	121 000	—	(121 000)	.97	(117 370)
2	86 000	210 000	124 000	.94	116 560
3	103 400	210 000	106 600	.92	98 072
4	128 400	210 000	81 600	.89	72 624
5	103 400	210 000	106 600	.86	91 676
6	128 400	210 000	81 600	.84	68 544
7	82 400	210 000	127 600	.79	100 804
Totals	£1 010 000	£1 260 000			£173 410

Comparison between the two cash flow valuations

The two examples for a scheme of residential development are relatively straightforward but we can see that the figures vary. In the period by period cash flow the profit is calculated to be £213 738 whereas using the discounted method it is reduced to £173 410. They suggest an error in the calculations although we should expect these figures to differ.

Basically there are three reasons. Firstly, in the period by period method when income exceeds outgoings and the scheme is starting to make a profit, interest is no longer paid. Some might contend that the surplus should accrue interest although most developers would argue that it is not possible to invest the money, that the interest received would be at a lower rate and that it would anyway be subject to tax. For most projects, and certainly for a project of this size, the difference would be negligible. Thus whilst interest would only be paid for part of the development period, in the discounted method interest is assumed to be constant throughout.

Secondly, the period by period approach is producing a profit on completion in two years time whereas the discounted method is calculating the profit as of today. If we currently had £173 400 to invest we would expect it to generate income over the next two years.

Thirdly, in the period by period method, interest is calculated at the end of each quarter, that is, in arrears, whereas in the DCF approach interest is assumed to be payable from day one. Thus we can see that the periods for paying interest and the methods for calculating payments differ and that different times are chosen for calculating the profit.

Both methods have their advantages and disadvantages for the developer. In the period by period cash flow approach the main advantage is that it can show the actual amount owed at any time in the development process. For example, we can see that the total outstanding debt at the end of the first year is £180 689. This figure is not readily available in the discounted cash flow.

A second advantage of the period by period approach is that if interest rates change during the development period, modifications can easily be incorporated into the appraisal as soon as they take effect and can be used thereafter. A disadvantage occurs when there are many periods to calculate although the use of a computer can overcome this.

The DCF approach has both advantages and disadvantages. If site value is to be calculated it can be done more quickly than by the other methods. It can also be used to assess a scheme's actual rate of return on the capital invested in it. It can be used to compare alternative investment options such as between developing different sites or between different proposals at the same site. Thus if archaeology is involved it can be used to help decide which site to develop or which proposal is the more viable option. If special foundations need to be considered this could be incorporated into the calculations to see which is the best option.

The effects of archaeology

What we now need to look at is how the late discovery of archaeological remains might affect the profitability of a scheme. Using the same example of housing development (Example 3) two scenarios are looked at to see how the

Example 5: Housing development – archaeological remains discovered as site prepared for development

In the table it is assumed that archaeological remains are discovered in Period 2 after site preparation costs have been paid and just as site works are about to start. Development is delayed for a period of three months with the developer contributing £25 000 towards archaeological investigation in the hope that this will speed things up.

Example 6: Housing development – archaeological remains discovered midway through project

In this scenario, which makes use of the same initials figures, it is assumed that discovery occurs later in the development process, at Period 5. A delay of three months is again assumed with the developer prepared to contribute a similar sum towards the costs of archaeological investigation. This is to make it easier to compare the impact of excavation at different phases in a development project.

Example 5 appraisal

Period 3 months	Activity	Total costs (£) (a)	Income (£) (b)	Net flow (£) (c = a − b)	Capital outstanding (£) (d)	Interest @ 3% (£) (e)	Capital outstanding (£ = c + d + e)
1	Land acquisition Acquisition costs (3%)	250 000 7 500 (257 500)		(257 500)		(7 725)	(265 225)
2	Site preparation Archaeological investigation	40 000 25 000 (65 000)	—	(65 000)	(265 225)	9 907	(340 132)
3	Site works Building costs Fees	25 000 50 000 7 000 (82 000)	—	(82 000)	(340 132)	12 664	(434 796)
4	Building costs Fees 2 houses sold	80 000 6 000 (86 000)	210 000	124 000	(434 796)	9 324	(320 120)
5	Building costs Fees 2 houses sold	95 000 8 400 (103 400)	210 000	106 600	(320 120)	6 406	(219 926)
6	Site works Building costs Fees 2 houses sold	25 000 95 000 8 400 (128 400)	210 000	81 600	(219 926)	4 150	(142 476)
7	Building costs Fees 2 houses sold	95 000 8 400 (103 400)	210 000	106 600	(142 476)	1 076	(36 952)
8	Site works Building costs Fees 2 houses sold	25 000 95 000 8 400 (128 400)	210 000	81 600	(36 952)	—	44 648
9	Building costs Fees 2 Houses sold	75 000 7 400 (82 400)	210 000	127 600	44 648	—	172 248 (profit)

NB Fees include both professional and agent's fees for convenience.

Example 6 appraisal

Period 3 months	Activity	Total costs (£) (a)	Income (£) (b)	Net flow (£) (c = a − b)	Capital outstanding (£) (d)	Interest @ 3% (£) (e)	Capital outstanding (£ = c + d + e)
1	Land acquisition	250 000					
	Acquisition costs (3%)	7 500					
		(257 500)		(257 500)		(7 725)	(265 225)
2	Site preparation	40 000					
	Site works	25 000					
	Building costs	50 000					
	Fees	6 000					
		(121 000)		(121 000)	(265 225)	(11 587)	(397 812)
3	Building costs	80 000					
	Fees	6 000					
		(86 000)					
	2 houses sold		210 000	124 000	(397 812)	(8 214)	(282 026)
4	Building costs	95 000					
	Fees	8 400					
		(103 400)					
	2 houses sold		210 000	106 600	(282 026)	(5 263)	(180 689)
5	Site works	10 000					
	Archaeological investigation	25 000					
		(35 000)					
			—	(35 000)	(180 689)	6 471	(222 160)
6	Building costs	95 000					
	Remaining site works	15 000					
	Fees	8 400					
		(118 400)					
	2 houses sold		210 000	91 600	(222 160)	3 917	(134 477)
7	Building costs	95 000					
	Fees	8 400					
		(103 400)					
	2 houses sold		210 000	106 600	(134 417)	835	(28 652)
8	Site works	25 000					
	Building costs	95 000					
	Fees	8 400					
		(128 400)					
	2 houses sold		210 000	81 600	(28 652)	—	52 948
9	Building costs	75 000					
	Fees	7 400					
		(82 400)					
	2 houses sold		210 000	127 600	52 948	—	180 548 (profit)

NB Fees include both professional and agent's fees for convenience.

figures might vary. In the first (Example 5), it is assumed that archaeological remains are discovered as initial site works are about to commence. In the second (Example 6), the discovery of remains occurs midway through the development process.

Comments on the effects

It is to be expected that the profits will be reduced but the question is by how much and what conclusions can be drawn. In Example 5 with profits down to £172 248, the reduction of £41 490 is some 66% more than the outlay of £25 000 for archaeological excavation. With no increases in building costs virtually the whole of this additional cost can be explained by an increase in interest charges. In Example 6 a similar situation occurs but, extra charges amount to only £8910. This, however, is to be expected. Occurring later in the development process there is less build-up of charges because more houses have been sold or are about to be sold. It suggests that later discovery might be preferred although this need not be the case. The developer has already spent over £600 000 indicating that there will be strong commitment to complete as quickly as possible. The outstanding site works could also be important, not least for the occupiers of properties which have already been sold. Complaints could be forthcoming if the scheme is not satisfactorily completed, further reinforcing the commitment.

In Example 5 the outstanding sum is contained mainly in site costs. Initial appraisal costs, the preparation of detailed drawings for approval and costing purposes and the purchase of some of the building materials must be added but the total will amount to around £370 000 or nearly two thirds of the sum outstanding in Example 6.

No hard and fast rules can be applied as to which situation is better or worse. The important factors will be in respect of the standing, financial situation and other commitments of the developer, and how he or she copes with these. Note too that the examples are relatively simple: no account has been taken of other problems or issues which might present themselves or where the development project is more complex.

16.3 ARCHAEOLOGY IN THE CONTEXT OF OTHER FACTORS

Many factors can affect viability as we have seen in previous Chapters. Some will be relatively easy to estimate or will be known in advance and will have little or no adverse effect. Others such as demand for the property, short-term

---

Example 7: Housing development – archaeological excavation coupled with increase in interest rate

In this example, which draws on the same basic details as Example 3, it is assumed that archaeological discovery requires an excavation to be undertaken three months after site acquisition, immediately after the site has been prepared for development. It is now assumed that interest rates go up from 3% to 4% nine months after purchase.

Example 7 appraisal

Period 3 months	Activity	Total costs (£) (a)	Income (£) (b)	Net flow (£) (c = a − b)	Capital outstanding (£) (d)	Interest @ 3% (4% from*) (£) (e)	Capital outstanding (£ = c + d + e)
1	Land acquisition + aquisition costs (3%)	(257 000)		(257 000)		7 725	(265 225)
2	Site preparation/ archaeological investigation	40 000 25 000 (65 000)	—	(65 000)	(265 225)	9 907	(340 132)
3	Site works Building costs Fees	25 000 50 000 7 000 (82 000)	—	(82 000)	(340 132)	12 664	(434 796)
4	Building costs Fees	80 000 6 000 (86 000)					
	2 houses sold		210 000	124 000	(434 796)	12 432*	(323 228)
5	Building costs Fees	95 000 8 400 (103 400)					
	2 houses		210 000	106 600	(323 228)	8 665	(225 293)
6	Site works Building costs Fees	25 000 95 000 8 400 (128 400)					
	2 houses sold		210 000	81 600	(225 293)	5 748	(149 441)
7	Building costs Fees	95 000 8 400 (103 400)					
	2 houses sold		210 000	106 600	(149 441)	1 714	(44 555)
8	Site works Building costs Fees	25 000 95 000 8 400 (128 400)					
	2 houses sold		210 000	81 600	(44 555)	—	37 045
9	Building costs Fees	75 000 7 400 (82 400)					
	2 houses sold		210 000	127 600	37 045	—	164 645 (profit)

NB Fees include both professional and agent's fees for convenience.

borrowing costs, building costs, rent and yield are more difficult to assess and yet can have a tremendous impact. They are where the developer is likely to pay greater attention. Small variations can have a disproportionate effect on viability as can be seen from Example 7.

From this we can see that the overall profit is reduced to £164 645, a reduction of £49 093 from the original estimate of £213 738. Not known nor anticipated at the commencement of development, it shows how susceptible development can be to changing circumstances. We should also bear in mind that these figures relate to a relatively simple example whereas in many cases there will be greater complexity.

Conclusions

What these figures and uncertainties show is that archaeology should not be seen in isolation from the development process. It emphasizes the need for early and careful evaluation but, in addition, it emphasizes a case for weighing archaeological considerations against other development constraints. In the same way that archaeology is judged against other planning considerations, so perhaps the same argument should be applied between archaeology and development. Clearly there needs to be a greater understanding of the different roles and interests in the archaeological, planning and development processes. This book attempts to go some way towards meeting this objective.

Index

Page numbers appearing in **bold** refer to figures and page numbers appearing in *italic* refer to tables.